American Art at Mid-Century
THE SUBJECTS OF THE ARTIST

American Art at Mid-Century

THE SUBJECTS OF THE ARTIST

E. A. CARMEAN, JR., and ELIZA E. RATHBONE

with THOMAS B. HESS

National Gallery of Art, Washington   1978

This publication was produced by the Editor's Office, National Gallery of Art, Washington.
Printed by Eastern Press, New Haven, Connecticut.
The type is Sabon, set by Composition Systems Inc., Arlington, Virginia.
The text and cover papers are Warren Lustro Offset Enamel Dull.

Library of Congress Cataloging in Publication Data
Carmean, E. A.
American art at mid-century.

Catalog of an exhibition held at the National Gallery of Art June 1, 1978—January 14, 1979
1. Serial art—United States—Exhibitions.
2. Abstract expressionism—United States—Exhibitions.
3. Art, Modern—20th century—United States—Exhibitions.
I. Rathbone, Eliza, 1948- joint author.
II. Hess, Thomas B., joint author.
III. United States.
National Gallery of Art. IV. Title.
N6512.5.S43C37   709'.73'0740153   78-4595

Frontispiece: Jackson Pollock. *Number 1, 1950 (Lavender Mist)*: detail. National Gallery of Art, Washington, Ailsa Mellon Bruce Fund, 1976

Cover: David Smith. *Voltri VII*: detail. National Gallery of Art, Washington, Ailsa Mellon Bruce Fund, 1977 [photo: Ugo Mulas, courtesy Antonia Mulas, Milan]

Contents

Foreword

It has been the policy of the National Gallery of Art to supplement the exhibition of its permanent collection with loan shows surveying the various facets of the history of art, from earliest archeological times to the present day. A good number of these exhibitions has been devoted to the art of the twentieth century, including such shows as *American Art at Mid-Century I; Matisse: The Cut-Outs; Morris Louis: Major Themes and Variations; British Painting and Sculpture 1960-1970; Painting in France, 1900-1967; Paintings from the Albright-Knox Art Gallery; Paintings from the Museum of Modern Art, New York,* among others.

In the Gallery's new East Building, the spaces designed to house, long-term, the program of temporary exhibitions from all fields are located on the Concourse level. For the opening of the building and the period of this exhibition, these Concourse level spaces are being used for a survey of five centuries of art collecting focusing on objects from the museums of Dresden and, following that, a major exploration of the art of Edvard Munch.

For the opening of the building we also planned to mount simultaneously another large-scale loan exhibition. The additional space required was available, as the purpose for which the East Building was designed also includes provision for the future growth of the Gallery's collections; and since this is America's national gallery, it was decided to have that show be devoted to a cardinal moment in the history of American art. This exhibition, *The Subjects of the Artist,* is the second part of a series of explorations, at the Gallery, of American art at mid-century. It is intended to be a core sample of the abstract-expressionist movement, focusing on works that form a series or emphasize a particular theme by each of seven artists.

The East Building provides a wide variety of exhibition capabilities. Rooms can be constructed in loft spaces to follow the requirements of individual sections of an exhibition. Daylight is also available in certain galleries, and, for the first time we know of in the history of museum architecture, the ceiling height of the daylit galleries can be adjusted. Thus the full thirty-five-foot height of the northwest gallery has allowed us to evoke the outdoor ancient Roman arena in which David Smith first exhibited his Voltri series. Moreover, the flexibility of the building design is such that the installation of this exhibition could have been virtually reversed, with the Pollocks and Motherwells occupying their two rooms with lower ceilings in the space here devoted to the Smiths.

The scholarship of this recent period in American art history is still in its pioneering phase. We are fortunate to have on the Gallery's staff a curator who is deeply immersed in this field. E. A. Carmean, Jr., conceived of the show and selected its contents, and the catalogue is a result of his work and that of Eliza E. Rathbone, assistant curator at the Gallery. The research of the photographic material was provided by Trinkett Clark. Thomas B. Hess has allowed us to reprint his discussion of Newman's Stations of the Cross as one of the seven essays here.

To them, and to all those members of the National Gallery staff and outside contributors who have helped bring about this major art and publishing undertaking, go our warmest thanks.

It is, above all, to the lenders to this exhibition that we are most deeply indebted. Her Imperial Highness, the Empress of Iran has taken a deep personal interest and has been very helpful in securing the loan of the important de Kooning from Tehran; other loans have come from as far away as Düsseldorf, Germany, and Canberra, Australia. Many of our museum and private lenders have had to make special exceptions to make possible the loan of very fragile and valuable material. To all of these trustees and staffs, and to the collectors who have given up these objects from their own walls, we wish to extend our deepest gratitude.

J. Carter Brown, *Director*

Lenders to the Exhibition

Albright-Knox Art Gallery, Buffalo, N.Y.
Allen Memorial Art Museum, Oberlin College, Ohio
Anonymous lenders
H. H. Arnason, New York
The Art Institute of Chicago
Australian National Gallery, Canberra
The Cleveland Museum of Art
Fogg Art Museum, Harvard University, Cambridge, Mass.,
and Reginald and Charlotte Isaacs and family and friends
Mr. Milton A. Gordon, New York
Estate of A. Gorky
Hirshhorn Museum and Sculpture Garden, Smithsonian
Institution, Washington
Mr. and Mrs. Gilbert H. Kinney, Washington
Kunstsammlung Nordrhein-Westfalen, Düsseldorf
Lois and Georges de Ménil, Paris
The Metropolitan Museum of Art, New York
Mr. Robert Motherwell, Greenwich, Conn.
Museum of Art, Carnegie Institute, Pittsburgh
The Museum of Modern Art, New York
Nelson Gallery-Atkins Museum, Kansas City, Mo.
Annalee Newman, New York
Mr. and Mrs. Stephen D. Paine, Boston
Rijksmuseum Kröller-Müller, Otterlo, The Netherlands
Nelson A. Rockefeller
Estate of Mark Rothko, New York
Mr. and Mrs. Robert Schwarz, Palm Springs, Calif.
Estate of David Smith, Bolton Landing, N.Y.
Mr. and Mrs. Harold P. Starr, Philadelphia
Tehran Museum of Contemporary Art
Whitney Museum of American Art, New York
Yale University Art Gallery, New Haven

Acknowledgments

This exhibition and the catalogue which accompanies it would not have been possible without the time and efforts of a great many people. Eliza Rathbone and I would like to thank especially Trinkett Clark, also of the Gallery's Department of Twentieth-Century Art, who assisted in all phases of the project and undertook the arduous task of photographic research. Polly Roulhac, of the Editor's Office, guided this publication through the press.

For their assistance we would like to thank: Ronnie Baer, Michael Blackwood, Dan Budnik, Rudolph Burckhardt, Anthony Caro, Lee Eastman, Betty Fiske, Xavier Fourcade, Cathy Gebhard, John Gernand, Clement Greenberg, Thomas B. Hess, Jim Jordan, Jacob Kainen, Hilton Kramer, Alexander Liberman, Ira Lowe, Mrs. John Magruder, M. Marsh, Shirley Matzky, Miranda McClintic, Garnett McCoy, Marian Moffett, Karlen Mooradian, Robert Motherwell, Antonia Mulas, Sybil Meyersburg, Hans Namuth, Annalee Newman, Kenneth Noland, Francis O'Connor, Brian O'Doherty, Alfonso Ossorio, Beverly Pepper, Agnes Phillips, Lee Krasner Pollock, Renate Ponsold, V. V. Rankine, James Rosati, Barbara Rose, Harold Rosenberg, Irving Sandler, William Scharf, Seymour Slive, Admiral and Mrs. William Small, the estate of David Smith, Tony Smith, Clyfford Still, Anne Truitt, Mr. and Mrs. Burton G. Tremaine, Phyllis Tuchman, Diane Waldman.

E. A. Carmean, Jr.

David Smith, Voltri, Italy, June 1962 [photo: Ugo Mulas, courtesy of Antonia Mulas, Milan]

Introduction

E. A. CARMEAN, JR.

"I accept the fact that the important painting of the last hundred years was done in France," wrote Jackson Pollock in 1944.

American painters have generally missed the point of modern painting from beginning to end. . . . Thus the fact that good European moderns are now here is very important, for they bring with them an understanding of the problems of modern painting.[1]

But within a short period of time—by mid-century—the situation described by Pollock had changed. American painters, far from seeing themselves as missing the point of modern painting, had assumed its leadership. The movement we call abstract expressionism emerged in this context; the "problems of modern painting" were now given in new terms, and this change meant a radical shift in character.

Given the particularities of its development, abstract expressionism is probably the most complex movement in art during the last century. We usually define directions in art as the shared endeavors of certain artists, giving our attention primarily to one or more principal figures and studying collective features of either style or iconography, or both. But these criteria, when used according to convention, do not apply to abstract expressionism as a movement. The works by its artists coincide neither in terms of formal characteristics nor in areas of particular thematic concerns. And this very diversity denies any artist the position of central figure.[2] However, one major factor does seem to connect the abstract expressionists—their repeated affirmation that while their works by and large reject representational manners, they nevertheless have subjects. "Neither Mr. [Adolph] Gottlieb's painting nor mine should be considered abstract paintings," stated Mark Rothko in 1958. "It is not their intention either to create or to emphasize a formal color-space arrangement. They depart from natural representation only to intensify the expression of the subject."[3]

Rothko's insistence on this point is paralleled in the statements and writings of many of the other artists. "We are raising the question of subject matter and what its nature is," said Barnett Newman in the discussions held at Studio 35 in New York in 1950.[4] These "Artists' Sessions" constituted the closest thing to a group statement made by the abstract expressionists; indeed its discursive rather than manifesto form is revealing, and it is significant that the question of subjects is the dominant topic.

The emphasis on this point is perhaps most clearly underscored in the school begun in 1948 by William Baziotes, David Hare, Robert Motherwell, Newman, Rothko, and Clyfford Still, which was entitled *The Subjects of the Artist: a new art school*. "The title was Barney's [Newman]," recalls Motherwell, "and I remember we all agreed that it was right because it made the point that our works did have subjects."[5] The curriculum included on the printed announcement for the school's first term can be seen as a further indication of these artists' concerns:

CURRICULUM: . . . as a spontaneous investigation into the subjects of the modern artist—what his subjects are, how they are arrived at, methods of inspiration and transformation, moral attitudes, possibilities for further explorations, what is being done now and what might be done, and so on.[6]

We have borrowed the school's title for this exhibition because it—and the curriculum—serve as a sign of the broader interests and procedures which informed the movement as a whole. An exhibition cannot be "spontaneous," given the requirements of loans, installation, cataloguing, research, and writing; our *Subjects of the Artist* is intended as an investigation into "what subjects are in abstract expressionism," and "how they are arrived at."

The exhibition brings together works by seven artists. Those by Arshile Gorky, Willem de Kooning, Motherwell, and Newman each form a series which is concentrated on a particular theme. The paintings and sculpture here by Pollock, Rothko, and David Smith are more the results of an exceptionally focused period in the artist's work, and while each may share his subject with the larger part of his oeuvre, nevertheless each stresses it through certain emphases and/or restrictions. For the former group, the question of subject seems more easily broached, at least; de Kooning's Women, for example, is a series consisting of six paintings, each of which displays a female figure. Motherwell's Elegies to the Spanish Republic is also a series, with a definite formal topography, even though the question of their precise subject—and how it is present—is not so readily closed. Pollock's classic paintings of 1950 are perhaps at the other end of this scale; given their high degree of abstraction and their interconnections to his other works, the paintings may seem to be less related to, or even participants in, the topic of this exhibition.

Given the complexity of defining subjects for abstract expressionism as a whole as well as in individual works, we have tried to give some coherence to the exhibition by selecting the more focused works by these artists, although even here the range stretches from Gorky's seemingly serial works to Pollock's paintings (which are not a proper series but, rather, have been gathered on the basis of the artist's own formal designations). But our selection of these seven artists, although each is a major figure, should not be seen as denying subjects in the works of any of the other abstract expressionists or in other works by these seven artists. Our limitation, which is to examine only focused works, has, however, been revealing in itself about the nature of the subjects here.

This exhibition's attention to subjects should not be taken as a proposal that this is the exclusive—or most correct—way of approaching this group of artists. The study of all art benefits from a variety of approaches, provided such approaches can be weighed against the works themselves. But it is a key to the diversity of abstract expressionism that it requires more divergent means of address. Preceding studies of abstract expressionism or of individual artists of this movement have, for the greater part, avoided confronting questions of subject matter and have instead divided into formal or sociological/biographical discussions.[7] As Eliza Rathbone and I have discovered, they have shed invaluable light upon the problems of dealing with subjects in these works; in return, it is hoped the ensuing discussions of this topic will open new ways of understanding the works by these seven artists.

It was the nature of earlier studies to treat the artist's works in a broad fashion, either relating general stylistic features to the fabric of the modern vocabulary or viewing the works as successive evidence of the influences upon, and the unfolding and reception of, the artist's career. Other studies have offered an interpretation of the meaning of the artist's oeuvre as a whole. Given this more general background, we found it necessary in examining only a small segment of an artist's work—here thirteen out of Smith's total oeuvre of 676 works of sculpture, for example[8]—to use a process akin to connoisseurship, not in the sense of establishing authorship, but in the placing of works in proper chronological orderings and determining, where possible, more about how each was created. This is especially pronounced in the case of Pollock's poured works but is also a major aspect of the studies of Gorky and de Kooning as well. And here again the heritage of formal and biographical discussions was instructional.

Finally we must caution that this study is not only discretionary but preliminary. Even within our restrictions the study of subjects revealed multiple new ways of understanding each of these artists individually, and only some of these ways could here be cogently advanced, in the separate essays which follow. Collectively the abstract expressionists remain a disparate group; but in light of their joint concern about subjects, some unifying factors have emerged. While one need not view all art in the manner of Newman's 1950 statement—"the central issue of painting is the subject matter"[9]—nevertheless it is clear that this issue was common to the abstract expressionists.

EXHAUSTION

As with other major shifts in art, the maturation of abstract expressionism occurred amidst numerous and complex developments, which are only now becoming clear. But a major factor was clearly the lessening of the avant-garde strength of European modernism during the 1940s, during the *emigré* period of the war. In a sense, history passed the "opening" to those New York artists who, on one hand, were striving to be a part of modernism and, on the other, knew they were not European—and thus not directly part of the avant-garde though they were equally eager to avoid provincialism. We need only contrast Pollock's statement of 1944, quoted above, with Smith's recollection of the situation later:

It has been very rewarding to us to have men like Lipchitz, and Mondrian, and Gabo become Americans and live here with us; that is good and it's been very nice. We have met them and we have found that they were humans like we were and they were not gods and they were fine artists. And so we know more about the world now.[10]

Concurrent with this modification in the measure of European artists was the emergence of a determination to make modern—and unprovincial—art in America. Again Smith:

The one thing when I came back [from Europe in 1936] that I realized was that I belonged here; my materials were here, my thoughts were here, my birth was here, and whatever I could do had to be done here. I thoroughly gave up any idea of ever being an expatriate. So I laid into work very hard. That must have been in the minds of other men. Otherwise, there wouldn't be so many of us here now.[11]

But it is also clear that Smith and the other abstract expressionists worked in a style which was fully informed by European art. What occurred during the decline of the pressure of European modernism was the Americans' ability to see this tradition more dispassionately and thus more independently. The Americans were able to judge it broadly and to attend to those elements which were more appropriate to their personal developing styles. As Hilton Kramer has proposed:

The term "abstract expressionism" . . . points to the essentially synthetic character of this art—to the extent to which it is itself an energetic synthesis, summary and elaboration of pre-existing styles. For the New York School came into existence at the end of the modernist era, when each of its separate styles and impulses was in a state of exhaustion. The American painter in the forties was free at last to create his own amalgam of modern European styles precisely because none was any longer vital enough to command his absolute loyalty. The result was a series of inspired refinements on the inherited vocabulary of modernism. . . .[12]

Kramer's term "exhaustion" is well chosen, for European modernism—the surrealism of Picasso, Miró, and Masson, for example, or the abstraction of Mondrian—had not died or even entered into a period of decline; nonetheless, the Americans saw it (partially due to the effects of the war) at the moment when its energy for on-going high development was spent. (Although Matta, and to a large degree Gorky as a surrealist, maintained some momentum of creativity.) Simultaneously, early movements in modern art—impressionism, fauvism, cubism, and dada—were either undergoing reevaluation by the abstract expressionists or were being seen for the first time with clarity and/or depth with the arrival of major works in New York, as we can see in de Kooning's interest in futurism in the mid-1940s.

Major movements in modern art have usually been keyed to either a reaction against a dominant style or a reinterpretation of some of such a style's salient elements; in each case the resultant new style achieves its own definite character. But for abstract expressionism the conditions of the situation were such that the view of the abstract expressionists was synoptical rather than political (in the sense of contending art movements) and the resultant styles were decidedly individual. Thus Pollock's classic paintings, which draw upon impressionism, the late Monet, and analytical cubism, could be companioned by Motherwell's Elegies, which fuse post-impressionism, Matisse, and the cubism of the synthetic phase.

Abstract expressionism as a movement might have had the nature of a conglomerate of styles save for one amalgamative factor: the influence of surrealism. William Rubin notes that the abstract expressionists

produced a kind of abstraction markedly different from that to which Cubism and Fauvism alone might have been expected to lead. These movements had already lost their momentum in Europe in the 1930s, and the American practitioners of Cubism and abstraction in that decade found themselves at a dead end. Only a new spirit could have freed them; the American painters' experience of Surrealism in the early and middle forties enabled them to "open up" the language they had inherited from Cubism and Fauvism, and thus preserve what was still viable in those styles. And while it is true that they expunged the quasi-literary imagery that had earlier related their paintings to Surrealism, the visionary spirit of their wholly abstract art retained much of Surrealism's concern with poetry albeit in a less obvious form.[14]

Although New York artists had seen surrealism in depth in the Museum of Modern Art's 1936 exhibition *Fantastic Art, Dada and Surrealism,* it was not fully comprehended, especially the formal practices and ideas of surrealism. New Yorkers did not turn to surrealism in any important way until the early 1940s. Curiously, when the war occurred, the two major artistic figures, Picasso and Miró, did not emigrate to America. ("The two artists I admire most, Picasso and Miró, are still abroad," said Pollock.)[15] Surrealism was thus seen close up in the United States not only in its moment of exhaustion, but in the hands of its lesser talents, although this must be qualified in the case of André Masson, whose works affected Pollock, and of Matta, who exerted strong influences upon the art of Gorky. And while Rothko, Newman, and Smith also made works in the early 1940s in the surrealist manner, nevertheless it was ultimately surrealist ideas—rather than their particular results in pictures—which were primary.

On the formal level it was the surrealists' concept of automatism which was of crucial importance. Abstract expressionism is often described as a "painterly" style: "loose, rapid, handling, or the look of it; masses that blot and fuse instead of shapes that stay distinct, large conspicuous rhythms, broken color; uneven saturation or densities of paint; exhibited brush, knife, finger or rag marks" are the characteristics cited by Clement Greenberg for the movement.[16] While not all of these features fit all of the painters (Pollock's works do not exhibit directly the tools of their making, and Motherwell's shapes generally stay quite sharp), nevertheless it is a useful description. Greenberg is certainly correct in viewing this style as "a reaction against the tightness of Synthetic Cubism, [although] it used the same vocabulary at first."[17] But there is another factor as well: that the looseness of both definition and

structure could create a form of picture making that was more spontaneous or automatic. This side of painterliness would allow for a wider latitude of personal invention on the one hand, and the enrollment of broader aspects of the modern language on the other. This same automatic flexibility is found in works of a less painterly nature as well—say those of Rothko and Newman, where their more reductive styles place greater emphasis on nuances thereby opening possibilities of expression.

It is important to distinguish the surrealists' imaginal automatism from the abstract and synthesizing variant we discover in the painterliness of abstract expressionism. For the surrealists, as in the works of Miró and Masson, for example, automatism consists of beginning the picture with random, nondescriptive markings. But as the surrealist artist finds figures suggested in these markings, automatism is replaced by more traditionally oriented practices of description, which are used to articulate the images. The abstract expressionist's variant of automatism is not used to create figuration—or even create a situation of finding figuration—out of random markings. Rather it is confined (generally) to abstraction and plays a more continuous role in the work. Pollock's poured pictures are a case in point. Although many of them began with a spontaneously generated pattern—as in, and perhaps partially learned from, Masson's works—in Pollock's art this randomness is articulated into an abstract coherence, not a representational image. In Gorky's work, which is viewed traditionally as transitional between surrealism and abstract expressionism, what the Plow and the Song series reveals is a diminution of the representational in favor of a more poetic and abstract nature.

De Kooning's Women might also suggest a stronger connection to surrealism given their "representational" aspects. The female image did not appear, however, in the midst of random markings; rather, de Kooning began these works with the figural image, and his automatism is the evolutional process he used to clarify the figure and to create a pictorial structure which would in itself effect a particular statement. We also find figuration in Smith's Voltri works, but it is also different from that of surrealism. Smith noted that

I try to approach each thing without following the pattern that I made with the other one. They can begin with any idea. They can begin with a found object, they can begin with no object. They can begin sometimes even when I'm sweeping the floor and I stumble and kick a few parts and happen to throw them into an alignment that sets me off thinking and sets off a vision of how it would finish if it all had that kind of accidental beauty to it. I want to be like a poet, in a sense. I don't want to seek the same orders.[18]

Certainly the Voltri works indicate this inventive variety and, for the most part, differ widely among themselves. But they are joined as a series because of a particular Italian vocabulary. "I think it was climate—locale—at least it seems to me that my Italian work took on a different feeling than my USA work ever had—yet it was natural and without intention. . . ," said Smith.[19] Many of the works make references to discrete images—suns, figures, chariots among them—and certain pieces evoke ancient and classical associations. But Smith did not pile up metal, recognize an image, and then change to a

1. Arshile Gorky. Three plows, 1944(?). Mr. Karlen Mooradian, on loan to The Art Institute of Chicago [photo: John Mahtesian]. Not in exhibition

2. Arshile Gorky. Study for *The Plow and the Song*, 1944. Allen Memorial Art Museum, Oberlin College, Oberlin, Ohio

3. Arshile Gorky. *The Plow and the Song*, 1946. National Gallery of Art, Washington, Avalon Fund

4. Arshile Gorky. *The Plow and the Song II*, 1946. The Art Institute of Chicago, Mr. and Mrs. Lewis L. Coburn Fund

5. Arshile Gorky. *The Plow and the Song,* 1947. Collection, Milton A. Gordon, New York

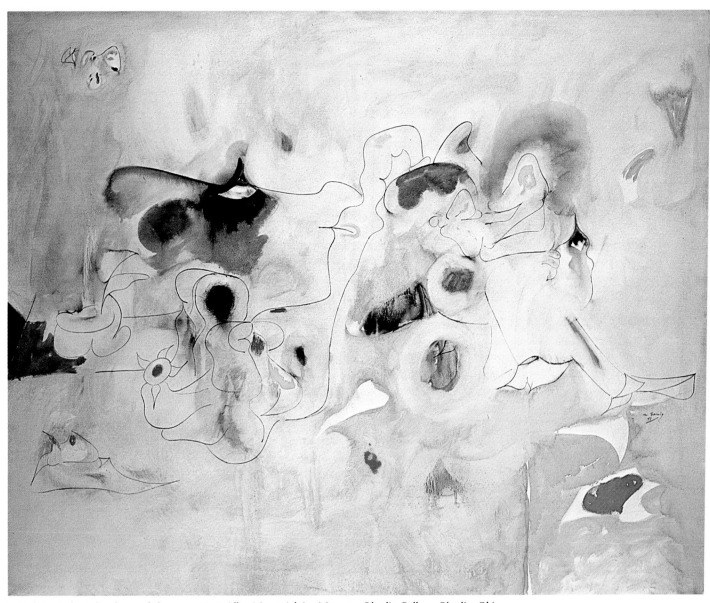

6. Arshile Gorky. *The Plow and the Song,* 1947. Allen Memorial Art Museum, Oberlin College, Oberlin, Ohio

7. Willem de Kooning. *Woman I*, 1950-1952. The Museum of Modern Art, New York, Purchase, 1953

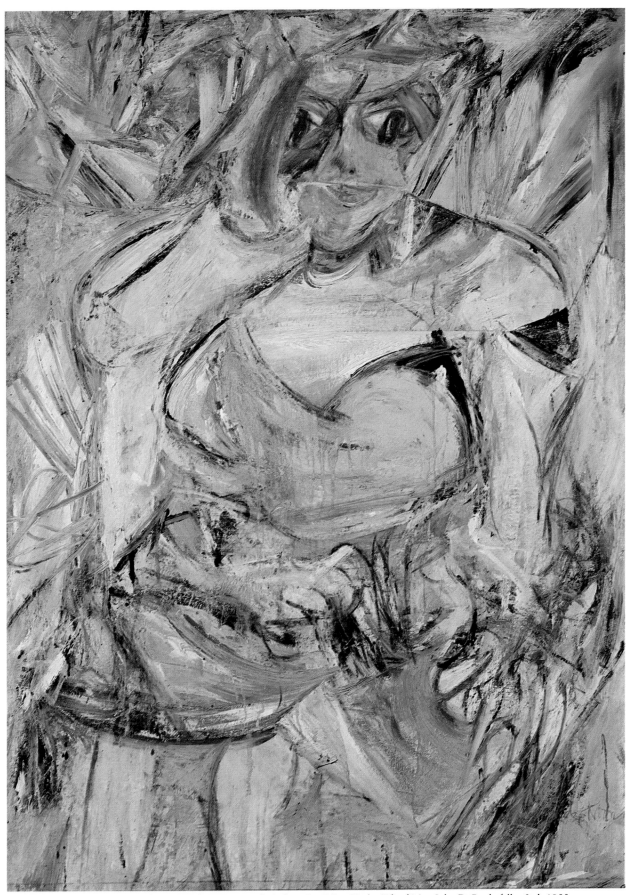

8. Willem de Kooning. *Woman II*, 1952. The Museum of Modern Art, New York, Gift of Mrs. John D. Rockefeller 3rd, 1955

9. Willem de Kooning. *Woman III*, 1951-1952. Tehran Museum of Contemporary Art

10. Willem de Kooning. *Woman IV*, 1952-1953. Nelson Gallery-Atkins Museum, Kansas City, Mo., Gift of Mr. William Inge

11. Willem de Kooning. *Woman V*, 1952-1953. Australian National Gallery, Canberra

12. Willem de Kooning. *Woman VI*, 1953. Museum of Art, Carnegie Institute, Pittsburgh

13. Robert Motherwell. *Elegy to the Spanish Republic, No. 34*, 1953-1954. Albright-Knox Art Gallery, Buffalo, N.Y., Gift of Seymour H. Knox

14. Robert Motherwell. *The Figure 4 on an Elegy,* 1960. Collection, H. H. Arnason, New York [photo: courtesy of Robert Motherwell]

15. Robert Motherwell. *Elegy to the Spanish Republic, No. 124,* 1971-1972. Collection, Robert Motherwell, Greenwich, Conn.; on extended loan to the National Gallery of Art, Washington

descriptive technique to present the image. The images in the Voltris were seen by Smith in the union of the disparate elements; their existence lies entirely within the construct of the work, which effects rather than educes them: the "finding" of the construct immediately produces the image, rather than its being recognized and then described.

Thus, on the formal level, abstract expressionism is more an extrapolation from the surrealist's concept of automatism than a technique derived from their actual practices. "What Pollock really took from surrealism was an idea—automatism—rather than a manner," Rubin notes.[20] Nevertheless it was this ingredient which provided a formal method for the combination of originality and synthesis so uniquely fused in abstract expressionism.

In general terms, the early development of abstract expressionism can be seen as the movement toward painterly/automatic abstraction by various artists of differing formal persuasions.[21] Probably most central was the fusion of surrealist automatism with certain formal postulates of cubist composition, especially its tendency to an even density, frontality, and a more apparent pictorial structure. In 1944 Sidney Janis observed "That abstract painters are able to bridge the gap to surrealism is indicated in the work of Mark Rothko . . . Gottlieb . . . and . . . Gorky. . . . It is also true that the opposite takes place. Motherwell, formerly a member of the Surrealist circle, still retains Surrealist ideas while approaching pure abstraction."[22] In 1945, Greenberg noted, more specifically, that certain artists "have accepted just enough of surrealist cross-fertilization to free themselves from the strangling personal influence of cubist and post-cubist masters. Yet they have not abandoned the direction these masters charted."[23]

For Pollock in his poured paintings and for de Kooning in his *passage*-dominated Women, automatism—or more precisely the abstract-expressionist variant of it—was a method for prying open a firm style and creating new pictorial structures. With Motherwell it was "a plastic weapon with which to invent new forms."[24] What is central is that the structures, forms, procedures, and even the images which developed out of these automatic procedures at the same time introduced the artist's subject into abstract-expressionist work.

VOYAGING

If the formal character of abstract expressionism is synoptic, enrolling both individual invention as well various aspects of the formal language of the modern tradition, it is also true that, by and large, these traits are present in a more abstract sense. While the historical situation in New York allowed—or even encouraged—the synthesis of formal styles, it did not support the transfer of overt European themes. Thus Pollock's works may correspond in particular ways with Cézanne's, but *Lavender Mist* does not in any manner refer to *Mont Sainte Victoire,* or even depict the Long Island landscape as a substitute. And while admixtures of disparate styles could take place under the variations of automatism, the joining of disparate themes would have been far more difficult, and—given their connections to Europe—not of much importance to New York.

There were some attempts at the transfer of themes: Bradley Walker Tomlin's early pictures present still-life objects with a fusion of impressionist and cubist touches. But as these two styles were more resolved in his work, the references to this discrete—and traditionally cubist—subject was abandoned. During this same time, some abstract themes of surrealism were also picked up; Pollock, Rothko, Smith, and others used surrealist ideas of mythology in their work in the early 1940s, adopting the practice of symbolic imagery and a tendency toward biomorphic forms. But again, as the formal language developed, these explicit themes were dropped or altered, although they may have had some effects upon the nature of mature abstract-expressionist subjects. In some cases— Rothko and Adolph Gottlieb in particular—the choice of the new and more abstract themes of mythology were as important as the use of automatism; it too could change the formal language. "Mark chose to do some themes from the plays of Aeschylus and I . . . played around with the Oedipus myth which was both a classical theme and a Freudian theme," recalled Gottlieb.

[As a result] we very quickly discovered that by a shift in subject matter we were getting into formal problems that we hadn't anticipated. Because obviously we weren't going to try to illustrate these themes in some sort of a Renaissance style. We were exploring. So we suddenly found that there were formal problems that confronted us for which there was no precedent. We were in unknown territory.[25]

As abstract expressionism matured and its amalgamation of European styles grew more complex and more tightly integrated, it became increasingly abstract and removed from any borrowed iconography. This was the "unknown territory" in which they found themselves, although their works represented, in formal terms, an extension of the modern language of impressionism, fauvism, cubism, and surrealism. Yet, as a synthesis, this language was new and unconnected to any preexisting thematic concerns.

We modern artists have no generally accepted subject matter, no inherited iconography [said Motherwell in 1950]. But to re-invent painting, its subject matter and its means, is a task so difficult that one must reduce it to a very simple concept in order to paint for the sheer joy of painting, as simple as the Madonna was to many generations of painters in the past. An existing subject matter for me—even though I had to invent it to begin with—variations gives me moments of joy. . . . The other mode is a voyaging into the night, one knows not where, on an unknown vessel, an absolute struggle with the elements of the real.[26]

What Motherwell indicates by inventing subject matter out of a "struggle with the elements of the real" is at the heart of the question of theme in abstract expressionism. As we have seen, the automatic procedures and the more abstract nature of the movement could not accommodate traditional themes in these works. If subject matter was to exist in them it would have to be "invented" within the painting or sculpture itself; or more accurately, it would have to arise within the concerns of the artist.

This was probably the central argument of Harold Rosenberg's description of abstract expressionism:

At a certain moment the canvas began to appear to one American painter after another as an arena in which to act—rather than as a space in which to reproduce, re-design, analyze or "express" an object, actual or imagined. What was to go on the canvas was not a picture but an event.

The painter no longer approached his easel with an image in his mind; he went up to it with material in his hand to do something to that other piece of material in front of him. The image would be the result of this encounter. . . .

Call this painting "abstract" or "Expressionist" or "Abstract-Expressionist," what counts is its special motive for extinguishing the object, which is not the same as in other abstract or Expressionist phases of modern art.

The new American painting is not "pure" art, since the extrusion of the object was not for the sake of the esthetic. The apples weren't brushed off the table in order to make room for perfect relations of space and color. They had to go so that nothing would get in the way of the act of painting.[27]

Analysis has shown that Rosenberg's thesis must be qualified—or challenged—in significant ways.[28] Clearly the abstract-expressionist artist did not "approach his easel" like a *naïf*. As we have seen, he had the battery of the modern tradition at his side, and more importantly, he used major components of it in making his work. They certainly gave the artist a language (though limited by time and range of expression) that did "get in the way of the art of painting"; Pollock's art, which was often seen as pure painting, is the case in point here, as it was so fully informed by this tradition. As Mary McCarthy observed, "You cannot hang an event on the wall, . . . only a picture."[29] In the final analysis, the abstract expressionists were making pictures.

When read in reference to the subjects in abstract-expressionist works, Rosenberg's thesis reveals a crucial perception. As we have seen, for the abstract-expressionist painter the painting was not to "reproduce, re-design, analyze or express an object, actual or imagined." The transference or the a priori existence per se of these subjects, as independent entities, was not permissible. De Kooning's *Woman I* may have existed as a general idea, but her character and her presence merged in the process of making the work. Newman is quite precise on this point:

Most people think of subject-matter as what Meyer Schapiro has called "object-matter." It is the "object-matter" that most people want to see in a painting. That is what, for them, makes the painting seem full. For me both the use of objects and the manipulation of areas for the sake of the areas themselves must end up being anecdotal. My subject is anti-anecdotal.[30]

"The image would be the result of this encounter [between the artist and his work]," writes Rosenberg. While this is not accurate or even distinctive as stated (after all, all images in art are the result of the artist's work with his materials), what Rosenberg suggests—and is proposed here as central to abstract expressionism—is, that the subject of each work is a result of the work, which is the use of materials.

PROCESS

Motherwell stated this thesis very early in the development of abstract expressionism in a review of Pollock's 1944 show at the Art of This Century Gallery:

In his exhibit Pollock reveals extraordinary gifts: his color sense is remarkably fine, never exploited beyond its proper role; and his sense of surface is equally good. His principal problem is to discover what his true subject is. And since painting is his thought's medium, the resolution must grow out of the process of his painting itself.[31]

What does it mean to say that the subject will "grow out of the process of painting itself"? In a general manner we can propose that in the painting of the abstract-expressionist picture (or the making of sculpture) the artisanal choices are made as part of the process of painting itself—its automatic aspect—and are also evaluated against the developing work, rather than being measured against any external program. In Newman's work, for example, the choices about placement and proportions of the vertical bands, and about how they are painted and in what color, etc., do not derive from a model, nor can they be related to any a priori system, as in the case of Mondrian's work.[32] Indeed, Mondrian—or more specifically his followers in America—were producing a nonobjective painting against which the abstract expressionists reacted precisely because the abstract expressionists used automatic procedures and insisted upon expression of a subject. Nonetheless, both Motherwell and Newman learned from Mondrian's classic works,[33] and Pollock's art was undoubtedly influenced by his "cubist" façades and his plus-and-minus pictures. From their perspective, Mondrian was not totally nonobjective; Motherwell has written of Mondrian's "intensity of feeling" and de Kooning's analysis saw Mondrian's work as expressive:

If we talk in terms of what kinds of shapes or lines we are using, we don't mean that and we talk like outsiders. When Motherwell says he paints stripes, he doesn't mean that he is painting stripes. That is still thinking in terms of what kinds of shapes we are painting. We ought to get rid of that. If a man is influenced on the basis that Mondrian is clear, I would like to ask Mondrian if he was so clear. Obviously, he wasn't clear, because he kept on painting. Mondrian is not geometric, he does not paint straight lines. A picture to me is not geometric—it has a face. . . . It is some form of impressionism. . . .[34]

This concept—that the forms in the work, or the combination of them, are expressive of a subject—is central to the abstract-expressionist movement. The fact that they are so varied from artist to artist with abstract expressionism was pointed out by Gottlieb: "What is it that makes each person use those particular forms that they use?" he asked in a Studio 35 session.[35] We have seen that the development of these forms in the abstract-expressionist work was automatic—either discovered or altered as formal developing took place—although they might derive indirectly from the modern tradition. Confronted with the necessity to articulate these forms independently, self-expression, we can propose, was the natural result. But this expression—while spoken in a language derived from the formal beginnings of the modern tradition—was given in terms of the work itself.[36]

But in another sense the abstract expressionists did not express themselves, at least in the sense in which we regularly use that term. Rather they discovered in the painting (or sculpture) a visual construct which constituted a subject that they recognized as expressive of certain of their ideas, opinions, experiences, and so forth. In this sense the abstract-expressionist picture can be said to have a dual identity: an almost objective existence, as the subject of the work was separate from them and appeared much as it might to the viewer of their works; and a subjective one, as the subject arose out of, and was capable of expressing, personal concerns. (Rothko's work especially forces the issue of the subjective/objective quality, and the tightly focused characteristics of his art make this quality of experience that of the viewer in a more pronounced manner than that of the others.)

Motherwell states that when he makes an Elegy it is "not that I'm going to paint something I know, but through the act of painting I'm going to find out exactly how I feel."[37] In Motherwell's view—which he extends to abstract expressionism as a whole—the markings on the surface, the forms, their arrangement, and so forth—parallel, not correspond or depict, the proportions or felt rhythms or placements we experience in life. Thus Pollock's arching order of the potential chaos of his technique—commandingly reached at the level of complexity (or delicacy) of his 1950 works—is a subject, which parallels our own sense, however fleeting, of order in the world.

This general thesis proposes a more formal origin for the subjects of abstract-expressionist painting, as meanings lie within, or are derived from, structural qualities. The record of the artists' discussion of this thesis is supportive: "There is always a subject that is uppermost in my mind," wrote William Baziotes in 1945.

Sometimes I am aware of it. Sometimes not. I work on my canvas until I think it is finished. Often I recognize my subject at completion of the picture and again I may wait a long time before I know what it is about.[38]

De Kooning approached the issue from the opposite side, raising the question directly as to whether the subject itself was not the formal treatment, in earlier art, rather than the iconography: "I wonder about the subject matter of the Crucifixion scene—was the Crucifixion the subject matter or not? What is the subject matter? Is an interior subject matter?"[39]

Rothko raises a similar point, but less directly related to the question of subjects:

It must be noted that the great painters of the figure had this in common. Their portraits resemble each other far more than they recall the peculiarities of a particular model. In a sense they have painted one character in all their work. What is indicated here is that the artist's real model is an ideal which embraces all of human drama rather than the appearance of a particular individual.[40]

Rothko's statement about the large size of his works has often been quoted in explanation of the impact on the viewer made by his pictures (and that by the giant paintings of the other abstract expressionists as well)—specifically their ability to surround and draw in the viewer. But within Rothko's discussion of this aspect of his work he indicates other reasons for the large scale, related to the subject and his dialogue with it:

I paint very large pictures. I realize that historically the function of painting large pictures is painting something very grandiose and pompous. The reason I paint them, however—I think it applies to other painters I know—is precisely because I want to be very intimate and human. To paint a small picture is to place yourself outside your experience, to look upon an experience as a stereopticon view or with a reducing glass. However you paint the larger picture, you are in it. It isn't something you command.[41]

Pollock, it is recorded by Goodnough, thought his art was "concrete,"[42] implying that its meaning lies within its formal properties. And Newman states a similar thesis, using the same term:

Instead of making cathedrals out of Christ, man, or "life," we are making it out of ourselves, out of our own feelings. The image we produce is the self-evident one of revelation, real and concrete, that can be understood by anyone who will look at it without the nostalgic glasses of history.[43]

Even if Newman made his "cathedral" out of himself, the subject of his works was revealed only in the process of making them, as Thomas Hess discusses in his essay on the Stations of the Cross (below). Indeed as Lawrence Alloway first recorded,[44] this particular subject was "found," as Newman had painted four of the works before he realized what the particular subject was. In a similar manner Motherwell painted thirty-three Elegies—mostly small sketches—before he fully realized what the subject was and how it was tied directly to particular formal characteristics in the thirty-fourth. In this case, the original Elegy schema—the arrangement of black ovals and panels against a white ground—was actually intended for another purpose; only in making subsequent versions did Motherwell come to recognize that the Elegies' theme was a part of this structural invention.

In the practice of sculpture, the procedures and the simple facts of mass and weight argue against the improvisational nature of abstract-expressionist painting. But Smith's use of the welding technique in collagelike structures enabled him to work from a much wider position and assimilate modifications and new images into his works. Furthermore, Smith worked from found materials or stockpiles of fabricated elements, so that he could continue the flow of work, not stopping to fabricate or fashion a particular part.[45] Smith created works which were a synthesis of thematic concepts and particular images suggested to him by his materials. At Voltri he found a large sheet of steel folded up "like a giant stick of gum—I . . . watched it in many positions until I found its relationship."[46] This was the figural composition of Voltri VIII. "Voltri XI started from a tong head demanding a thick, oval, curved, supplicated hood held up by a vertical. It started in the fly ash of the floor; it never changed from the first few minutes of seeing."[47]

Many of the Voltri works are joined together because the "found" relationships of the parts also related to compositions, details, or just a general feeling of ancient and classical art. And they share (or the majority of them do) with Smith's other work a vocabulary drawn from the cubist collage, Gonzalez's and Picasso's constructed sculpture, and from Giacometti's surrealist pieces.

We see in Smith's work and in those of the other abstract expressionists that the forms presented are a result of the use of materials in a more automatic or improvisational manner, and the final structure has been determined by internal rather than programmatic requirements, however much each structure invokes a synthesis of the formal language of the modern tradition. The subjects in these works are thus derived from the found elements; the subjects do not exist separately only to be "correctly described" by the works. Rather the subject in these works is found or recognized in these formal properties.

METAPHORS

Because of this identity with formal structure, the subject in abstract-expressionist works is stated metaphorically rather than descriptively. It does not exist symbolically—as *immortality* does in a pomegranate in a Renaissance picture—nor has one kind of figuration been substituted for another, in the sense of a trope. Rather the arrangement of shapes, colors, etc., in the work itself constitutes a metaphor for something else, or rather it constitutes a subject which we can extrapolate to our experience of the actual world—or our ideas—in a metaphorical manner.

Because this was the direction of abstract expressionism—given its formal basis—it accounts for the greater abstraction in these artists' works: "It was with the utmost reluctance that I found the figure could not serve my purposes. . . . But a time came when none of us could use the figure without mutilating it," said Rothko in 1958.[48]

One of the rigors of abstract-expressionist painting is that because the subject is not descriptive, the articulation of it is key to its formal terms of existence. Thus Pollock, in emphasizing his subject—the ordering of chaos—had to work within the decisively fixed limits of his allover poured style; to change that style distinctly, by introducing figuration, for example, was to change the metaphorical subject of the works.

For Gorky, as Miss Rathbone proposes in this catalogue, the Plow and the Song works are most cogently viewed as Gorky's stating the subject increasingly in a metaphorical fashion—a direction clearly more abstract expressionist in orientation and character than it is surrealist. In a similar way, de Kooning's *Woman I* is concerned not simply with woman's femininity, but more with the ways in which her characteristics are linked with the pictorial style, and the way it records this as an evolutionary achievement.

It is clear that the relationship of the abstract-expressionist picture to the formal language of the modern tradition is not direct. Thus, Pollock's webs of paint produce a structure that parallels the cubist armature rather than borrows from the earlier style. In a similar way, if Rothko's works are related to certain precedents in Bonnard's pictures—even if they influenced the early Rothko—in his mature works this relationship is one of similarity rather than transference. Many artists' works in the early 1940s involved the direct translations or whole borrowings of European forms, and the subjects were often "borrowed" as well. In a general sense—at least—if the abstract expressionists rejected or transformed subjects, preferring to find them in their paintings' structure, the parallel isolation of their formal language increasingly made the language spontaneous, more of a simile to European precedents than a translation.

ABSTRACTION AND MEANING

"I think we start from a subjective attitude, which, in the process of our endeavour, becomes related to the world," said Newman in 1950. But that relationship between the subject of the work and the world remains metaphorical and bound to formalism. While extending the language of the modern tradition and placing the origin of their subjects within that extension and their own formal inventions, the abstract expressionists found themselves in a situation where they "could perceive no other way in which to go in order to say something personal, therefore new, therefore worth saying," according to Greenberg.[49] This may also account for the anxiety which pervades abstract-expressionist work; not that these artists lived in unanxious times, but rather their sense that the subject, derived from the difficult fusion in their art—"the voyage"—had to be communicated in formal and usually abstract terms.

Because the abstract-expressionist picture must speak in metaphors, its subject is conveyed through feelings, rather than precisely stated. The lack of the specific in the metaphor was of concern to these artists during this period, as we can see in the following exchange in the Studio 35 discussion in 1950:

Moderator Motherwell: . . . what is the content of our work? What are we really doing? The question is how to name what as yet has been unnamed.

Baziotes: Whereas certain people start with a recollection or an experience and paint that experience, to some of us the act of doing it becomes the experience; so that we are not quite clear why we are engaged on a particular work. And because we are more interested in plastic matters than we are in a matter of words, one can begin a picture and carry it through and stop it and do nothing about the title at all. All pictures are full of association.

Reinhardt: Titles are very important in surrealist work. But the emphasis with us is upon a painting experience, and not on any other experience. The only objection I have to a title is when it is false or tricky, or is something added that the painting itself does not have.

De Kooning: I think that if an artist can always title his pictures, that means he is not always very clear.

Newman: I think it would be very well if we could title pictures by identifying the subject matter so that the audience could be helped. I think the question of titles is purely a social phenomenon. The story is more or less the same when you can identify them. I think the implication has one of two possibilities: (1) We are not smart enough to identify our subject matter, or (2) language is so bankrupt that we can't use it. I think both are wrong. I think the possibility of finding language still exists, and I think we are smart enough. Perhaps we are arriving at a new state of painting where the thing has to be seen for itself.[50]

This lack of specificity outside of "the thing itself" is bound up with the broader venture of abstract-expressionist subjects. While Motherwell's Elegies are related to the Spanish Civil War in the sense that his feelings about that event are paralleled by certain properties and rhythms in the Elegy schema, he insists as well that "the pictures are also general metaphors of the contrast between life and death, and their interrelation."[51] As this metaphor stems from particular formal properties, it has the qualities of their more abstract speech. Again Motherwell:

The slightest touch will produce a whole, new-felt tone—and yet they still remain Elegies. To me this raises a profound question: [are the colors and shapes] . . . an iconography or a tone of voice. I'd argue that the subject matter of all of the Elegies—of all Abstract Expressionism—is a tone of voice.[52]

Motherwell's description of the words producing a "tone of voice" is paralleled by Franz Kline's analysis of his subject matter and its connection to formal means. In an interview with David Sylvester in 1963 Kline noted:

It is nice to paint a happy picture after a sad one. I think that there is a kind of loneliness in a lot of them which I don't think about as the fact that I'm lonely and therefore I paint lonely pictures, but I like kind of lonely things anyhow; as if the forms express that to me, there is a certain excitement that I have about that. Any composition—you know, the overall reality of that does have something to do with it; the impending forms of something, do maybe have a brooding quality, whereas in other forms, they would be called or considered happier.

Sylvester: Are you aware of these qualities when you are actually painting or only after you have finished the painting?

Kline: No, I'm aware of them as I paint. I don't mean that I retain those. What I try to do is to create the painting so that the overall thing has that particular emotion; not particularly just the forms in it.[53]

Given these factors—the abstraction of the works (or, in de Kooning's and Smith's cases, of the structures), the inextricable relationship between form and subject, and the need for the subject to speak in a metaphorical and thus tonal, or nonspecific, way—the subjects of their works seem to be addressed to universal concepts or ideas, rather than focused on thoughts or images of a particular culture or time (although it is historical and cultural that they stated them in this fashion). It is interesting that the surrealists and abstract expressionists in the early 1940s would use myths as subjects and that these were seen as more broadly based references to life. These myths were perhaps transitional to the abstract expressionists' subjects. The "abstraction" inherent in myths certainly is a partial precedent for the formal abstraction of the subject in abstract expressionism. Thus we find themes that are grand, poetic, tragic: the benevolent "order out of chaos" in Pollock, the "death (and life)" in Rothko and Motherwell.

SERIES

Our discussion to this point may suggest that the abstract expressionist introduces a new subject every time he makes a work; that each creative act is a Mallarméan "toss of the dice." This is not necessarily untrue for certain artists: Kline, for example, may in his works suggest certain affinities to the urban environment, which link his mature work as a whole, as does his personal touch. Nonetheless within his oeuvre, there is nothing that signifies any particular theme, or makes his more general subjects more focused. By contrast some of Pollock's works—the classic paintings, for example—can be seen as related in the manner in which the broader theme of his art is more pronounced.

By contrast to Kline and Pollock, Still's works are seen by the artist as comprising one grand subject. He calls it "Orchestral. My work in its entirety is like a symphony in which each painting has its part."[56]

For other artists—the seven in this exhibition—certain subjects are singled out in particular works which form a series—

Gorky, de Kooning, Motherwell, or Newman. Others stress certain thematic ideas that underlie the larger part of the works—as with Pollock and Smith—or do both, as in the case of Rothko.

In the works of Gorky, de Kooning, and Motherwell, it is a matter of repetition or recalling particular compositional elements; Gorky's Plow and the Song series—his longest continuing mature theme, stretching from 1942 through 1947 and encompassing more works than any other theme—is marked by his use of roughly the same layout and a majority of the same forms from picture to picture. De Kooning's Women are marked not only by similarities of image—a woman and her activities, a bather—but by his formal presentation in a manner at once surrealist and Cézannesque. Gorky's and de Kooning's works can also be joined in the way that they reveal an evolution of their theme: Gorky's gradual move to a more personal and metaphorical painting, and de Kooning's development of the woman form as existing in a landscape to being the landscape.

Motherwell's works differ from those of Gorky and de Kooning in that they are abstract and the paintings in the series differ widely in appearance. Yet, what makes them Elegies and gives them their subject is the particular manner in which the component black forms are linked together, to make a schema which is at once unified and composite. In this sense the Elegies do not evolve, rather the subject is revealed in its different faces by various versions.

Newman's Stations of the Cross are different as well. Although there are fourteen paintings (and one concluding work), they are in effect a thematic unit. "Do not the Stations tell of one event?" asked Newman.[57] Here, rather than unifying the composition by similar formal elements, Newman used canvases of the same proportions, which further emphasize the processional aspects of the works.

Pollock's classic works are not linked together by any means which might suggest a series, although three works—*Number 32, 1950, One,* and *Autumn Rhythm*—may share some particular formal traits. Further, in Pollock's works certain pictures are singled out and the subject matter clearly identified in the way in which he extended his resolution over technique. Indeed Pollock's subject denied his making a "series"; if his achievement of order in the works was explicitly the subject, it had to be stated anew in each work. A program image would have prevented this.

Smith's Voltri sculpture can be seen as constituting a series simply on the basis of the time they were done, the conditions surrounding their creation, and the specific materials incorporated in them. But if the body of Smith's work can be seen as linking with forms and themes from across the range of the history of art, at Voltri many of the works single out more restrictive connections to ancient and classic precedents. Here the works do not reveal facets of a subject—as in Motherwell, for example—so much as they each, with their separate identities, constitute a constellation which has a more precise form.

Rothko is in many ways the most summary and the most complex of the artists with respect to a subject which is present in more than one work. The Brown and Gray series consists of works that are related by virtue of their material, paper, format (even the white edges), and general layout—the brown areas above gray areas. Yet, as Miss Rathbone discusses in her essay, in the case of Rothko the union of the works in series reveals more of the subject than the study of each of them in isolation.

Because the subject is endemically a part of its form and cannot be isolated, its presence can only be recalled by formal means. Subject is not separated into theme and presentation; and to restate the subject the artist must restate—in part—the means of presentation. As Motherwell suggested in 1950,

When one looks at a Renaissance painter, it is evident that he can modify existing subject matter in a manner that shows his uniqueness and fineness without having to re-invent painting altogether. But I think that painters like Mondrian tend to move as rapidly as they can toward a simple iconography on which they can make variations. Because the strain is so great to re-invent reality in painting.[58]

ISOLATING ASPECTS

The creation of a series by recollection of formal properties in abstract expressionism might suggest that these works are precursors for the serial imagery used by Noland in his target paintings, Stella in his Black series, or Warhol in his Brillo boxes, for example. But the particular composition for these later artists constitutes a "successful" format from which they could move outwardly into variations and new inventions, whereas in abstract expressionism the repetition of format is for an opposite reason: to move inwardly or to stay in closer contact with a specific theme. Neither of these stylistic tendencies is a prerequisite for quality, but it does underscore a specific difference between the two generations.[59]

Nevertheless the painting that followed abstract expressionism did borrow from it, especially the manner in which abstract expressionism approached the art of the past synoptically and formally, ignoring direct thematic traditions. But for this next generation, the subjects in their works were either ignored or made implicit. The works of Morris Louis, who was a transitional figure from abstract expressionism to the abstract painting of the 1960s, are a case in point; for his large Unfurled paintings ask for direct comparison with the grand paintings of the abstract expressionists. But where the sublime aspects of the abstract-expressionist works are a part of their subjects (and their metaphorical nature) Louis' ambition was to achieve a grandness in more purely pictorial terms, and that grandness itself would then work metaphorically.

Because of its position between the more literary works of the surrealists and the more endemically abstract paintings of the 1960s, abstract expressionism is viewed as transitional, and it is understood differently when seen from the opposite sides of its linkage. The very presence of subjects suggests that abstract expressionism was understood as an extension of the traditional means of expression used in surrealism, while its very real formalism suggests that its concerns should be joined with those of the formalist art of the next generation. Following the latter perspective, Geldzahler has united abstract expressionism, and color painting as part of a New York movement, writing that for both "artistic problems become the subject of art."[60]

As we have seen, abstract expressionism was unique in its synoptical view of modern art. But the selection and use of "art"—its intrinsic formal qualities—was, in the abstract expressionists' hands, for purposes of finding a subject.

"Art always gets its moral support from a tradition—the church, governments, etc.—here [in abstract expressionism] it gets its support from itself, from the culture of art," Motherwell said recently.[61] While this is not the place to chronicle why modern art arrived at such a position, it is important to note that in abstract expressionism art gets its support—rather than its full meaning—from the "culture of art."

The insistence on the presence of subjects in their works belies any "art for art's sake" analysis of abstract expressionism; rather, one might say, these artists were forced into a position of "art for their subjects" sake. As Smith discussed:

But how can a man live off of his planet? How on earth can he know anything that he hasn't seen or doesn't exist in his own world? Even his visions have to be made up of what he knows, of the forms and the world that he knows. He can't go off his planet with visions no matter how they're put together. And he naturally uses his proportion and his sort of objectivity. He can't get away from it. There is no such thing as truly abstract. Man always has to work from his life.[63]

The more recent trend in the analysis of abstract expressionism has been to isolate its other side, that of subjects, by proposing there exists, in one way or another, extractable imagery and iconography.[64] But as Greenberg recently noted, "If there is anything Pollock was set against in his poured pictures it was iconography. They have a subject—Jackson was sure of that—but it wasn't there because of iconography."[65]

The problem with an isolated imagistic, and iconographic program as applied to abstract expressionism is that no one has been able to demonstrate its existence across the board. Yet recent analysis of the movement has accounted for it by suggesting that a patently traditional system of images is—or was—present, but that it has been hidden or camouflaged by the artist in some way. This is perhaps the most serious charge against abstract expressionism because it portrays a different set of motivations behind the works. As is stated above, the artistic anxiety in abstract expressionism may come, in part, from the artists' ability to pinpoint the subject in the work, and their inability to state it in any terms save its pictorial ones. The case is probably the most pronounced—and most difficult—in the works of Pollock, who has been repeatedly charged with layering paint over traditional iconographic images. But in understanding Pollock's works it is central to recognize that far from working to disguise his subject, his efforts were certainly to make it explicit and yet still within the concrete and absolute fabric of his abstractions. To misread this struggle by Pollock and the abstract expressionists and to accuse them of camouflage is a major misunderstanding of their enterprise.

The linking of subjects to format is the crucial distinction in abstract expressionism and is, perhaps, its most salient feature. Only by understanding this inextricable bondage can we hope to comprehend the full origin and meaning of these works. As was suggested in the first remarks in this essay and is exhibited at length in the texts which follow, the works of the abstract expressionists cannot be separated into categories of form or iconography as a group nor, even, individually.

Further analysis of abstract expressionism may reveal other connecting threads, and our topic will await further and more complex interpretation of this movement's origins, development, and import. But thematic concerns arising out of formal inventions are one of its salient features. As Hans Hofmann said in 1950, "I think the question goes all the time back to subject matter. Each subject matter depends on how to use meaning."[66]

NOTES

1. Jackson Pollock, in a questionnaire in Feb. 1944 issue of *Arts and Architecture*; quoted in Francis O'Connor, *Jackson Pollock*, exh. cat. (New York: Museum of Modern Art, 1967), 31.

2. The dada movement offers interesting parallels along these lines, although it might be said to be more a case of a unifying idea expressed in different ways. Comparison is also complicated because dada appeared in various cities. Surrealism follows along in this way, divided into abstract and veristic styles but each concerned with similar themes. In the 1950s de Kooning was seen as the leading figure of abstract expressionism and was the focus of an enormous amount of following in the so-called "10th Street touch." But this position does not mean de Kooning was central *within* the development of abstract expressionism. Certain critics and historians have used the terms *abstract expressionism* and *New York School* interchangeably, but this can often suggest that abstract expressionism was not a movement so much as a group bound together by geography and time, an American equivalent of the *École de Paris*. This is precisely what Henry Geldzahler's exhibition, *New York Painting and Sculpture: 1940-1970*, for the Metropolitan Museum of Art (1969) implies, and he suggests that the term *New York School* can be extended to include pop and color field painters. To avoid this confusion, the term *New York School* will not be used here.

3. Mark Rothko; quoted from the Pratt Lecture by Dore Ashton, in Maurice Tuchman, ed., *New York School: The First Generation: Paintings of the 1940s and 1950s*, exh. cat. (Los Angeles: Los Angeles County Museum of Art, 1966), 30.

4. Barnett Newman, in "Artists' Sessions at Studio 35" (1950); quoted in Tuchman, *New York School*, 40.

5. Robert Motherwell, in conversation with the author, Aug. 17, 1977 (on file in the Department of Twentieth-Century Art, National Gallery of Art, Washington).

6. Excerpt from the curriculum of the "Catalogue for 1948-49" of The Subjects of the Artist: A New Art School announcement sheet; original on file in Department of Twentieth-Century Art, National Gallery of Art, Washington.

7. See William Rubin's "Jackson Pollock and the Modern Tradition, Part I: The Myths and the Paintings" (Feb. 1967); "Part I: 2. The All-over Compositions and the Drip Technique" (Feb. 1967); "Part II: 3. Impressionism and the Classic Pollock; 4. Color and Scale; Affinities with the Late Monet" (Mar. 1967); "Part III: 5. Cubism and the Later Evolution of the All-over Style," (Apr. 1967); "Part IV: 6. An Aspect of Automatism" (May 1967), *Artforum*, vol. 5; Irving Sandler, The *Triumph of American Painting: A History of Abstract Expressionism* (New York: Praeger Publishers, 1970); and Brian O'Doherty, *American Masters: The Voice and the Myth* (New York: Random House, 1973).

8. As recorded in Rosalind Krauss, *The Sculpture of David Smith: A Catalogue Raisonné* (New York: Garland, 1977).

9. Barnett Newman; quoted by Dorothy Seckler, "Interview with Barnett Newman," *Art in America, 50* (Summer 1962): 83.

10. David Smith, in an interview with David Sylvester, in *David Smith*, ed. Garnett McCoy (New York: Praegar Publishers, 1973), 170.

11. Smith; quoted in *David Smith*, 170.

12. Hilton Kramer, "30 Years of the New York School," *The New York Times Magazine*, Oct. 12, 1969, 94.

13. See Sandler on this point in his *Triumph of American Painting*, 125, 128, 129.

14. William Rubin, *Dada, Surrealism, and Their Heritage*, exh. cat. (New York: Museum of Modern Art, 1968), 182.

15. Pollock; quoted in O'Connor, *Jackson Pollock*, 31. This absence may have been crucial for Gorky as well, for his art had evolved along lines drawn from Picasso and Miró.

16. Clement Greenberg, "After Abstract Expressionism" in Henry Geldzahler, *New York Painting and Sculpture: 1940-1970* (New York: Dutton, 1969), 361.

17. Greenberg, "After Abstract Expressionism," in Geldzahler, *New York Painting*, 361.

18. Smith; quoted in *David Smith*, 171.

19. Smith, "Letter to David Sylvester," Dec. 11, 1962; quoted in Giovanni Carandente, *Voltron* (Philadelphia: Institute of Contemporary Art, University of Pennsylvania, 1964), 14.

20. Rubin, *Dada, Surrealism, and Their Heritage*, 177.

21. The following discussion of automatism and cubism is adapted from this author's *The Collages of Robert Motherwell*, exh. cat. (Houston: Museum of Fine Arts, 1972), 18-21.

22. Sidney Janis, *Abstract and Surrealist Art in America* (New York: Reynal and Hitchcock, 1944), 2.

23. Clement Greenberg, "Art," *The Nation, 160* (June 9, 1945): 657.

24. Robert Motherwell, "The Modern Painters' World," *Dyn, 6* (Nov. 1944): 13.

25. Adolph Gottlieb, in an interview with Andrew Hudson; in Karen Wilken, "Adolph Gottlieb: The Pictographs," *Art International, 21* (Dec. 1977): 28.

26. Robert Motherwell; quoted in Tuchman, *New York School*, 39.

27. Harold Rosenberg, *The Tradition of the New* (New York: Horizon Press, 1959), 25, 26.

28. For discussion of this point see the correspondence between Rosenberg and William Rubin in *Artforum, 5* (Apr.-May 1967).

29. Mary McCarthy; quoted by Rosenberg in *The Tradition of the New*, 5.

30. Newman; quoted in Seckler "Interview," 86.

31. Motherwell; quoted in O'Connor, *Jackson Pollock*, 31.

32. Hess has suggested that Newman may have used a system of proportioning, in his *Barnett Newman*, exh. cat. (New York: Museum of Modern Art, 1971).

33. For Motherwell, see the author's *Collages*, 11-15, 48-49; and for Newman, see Barbara Rose, "Mondrian in New York," *Artforum, 10* (Dec. 1971): 54-63.

34. Willem de Kooning in "Artists' Sessions at Studio 35"; quoted in Tuchman, *New York School*, 39-40.

35. Adolph Gottlieb in "Artists' Sessions at Studio 35"; quoted in Tuchman, *New York School*, 37.

36. This discussion is adapted from this author's analysis of Motherwell's Elegies in this catalogue (see "Robert Motherwell: The Elegies to the Spanish Republic").

37. Motherwell, in conservation with the author, Aug. 17, 1977.

38. William Baziotes, "Personal Statement, 1945"; quoted in Tuchman, *New York School*, 10.

39. De Kooning in "Artists' Sessions at Studio 35"; quoted in Tuchman, *New York School*, 40.

40. Rothko; quoted in Tuchman, *New York School*, 30.

41. Rothko, *Interiors, 110* (May 1951): 104.

42. Robert Goodnough, "Jackson Pollock Paints a Picture," *Art News, 60* (May 1951): 38.

43. Newman, "The Sublime is Now," *Tiger's Eye, 1* (Dec. 15, 1948): 53.

44. Lawrence Alloway, "The Stations of the Cross and the Subjects of the Artist" in *The Stations of the Cross*, exh. cat. (New York: Solomon R. Guggenheim Museum, 1966), 11.

45. Both Anthony Caro and Kenneth Noland have repeatedly emphasized in conversations with the author this central aspect of Smith's art, his ability to keep it constantly moving and open.

46. David Smith, "Report on Voltri," in *David Smith*, 163.

47. David Smith, "Report on Voltri," in *David Smith*, 162.

48. Rothko; quoted in Tuchman, *New York School*, 29.

49. Greenberg, "After Abstract Expressionism"; in Geldzahler, *New York Painting*, 360.

50. Discussion from "Artists' Sessions at Studio 35"; in Tuchman, *New York School*, 35.

51. Motherwell, *Robert Motherwell*, exh. cat. (Northampton, Mass.: Smith College, 1963), cat. no. 16.

52. Motherwell, in conversation with the author, Aug. 17, 1977.

53. Franz Kline; quoted in Tuchman, *New York School,* 20.

54. The surrealists' interest in the unconscious as a source for subject matter may have also been of importance in the development of the abstract expressionists; this interest certainly influenced the works of Gottlieb, Motherwell, Rothko, and Pollock. However, the latter's earlier painting *Search for a Symbol,* 1944 (collection of Lee Krasner Pollock, New York) is a case in point, as the surrealists' subjects were expressed by symbols—even archetypal forms—that had a standard repertoire (which we can see transformed in Gottlieb's work). But it is argued here that in the abstract expressionists' painting, the metaphors are stated not symbolically but structurally. A study of this transformation of the subject from symbol to structure would clearly be of importance, if it were possible; however, to identify earlier themes stated symbolically and then to propose these themes form a "hidden symbolism" in the full abstract-expressionist work is incorrect (Rothko may be an exception).

55. Kline said in Sylvester interview: "If someone says, 'That looks like a bridge' it doesn't bother me really. A lot of them do.... I don't have the feeling that something has to be completely non-associative as far as figure form is concerned ..." (in Tuchman, *New York School,* 20).

56. Clyfford Still; quoted in "An Interview with Clyfford Still" by Benjamin Townsend in *Gallery Notes, 24,* Albright-Knox Art Gallery (Summer 1961): 16. Because certain of his works use a restricted palette or composition, Charles Parkhurst and the author discussed this exhibition with Still in the fall of 1976 and inquired if within his works certain paintings did stress a particular theme. His reply was that "all of his work was one subject" and stated that it would not be appropriate to select a group of paintings for this exhibition. Still's preference for showing his work in a large grouping has often been noted.

57. Barnett Newman, in statement in *The Stations of the Cross.*

58. Motherwell in "Artists' Sessions at Studio 35"; quoted in Tuchman, *New York School,* 39.

59. For a different view of "series" in abstract expressionism, see John Coplan's *Serial Imagery* (Pasadena: Pasadena Art Museum, 1968), 9.

60. Geldzahler; quoted by Kramer, "30 Years," 97.

61. Motherwell, in conversation with the author, Aug. 17, 1977.

62. Both Greenberg and Rosenberg have suggested some origins lie in the shift away from politics in the 1940s—Greenberg in "The Late Thirties in New York" in *Art and Culture* (Boston: Beacon Press, 1961), 230, and Rosenberg in *The Anxious Object* (New York: Horizon Press, 1966), 39.

63. David Smith; quoted in *David Smith,* 171.

64. See, for example, Charles Stuckey's "Another Side of Jackson Pollock," *Art in America, 65* (Nov. 1977): 80-91.

65. Greenberg, in conversation with the author, Mar. 1978 (on file in the Department of Twentieth-Century Art, National Gallery of Art, Washington).

66. Hans Hofmann in "Artists' Sessions at Studio 35"; quoted in Tuchman, *New York School,* 40.

16. Barnett Newman. *Be II,* 1961-1964. Collection, Annalee Newman, New York [photo: Malcolm Varon, courtesy of Annalee Newman]

17. Jackson Pollock. *Number 1, 1950 (Lavender Mist)*, 1950. National Gallery of Art, Washington, Ailsa Mellon Bruce Fund, 1976

18. Jackson Pollock. *Number 2, 1950,* 1950. Fogg Art Museum, Harvard University, Cambridge, Mass.; in part given and in part lent by Reginald and Charlotte Isaacs and family and friends, and in part purchased from the Contemporary Art Fund

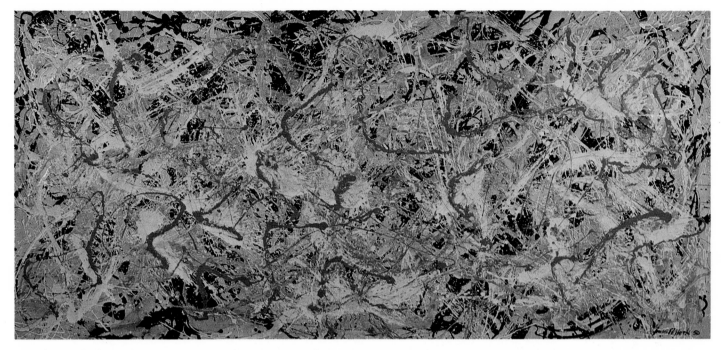

19. Jackson Pollock. *Number 27, 1950,* 1950. Whitney Museum of American Art, New York [photo: Geoffrey Clements]

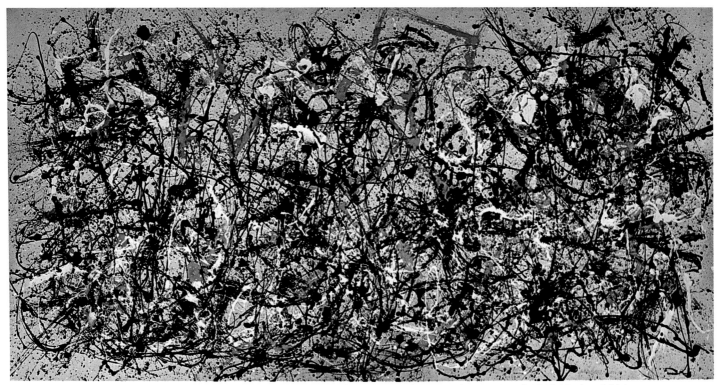

20. Jackson Pollock. *Autumn Rhythm,* 1950. The Metropolitan Museum of Art, New York, George A. Hearn Fund, 1957. Not in exhibition

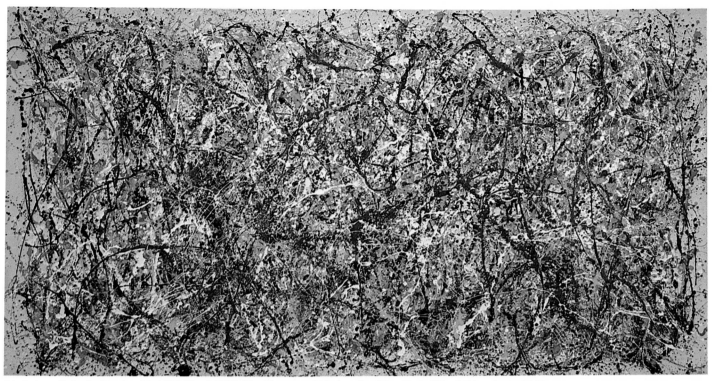

21. Jackson Pollock. *Number 31, 1950 (One)*, 1950. The Museum of Modern Art, New York, Gift of Sidney Janis, 1968

22. Mark Rothko. *Brown and Gray,* 1969. Anonymous loan

23. Mark Rothko. *Brown and Gray*, 1969. Private collection

49

24. Mark Rothko. *Brown and Gray*, 1969. Estate of Mark Rothko

25. Mark Rothko. *Brown and Gray,* 1969. Anonymous loan

26. Mark Rothko. *Brown and Gray,* 1969. Estate of Mark Rothko

27. Mark Rothko. *Brown and Gray,* 1969. Anonymous loan

28. Mark Rothko. *Brown and Gray,* 1969. Private collection

29. Mark Rothko. *Brown and Gray,* 1969. Private collection

30. David Smith. *Voltri VII*, 1962. National Gallery of Art, Washington, Ailsa Mellon Bruce Fund, 1977 [photo: Dan Budnik, courtesy of Woodfin Camp & Associates]

American Art at Mid-Century

THE SUBJECTS OF THE ARTIST

ARSHILE GORKY:
The Plow and the Song

Figure 1. Arshile Gorky, shown drawing at Crooked Run Farm, 1943 or 1944. [Photo: Mrs. John H. Magruder]

CHECKLIST

1. Study for The Plow and the Song   1944 *ill. p. 67, fig. 9.*
   pencil and crayon on paper
   48.2 × 64.3 cm (19 × 25¼ in)
   Signed and dated center right: A. Gorky 44
   Allen Memorial Art Museum, Oberlin College, Ohio

2. The Plow and the Song   1946
   pencil, charcoal, crayon, pastel and oil on paper *ill. p. 69 fig. 13*
   121.5 × 150.8 cm (47⅞ × 59⅜ in)
   Signed lower right: A. Gorky
   National Gallery of Art, Washington, Avalon Fund

3. The Plow and the Song II   1946 *ill. p. 79, fig. 36*
   oil on canvas
   131.8 × 155.9 cm (51⅞ × 61⅜ in)
   The Art Institute of Chicago, Mr. and Mrs. Lewis L. Coburn Fund

4. The Plow and the Song   1947
   oil on burlap
   132.4 × 162.9 cm (52⅛ × 64⅛ in)
   Signed and dated lower right: A. Gorky 47
   Mr. Milton A. Gordon, New York

5. The Plow and the Song   1947 *ill. p. 85 fig. 47*
   oil on canvas
   128.9 × 159.4 cm (50¾ × 62¾ in)
   Signed and dated lower right: A. Gorky 47
   Allen Memorial Art Museum, Oberlin College, Ohio

6. Untitled   1944-1945
   pencil and crayon on paper
   48.0 × 59.7 cm (18⅞ × 23½ in)
   Estate of A. Gorky

   see ill. p. 75 - fig. 21

BIOGRAPHY

Arshile Gorky (Vosdanik Manoog Adoian). Born 1904, village of Khorkom, province of Van, Armenia. In 1915, following Turkish seige of Van, leaves home with family. 1915-1919, lives in, and subsequently just outside, town of Yerevan; holds various jobs, including carpentry. In 1920 Gorky and sister Vartoosh arrive in United States. In 1922 Gorky teaches art at Boston's New School of Design, 248 Boylston Street. Moves to New York in 1925 and teaches at Grand Central School of Art until 1931. In 1930 moves into studio at 36 Union Square; work included in group show at Museum of Modern Art. 1933-1941, is involved in the WPA. Marries Agnes Magruder in 1941. Visits Saul Scharys in Connecticut in 1942 and in 1943 makes first visit to Magruder Farm, Hamilton, Virginia. In 1944 begins The Plow and the Song. In 1945 exhibits at Julien Levy Gallery. In January 1946 fire destroys studio in Sherman, Connecticut; in February, Gorky undergoes colostomy operation for cancer and, during the summer, does 292 drawings in Virginia. On June 26, 1948, his neck is broken and his painting arm paralyzed in automobile accident with Julien Levy; mid-July, Agnes Gorky leaves Gorky, taking their two children; July 21, Gorky hangs himself, Sherman, Connecticut.

ARSHILE GORKY:
The Plow and the Song

ELIZA E. RATHBONE

INTRODUCTION

No discussion of Arshile Gorky's The Plow and the Song would be complete without addressing the issue of Gorky's art in light of the work of his contemporaries. Few artists of this century have provoked as much discussion regarding which school or movement they should be considered a part of. Just as the heading *post-impressionism* comfortably embraces artists as different from one another as van Gogh, Gauguin, and Cézanne, so the name *The New York School* has been used sufficiently loosely to include Gorky with the artists that came to be known as the abstract expressionists. Van Gogh and Cézanne, even more than Gauguin, who formed the school of Pont-Aven around him, after a period of painting in the impressionist style, pursued a highly independent tack and shared no group aesthetic or program.

Similarly it is tempting to consider that Gorky most accurately falls into what we might call a "post-surrealist" camp. While in the 1930s the works he emulated most highly, besides Cézanne's, were Picasso's of the late 1920s and his surrealist paintings of the thirties, Gorky was never involved with the surrealist movement proper, nor did he actively involve himself in the formation of abstract expressionism. In view of the present exhibition concerned specifically with the content of abstract-expressionist painting and its manifestation, Gorky's relation to the rest of the artists included must be clarified.

Gorky's tragic and early death by suicide occurred in 1948, the year that Baziotes, Motherwell, Rothko, and Still gave the name *The Subjects of the Artist* to the "school" at 35 East 8th Street. Most of the artists involved were just embarking on their mature styles of painting, and what came to be known as The Club provided a forum for the discussion of ideas which were to change radically the course of American painting.

In 1943 Adolph Gottlieb and Mark Rothko, with Barnett Newman's assistance, wrote a letter to the art editor of the *New York Times,* Edward Alden Jewell. This manifesto, one of the first, indicated the direction to be taken by the abstract expressionists. While some of its ideas clearly derive from surrealism, automatism in particular, it also put forward in points four and five certain principles of content and form which were to distinguish the work of the abstract expressionists from anything that had gone before:

4. We favor the simple expression of the complex thought. We are for the large shape because it has the impact of the unequivocal. We wish to reassert the picture plane. We are for flat forms because they destroy illusion and reveal truth.

5. . . . We assert that the subject is crucial and only that subject matter is valid which is tragic and timeless.[1]

Gorky was not involved in the formation of this new ideology, already germinating as early as 1943. While he shared his contemporaries' dedication to subject matter, the attitudes outlined in point four of the letter, embraced by the others, led, by the late 1940s, to a manner of painting to which Gorky's work bears only tangential resemblance.

One of the fundamental aspects to emerge with the full flowering of abstract expressionism was the size of the paintings. Despite the size of some of Gorky's paintings, the largest being one of his last works, *Summation* (78⅜ x 100¼ inches; 1947), they maintain their own internal scale—"windows" on the world, as he called them—rather than addressing themselves to the scale of the spectator outside the painting.[2] The abstract expressionists created their formal vocabulary, rather than abstracting or deriving it from nature, whereas not only did Gorky turn continually to the visible world for his subject but also the creative process of his mature work entailed a direct dialogue with nature.

Gorky's unshakeable attachment to reality and to the specific and concrete content of a work in itself imposed a limit on any given series—a limit of a kind that would not apply to paintings of a more metaphysical nature, for example, by Newman, Rothko, Motherwell, or Still.[3] Gorky shared with the abstract expressionists a moral commitment to his subject that differentiates them collectively from the surrealists. From his first series, Portrait of the Artist and His Mother, onward, he continued to choose subjects rich in personal association.

While Gorky never fully freed himself from representation as the abstract expressionists did, his process often involved a sufficient remove from nature to allow the evocative power of a form to reveal to him an unanticipated subject. Thus he wrote of abstraction as "the probing vehicle" for creating "new infinities."[4] In that respect his process parallels the "finding" of a subject that is the genesis in many instances of an abstract-expressionist theme. To "find" a subject in such a manner is, of course, ultimately derived from surrealist automatism. In some respects, however, Gorky developed a greater polarity between his source of inspiration and its ultimate form of expression than had either the surrealists or, indeed, the abstract expressionists. Given a concrete visible starting point, he translated it freely, sometimes in the adopted manner of another artist. He then and only then might find other images—in the manner of André Masson finding specific forms in an au-

Figure 2. Arshile Gorky. *The Artist and His Mother*, 1926-1929. Oil on canvas, 152.9 x 127.0 cm (60 x 50 in). Whitney Museum of American Art, New York, Gift of Julien Levy for Maro and Natasha Gorky in memory of their father [photo: Oliver Baker]. Not in exhibition

tomatist drawing. One would be hard pressed to think of another artist who proceeded through such a complex sequence of translation, derivation, and invention.

The process of both the surrealists and the abstract expressionists, on the other hand, usually involved a more direct relation between the point of departure and the ultimate realization of the work. Their starting point did not lie in the outside world; in place of nature as a starting point, they created their own "given" situation—a pictorial one. Such a "given," in one way or another, entailed a deliberate restriction of conscious control. (Only after the initial action with paint and canvas would Pollock "get acquainted" with what he had done; Ernst would transform a frottage of floor boards into a gothic forest.) From beginning to end the process involved a more consistently self-referential sequence—of one pictorial situation giving rise to another. In the mature work of the abstract expressionists, the dialogue of "given" and "found" merges as the artist exerted more and more control throughout. It was Gorky's reference to something outside himself that provided a constant variety of sources for his interpretation, even within one work or series, and that from the start distinguishes his process from that of the surrealists and that of the abstract expressionists.

Gorky can, nevertheless, be considered a bridge between both movements.[5] Two of the major features of surrealism that were adopted by the abstract expressionists were central to

Gorky's style. Not only did he employ forms—particularly biomorphic ones—for their intrinsic evocative power, but also he used gesture as a spontaneous recording of unconscious impulses. The individual and expressive execution of his line drawings or of such freely painted works as *Water of the Flowering Mill* (fig. 3), despite its source in the surrealist principle of automatism, is unlike most surrealist painting in which the actual facture tends to be either carefully finished (as in the work of Magritte or Dali) or to be based upon a technique that distances the artist by way of such "givens" as a frottage or a collage (Ernst or Miró). Gorky never introduced extraneous materials into his work. His love of the physical properties of paint for their own sake and his understanding of the expressive potential of the artist's gesture is that aspect of his style that most justifies his kinship with the abstract expressionists. The concept of spontaneous gesture was probably introduced to Gorky by his friend John Graham, Russian expatriate painter and theorist whom Gorky met in the late twenties.[6] Graham brought to this country from Paris his own particular interpretation of the possibilities of surrealist automatism and expostulated his views in his *System and Dialectics of Art* (1937). In example, however, Gorky's work derives more from the early abstractions of Kandinsky which New York artists were given the opportunity to study with the opening of Peggy Guggenheim's gallery, Art of This Century, in 1939. The Chilean surrealist, Matta Echaurren, whom Gorky met in 1941, also provided significant encouragement to his unleashing of the flow of paint.

If surrealism essentially consisted of a tempering of consciously conceived reality, with subconscious or irrational associations—a marriage of inner and outer, dream and reality—Gorky was naturally inclined toward it from his early work onward. His *Portrait of the Artist and His Mother* (1926-1936; fig. 2) presages the psychological intensity invested in later work, including others based on memories of his past. Gorky's autobiographical inclination may have been encouraged by John Graham, who had written and illustrated his own autobiography, entitled *From White to Red*.

[He] illustrated it with colorful and fanciful crayon drawings . . . it presented a dreamlike concept of his infancy and childhood, in part real, in part fantasy. It had Freudian overtones and evoked surrealist imagery. It seemed . . . to be wrought in rich enamels and embroidery, to summon up the spirit of Russian icons.[7]

As early as the mid-thirties Gorky had the opportunity to further acquaint himself with surrealist art and thought at the gallery of Julien Levy, pioneer in bringing surrealism to this country. Upon Gorky's first visit to his gallery, when Levy lent him his book on surrealism (published 1936),

Gorky read it in the back room of the gallery and later borrowed it to take home. *Surrealism* was the first American version of what Levy called the "surrealist point of view," and it gave the small band of artists attracted to the modern European art a framework and language with which to pursue their dialogue with Europe.[8]

Gorky himself identified with surrealism to a considerable extent. His paraphrases of Eluard and Breton *(Simulation of General Paralysis Essayed)* in his love letters of the mid-thirties is well known, and he continued to allow surrealist titling of his

Figure 3. Arshile Gorky. *Water of the Flowery Mill,* 1944. Oil on canvas, 108.0 x 123.9 cm (42½ x 48¾ in). The Metropolitan Museum of Art, New York, The George A. Hearn Fund, 1956. Not in exhibition

Figure 4. Joan Miró. *The Tilled Field,* 1923-1924. Oil on canvas, 66.0 x 94.0 cm (26 x 37 in). The Solomon R. Guggenheim Museum, New York [photo: Robert E. Mates]. Not in exhibition

paintings in the forties. In 1941 he described his murals as "surrealistic" and continued,

Of course, the outward aspect of my murals seemingly does not relate to the average man's experience. But this is an illusion! What man has not stopped at twilight and on observing the distorted shape of his elongated shadow conjured up strange and moving and often fantastic fancies from it? Certainly we all dream and in this common denominator of every one's experience I have been able to find a language for all to understand.[9]

The meeting point of dream and reality was to be found in the artist's subjective response to objective reality. For Gorky that sense of the surreal involved intense concentration on chosen details of his visual experience. Ethel Schwabacher related some pertinent remarks Gorky made to her in the Metropolitan Museum:

"Vermeer is not a sun painter, but rather a moon painter—like Uccello—that is good, it is the pure, final stage of art, the moment when it becomes more real than reality." He paused thoughtfully. "One aspect," he continued, "of this super-reality is an extraordinary concentration on detail; see how he has drawn the snake so exactly with the red blood trickling onto the black and white diamond tiles of the floor. He has painted as Marianne Moore suggested a poet should write—'imaginary gardens with real toads.'"[10]

While surrealism was essentially a literary movement, Gorky turned to works of art for inspiration, not in general to literature. Although his knowledge of surrealist thought encouraged the development in his work of sexual associations, Gorky's erotic overtones are only an echo of the Freudian interpretations of the surrealists, not an explication of Freud's theories. Freud's concept of sexuality as fundamental to understanding human feeling and behavior were absorbed by Gorky and subsumed. Rather than being the explicit subject matter of a work, sexual associations are encompassed by themes that are broader in scope and more generalized in depiction. Birth,

fertility, death, the whole cycle of life may come into play and thus find a natural corollary in nature. The surrealists who influenced Gorky, primarily Picasso, Miró, Matta, and Masson, were also the major influence on other artists of the New York School, who in turn broadened Freudian subject matter into a more generalized mythological content.

Gorky was always more closely related to those surrealists who had painted first in a cubist style, like Picasso and Miró, than to Matta, for example, who combined the deep space of Dali and Tanguy with the biomorphic form. Thus, even after he broke away from his "apprenticeship" to Picasso in his work of the forties, the interrelationship of forms on the surface continued to play an important role in his work.

Unlike either the surrealists or the abstract expressionists, Gorky's work was often autobiographical; his mythology originated in a private experience. Of all the surrealists, with the exception of Picasso, it was from Miró that Gorky derived the most, and this kinship extended to the autobiographical content of his work. In Miró's first surrealist works of the mid-1920s, where he drew upon his nostalgia for Catalonia in numerous paintings, he expressed this nostalgia not in narrative form but rather in remembered images whose distillation opened the door to poetic associations. Gorky did the same, especially in works based on memories of his homeland in Armenia. If, however, qualities fundamental to surrealism, which are often given full play by Miró, consist either of the juxtaposition of the unlikely or irrational (an ear on the trunk of a tree in *Tilled Field* [fig. 4] or a hobbyhorse with an onion behind in *Family*) or of such juxtapositions married metaphorically into one—often biomorphic—form, the essential difference between Gorky and Miró lies in the identifiability of the object. In Miró's work the identity is usually self-evident, whereas in the case of Gorky's mature work, the title often provides a key without which the subject could remain enigmatic. It was this unique talent to translate surrealist concerns into abstract painting that provided an important stimulus to other New York artists who were evolving a new style of American painting. As Adolph Gottlieb acknowledged in the catalogue of the Gorky show at the Kootz Gallery two years after his death, for him, as for a few others, the vital task was a wedding of abstraction and surrealism. Out of these opposites something new could emerge, and Gorky's work is part of the evidence that this is true.[11]

In his illuminating article for *Art International,* William Rubin noted a crucial point: that Gorky's attitude differed from that of the surrealists;[12] while their program was revolutionary, Gorky looked to the past. He combed museums and always returned to the old masters for inspiration. Indeed, the Museum of Modern Art provided a certain pedigree for dada and surrealism in its exhibition of 1936-1937, *Fantastic Art, Dada, Surrealism,* which presented surrealism's heritage in the fantastic art of the past—of Giovanni di Paolo, of Bosch. Surrealism nevertheless represented a break from the immediate past. Gorky's sense of tradition extended not only to his attitude to art history and his place in it, of which he was very conscious, but also to his method. Most of his important paintings are preceded by preparatory drawings, often squared for transfer in the tradition of past masters.

During his lifetime, however, Gorky was consistently grouped with the surrealists, and it is only through the advantage of historical perspective that his kinship with the abstract expressionists fully emerges. One could speculate that abstract expressionism would have been born without him. His impact on these artists was more in terms of the nature of his achievement than of specific influence. What his work would have been like had he lived on past the age of forty-three, into the fifties when abstract expressionism came into its own, one cannot predict but only suspect that it would have continued along its already established course.

As late as 1947, André Breton, forever eager to perpetuate the movement, included Gorky in an exhibition in Paris he had arranged entitled *Surrealism in 1947.* By 1944 Gorky had met not only Breton but also other surrealists who came to the United States during the war. De Kooning, whom Gorky met in 1927 and with whom he shared a studio (in the late thirties), noted that Gorky "had this extraordinary, extrasensory perception. He had that other sense. He had all those things before the Surrealists and the Surrealists told him he had it already."[13] Robert Jonas similarly remarked: "Gorky had surrealism innate in him. . . ."[14]

Yet, in the person of André Breton Gorky found support and encouragement (see fig. 5). In 1945 Breton wrote the well-known foreword for Gorky's show at the Julien Levy Gallery, a foreword which he added to that year's new edition of his book, *Surrealism and Painting.* His piece allows for those aspects in which Gorky's work differs from that of the surrealists and yet falls into their camp, and he writes of Gorky's treating nature "like a cryptogram."

Those who love easy solutions will find slim pickings here; despite all warnings, they will continue in their attempts to discover still lifes, landscapes and figurations in these compositions, simply because they do not have the courage to recognize the fact that all human emotions tend to be precipitated in *hybrid* forms. By "hybrid" I mean to signify the end result produced by the contemplation of a natural spectacle blended with the flux of childhood and other memories provoked by

Figure 5. Gorky, Maro Gorky, and André Breton, c. 1946. [Photo: Elisa Breton, reproduced from Ethel K. Schwabacher, *Arshile Gorky* (New York, 1957)]

intense concentration upon this spectacle by an observer endowed with quite exceptional emotional gifts. It should, indeed, be emphasized that Gorky is unique among surrealist painters in remaining in direct contact with nature by standing *in front of it* in order to paint. He is not concerned, however, with translating nature as an *end in itself,* but rather with extracting from it sensations capable of acting as springboards toward the deepening, in terms of consciousness as much as of enjoyment, of certain spiritual states.[15]

Elaine de Kooning recorded that Gorky's formal recognition by the surrealists gave him "much satisfaction."[16] He esteemed Breton highly, and when Breton suggested that he should come to Paris, he talked of it with serious consideration.[17] In 1946 he made two illustrations for Breton's book of poetry, *Young Cherry Trees Secured Against Hares.* What greater stamp of authenticity or entrance-pass into the surrealist circle than that of André Breton, the principle pundit of the movement!

Yet Gorky himself must have begun to see his inclusion in this group that had christened him with a status he sought as inhibiting a true understanding of his objectives. Clement Greenberg had leveled harsh criticism at Gorky's first exhibition of paintings at the Julien Levy Gallery; reviewing the show for *The Nation,* he wrote, "[Gorky's] prismatic, iridescent [*sic*] color and open forms of abstract, 'biomorphic' surrealist painting . . . emphasizes the dependent nature of his inspiration," and continued, "Gorky has at last taken the easy way out—corrupted perhaps by the example of the worldly success of the imported Surrealists."[18] In 1947, Gorky expressed his objections to what he found to be a lack of seriousness in surrealist art. In his disgust for their emphasis on novelty and their shunning of the aesthetic, his own quest, evincing a degree of self-examination that he shared with the other members of the New York School, points to the fundamental aspects in which he differed from the surrealists, both in method and intent:

Surrealism is academic art under disguise and anti-aesthetic and suspicious of excellence and largely in opposition to modern art. To its adherents the tradition of art its quality mean little. . . . Art must be serious, no sarcasm, comedy. . . . They feel it is play. . . . It is not new things that are important, but new ways of expressing universals in the tongue of modern times. The deification of novelty can rob art of its painstakingly acquired aesthetics. . . .[19]

In his late work Gorky reversed his earlier procedure to make formal considerations the servant of inner feelings. While Baziotes, Pollock, Rothko, and David Hare were all grouped with Gorky as surrealists in 1944,[20] by 1947 their work already began to show signs of a new aesthetic that eliminated many of the ties to the art of the past that Gorky retained. Gorky's position as a pivotal figure lies in the manner in which he brought the foregoing artistic thought and tradition together in a dialogue of form and content.

SERIES

Gorky's work stands apart for a reason other than the art historical view that he was, as it were, riding on the crest of one wave, surrealism, before the breaking of the next, abstract expressionism. That reason lies in his strong sense of himself as an alien in this country. Rather than disguising his differences, he played them up. That the subjects he painted often arose from an intense feeling of individuality, moreover, was accentuated by his alienation from his homeland. Robert Jonas, artist, writer, and close friend of Gorky, said:

You felt it all the time, as if he was never here, as if his umbilical cord to the past was never broken. Gorky's isolation in the United States forced him to work and to dream of where he came from.[21]

Gorky's sense of world culture, moreover, made him feel responsible as an artist to the unique contribution of the artistic tradition of his country. Thus he chose not to minimize his Armenian heritage but to incorporate it in his ideal of achieving a universal statement.

I shall resurrect Armenia with my brush for all the world to see, and when we return to clay as we all must, then perchance they might say, "as a son of the Armenian mountains he offered his modest share to the accumulation of our world's great culture."[22]

Gorky did many groups of works on the same theme that may be considered series. Several of these were based on his memories of the province of Van, in Armenia. He was born there in the village of Khorkom, in April 1904, the son of a carpenter and trader. There Gorky spent the formative and impressionable years of his life. He had been named Vosdanik Manoog Adoian, after the nearby town of Vosdan which

Figure 6. Arshile Gorky. *Image in Khorkom*, c. 1936. Oil on canvas, 83.5 x 109.2 cm (32⅞ x 43 in). Estate of Arshile Gorky [photo: Xavier Fourcade, Inc.]. Not in exhibition

means "Land of Luxurious Growth."[23] At the age of twenty-one, after five years in this country, he changed his name to Arshile Gorky, the first of Gorky's adopted identities.[24] Gorky had been only ten years old when the Turks began the seige of Van in 1914, forcing the Adoians to leave. The grim sequel to the story is well known: Gorky saw his mother starve to death, and he and his sister fled Armenia, following their father, who had left some years before, to America. They arrived at Ellis Island March 1, 1920. Gorky never saw his native land again, but his continued contact with his sister Vartoosh, through correspondence or visits, kept alive the memories he cherished of Armenia.

Gorky consecrated to the memory of his mother a series of drawings and paintings (1926-1936) derived from a photograph made in his youth of himself standing beside her. And in the years that followed he returned repeatedly to themes drawn from his childhood in Armenia, now derived from remembered images. There are three series of works based specifically on the landscape and its traditions: Image in Khorkom (fig. 6), begun in 1936; Garden in Sochi, begun in 1940; and finally The Plow and the Song, begun in 1944.

No real understanding of the meaning of The Plow and the Song can come about without considering it in light of its serial evolution. Gorky's conception of each work alone and of the cumulative meaning of the series can only be approached by following the transformations as they occurred from one work to the next. In his discussion of the Garden in Sochi, William Rubin has demonstrated how an apparently more "finished," or detailed, rendering is not necessarily the last in a series; on the contrary, Gorky was more inclined to work away from the tighter control and more specific description of an earlier work to a more generalized version.[25] The same applies to the later series. It has been suggested that Gorky worked toward such painterly and less descriptive versions through an intent to obscure his highly personal subject matter.[26] I would choose to think that, particularly with regard to Gorky's late work, there must have been other reasons for continuing a series and that a last version was not necessarily further removed from its subject or source.

It seems that the issue of camouflage can be taken too far. It may be a case in which the myth of the man has clouded perception of the artist. Gorky's early works after the masters were motivated by a sense of apprenticeship; it was a question of learning rather than one of hiding behind them. The masters were the yardstick against which he measured himself. Clearly Gorky's crucial role in the evolution of modern art was made possible by his genius for gathering the threads of myriad aspects of the art of the past and bringing them to bear on his own in a highly original marriage of surrealism and abstraction.

As he himself stated, "It is my feeling that form is the language of a given time and it is that which must be constantly sought . . ."; and even more to the point in question, "What else is an artist but a creator who wants to share? I seek a form or language which will express my ideas for our time."[27]

John Graham's conception of serial painting may well have influenced Gorky. Graham stated that his painting *Studio* of 1941

is the fifth of a series. It started with a realistic interior consisting of an old armchair with a little lamb's hide thrown over its back, a green plant, a square antique mirror above the chair and secretaire to the right. Every subsequent painting of this subject became a further abstraction or summation of the phenomena observed.[28]

Clearly, however, Gorky was not abstracting in the sense that Graham was. He was not summing up or removing himself from his subject. Rather his process of distillation simultaneously involved the creation of a form that bore an intrinsic potential to evoke layers of identity. Those layers or allusions might not be simultaneously present and constant throughout the series in each given form, but rather they grow or transform through each successive version.

Therefore, if we accept that Gorky's sources were manifold rather than looking at Gorky's shapes for a single source or identity, we might conclude that his intention was not to obscure but rather to explore the possibilities of line and color to enhance his subject and, in the process, to bring to bear upon it the rich scope of his own feelings and associations. Thus Gorky's reasons for working in a series were both pictorial and contextual.

Gorky had always had an inclination to overpaint. Stuart Davis recalled the wealth of materials, quantities of canvases, paints, and brushes in Gorky's studio in the 1930s, and stated that Gorky "intensified" his "poverty" "by his method of painting." Davis described the "small fortune in pigment" that Gorky would apply to his canvases only to scrape it all off the next day.[29] Indeed, many of his paintings of this period are heavily painted. He would even submerge canvases in the bathtub to reduce the surface to a mere "ghost," as he called it, from which to start again.[30] This search for perfection continued in the 1940s. Just as the last version of Garden in Sochi is the most thinly painted one, in the several series of 1946-1947, Gorky explored more intensively a means of avoiding such overworking of a painting (figs. 7, 8). Rather than overload one

Figure 7. Arshile Gorky. *Garden in Sochi,* 1941. Oil on canvas, 112.4 x 158.1 cm (44¼ x 62¼ in). The Museum of Modern Art, New York, Purchase and gift of Mr. and Mrs. Wolfgang S. Schwabacher. Not in exhibition

Figure 8. Arshile Gorky. *Garden in Sochi,* 1943?. Oil on canvas, 78.8 x 99.0 cm (31 x 39 in). The Museum of Modern Art, New York, Acquired through the Lillie P. Bliss bequest [photo: Geoffrey Clements]. Not in exhibition

canvas, he chose to commence afresh to allow other associations to come into play. As early as 1942, after completing various versions of Garden in Sochi, he expressed this desire to allow the layers of meaning in one given theme to unfold in the course of a series. In a letter to his sister, Vartoosh, he wrote

Dearest one, I search for new infinities. I paint in series for an important reason. If one painting, Vartoosh dearest, is a window from which I see one infinity, I desire to return to that same window to see other infinities. And to build other windows looking out of known space into limitless regions. Continuously imposing new ideas of changes on one canvas mars the window by fogging it, in elaborating upon the completion of one window or canvas. By that I mean one finite. In doing that I attempt to extract additional unknowns. I place air in my works. They are the windows viewing infinity.[31]

The Plow and the Song may present a special case in this regard. It was Gorky's Armenian heritage that was in large part

Figure 9. Arshile Gorky. Study for *The Plow and the Song*, 1944. Pencil and crayon, 48.2 x 64.3 cm (19 x 25¼ in). Allen Memorial Art Museum, Oberlin College, Ohio. Cat. no. 1, pl. 2

responsible for what may be considered the poetic aspect of his art. To perceive the ambiguities of a form, its potential for metaphor or a metamorphosis, was apparently second nature to Gorky (see Noguchi's account in the iconography discussion that follows); it was exactly that trait that caused other artists like de Kooning to consider Gorky a surrealist before the surrealists. What de Kooning was referring to was the imagination, the sense of the fantastic kindled in Gorky as a child by the art of his homeland. The metamorphoses of plant and animal, animal and human, to be found in medieval Armenian manuscripts and sculptures lived on for Gorky as a lodestar of the direction his art should take. He was continually enriching his knowledge of the art of Armenia and the other ancient cultures he considered ancestral—the Hittites, the Sumerians. He visited the Boston Museum of Fine Arts and the Metropolitan in New York—not only for those masters of Western painting he admired, but also to study their primitive collections. He pored over periodicals and magazines reporting archeological finds in the Near East or pictures of his homeland. His letters to his family, written in Armenian, overwhelm one with the depth and sincerity of his attachment to his Anatolian roots, and he always entertained the hope of revisiting Armenia. In the letter of February 9, 1942, Gorky wrote to Vartoosh:

In trying to probe beyond the ordinary and the known, I create an inner infinity. I probe within the confines of the finite to create an infinity. Liver. Bones. Living rocks and living plants and animals. Living dreams . . . to this I owe my debt to our Armenian art. Its hybrids, its many opposites. The inventions of our folk imagination. These I attempt to capture directly, I mean the folklore and physical beauty of our homeland, in my works.[32]

Thus it is hardly surprising that a series based on memories of his homeland could create more overlay of meaning, a greater ambiguity of form, than other subjects. While in the

much earlier series, Portrait of the Artist and His Mother, Gorky kept referring back to the original photograph, as he progressed from one version to the next of The Plow and the Song, he brought to bear on it a wealth of sources that had expanded to include nature, the work of other artists, and works of his own, for further layers of meaning or reference in a given form.

DATING

In a discussion of a group of works gathered under the heading Pastoral, Jim Jordan presents a sequence based on "an increasing refinement of technique, an increasing exactitude of shape, and an increasing sureness of spatial relationships."[33] The same can be applied to the evolution of Gorky's conception of The Plow and the Song. That a sequence of execution for the six extant works bearing the title The Plow and the Song may nevertheless be difficult to ascertain, however, is complicated by the fact that Gorky frequently neglected to date his works, or even sign them, and was not above giving his work an earlier date than that of their actual execution.[34] Of the six versions of The Plow and the Song, three are both signed and dated. A drawing bears a date of 1944 and two paintings, one of which is almost certainly the last in a series, have both been dated 1947. The dates of the other three works executed between 1944 and 1947 are problematic. The Oberlin study, signed and dated 1944 (fig. 9), is clearly the first in the series; it differs most markedly from the rest of the works, particularly in the relative size and positioning of the vertical form to the left and in the distribution to the edges of the sheet of all the forms which have been more centrally consolidated in all the later versions. In a letter of June 1945, Gorky mentions having already begun work on The Plow and the Song theme.[35] In

Figure 10. Arshile Gorky.
Study for *The Plow and the Song,* 1946?.
Pencil and crayon, 50.8 x 63.5 cm (20 x 25 in).
Fogg Art Museum, Harvard University,
Cambridge, Mass., Anonymous loan.
Not in exhibition

Figure 11. Arshile Gorky. *The Artist and His Mother,* c. 1936. Pencil on
squared paper, 61.0 x 48.3 cm (24 x 19 in). Estate of Arshile Gorky [photo:
Paulus Leeser, courtesy Xavier Fourcade, Inc.]. Not in exhibition

Figure 12. Arshile Gorky. Study for *The Betrothal,* 1946. Pencil and crayon,
60.7 x 47.0 cm (23⅞ x 18½ in). Estate of Arshile Gorky [photo: Xavier
Fourcade, Inc.]. Not in exhibition

Figure 13. Arshile Gorky. *The Plow and the Song*, 1946. Pencil, charcoal, crayon, pastel, and oil on paper, 121.5 x 150.8 cm (47⅞ x 59⅜ in). National Gallery of Art, Washington, Avalon Fund. Cat. no. 2, pl. 3

January 1946 a fire in his studio in Sherman, Connecticut, destroyed twenty-seven works, including two paintings of The Plow and the Song.[36] Thus the first extant drawing must have almost certainly been executed prior to 1946 as a study for the lost paintings, although possibly as late as 1945.

Although one might assume that the unsigned and undated squared drawing (fig. 10) must also have preceded the paintings lost in the fire, during the period 1943-1945 Gorky rarely squared drawings for transfer. While smaller versions or studies exist, there are no known squared drawings for such important paintings of those years as *The Liver Is the Cock's Comb, Good Afternoon Mrs. Lincoln,* or *The Unattainable.* The greatest number of such drawings were executed for paintings of 1947 and are generally assigned (if not dated) to 1946. Four examples may be cited: *The Limit, Betrothal* (fig. 12), *Orators,* and *Dark Green Painting,* all of which share approximately the same dimensions (19/20 x 24/25 inches) and stylistic traits with the square drawing for The Plow and the Song.

Gorky had begun the process of squaring a drawing in the 1920s. One of the few known drawings squared for transfer since that for the portrait of *The Artist and his Mother* (fig. 11) and prior to 1946 not only differs in dimension and style from the drawings of 1946 but also does not inaugurate an important series.[37] I would consequently propose that the squared study for The Plow and the Song in fact postdates the fire of January 1946 and was probably done the following summer.[38]

Peculiar to the Orswell drawing is the faint delineation of figures in the upper left and the pink staining in the lower right corner. A close examination reveals that they existed before the sheet was squared. While they do not recur in any of the other versions, the pink staining appears to have triggered the shift of the whole composition to a position higher on the sheet and an extension, in all the subsequent versions, of the vertical form to balance the development of the lower right corner. Such a use of the accidental is rarely so apparent in Gorky's work.

The large grisaille for The Plow and the Song is clearly the first large-scale version to follow the squared study (fig. 13). While some of the pentimenti and detailing of the central portion of the Orswell drawing have been eliminated here, no clear forms have yet emerged in the lower right corner and a close examination reveals that Gorky was still shifting his contours. The faint lines in the study, linking the central portion to the frame at the top, are again indicated in the hastily sketched pencil lines in the grisaille. Whatever Gorky's intention, these are eliminated in all the subsequent versions, indicating his decision to allow for an unobstructed horizon. In the Chicago painting the entire top register is filled with varying shades of blue, imposing an unavoidable reading of the painting as an outdoor landscape. Thus it appears not only that an, albeit undeveloped, formal instinct at work has been overthrown for the sake of content but also that color has been employed not only for formal reasons but to reinforce that content.

One of the paintings by Ingres that Gorky most admired was the *Odalisque en Grisaille* in the Metropolitan Museum. Both Ingres' practice of executing several versions of the same theme, together with the particular refinement of a grisaille rendering, must have encouraged Gorky and given him the sanction that only an old master could to follow such procedures himself. Above all, it was the intensive search for formal

Figure 14. Detail of *The Plow and the Song,* 1946 (fig. 13)

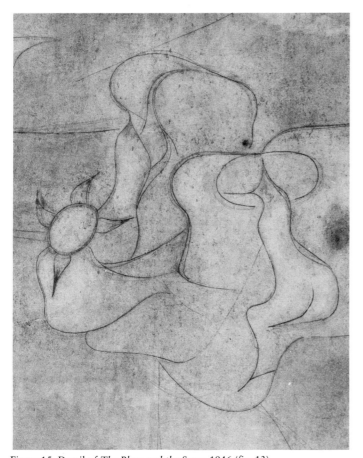

Figure 15. Detail of *The Plow and the Song,* 1946 (fig. 13)

perfection that Gorky studied and admired in Ingres' work. Studying paintings with Ethel Schwabacher in the Metropolitan, he remarked,

It is true, is it not, that even Ingres had to revise—yes, the surface of the painting is smooth, finished and incorruptible as a diamond, but under the accomplished surface are *pentimenti*—see there at the shoulders, how the line of the black dress was lowered a fraction and

the hand was extended to give greater elegance.... Are these not signs of the patient revision that even a genius has to make?[39]

The quality of Gorky's line, which appears to flow with extraordinary ease and elegance, only reveals on close examination the physical intensity, even aggression, he exerted toward his materials. The grisaille may well have been one of those works submerged in water, then dried in the sun and scrubbed, so totally wed to the paper is the charcoal surface. The "highlights" in the upper and lower right corners and of the vertical form on the left are due to such a scrubbing away (figs. 14, 15).

Evidence for the proposed date of 1946 for the large grisaille lies in examination of works comparable to it in method and intention. The only works that can be compared, in both their predominantly gray-brown coloration and their position within a series, are the first fully developed version of *The Calendars* (fig. 16) and the *Study for the Betrothal* (fig. 17). The former is dated 1946 and the latter 1946-1947. The *Study for the Betrothal* bears particular comparison to the Plow and the Song grisaille not only in its use of mixed media—pencil, charcoal, pastel, and wax crayon—but also in that it is virtually exactly equal in size to its related paintings. Indeed, the term *study* begins to strike us as something of a misnomer in view of their scale and quality of completion.[40] An outstanding example of Gorky's consideration of these works not as studies but as finished works in their own right is *Summation* of 1947 (fig. 18). In pastel, pencil, and oil on buff paper, it constitutes a large grisaille, measuring 78⅜ × 100¼ inches, and is the final version for which there is only one, much smaller, study. If, in fact, all the existing Plow and the Song works, with the exception of the drawing of 1944, postdate the fire in which two paintings on the theme were destroyed, it would help explain the titling of the Chicago painting, *The Plow and the Song II,* possibly suggesting that the grisaille is *I.*[41] Since, moreover, there is no other instance of two so meticulously rendered preparatory drawings on the same theme in Gorky's oeuvre, it seems probable that more than a year passed between the two.

The Plow and the Song II is generally assigned a date of 1946. If this date is correct, it precedes the other two paintings, both of which are dated 1947. Such a sequence can be substantiated by the retention in this painting of particular elements existing in the grisaille, from the fine loop that swings out in an arc to the right of the central cluster of forms to the dancing plant form at the lower center of this complex, which is encased in an egg shape in *The Plow and the Song II* and finally blocked in altogether in the Milton Gordon version (collection of Milton Gordon, New York). Although it is one of the few works Gorky painted on burlap rather than canvas, it has been primed to eliminate the texture of the material and thinly painted in more predominantly golden tones that look toward the lyrical delicacy of the last painting of the series. This almost monochromatic version of The Plow and the Song may be the most eloquent example of Gorky's application to his own ends of Matta's technique of thinning paint with turpentine until it's nearly a wash.

Figure 18. Arshile Gorky. *Summation,* 1947. Pencil, pastel, and oil on buff paper, 199.1 x 254.7 cm (78⅜ x 100¼ in). The Museum of Modern Art, New York, Mr. and Mrs. Gordon Bunshaft Fund. Not in exhibition

Figure 16. Arshile Gorky, *The Calendars,* 1946. Charcoal and colored chalk, 82.5 x 101.6 cm (32½ x 40 in, sight). Fogg Art Museum, Harvard University, Cambridge, Mass., Gift of Mrs. Culver Orswell. Not in exhibition

Figure 17. Arshile Gorky, *The Betrothal,* 1947. Pencil, charcoal, pastel, and crayon, 124.5 x 99.1 cm (49 x 39 in). Formerly, collection of Jeanne Reynal; present location unknown [photo: reproduced from Julien Levy, *Arshile Gorky* (New York, 1966)]. Not in exhibition

DRAWINGS

Gorky's late work is intimately related to his drawings, of which he executed an unprecedented number during the last four years of his life. Gorky had been in the habit of drawing from nature in New York's Central Park. In 1942, however, he spent three weeks with the artist Saul Schary in Connecticut, and it is this sojourn in the country that is generally considered to mark the crucial rediscovery of nature so essential to his late work. As late as 1940-1942, Gorky was still drawing in a Cézannesque manner (which dates back to his drawings of the mid-twenties; fig. 19). While in the drawings of 1943, and in most thereafter, he eliminated the cross-hatching of Cézanne, he retained a concentration of volumetric forms along a horizontal axis, often defined by dense indications of recesses (fig. 20). These drawings, are, however, already removed from naturalistic landscape renderings in which near, middle, and far distance are suggested. Instead, the forms, compressed in the immediate foreground, take on a life of their own and exhibit the erotic overtones characteristic of such paintings of that year as *The Liver Is the Cock's Comb* (fig. 21). The influence of Matta has been noted in the pencil and crayon drawings of 1943. While the forms in these drawings by Gorky may be "more disjointed" (as William Rubin has stated) than in earlier drawings, and in some cases manifest striking resemblance to particular works by Matta, Gorky's forms are at once more clearly delineated and interrelated.[42] The differences between the two artists' work are as revealing as their similarities. Neither Gorky's drawings nor his paintings exhibit the suspension of forms in infinite space characteristic of Matta. Movement in Gorky's late work is conveyed by the sinuous delineation of the forms themselves or by the line that links one to another. Whereas Matta's indeterminate and evolving contours suggest a futuristic transformation of matter in time and space, Gorky's dialogue with nature produced

Figure 19. Arshile Gorky. *Landscape*, c. 1928. Pencil, 31.1 x 48.3 cm (12¼ x 19 in). Estate of Arshile Gorky [photo: reproduced from Julien Levy, *Arshile Gorky* (New York, 1966)]. Not in exhibition

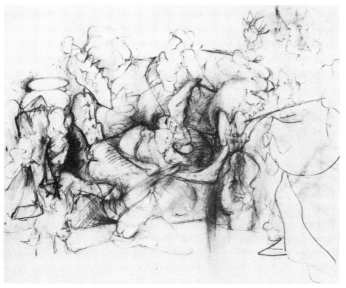

Figure 20. Arshile Gorky. *Drawing*, 1944. Pencil, 47.7 x 62.9 cm (18¾ x 24¾ in). Julien Levy Gallery, New York [photo: reproduced from Julien Levy, *Arshile Gorky* (New York, 1966)]. Not in exhibition

instead figurations whose potential to transform is related to organic patterns of growth.

From the masters, Cézanne and Picasso, Gorky had learned the value of negative space. In the first version of Garden in Sochi, for example, background spaces are painted in on top of positive elements as if carving their contours. His spaces in drawings as well as paintings continued to have a concrete pictorial presence, diametrically opposed to the illusion of infinite space of Matta.[43] While Gorky strayed far from conventional landscape composition, an aspect of continuing faithfulness to nature in his work is relevant to the composition of The Plow and the Song, one of the rare late works to exhibit clear indications of an outdoor landscape.

In 1943 Gorky and his wife Agnes Magruder spent their first summer at her parents' farm near Hamilton, Virginia. Gorky felt immediately at home there. This was the landscape with its endless succession of hills and a stream through the bed of the

valley that inspired the hundreds of drawings which provided the source for the paintings of his last years. Jim Jordan, who pioneered the idea of visiting Crooked Run Farm itself, noted correspondences in the landscape with Gorky's drawings.[44] One of the more finished drawings Gorky did at Crooked Run (and gave to his neighbor there) bears a clear topographical correspondence to the landscape. Gorky could point out specific trees on the Magruder property in the drawing and the particular vantage point from which he had sketched the scene before him. Another friend who saw him there has related how upset he was when the milkweed he had been drawing had blown away.[45] This story is one of many indicating an existing correlation between landscape and drawings as well as Gorky's tendency to concentrate on, or extract, one particular feature of the landscape and examine it with rapt attention.

In 1944 Gorky and his wife returned to Crooked Run in the spring and stayed for nine months. Gorky began to draw in a style unlike anything he had done before. A year earlier, his use of paint had been freed in an unprecedented way; under the influence of Kandinsky, he had nearly eliminated line from his paintings. In his drawings of 1944 and from the succeeding summers spent in Hamilton, he explored the potentialities of line with an equally unprecedented abandon. In these pencil drawings crayon is also introduced—but often in patches, independent of any linear contour. It was through this liberation of first color, then line, that Gorky arrived at a new synthesis in the paintings of 1946-1947.

These free and open line drawings of 1944 and those of the summers that followed bear a much less recognizable relation to natural landscape. Little suggestion of volume remains; lines glide across the surface or describe amorphous and fanciful plant or animal forms that in some cases grow onto the sheet from outside it, emphasizing its two-dimensionality.

Although Gorky had long been known for his unique talent as a draftsman, such intensive exploration of line and unleashing of its potential never occurred before in his work. We are told that he could not resist drawing wherever he went (even on napkins in restaurants) and was the envy of other artists for this facility. Impecunious in 1932, he had been forced to spend the entire year exclusively drawing.

Gorky's love of line attracted him to the art of the Egyptians and to Ingres. De Kooning claims that he would carry a pocketknife with him to keep his pencils very sharp. It was in 1945 that de Kooning introduced Gorky to the possibility of making such fine lines in paint, with a brush used by sign painters called a *liner* and his well-known account is worth quoting:[46]

One day de Kooning found Gorky unsuccessfully struggling to produce long lines with "fat Rubens brushes", and was amazed to discover that Gorky did not know a brush had been expressly designed for that purpose. "Having bought one," de Kooning remembers, "Gorky sat around all day in an ecstasy painting long beautiful lines."[47]

This extraordinarily free and fluid yet perfectly controlled line that Gorky discovered in the liner only began to emerge in his paintings the following year, and the excitement of this discovery dominates the paintings of 1945 particularly. Line

Figure 21. Arshile Gorky. *The Liver Is the Cock's Comb,* 1944. Oil on canvas, 182.9 x 249.9 cm (72 x 98 in). Albright-Knox Art Gallery, Buffalo, N.Y., Gift of Seymour H. Knox. Not in exhibition

Figure 22. Arshile Gorky. *The Unattainable,* 1945. Oil on canvas, 104.8 x 74.3 cm (41¼ x 29¼ in). The Baltimore Museum of Art. Not in exhibition

Figure 23. Joan Miró. *The Farm,* 1921-1922. Oil on canvas, 132.1 x 147.3 cm (52 x 58 in). Ernest Hemingway Collection, New York. Not in exhibition

remained, however, an essential element of most of his late work. In a letter of May 1947 Gorky wrote: "try to develop a beautiful, clear and sensitive line—this is drawing—line is all important." Line as Gorky had used it not only became an extraordinary vehicle of expression, of tension, growth, even anguish, but also seems to have allowed him a freedom of composition which need no longer depend for coherence on the interlocking of planes or the modeling of forms in a defined shallow space, or on a surface handling of paint which would run one form into another, as it had before.

In such paintings as *Child's Companions* and *The Unattainable* (fig. 22) of 1945, color and line work independently. As neither suggest volumes in space, the loss of a horizon does not provoke a sense of suspension in the forms; rather color and line exist on the surface, devoid of allusion or illusion. As line became contour once again in the drawings and paintings of 1946, the most personal, and essentially Gorky, forms emerged. This fresh approach to composition allowed for an inventive arrangement of forms across the surface which could be transformed and modified, some elements more than others, from one version of a series to the next.

The world of forms Gorky began exploring as early as 1943 only gradually emerged in his paintings. Thus the rich painterly quality of *The Liver Is the Cock's Comb* of 1944 was followed by the spare and pellucid paintings of 1945, representing the furthest remove from the thick paint application of works of the thirties and early forties. The paintings of 1946-1948, derived from those drawings so freely responding to nature's stimulus, exhibit a distillation of these forms in a context of greater restraint, at times even austerity. Color and line coalesce again in the discrete forms of the late series.

Concurrent with this rediscovery, as it were, of line, Gorky appears to have revived his interest in Miró. Gorky had ample opportunity to see Miró's work, at the Pierre Matisse Gallery, regularly throughout the thirties and forties, at the Museum of Modern Art, and most particularly at the large one-man show

Figure 24. Joan Miró. *The Potato,* 1928. Oil on burlap, 100.7 x 81.6 cm (39⅝ x 32⅛ in). Collection, Mr. and Mrs. Gelman, Mexico City. Not in exhibition

Figure 25. Arshile Gorky. *Drawing,* 1944. Pencil and crayon, 45.8 x 61.0 cm (18 x 24 in). Julien Levy Gallery, New York [photo: reproduced from Julien Levy, *Arshile Gorky* (New York, 1966)]. Not in exhibition

there in 1941—not to mention Miró's work in reproduction. Frequently featured in *Cahiers d'Art,* it was accompanied by articles by such heroes of Gorky as Eluard. Gorky must have been well aware of Miró's evocation of his homeland in Catalonia in his work of the twenties; and an article in *Cahiers d'Art* featuring Miró was followed by one on Catalonian art. Sweeney's essay on Miró in the 1941 Museum of Modern Art catalogue describes Miró's process of distilling memory images in a manner similar to Gorky's. The specificity of Miró's remembered images of Catalonia, such as a plant, a bucket, or a rooster (fig. 23), might have reinforced Gorky's inclination to select such specifics from his own memories, like the plow or the apricot of his homeland.

Few people are aware that Gorky and Miró met. Ethel Schwabacher, however, has provided us with a delightful account of a party given for Miró at Gorky's studio at 36 Union Square.

And Gorky was in many places at once. He had scrubbed the floor that morning; it was immaculate. Many kinds of Armenian food were already laid out; everything had been ready for hours. As Agnes came out from the pantry alcove Gorky had built for her they moved forward to welcome us. Gorky tall, and Agnes tall too, singular in her grace and youth. They introduced us to the others—Joan Miró, his friend, a Spanish architect, and Margaret La Farge Osborn.

After supper we sat about the enormous low table. Gorky offered wine in a bottle and without glasses. With reversed hand and arm bent sharply at the elbow he raised the flask to his lips, and tilting his head back, drank deeply from the curved spout. Then he passed the flask. No one could manage it, the wine spilled, faces were dripping, laughter mixed with the wine. Gaily Miró took the flask, sat straight, his legs firmly planted wide apart, then with a gesture of bravado and virtuosity, accomplished the feat. Waves of applause greeted him.

Now there were requests for song. Gorky sang the wailing trills and arpeggios of the East, songs of Armenia and Georgian Russia, and Miró countered with Catalan songs, close in spirit, high-keyed, ringing, intensely melancholy. Gorky answered the request for dance with a few steps suited to the music.[48]

Gorky's drawings of 1944 reveal the extent to which he had absorbed not only aspects of overall composition but also some particulars of Miró's visual language. Two drawings especially (figs. 25, 26) derive a good deal from Miró, though no one specific source can be cited. Rather Gorky has extracted elements from Miró's *Tilled Field, Potato* (fig. 24), and *Catalan Landscape* (all of which were included in the 1941 MOMA exhibition) and put them to his own use. Although Miró was the dominant influence on Gorky's late style, Gorky's sources at this time were manifold. The drawings of this period manifest his ability to dissect, extract, recompose with a selective eye and an independence of intention that is never the case in his early work in the manner of Cézanne or even those in the manner of Picasso.

This talent to select only what he wanted from the work of another artist—not entire compositions or techniques but aspects thereof—and from nature—particular features rather than a slavish notation of the scene—was precisely the factor that allowed many sources to come simultaneously into play in his late work. Gorky's practice of selection and distillation of the most significant or iconographic forms dates back to his Aviation murals of 1936. He employed a similar process of isolating and recomposing according to pictorial demands in his late work, but his drawings liberated him from any trace of the geometric into a highly personal use of line and biomorphic form. A sense of surface composition he had derived from cubism remained, but the completely original handling of space that emerges in his late work entailed a rejection of the rectilinearity he associated with what he termed "urban cubism." Rather he sought to free an innate Armenian sensibil-

Figure 26. Arshile Gorky. *Drawing*, 1944. Pencil with color, 50.8 x 66.0 cm (20 x 26 in). Collection, Bowdoin College Museum of Art, Brunswick, Me., Gift of Mr. Walter Gutman, '24. Not in exhibition

Figure 27. Arshile Gorky. *Untitled*, 1944-1945. Pencil and crayon, 48.0 x 59.7 cm (18⅞ x 23½ in). Estate of Arshile Gorky [photo: M. Knoedler & Co., Inc.]. Not in exhibition

ity that would guide the evolution of a spatial dimension attuned to his "rediscovery" of nature.

Recently, I came across an Armenian book with a picture of the Shamiram Canal of our Van. Such beauty. Such sensitive beauty. Aesthetic technology. A very human-feeling technology. So different from the soulless technology here. . . .

I am an Armenian and man must be himself. For that reason urban cubism hinders my self-expression for its technological direction is couched in an unfeeling tongue that grates against my ears which are accustomed to different songs. Its lines are straight, but I am a curved line.

and

I must . . . speak as part of this century but in my own accent, must convey the inherent freedom of my experience, else it becomes unnatural. This special vernacular of mine is far removed from the rigidities and closed structuring of urban cubism, which to me is the child of the utilitarian, rectilinear life. And because I am a son of Ararat, mine is the speech of a different motion, of expansion, of growth in the sense that anything that grows is constantly in movement.[49]

Since the first known drawing on The Plow and the Song theme is already executed with greater precision and finish than a sketch, antecedents for its various forms probably lie in numerous landscape sketches. Only one that bears a marked resemblance has come to light (fig. 27). It includes the dotted circle, out of which emerge two trunklike forms, and below which a concentration of other forms are described in cursory fashion: the suggestion of a hillside, a vertical form rising to the left, and a petaled shape surrounded by a larger flowering ovoid, lower center. It is, moreover, squared, which in itself suggests transferral of certain elements for further refinement of the idea.

Many aspects of the drawings that appear to derive from Miró, such as the dotted circle, are eventually blocked out in the paintings that follow, while other Miróesque qualities emerge such as the scumbled patches of color in a landscape (*The Plow and the Song II*) and the absence of highlights or

texture. When Raphael Soyer was working on a portrait of Gorky, c. 1940-1941, Gorky said, regarding highlights:

You know this disturbs the painting. If you just make the shape of the hair and eliminate the shine, retain the shape and color at the expense of the hair texture, it will play a stronger part in the picture. The shine disturbs it, the highlights destroy the shape. By elimination it becomes part of the entire design.[50]

A clear indication that this continued to be a quality he admired in Miró lies in a comparison of Gorky's *Landscape Table* (1945; fig. 28) with Miró's *Maternity* (1924; fig. 29) in which the flat, black head shape with feelerlike hairs has been almost directly quoted from one to the other.[51] Yet Gorky's work consistently evokes a mood—a romantic intensity—that has no part in Miró's work. Gorky's forms are soft, sometimes of a maleable or spongy quality, his colors subtle and rarified. The fantasy in Miró's work is rarely present in Gorky's. Its absence could well reflect the very different experience each artist had in that homeland for which he felt such nostalgia. The tragedy experienced by Gorky as a child always infuses those works ostensibly about sweet memories of smells and sensations with the sorrow and bitterness of his experience.

ICONOGRAPHY

The understanding of the iconography of Gorky's late work, which was initiated by Ethel Schwabacher, owes a great deal to the more recent research of both Harry Rand and Jim Jordan. All three scholars, to a greater or lesser degree, have challenged the general assumption that Gorky had eschewed all traces of the representational by the mid-forties. In her book, the first monograph published on Gorky, Schwabacher makes many allusions to the content of his work. In some cases she states a general theme; in others she makes more specific reference to interior scenes and figures. Rand has interpreted convincingly—albeit perhaps too specifically—many subjects of Gor-

Figure 28. Arshile Gorky. *Landscape Table,* 1945. Oil on canvas, 91.5 x 121.9 cm (36 x 48 in). Musée National d'Art Moderne, Centre Georges Pompidou, Paris. Not in exhibition

Figure 30. Arshile Gorky. *The Calendars,* 1946-1947. Oil on canvas, 127.0 x 152.9 cm (50 x 60 in). Destroyed by fire, 1961 [photo: Estate of William C. Seitz]. Not in exhibition

of his subject matter. Gorky did not evolve a vocabulary of forms in earlier years that might later be employed as purely aesthetic elements; rather each new subject provided a fresh point of departure that could unleash a variety of deeper personal associations. If anything, he moved farther from abstraction and more toward surrealism.

Most other iconographic interpretation has not gone beyond generalization. Even Harry Rand, who has pursued the iconography of numerous works, has found The Plow and the Song enigmatic.[53] Ethel Schwabacher went so far as to state that the theme of the series is fertility, and in her brief analysis, she wrote,

We find the sun-warmed fertility of the earth, plow-turned; the sheltering bone, the winding birth passage and spacious exit chambers out of which the seed passes into space.

She also found present the plow and "metaphors of plow, flower and bone."[54] Nevertheless, the fact that the forms in The Plow and the Song, from the beginning of the series, are so advanced in their development seems to have thwarted attempts to interpret them in any depth.

From its inception, The Plow and the Song does indeed appear to be the most clearly worked out composition of all the late series. The contours are more precisely delineated, each form more clearly distinguished from another; there is little overlapping. All of these particulars suggest a more specific subject in Gorky's mind. Nor can we ignore Agnes Gorky's special mention of The Plow and the Song—the only paintings she mentions by name—in her account of the fire in Gorky's studio.[55] That Gorky felt compelled to return to the subject after the disaster, and consistently titled the paintings from beginning to end of the series, further suggests the particular importance of this opus to him. Finally the configuration of The Plow and the Song never dissolves in later versions into a

Figure 29. Joan Miró. *Maternity,* 1924. Oil on canvas, 92.1 x 73.0 cm (36¼ x 28¾ in). Private collection, London. Not in exhibition

ky's late years. In *The Calendars* (fig. 30), for example, he finds Gorky's daughter Maro sitting in the window; Gorky himself reading the newspaper; his wife Agnes, dog, pram, fire on the hearth; and even a floorlamp, lit.[52] Such a reading suggests not only the extent to which Gorky did find his sources in the world around him but also the intimate and personal nature of much

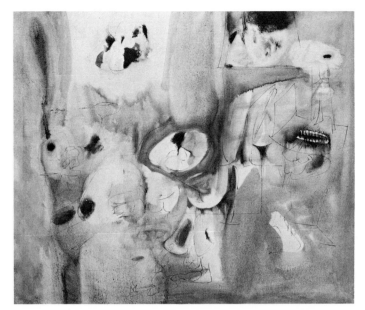

Figure 31. Arshile Gorky. *Making the Calendar,* 1941 (1947?). Oil on canvas, 86.4 x 104.2 cm (34 x 41 in). Munson-Williams-Proctor Institute, Utica, N.Y., Edward W. Root Bequest. Not in exhibition

Figure 32. Arshile Gorky. *The Opaque,* 1947. Oil on canvas, 86.4 x 104.2 cm (34 x 41 in). Estate of Arshile Gorky [photo: Tony Rogers, courtesy Xavier Fourcade, Inc.]. Not in exhibition

rendering as free as, for example, does that of The Calendars in *Making the Calendar* or *The Opaque* (figs. 31, 32).

Sometimes Gorky invented his titles; sometimes Julien Levy, Breton, or Max Ernst provided them. Unlike The Plow and the Song, several of his titles suggest visual metaphors—*The Leaf of the Artichoke Is an Owl,* or *The Liver Is the Cock's Comb*—metaphors which suggest the degree to which large and small, animal and vegetable, inner and outer, coexist in a poetic framework, where sight and sensation are inextricably intertwined.[56]

In view of the fact that The Plow and the Song was inspired by his summers in the Virginia countryside, which, in turn, reminded him of his youth in Armenia, and that in the midst of the series he executed many drawings from nature, it is hardly surprising that with each new version, new layers of meaning, often relating to forms in nature, might suggest themselves. Of the three nostalgic subjects dealing with his memories of the Armenian countryside that exist in series—Image in Khorkom, Garden in Sochi, and The Plow and the Song—The Plow and the Song is unique in that it was begun *after* Gorky's return to nature. In July of 1943, Gorky wrote, "The State of Virginia reminds me of Armenia's lowland," and in February 1944, "My recollections of Armenia open new visions for me."[57]

Some years earlier, Gorky himself affirmed that his forms harbor specific meaning. In a published statement in *The New York Sun* in 1941, Gorky stated:

I might add that though the various forms all had specific meanings to me, it is the spectator's privilege to find his own meaning here. I feel that they will relate to or parallel mine.[58]

Although the extent of that personal meaning may never be fully disclosed, in Gorky's published statements and letters the content of two series of paintings above all, the Garden in Sochi and The Plow and the Song, seem to have merited special reference.

Gorky was an exceptionally articulate man, particularly in his native tongue. Those who met him were virtually enthralled by his ability to discourse on art, by the acuity of his perceptions.[59] His letters to his sister and her family are due the same consideration as those of van Gogh to his brother Theo; they are an invaluable source for the understanding of his artistic intentions.

While working on Garden in Sochi he wrote,

For many days now I have been absorbed completely with memories of our Armenia's Van. . . . I am at work on a picture deriving from an extremely intense recollection of our home on Lake Van. At times I can smell its salt. At times I race to capture the subtleties which attempt to escape me.[60]

The statement which Dorothy Miller asked Gorky to write, about the version of the Garden in Sochi acquired by the Museum of Modern Art in 1952, is most revealing:

I like the heat the tenderness the edible the lusciousness the song of a single person the bathtub full of water to bathe myself beneath the water. I like Uccello Grunewald Ingres the drawings and sketches for paintings of Seurat and that man Pablo Picasso.
I measure all things by weight.
I love my Mougouch. What about Papa Cézanne.
I hate things that are not like me and all the things I haven't got are god to me.
Permit me—
I like the wheatfields the plough the apricots the shape of apricots those flirts of the sun. And bread above all.
My liver is sick with the purple.[61]

He continues to describe the garden, the Holy Tree and the traditions associated with this "Garden of Wish Fulfillment." Gorky's letter of July 1943 to the Mooradians makes it apparent that it was not only due to Dorothy Miller's prompting that he was as specific as he was in his description for the Museum of Modern Art of the content of the painting.

Figure 33. Arshile Gorky. *Garden in Sochi,* 1940. Oil on canvas, 63.5 x 73.7 cm (25 x 29 in). Estate of Arshile Gorky [photo: Nathan Rabin]. Not in exhibition

Figure 34. Arshile Gorky. Plow, 1944?. Wood, 20.6 x 72.7 x 15.2 cm (8⅛ x 28⅝ x 6 in). Mr. Karlen Mooradian, on loan to The Art Institute of Chicago [photo: John Mahtesian]. Not in exhibition

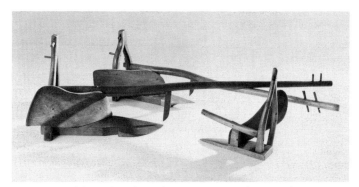

Figure 35. Arshile Gorky. Three Plows, 1944?. Wood. Mr. Karlen Mooradian, on loan to The Art Institute of Chicago [photo: John Mahtesian]. Not in exhibition , pl. 1

Vartoosh dear, do you realize how the critics ramble, the mask that hides their vacuum? In that series I have, for example, depicted most prominently the beautiful Armenian slippers father and I used to wear, the ones we purchased in Armenia's Van. . . .

And farther on,

You will be happy to know that also included in it are my interpretations of Mother's soft Armenian butterchurn. . . .[62]

In his free-verse description of Garden in Sochi, Gorky mentions both "the song" and "the plough." An examination of the various versions of The Plow and the Song reveals that Gorky reverted to many other aspects of the imagery he originally associated with Garden in Sochi. In the paragraph that follows this evocation of the garden he continues, "There was a blue rock half buried in the black earth with a few patches of moss placed here and there like fallen clouds."[63] Ethel Schwabacher has noted the presence of the blue rock in Garden in Sochi. From the first version of The Plow and the Song, incorporating color, to the last, a smoothly rounded form is nestled in the central section of the composition. While it varies in tonality, it is consistently blue. A brilliant blue passage enters the composition on the left of one version of Garden in Sochi (fig. 33) but a blue rock is in no wise so succinctly indicated or identifiable in that series as it is throughout The Plow and the Song. This more iconic depiction of content in the later series suggests the possibility of more specific readings for other such isolated forms in The Plow and the Song. Further examination will reveal the extent to which the Garden in Sochi and The Plow and the Song are both formally and iconographically linked, and are perhaps the most programmatically complex of all Gorky's works.[64]

* * * * * * *

O, Moorad, sing when you receive this letter—sing 'kashesh gutan ari yar vyle lele' (Pull the plow, O come my sweetheart). . . .

So wrote Gorky in a letter to his sister's family, the Mooradians.[65] In Armenia the tilling of the wheatfields was always accompanied by song. Just as Gorky kept phonograph records of Armenian songs that he would bring to parties in New York, so too he also made several miniature Armenian plows. His sense of craftsmanship as a painter had its roots in his boyhood, when he would carve flutes out of willow wood. Remembering the lessons of his uncle, who had a carpentry shop in Yerevan, he set about making a plow with a boyhood friend whom he rediscovered in this country. Yenovk der Hagopian recalled:

He would draw the shapes and I would cut them with a hack-saw or chisel. I remember once we went to work on one and I bought small nails to put it together. "O no," Gorky said, "we didn't use nails like that in Van. We did this instead." And he made his own nails. Anyway, we finally made one about a foot long. In the old country, in Van, one pair of water buffalo and three pairs of oxen used to pull one of those original plows. And it would turn up the earth at least two feet deep. So Gorky pulled his miniature plow through some sand but it was so fragile that it broke. We were both heartbroken. But early next morning he was waiting for me in front of my studio in Watertown. "Come on, we have to finish a plow because tonight I'm going to take the train back to New York." We started one but didn't have time to finish it.[66]

While this first incident probably dates from the thirties, in 1944 he made another plow and related, in a letter to his sister, his use of it as a model for his drawings.[67]

Figure 36. Arshile Gorky.
The Plow and the Song II, 1946. Oil on canvas,
131.8 x 155.9 cm (51⅞ x 61⅜ in). The Art
Institute of Chicago, Mr. and Mrs. Lewis L.
Coburn Fund. Cat. no. 3 , pl. 4

Vartoosh, dear, I have been occupied in *drawing* the Armenian plows which we used in our Adoian fields near our house. Recall? I have carved one from wood which I will send Karlen. *You cannot imagine the fertility of forms that leap from our Armenian plows,* the plows our ancestors used for thousands of years of toil and gaiety and hardship and poetry. A plow must be the fitting tombstone for the Armenian man from Khorkom.[68]

In the same letter Gorky continues about the apricots and songs of Armenia and then states, "This I am painting." Clearly the drawings he mentions contributed directly to the evolution of the only series principally focused on the theme of the plow. His use of the plow he made as a model proves his need for a real object as a starting point. While drawings more clearly derived from the plow may exist, a comparison of certain shapes in The Plow and the Song with those of his plow itself (figs. 34, 35) reveals correspondences. In The Plow and the Song, a long straight form rises on a diagonal from the lower right of the composition to meet a group of convex forms. Each of these manifests a general correlation to the various components, curves, and blade shapes of the plow, although Gorky's drawn configuration is, of course, no longer linked to the functional structure of the plow. For Gorky, either contour or a direct linear transcription of an actual object was the key to the feeling elicited by that object; its convexity or concavity or its linear thrust was first expressed by line, which, fluid or taut, could convey substance as well, stiff or amorphous.[69] Extracting that essence opened the door to analogies. The words André Breton wrote for the catalogue of Gorky's first one-man show of paintings at Julien Levy's gallery in 1945 may well have encouraged Gorky in this pursuit. In this famous foreword in which he refers to Gorky as "the eye-spring," Breton went on:

[The eye] was made to cast a lineament, a conducting wire between the most heterogeneous things. Such a wire, of maximum ductility, should allow us to understand, in a minimum of time, the relationships which connect, without possible discharge of continuity, innumerable physical and mental structures. These relationships have been scrambled interminably by false laws of conventional proximity (the apple calls for a pear in the fruit compote) or of scientific classification (for better or for worse the lobster and the spider are 'brothers' under the shell). The key of the mental prison can only be found in a break from such absurd manners of perception: the key lies in a free unlimited play of *analogies*.[70]

The paintings that follow the first three versions of The Plow and the Song also introduce what is probably an allusion to the blade of a plow in the lower right corner. In both the Chicago (fig. 36) and Milton Gordon versions, the golden wheat color of the surrounding square field reinforces the interpretation of this series of shapes as a reference to the plow. The development of this section as a factor contributing to the imagery of the whole visual poem could denote a nod to Miró's *Tilled Field* with its flat schematic rendering of the field.

The plow probably has a sexual connotation as well. The likelihood of this is furthered by a possible source in a pastel drawing by Miró also included in the 1941 exhibition at the Museum of Modern Art. Entitled *The Lovers* (1934; fig. 37), the drawing's most prominent feature is the erect phallus of the male figure. It rises on a diagonal in a similar fashion to the plow form entering the composition at the right in The Plow and the Song. The song Gorky quoted to Mooradian, "Pull the

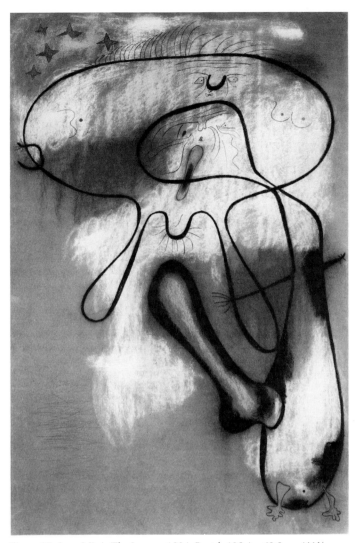

Figure 37. Joan Miró. *The Lovers*, 1934. Pastel, 105.4 x 69.9 cm (41½ x 27½ in). Philadelphia Museum of Art, The Louise and Walter Arensberg Collection. Not in exhibition

Figure 38. Arshile Gorky. *Untitled*, c. 1940. Watercolor, gouache on gessoed wood panel, 10.2 x 19.4 cm (4 x 7⅝ in). Collection, Mrs. Satenig Avedisian [photo: Muldoon Studio]. Not in exhibition

plow, O come my sweetheart," might also have prompted an association in Gorky's mind between the act of tilling the field with a kind of love song. Gorky had, moreover, incorporated such an analogy directly into one of his carved pieces. Jeanne Reynal, mosaicist and dear friend of Gorky, recounted to Hayden Herrera in 1974: "At home in the evenings, he whittled flutes, whistles, plows, toys and even a crossbow shaped like a dead bird with a phallus for the trigger."[71]

Just as the plow form embraces a dual identity, the vertical form to the left of the composition has generally been referred to as a hybrid. Its more squat rendition in the first drawing of The Plow and the Song appears related to the figuration on the left in Garden in Sochi, similarly articulated with protuberances and rising in the two later versions from a shape analogous to the slipper shape in the center of Garden in Sochi. Significantly, in the watercolor and gouache on gessoed wood panel from which Garden in Sochi is directly derived, that form is a Miróesque personnage—with a face, skirt, and hand—that seems to grow from rootlike extensions below (fig. 38). Considering the extent to which the form in The Plow and the Song

is transformed, following the first version, more than any other, Gorky's absorption with nature between the time of the first and the second drawing must account for its more vegetal quality in the later versions. It is a well-documented fact that Gorky would "look into the grass." He would get down close enough to the earth to hear it and smell it, he said, and fix on a particular plant or insect inches away so that it would become monumental on his sheet. From these he would select forms for his paintings.[72] Such a plant as that in the photograph (fig. 39), found in the fields of Crooked Run Farm, may well have provided the stimulus for elongating the form into jointed sections and organizing its leafy protuberances more in accord with the structure of natural organisms. Ethel Schwabacher's description of Gorky before nature is expressly descriptive of Gorky's "translations":

Further, the stiff core of the waving pliant grasses interested him; he translated this stiffness as bone, contrasting the stasis of the bone with the metamorphosis of the leaf.[73]

From the squared sheet to the grisaille this element undergoes further elongation and the base is made more blocky and analogous to the plow shapes. The long slipper shape returns, however, in all three paintings. It has been sufficiently simplified to resemble the pointed leaf toward the base of the farm weed (fig. 39), yet exhibits those salient slipper qualities as well, suggesting that Gorky wished to retain that aspect of a personage. Given the liberties that Gorky took with the human figure elsewhere—traits conspicuous in those artists he most admired, Picasso and Miró—the connotation of a human does not seem farfetched.[74] In manipulating elements of both plant and human, Gorky distilled a hybrid.

Surely Gorky's study of Armenian painting with its decorative play of shapes inspired some of the motifs in The Plow and the Song. The general silhouette of Gorky's plow and slipper forms both recur in Armenian manuscript illumination. The slipper in a fifteenth-century Armenian miniature is bootlike; it is more like the slipper in Garden in Sochi, which then appears in reduced form in The Plow and the Song. The form that

Figure 39. Weed, Crooked Run Farm, Hamilton, Va. [Photo: E. A. Carmean, Jr., July 1977.] Not in exhibition

Figure 40. Miniature from Armenian manuscript (W543), of the four Gospels, A.D. 1455. Walters Art Gallery, Baltimore. Not in exhibition

Figure 41. Miniature from Armenian manuscript (W543), of the four Gospels, A.D. 1455. Walters Art Gallery, Baltimore. Not in exhibition

occurs to the right of the diagonal plow echoes the decorative motif in another miniature (figs. 40, 41).[75]

By contrast, the large form that insinuates itself through the central portion of the composition remains virtually unaltered from one version to the next in the The Plow and the Song series. Unlike the forms it encloses, its contour and internal details (like the four-petal motif) remain intact even in the last thinly painted version, in which most forms have been washed to mere suggestion. Its principal color touches of yellow and red also remain consistent throughout the series. Nevertheless, neither an interpretation nor a source for this form are easy to determine.

The movement initiated by the diagonal thrust of the plow, set at an angle as if engaged in the act of tilling, is picked up in an undulating flow that reaches its resolution in the spreading area in the foreground. William Seitz has interpreted the circle, dotted in the earlier versions, at the culminating point of this form as an "ovary," "with flower anatomy inside."[76] The analogy between sowing the fields and lovemaking, or agricultural and human fertilization, suggests a consequent reading of the long white passage as a placenta—or "the winding birth passage and spacious exit chambers out of which the seed passes into space" described by Ethel Schwabacher. Lying between it and the plow, the forms depicted are those particulars of the field, like the blue stone, a memory image, or the leafy form below, probably derived from his landscape draw-

81

Figure 42. Arshile Gorky, *Virginia Landscape,* 1944. Pencil and crayon?, 43.2 x 58.4 cm (17 x 23 in). Private collection. Not in exhibition

ings, or finally, the isolated ivy-type leaf which echoes earlier use of the motif in *Painting* and *Composition,* both of 1936-1937. Thus a possible interpretation of the central form might be a kind of gestating cornucopia of the fruits of the earth, spilling out a snaillike creature and a star-petaled flower.[77] And we are reminded of der Hagopian's reminiscence that a real Armenian plow pulled by one pair of water buffalo and three pairs of oxen—that is, eight strong—would turn up the soil at least two feet deep.[78]

One might speculate on a formal source for this shape which has clearly puzzled scholars. Its only precedent in Gorky's work is in the landscape drawing of 1944. Akin to it is a similar but less articulated form, clearly derived from The Plow and the Song, in *Summation* (fig. 18). One possible source, however, presents quite a convincing case and may open doors to the understanding of other late works.

The old masters were Gorky's masters. Largely self-taught, he never stopped learning lessons in museums and through reproductions. He made copies of details from Ingres, Poussin, Rembrandt. Elaine de Kooning has described this process in detail:

he would twist the design as he worked, finishing abstract shapes he saw suggested in shadows or folds of material. Even in later years, forms in his abstractions were often directly inspired by these highly organized representations of reality. He would cut up prints and, turning the isolated fragments upside down, work from them as from a still-life.[79]

The elegance and refinement of this form (not yet present in the squared drawing of 1944) from the very first study onward suggests a study of drapery in an old master painting. Experimental tracings of a random detail like a full sleeve in Rembrandt's *Flora* or drapery as it falls around the knees of a seated figure tend to confirm this. Thus removed from their context, the gathers and tucks of material that spread into gentle curves are comparable to the large section at the base of the form. To the basic configuration derived from landscape drawings, Gorky brings refinement from an unexpected formal source.

Vartoosh described Gorky's method of isolating and extracting what he chose to focus on or to draw. V. V. Rankine, who

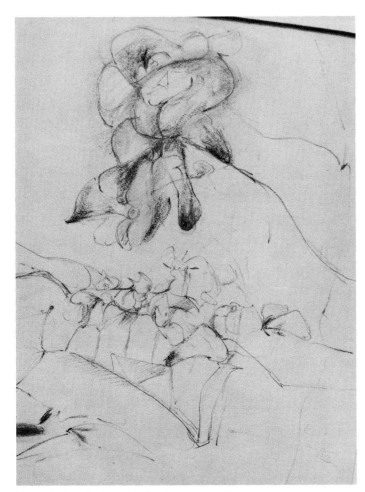

Figure 43. Detail of *Virginia Landscape* (fig. 42)

visited the National Gallery with Gorky when he came in from Hamilton, related how, sketchbook in hand, he would stop to draw before certain paintings. Both stories confirm that he continued this practice well into the time of working on The Plow and the Song. Vartoosh said that during these visits to museums,

He would often simulate a telescope with his hands to study paintings. "This way," he told me, "you can see only what you want, only the face, and you can study it more." And he would sit and draw there. . . .[80]

Similar to Gorky's practice of selecting a face or a passage of drapery and telescoping away the peripheral, his landscapes, even one as topographically descriptive as the *Virginia Landscape* (fig. 42), show like obsession with details. For Gorky the intensity with which he experienced the whole depended upon intimacy, or immediacy, with a particular part.

Elaine de Kooning noted this particularity of approach: "He never took a large vista, but preferred to find all his distances in the branches of one tree or in one cluster of weeds. . . ."[81] By taking a photograph from "an eye level close to the ground of the pasture," Jim Jordan made a study of Gorky's possible vantage points and his translation of what he saw into his drawings. He concluded with regard to the same *Virginia Landscape,*

In a reversal of the natural sequence, and for the purpose of control-

82

Figure 44. Arshile Gorky.
The Plow and the Song, 1947.
Oil on burlap, 132.4 x 162.9 cm (52⅛ x 64⅛ in).
Collection, Milton A. Gordon, New York.
Cat. no. 4, pl. 5

ling the depth of space, Gorky consistently makes his foreground forms most general and vague. His close-view details of leaves and grass are displaced to positions in middle and deep space.[82]

In The Plow and the Song two such "close-view" details have been radically displaced: the vertical element on the left and the form in the upper right.

The full spreading element projecting into the foreground of this drawing (fig. 43) has the effect of a repoussoir which throws the rest of the landscape into the distance. In The Plow and the Song a corresponding form has been isolated and placed in the far distance. Comparison of the composition of the drawing to that of The Plow and the Song suggests the topographical relation of the latter to the landscape and the manner in which Gorky has recreated it in terms of pictorial space.

Both compositions are framed by a vertical growth on the left and a blossom motif in the upper right. The depth conveyed by the delineation of rolling hills in the drawing is still hinted at in the tree that crowns the distant hillside of The Plow and the Song. The topographical description of the drawing has been sacrificed, however, for the introduction of the central form which, of all the major elements, is the only one to retain a suggestion of spatial recession. The rest of the composition has been developed in the series to allow the relative importance or varying iconographic context of the forms to evolve. Thus, no sooner is the sensation of depth perceived than the eye is brought back to the surface. A two-dimensional reading of forms is reinforced by the square field, lower right, introduced as an emphatic formal element only in the Chicago and Milton Gordon paintings and directly responding to the flat bar of color which enters the composition to the left. They serve to

anchor the composition and reassert it as a relation of surface elements.

The form in the upper right of The Plow and the Song probably developed out of the convoluted rococo shapes of the 1943 landscape drawings. It also appears to relate to the *Virginia Landscape* drawing, in which it can be read as a blossom or fruit on the branch of a tree which projects into the picture. Its location in the upper right corner of a landscape with a similar horizon suggests a parallel derivation of the shape in The Plow and the Song and its interpretation as a fruit form.

Here again, Gorky's letters of 1944, written as he began work on the first version of The Plow and the Song recapitulate the imagery of his free-verse description of those most salient memories of Khorkom that he had originally associated with the Garden in Sochi. He had described "the heat the tenderness the edible the lusciousness the song" and further on he included "the wheatfields the plough the apricots the shape of apricots those flirts of the sun." The richness of those intimately related sensations are echoed in a letter of February 14, 1944:

Man should learn to smell with his mind and thereby master yet another of memory's senses. Strange. Recently my mind was seized by the scent of Armenia's apricots, and though of course none are to be found in my studio, I smell them with my head just as surely as I climbed our orchard trees to pick them for Grandfather as his apricot messenger. I touch their softness with my nosetip. Now they float in my work as the humble procreators of delicate beauty. They are the many sunsets dancing silently on the horizon and opening as flower petals to allow Armenian maidens to folk-dance on their leaves to the grateful ovation of nature's grand audience. The scent of apricots on our fields.[83]

Figure 45. Crooked Run Farm, Hamilton, Va. [Photo: E. A. Carmean, Jr., July 1977]

Figure 46. Arshile Gorky. *Fireplace in Virginia*, 1946. Ink and crayon, 21.6 x 27.6 cm (8½ x 10⅞ in). Estate of Arshile Gorky [photo: reproduced from Ethel K. Schwabacher, *Arshile Gorky* (New York, 1957)]. Not in exhibition

The position of the form in The Plow and the Song—floating, dancing "on the horizon," its contour in the first two drawings opening into petal forms—suggests the apricot as at least one interpretation for this form, and perhaps the first drawing for The Plow and the Song as the very work to which he was referring. In the letter of the following December in which he describes his use of the plow as a model for drawing, he continues, again specifically in reference to his work in progress:

I smell the apricots hot on our orchard trees and they move for me in dances of old. And the songs, our ancient songs of the Armenian people, our suffering people. This I am painting and you will I am sure appreciate it. So many shapes, so many shapes and ideas, a secret treasure to which happily I have been entrusted the key.[84]

And in closing the same letter,

Beloved ones, write me and tell me of mountains and valleys. Sing of Van. Sing of apricots and wheatfields, of plows. Sing of songs.[85]

In *The Plow and the Song* (Milton Gordon; fig. 44), the form under discussion is a rich apricot color. In *The Plow and the Song II* (fig. 36), however, the form has been given a paler pink-orange hue that is virtually flesh color, to the end that it evokes nothing so much as a female torso in the sky. That such a reading for this form in this particular version of the series was Gorky's intention may be substantiated by two possible sources, one derived from nature and the other from a contemporaneous work of another series. Isamu Noguchi, with whom Gorky traveled to California in the summer of 1941, related a revealing story of the way in which Gorky's sense of fantasy was inclined to anthropomorphize natural phenomena.

His images were always sort of tinged with the Armenian viewpoint . . . he'd be always seeing some peasant woman up in the sky. And we had terrible arguments about it because I said, "that's just a cloud." He said, "Oh no, don't you see that old peasant woman up there?". . . . Nature didn't look the same to him as to somebody else. . . . He [Noguchi] feels that Gorky "was always sort of elaborating and weaving a lacework of imagery into whatever he saw."[86]

A typical cloud formation in that hilly region of Virginia is the fat cumulus variety that may well have entered his sketches from nature (fig. 45).

In the several versions of The Calendars the biomorphic form in the upper left has been identified quite convincingly by Harry Rand as a female torso. Such a reading is made all that more credible on the evidence of an earlier important crayon drawing from which The Calendars derives, entitled *Fireplace in Virginia* (1946; fig. 46).[87] Here, the form in question is depicted fringed with little hairs reminiscent of the schematic detailing of Miró's variety of erotic female figures and symbols. The female's sex is more overtly depicted in The Calendars than in The Plow and the Song. The form indeed appears to be not a mere torso but the entire figure, knees bent, her slightly spread legs tucked under her and either her arms folded against her chest or eliminated to allow the breasts to round the form, a quintessentializing of the female anatomy. The figure may also refer to a source in ancient art, for in its more generalized version in The Plow and the Song it bears a resemblance to Sumerian sculptures, particularly the goddess of fertility and the goddess of beauty. Gorky must have known of the surrealists' esteem for the art of ancient civilization and the influence of these sources on their art. *Cahiers d'Art* had published a book, *L'Art de la Mésopotamie* by Christian Zervos in 1934, which he might well have known since he had seen other *Cahiers d'Art* publications. Gorky's admiration for this art that he considered his heritage was often expressed in terms of the plasticity he discovered in the sculpture of the Near East and in the miniatures of medieval Armenia—particularly those of Toros Roslin, who also came from Van, and of Sardis Pidzak. Thus it appears that in the case of a particular image such as this, its various allusions, or identities, may only have occurred to Gorky once confronted with his own first rendering of the form before him.

Toros Roslin was one of the finest artists of the great period of Armenian manuscript painting in the thirteenth century. "He communicated a sense of movement not only to men and

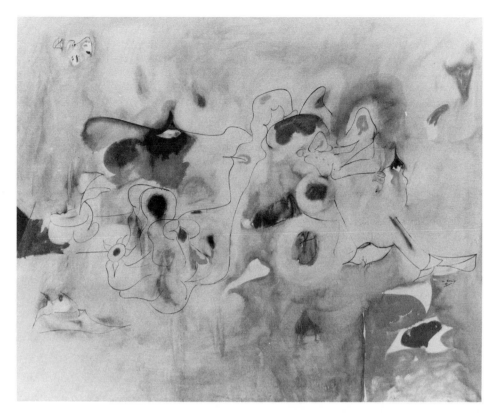

Figure 47. Arshile Gorky.
The Plow and the Song, 1947.
Oil on canvas, 128.9 x 159.4 cm (50¾ x 62¾ in).
Allen Memorial Art Museum, Oberlin College,
Ohio. Cat. no. 5, pl. 6

animals but even to plant motifs and decorated initials."[88] Gorky wrote to Vartoosh on June 14, 1945, "Above all I remember the medieval Armenian manuscript paintings with their beautiful Armenian faces, subtle colors, their tender lines and the calligraphy. And to this day I can still feel the chill of excitement at being introduced to a whole new world of plasticity."[89] He wrote often of his admiration for the colors used in these miniatures. *The Plow and the Song II* is the version in the series in which the entire spectrum of color comes closest to the delicate jewellike brilliance characteristic of the miniatures of Roslin. Thus in many respects this version presents a particular homage to his Armenian heritage.

That a fruit form in one version could evolve into a female one in the next may have been facilitated not only by the imaginative approach Gorky derived from his memories of Armenia and his subsequent education in that culture, but also by an awareness of a similar analogy of fruits to the female form in Picasso's paintings of Marie-Thérèse of the 1930s. The issue of *Cahiers d'Art* devoted to Picasso in 1935 reproduces one of the paintings, a nude of 1932, in which Picasso's mistress evokes ripe fruit forms and sprouts flowers and leaves suggesting her fecundity, and a nude of the year before in which the full forms have been arranged like a still life.[90]

No such overlay of meaning that I know of qualifies the related form in The Calendars. The Plow and the Song seems to have provoked an unusually rich succession of analogies for Gorky. In a letter of February 17, 1947 (that is, following *The Plow and the Song II*), Gorky wrote about the endless formal potential of the apricot and attributed the associations it inspired to his Armenian past:

Infinity is beyond space. The beautiful apricot of Armenia is finite in size. But if its interior is probed, if it is exploded or explored, infinities are reached. Therefore when I speak of infinity and finite objects I am not necessarily speaking of space alone, nor am I allowing size to define what is finite. Man's mind probing the finite Armenian apricot unearths its infinite properties, its infinite secrets. This is an instance of the glorious potentiality of the abstract mind. There is an abundance of abstractions in the Armenian experience and civilization. Fortunately for us these have produced a broad range of infinities for exploration. Tangible Armenia is replete with inner infinities and so too are intangible memories of Armenia, the intellectual ideas sired by it.[91]

While in the grisaille version, the whites act as highlights allowing the forms to project, however ghostly, like low relief, in the first two painted versions the whole surface is endowed with a physical presence in which, despite the flattening effect of the color patches and their scumbled treatment, the principle forms, by virtue of their silhouette, do not lose their plastic identity.

In the last version in the series (fig. 47) a thin application of golden yellow pigment veils into partial obscurity all the main elements of the composition but the central motif. Vartoosh's account of the period, when she and her husband were living with Gorky in New York (1935-late 1936), describes how he would ask her to sing the Armenian songs of Hovhanes Toumanian while he was painting. Then, she says, "He would mix his paints a great deal. He always wanted to obtain the colors of Van. Especially the yellow that is produced when we cooked the roots of the Van dandelion. It turned the water into a most beautiful yellow."[92]

During their first stay in Virginia Agnes Gorky reported that Gorky "was fearfully linked with the sun."[93] In reference to Garden in Sochi we are reminded that he described apricots as

Figure 48. Arshile Gorky. *Scent of Apricots,* 1947. Oil on canvas, 78.8 x 111.7 cm (31 x 44 in). Collection, Mr. and Mrs. Joseph R. Shapiro, Oak Park, Ill. [photo: Nathan Rabin]. Not in exhibition

"those flirts of the sun" and later, "they are the many sunsets." In The Plow and the Song the warmth and ripeness associated with the specific fruit is translated into the enveloping source of all heat and life. In the final radiant version this form, overlaid with symbols of fertility, nearly disappears as if it has become the overriding theme of the whole painting.

If we compare the sequence from *The Calendars* of 1946 to *Making the Calendar* and *Days Etc.,* both of 1947, Gorky appears to work through all the personal associations specifically described in the earlier versions of this series to one in which the paint has been thinned with turpentine allowing the consequent fluidity of the rendering to result in a work predominantly characterized by mood and feeling. In the contemporaneous *Scent of Apricots* (1947; fig. 48) the fruit forms burst and drip apricot color in a sensuous evocation of their memory.

Throughout The Plow and the Song Gorky maintains a balance between formal and iconographic concerns. Each is developed or modified in concert with the other. Color appears to be strongly associative, yet, for example, in the Milton Gordon version, it is a formal analogy of plow and slipper that is furthered by Gorky's use of lavender and black, unique to those two elements in the painting.

The theory that Gorky distilled from an external visual source a formal language that harbored less and less significant content cannot be seen to apply to The Plow and the Song.[94] We know from his drawings of the early 1940s the extent of Gorky's freedom from representation in these direct responses to nature. From these drawings he appears to have selected forms, more abstract in isolation, and only subsequently infused them with meaning, which may or may not relate to their original identity. Thus Gorky's forms became more and more rich in meaning and association in these late works. In the case of the vertical form on the left of The Plow and the Song, it appears to have been formally initiated in a painting that predates the series, then transformed through reference to the landscape. In the case of the fruit/cloud form, the opposite

probably occurred; its origin in landscape drawings, it only subsequently gained meaning in the course of serial evolution. It was only in such a consciously evolved series that Gorky could bring such a wealth of ideas and influences to bear.

The overall composition of The Plow and the Song, in which large and small, near and far are kaleidoscoped onto the surface, suggests Gorky's continuing admiration for Uccello's *Battle of San Romano* of which, Ethel Schwabacher records, he had nearly life-size photos "which he contemplated incessantly."[95] That this painting continued to be a source for Gorky may be confirmed by a letter of June 14, 1945, in which he places marked emphasis on the importance of Uccello and his lessons in dimensionality and space, and also by a comparison with two other late works, *Orators* and *Summation,* both of 1947, in which the seemingly random distribution of small elements in the foreground echo the broken spears in the Uccello.

The dominant role that Gorky's line plays in spatial organization, however, probably also depends upon his study of Armenian manuscripts in which he admired the colors but above all "the calligraphy." The vitality in the depiction of drapery alone in these miniatures and the linear play that organizes an entire composition is revived in Gorky's work. In a letter of 1945 Gorky, in the same breath almost, cites both Uccello and Armenian sources for his conception of space.

Toros Roslin is the first. But Uccello is the next step. The beginnings of what are considered modern paintings, the coming to grips with color and dimensionality and space, I discern in these two geniuses. Enclosed are some works by Uccello which you should study.[96]

Finally the composition of The Plow and the Song, particularly the central complex of forms that bear the principal burden of spatial organization appear to be echoed in a description Gorky wrote to his sister Vartoosh in 1941 regarding the methods and content of his paintings about Armenia. Although written while he was working on Garden in Sochi, it was not until The Plow and the Song that he seems to have fully realized this conception:

Visualize painting as the mobile positioning and partitioning of component parts of materiality. Houses built by man's labor and apricot trees by nature's formula and the artist making them all his own by controlling their motion as a conductor leads his orchestra. The rectangular walls with butterchurns and clay baking tools and Armenian rugs pasted on them stretch and twist in seeking contact with wheatfields and cloth trees and Armenian cranes and garden stones, all floating within one another and swept up by the universe's ceaseless momentum just as life-nourishing blood when flowing through the body nudges the artery walls on its journey.[97]

Thus both the form and content of The Plow and the Song were realized through Gorky's perception of the uniqueness of the Armenian sensibility. Whatever camp one tries to place him in—surrealist, abstract-expressionist—whatever myriad influences on his style may be cited, the contribution of his Armenian background (which he cultivated) to the formation both of his style and of the content of his work has often been underestimated. The subject matter of The Plow and the Song made it naturally conducive to the employment of all those particular Armenian qualities.

Gorky's free-verse about the Garden in Sochi is written in a surrealist style.[98] Other writings of 1941 exhibit that frequent occurrence in art history in which the artist's idea precedes its realization. In the case of The Plow and the Song Gorky has drawn upon a surrealist orientation to realize his remembered sensations of the "Land of Luxurious Growth" for which he was named. While the Garden in Sochi has been cited as the beginning of a turn toward a surrealist approach, The Plow and the Song can be seen to represent the fulfillment of those surreal qualities peculiar to Gorky and ultimately must be recognized as an extraordinary personal vision that was "innate in him."

Gorky was struck by the silence in the tilling of fields in this country.

What I miss most are the songs in the fields. No one sings them any more. . . . And there are no more plows. I love a plow more than anything else on a farm.[99]

In a lyrical and poetic dialogue with the landscape, Gorky forged the artistic language and traditions of Armenia into the idiom of his time.

NOTES

1. Dore Ashton, *The New York School* (New York: The Viking Press, 1973), 128.

2. Gorky wrote of his paintings as "windows" in a letter of Feb. 9, 1942. See discussion of his work later in this essay, under the heading *Series*. It is possible he derived the concept of a painting as a window from André Breton, who wrote in *Surrealism and Painting* (first published in English in his *What Is Surrealism?* [1936], trans. D. Gascoyne; London: MacDonald, 1972), 2: "it is impossible for me to envisage a picture as being other than a window, and . . . my first concern is then to know what it *looks out* on. . . ." William Rubin noted this attitude of Breton in "Arshile Gorky, Surrealism, and the New American Painting," *Art International,* 7 (Feb. 1963): 27.

3. Yet one might speculate whether Gorky's serial conception of painting did not influence the like approach of the abstract expressionists.

4. Karlen Mooradian, "A Special Issue on Arshile Gorky," *Ararat,* 12, no. 4 (Fall 1971): 39 (Gorky's letter of Feb. 17, 1947).

5. See William Rubin, "Gorky," for discussion of Gorky's position, in which he includes Harold Rosenberg's interpretation (p. 28): Gorky's peculiar historical position sustains the impression that his style is hybrid and identifies him as what we may truly call a *transitional* painter. The idea that he is thus a link between the European tradition and present-day American abstraction finds favor with many critics, but Harold Rosenberg rightly cautions that "the 'link' idea slips when it is applied to suggest that Gorky is nothing more than a transition to a body of painting more 'advanced' and more 'authentically American.' . . . Those to whom Gorky represents a link to something newer and better should be reminded that in art, as elsewhere, a chain is nothing *but* links, and there is no particular virtue in being the one at the end."

We can sympathize with Rosenberg's reaction to the general tendency to confuse novelty and quality, to attribute to the word "advanced" the implications it would have if we were talking about technological progress. But the word "newer", which Rosenberg paired with the word "better", need not go down the drain with it, for American painting after Gorky is manifestly newer, and it is new in ways that differentiate it collectively from Gorky.

6. Barbara Rose, "Arshile Gorky and John Graham: Eastern Exiles in a Western World," *Arts Magazine,* 50 (Mar. 1976): 62. No more specific date of their meeting is recorded here.

7. Dorothy Dehner, Foreword in Marcia Epstein Allentuck, *John Graham's System and Dialectics of Art* (Baltimore: The Johns Hopkins Press, 1971), xix-xx.

8. Dore Ashton, *School,* 94.

9. Arshile Gorky, *New York Sun* interview with M. Johnson, Aug. 22, 1941; quoted in Maurice Tuchman, ed., *The New York School, Abstract Expressionism in the 40s and 50s* (London: Thames and Hudson, n.d.), 57-58.

10. Arshile Gorky; quoted in Ethel K. Schwabacher, *Arshile Gorky* (New York: MacMillan Co. and Whitney Museum of American Art, 1957), 111.

11. *Arshile Gorky* (New York: Kootz Gallery, 1950); quoted in Lawrence Alloway, "Gorky," *Artforum, 1* (Mar. 1963), 28.

12. Rubin, "Gorky," 28.

13. Willem de Kooning; quoted in Karlen Mooradian, "Philosophy of Arshile Gorky," *Armenian Digest, 2* (Sept.-Oct. 1971): 55.

14. Robert Jonas; quoted in Mooradian, "A Special Issue," 48.

15. Breton, *Surrealism and Painting,* 200.

16. Elaine de Kooning, "Gorky: Painter of His Own Legend," *Art News,* 49 (Jan. 1951): 63.

17. Vivi Rankine, in conversation with the author, Oct. 14, 1977 (on file in the Department of Twentieth-Century Art, National Gallery of Art, Washington); hereafter referred to as Rankine, Oct. 14.

18. Clement Greenberg (*The Nation,* Mar. 24, 1945); quoted in Schwabacher, *Gorky,* 108.

19. Gorky; quoted in Mooradian, "A Special Issue," 39 (letter of Jan. 17, 1947).

20. Sidney Janis, *Abstract and Surrealist Art in America* (New York: Reynal and Hitchcock, 1944).

21. Robert Jonas; quoted in Mooradian, "Philosophy of Arshile Gorky," 56.

22. Gorky; quoted in Mooradian, "Philosophy of Arshile Gorky," 56-57 (letter of Apr. 22, 1944).

23. *Arshile* is the Georgian form of the Armenian royal name *Arshak; Gorky,* in addition to being the name of the renowned Russian writer Maxim Gorki, means "bitterness" in Russian. The most detailed chronology of Gorky's life has been compiled by Karlen Mooradian for the Armenian quarterly *Ararat* (see n. 4 above); details of biography/chronology in this essay, where not otherwise indicated, are derived from that text. Also see Karlen Mooradian, "The Unknown Gorky," *Art News,* 66 (Sept. 1967): 52.

24. Gorky's adopted identities extended to his particular inclination and gift for paraphrasing both other artists and writers. To enhance his love letters, Gorky paraphrased not only the surrealist poet Eluard but also the short-lived sculptor Henri Gaudier-Brzeska. About these letters, written to Michal West in 1936 and to Agnes Magruder in 1941, see: Nick Dante Vaccaro, "Gorky's Debt to Gaudier-Brzeska," *The Art Journal,* 23 (Fall 1963): 33-34.

25. Rubin, "Gorky," 28.

26. Harry Rand, "Arshile Gorky's Iconography" (diss., Harvard University, 1974), 26, 172. Elsewhere (pp. 89-90) Rand states more emphatically, "As the interaction of his [Gorky's] imagery and his personal life became more complete, at last he was nearly painting a diary, so also the obfuscation of these images increased, almost as if propriety dictated a certain civil distance be kept as the images became more terrible." In a note (n. 12, p. 81), Rand states, "Even when Gorky expressed himself explicitly on his subject matter, he allowed ambiguity to insinuate that a more fluid condition existed with regard to his content than may in fact have been the case."

Conclusions as to single or multiple meanings may indeed differ according to the work (or works) in question. Rand concludes that all of Gorky's "obfuscations were to one end: to make it harder for the viewer to determine 'what happened'" (p. 151). Rand's own frustration at thoroughly "decoding" Gorky's "subjects" should not be used as evidence that Gorky intended to hide his subject. To state that Gorky's complex evolution of a style of painting was to "one end," and that he was motivated by a desire to cover his tracks, seems to ignore, or relegate to lesser importance, a more relevant and positive artistic concern. Not only Gorky's entire oeuvre but also his writings attest to his continual preoccupation with questions of composition and handling of materials. I would propose that it was not a matter of deliberately obscuring his sources that motivated Gorky so much as it was a desire to explore, interpret, and enrich his subject through the act of painting in order to elevate it to a realm of universal art historical importance.

Diane Karp (*Arts Magazine, 50* [Mar. 1976]:82), who has written a brief study of Gorky's iconography, also presents an opposing view to that of Harry Rand: "He [Gorky] willed an understanding of his work and not, as so often [has] been assumed, obscure images beyond the reckoning of the observer." It must be noted, nevertheless, that in his discussion of The Calendars, Rand appears to acknowledge and elaborate upon the point of view with which I would agree, with regard to the late series particularly: "Only by seeing *what* he was treating can we begin to understand *how* he was distorting for expressive and formal ends."

27. Gorky; quoted in Mooradian, "A Special Issue," 20 (letter of July 3, 1937).

28. John Graham; quoted in Janis, *Abstract and Surrealist Art.* Harry Rand makes specific mention of this statement by Graham and observations on its possible relation to Gorky. See Rand, "Gorky's Iconography," 105-106.

29. Stuart Davis, "Arshile Gorky in the 1930's: A Personal Recollection by Stuart Davis," *Magazine of Art,* 44 (Feb. 1951): 57.

30. Rankine, Oct. 14. See also Schwabacher, *Gorky,* 97.

31. Gorky; quoted in Mooradian, "A Special Issue," 29 (letter dated Feb. 9, 1942).

32. Gorky; quoted in Mooradian, "A Special Issue," 29 (letter dated Feb. 9, 1942).

33. Jim M. Jordan, *Gorky: Drawings,* exh. cat. (New York: M. Knoedler & Co., 1969), 13.

34. Rubin, "Gorky," n. 9. Such misdating of works, however, generally applies to works executed prior to 1943 (Jim Jordan, in conversation with the author, Mar. 1978; on file in the Department of Twentieth-Century Art, National Gallery of Art, Washington).

35. Mooradian, "A Special Issue," 33. Earlier letters of 1944 refer to much of the imagery that occurs in The Plow and the Song (see discussion of iconography that follows) advocating a date of 1944 for the Oberlin drawing.

36. Schwabacher, *Gorky,* 115.

37. Harold Rosenberg, *Arshile Gorky: The Man, the Time, the Idea* (New York: Horizon Press Inc., 1962), 91.

38. Most of the literature concurs in assigning a date of 1946 to this drawing. Nevertheless, reasons for this date are assembled here in view of the more problematic circumstances of execution peculiar to The Plow and the Song which may have provoked some doubt as to the validity of the accepted dating.

39. Schwabacher, *Gorky,* 112.

40. Another possible source for these large grisaille renderings is Miró's *Self-Portrait* (1938) in pencil and oil on canvas which was included in the Miró exhibition at the Museum of Modern Art, 1941-1942. Again an instance of such a grisaille as a full-scale work in its own right does predate 1946, in *Diary of a Seducer* (dated 1945). This, however, like the exceptional squared study of 1944, was not executed as part of a series (see n. 37 above).

41. It should, nevertheless, be noted that *Betrothal I* and *Betrothal II* are both paintings.

42. Rubin, "Gorky," 32. A review of Gorky's exhibition at the Julien Levy Gallery (*Art News,* 45 [Apr. 1946]: 54) notes such correspondences between the work of Matta and Gorky and rightly stresses the technical aspect of Matta's influence:

Arshile Gorky's most recent manner, now shown at Julien Levy's is definitely reminiscent of Matta. This is not a case of aping or stealing, but rather a borrowing of technical means. He adopted Matta's thin washes, dripping colors, method of floating the pigment on the medium, and the linear background. But here the similarity ends. Where Matta is mathematical and sexual, Gorky is lyrical, almost sentimental, and decorative. . . .

43. Gorky met Matta in 1941. Matta was ten years younger than Gorky and a much less experienced artist. Although Matta had recently arrived from Paris and had a magnetic personality, it is unlikely that Gorky looked to him as a "master," or borrowed from him more than superficial characteristics. I am indebted for this view of Gorky's probable attitude toward Matta to John Loftus, "Arshile Gorky: A Monograph" (M.A. thesis, Columbia University, 1952), 45.

44. Jim Jordan, "Arshile Gorky at Crooked Run Farm," *Arts Magazine, 50* (Mar. 1976): 99-103.

45. Vivi Rankine (who knew Gorky from the early 1940s to the end of his life), Oct. 14.

46. William Seitz, "Abstract-Expressionist Painting in America: an Interpretation Based on the Work and Thought of Six Key Figures," (Ph.D. diss., Princeton University, 1955), 48.

47. Rosenberg, *Arshile Gorky,* 68.

48. Schwabacher, *Gorky,* 122-123.

49. Gorky; quoted in Mooradian, "A Special Issue," 30 (letter of Jan. 26, 1944).

50. Gorky; quoted by Mooradian, "Philosophy of Arshile Gorky," 58.

51. *Maternity* was included in the Miró exhibition at the Museum of Modern Art, 1941.

52. Rand, "Gorky's Iconography," 99. Although Rand makes no mention of it, one might speculate that Gorky was inspired, at least in part, by Miró's example for his "interior" subjects of 1945-1947. Miró's *The Family* (1924) and *Dutch Interior I* (1928) were included in the 1941-1942 exhibition.

53. Rand, "Gorky's Iconography," 161. Rand stated, in reference to The Plow and the Song, "Nothing suggests what the major theme of the work actually might be . . ." (p. 161).

54. Schwabacher, *Gorky,* 128. This book, published after Schwabacher's catalogue for the Gorky exhibition at the Whitney in 1951, draws upon the many years of their friendship. She met him in 1928 and in 1934 began studying with him.

55. Quoted in Schwabacher, *Gorky,* 115.

56. In the case of The Plow and the Song, the title is said to have been invented by Gorky's wife Agnes (Vivi Rankine, Oct. 14). Nevertheless, Mrs. Agnes (Gorky) Phillips stated in a letter to the author (Feb. 19, 1978; on file in the Department of Twentieth-Century Art, National Gallery of Art) that this is not the case.

57. Gorky; quoted in Mooradian, "A Special Issue," 30-31 (letters of July 1943 and Feb. 14, 1944).

58. Tuchman, *The New York School,* 57.

59. See Rosenberg, *Arshile Gorky,* 68. "One inclines to accept Thomas Hess's judgment that Gorky excelled in awareness of what was happening in art. . . . As a theoretician Gorky was inexhaustible; nothing could stop the flow of his speculation."

60. Gorky; quoted in Mooradian, "A Special Issue," 25 (letter of Feb. 25, 1941).

61. Gorky, written in June 1942, at the request of Dorothy Miller about the painting *Garden in Sochi,* which the Museum of Modern Art had just acquired. From the Collections Archives, Museum of Modern Art, New York, June 1942. Reprinted in Tuchman, *The New York School,* 60.

62. Gorky; quoted in Mooradian, "A Special Issue," 29 (letter of July 1943).

63. Tuchman, *The New York School,* 60.

64. The observation that the imagery of Garden in Sochi and that of The Plow and the Song might be linked was also independently arrived at by Cathy Gebhard, intern at the National Gallery of Art in the summer of 1977.

65. Gorky; quoted in Mooradian, "A Special Issue," 21 (letter of Mar. 1, 1938). Moorad Mooradian (also born in Van) married Gorky's sister, Vartoosh, in June 1923. In 1935 they had a son Karlen. The following year the family moved to Chicago (Mooradian, "A Special Issue," 5, 15). Between 1937 and 1948 Gorky wrote to his sister and her family many letters, thirty-four of which have been published in Mooradian, "A Special Issue."

66. See Karlen Mooradian's interview with Yenovk der Hagopian, sculptor and boyhood friend of Gorky, "A Special Issue," 55.

67. There are three such plows extant, belonging to Karlen Mooradian.

68. Italics mine. Arshile Gorky; quoted in Mooradian, "A Special Issue," 32 (letter of Dec. 1944).

69. Gorky's daughter Maro says her father believed that "if you look very hard at an object, a chair, and you look at the lines that the object makes in space, and you try to get an exact replica of it which may not look at all like a photograph of a chair, you will get very near the essence of the chair, the feeling of the chair." Quoted by Karlen Mooradian, "Philosophy of Arshile Gorky," 57.

70. André Breton ("The Eye-Spring: Arshile Gorky," trans. Julien Levy, in *Arshile Gorky,* exh. cat. [New York: Julien Levy Gallery, 1945]), quoted in Schwabacher, *Gorky,* 106.

71. Jeanne Reynal; quoted by Hayden Herrera, "The Sculpture of Arshile Gorky," *Arts Magazine,* Mar. 1976, 88.

72. James Johnson Sweeney was the first to record this in "Five American Painters," *Harper's Bazaar,* Apr. 1944. See also interview with Robert Jonas in Mooradian, "A Special Issue," 47.

73. Schwabacher, *Gorky,* 98. It is this hard bony quality to which William Seitz refers ("Arshile Gorky's 'The Plow and the Song,'" *Allen Memorial Art Museum Bulletin* [Oberlin College, Ohio], 12 [Fall 1954]: 9) in observing its affinity to the structures of Yves Tanguy, who, after arriving in this country in 1939, went to live in Woodbury, Connecticut. It is most probable that the two artists met (Tanguy owned a Gorky). Seitz also refers to the base as the "slipper" motif which "can resemble petals or leaves" (p. 9). The stiff, bony quality of the figure has been softened by a more vital biomorphism that brings to mind the work of another artist who combined human and vegetal forms, Hans (Jean) Arp—for example, *Growth* (1938). (Schwabacher has cited Gorky's interest in Arp.)

In the work of Miró, a single, profile foot is given similar prominence at the base of such biomorphic "personnages" as occur in *Person*

Throwing a Stone at a Bird (1926), *Statue* (1926), or *Drawing on Felt Paper* (1928)—all included in the 1941 MOMA Miró exhibition.

That analogies of human and botanical forms came naturally to Gorky is revealed in his reference to his child as a little tree (Schwabacher, *Gorky*, 133).

74. Harry Rand ("Gorky's Iconography," 157) has cited a photograph in the June 1942 issue of *Dance Index* magazine, which Gorky probably saw, as a possible source for the most prominent figurative element in *Agony* (1947). If indeed this photograph, entitled *Xochitl*, did provide a source for Gorky, it seems just as, if not more, related to the more totemic vertical form at the left in The Plow and the Song. The crested headdress, the feather protrusions at knee and loins, and particularly the medallion-studded belt (that might correspond with the section developed two-thirds of the way down in Gorky's form) are more clearly echoed in the form as it appears in the squared drawing than in any other version of the series.

75. Barbara Rose was the first to actually publish such an example in her article on Gorky and Graham ("Eastern Exiles," 66). I am indebted to her for the encouragement to present, again, such a direct comparison here.

76. Seitz, "'The Plow and the Song'," 9.

77. There are, of course, numerous sources for the motif of the leaf and flower in the work of Miró (*The Tilled Field, Self-Portrait,* etc.).

78. Jim Jordan, "Gorky at Crooked Run Farm," 101. In his description of the *Virginia Landscape* drawing belonging to neighbors of Crooked Run Farm, Jim Jordan explains the foreground terminus of the central delineation of rolling hills: "the triangular funnel or cornucopia form at the center foreground in the drawing Gorky called a pool of water, acknowledging in a bemused way that it was not from the observed landscape, but was an imaginative addition" (p. 101). While Jordan makes no comparison of this drawing to The Plow and the Song, that the same image of a cornucopia should be evoked by both further suggests that this very drawing may be one of the sources for the series.

79. Elaine de Kooning, "Gorky," 39.

80. Karlen Mooradian, interview with his mother Vartoosh Mooradian, "A Special Issue," 16.

81. Elaine de Kooning, "Gorky," 64.

82. Jim Jordan, "Gorky at Crooked Run Farm," 102.

83. Gorky; quoted by Mooradian, "A Special Issue," 31 (letter of Feb. 14, 1944).

84. Gorky; quoted by Mooradian, "A Special Issue," 32, 33 (letter of Dec. 1944).

85. Gorky; quoted by Mooradian, "A Special Issue," 32, 33 (letter of Dec. 1944).

86. Isamu Noguchi; quoted in Mooradian, "Philosophy of Arshile Gorky," 60.

87. Harry Rand also sees this as a possible reading for the shape in question in The Plow and the Song. Rand cites this drawing as antecedent to The Calendars.

88. Lidiía Alexandrovna Durnovo, *Armenian Miniatures* (New York: Harry N. Abrams, 1961), 111.

89. Gorky; quoted in Mooradian, "A Special Issue," 34 (letter of June 14, 1945).

90. *Cahiers d'Art,* 1935, issue devoted to Picasso: see *Peinture,* 1931 (p. 209), and *Peinture,* 1932 (p. 213). That Gorky was well acquainted with these paintings is suggested by their similarity to several Gorkys of the thirties: *Painting, Composition,* and *Image in Khorkom.*

91. Gorky; quoted in Mooradian, "A Special Issue," 40 (letter of Feb. 17, 1947).

92. Karlen Mooradian, interview with Vartoosh Mooradian, "A Special Issue," 18.

93. Agnes Gorky, quoted in Schwabacher, *Gorky,* 96. The image of the sun occurs in other works by Gorky. In a more schematized depiction, it is similarly situated on the tip of a hill in the distance, for example, in *Golden Brown Painting* (1946).

94. Harry Rand, "Gorky's Iconography," 148.

95. Schwabacher, *Gorky,* 131. Gorky wrote of Uccello as one of his heroes as early as 1931 (see Ashton, *School,* 27). John Graham shared Gorky's admiration for Uccello, and Breton reproduced Uccello's *Battle of San Romano* (detail) in *Surrealism and Painting* (1928).

96. Gorky; quoted in Mooradian, "A Special Issue," 34 (letter of June 14, 1945).

97. Gorky; quoted in Mooradian, "Philosophy of Arshile Gorky," 57.

98. The above passage, "Visualize painting as the mobile positioning. . . ," is also closely paralleled in some of Picasso's surrealist writings: "Chasuble of blood thrown on the nude shoulders of the green wheat trembling between damp sheets symphonic orchestra of torn-up flesh hung on flowering trees of the wall painted ochre agitating its great apple green wings and white mauve tearing its nose against the windows. . . ." Quoted from *Cahiers d'Art,* 1948 (from a notebook of 1941 of Picasso), in Dore Ashton, *A Reading of Modern Art,* rev. ed. (New York: Harper and Row, 1971), 76.

99. Schwabacher, *Gorky,* 128.

ROBERT MOTHERWELL:
The Elegies to the Spanish Republic

Figure 1. Robert Motherwell painting *Elegy 124* in the winter of 1971. [Photo: Blackwood Productions]

CHECKLIST

1. Ink Sketch (Elegy No. 1)   1948
   ink on paper
   26.8 × 21.6 cm (10½ × 8½ in)
   Signed lower right: RM
   Mr. Robert Motherwell, Greenwich, Conn.

2. At Five in the Afternoon   1949
   casein on board
   38.1 × 50.8 cm (15 × 20 in)
   Signed lower right: Motherwell 1949
   Private collection

3. Elegy to the Spanish Republic, No. 34   1953-1954
   oil on canvas
   203.2 × 254.0 cm (80 × 100 in)
   Signed upper right: RM
   Albright-Knox Art Gallery, Buffalo, N.Y., Gift of Seymour
   H. Knox

4. Elegy to the Spanish Republic, No. 55   1955-1960
   oil on canvas
   177.8 × 193.3 cm (70 × 76⅛ in)
   Contemporary Collection of The Cleveland Museum of Art

5. The Figure 4 on an Elegy   1960
   oil on paper
   58.4 × 73.7 cm (23 × 29 in)
   Signed and dated lower left: RM—60
   Collection H. H. Arnason, New York

6. Elegy to the Spanish Republic, No. 70   1961
   oil on canvas
   175.3 × 289.6 cm (69 × 114 in)
   The Metropolitan Museum of Art, New York

7. Elegy to the Spanish Republic No. 78   1962
   oil and plastic on canvas
   180.4 × 335.9 cm (71 × 132¼ in)
   Signed upper right: R. Motherwell 62
   Yale University Art Gallery, New Haven, Gift of the Artist

8. Elegy to the Spanish Republic, No. 124   1971-1972
   acrylic on sized canvas
   260.4 × 444.5 cm (102½ × 175 in)
   Signed and dated: Motherwell
   Mr. Robert Motherwell, Greenwich, Conn.; on extended loan to
   the National Gallery of Art, Washington

9. Spanish Death   1975
   acrylic on oil-sized canvas
   243.9 × 198.1 cm (96 × 78 in)
   Signed and dated: Motherwell 30 August 75
   Mr. Robert Motherwell, Greenwich, Conn.

10. Elegy to the Spanish Republic, No. 100   1963-1975
    acrylic on oil-sized canvas
    213.4 × 609.6 cm (84 × 240 in)
    Signed and dated: Motherwell 1965-1975
    Mr. Robert Motherwell, Greenwich, Conn.

BIOGRAPHY

Robert Burns Motherwell. Born 1915 in Aberdeen, Washington; is raised in San Francisco. Studies at Stanford, Harvard, and Columbia universities. Moves to New York in 1940. Begins painting in 1941. In 1943 collage becomes a major interest. First one-man exhibition at Art of this Century Gallery in 1944. In 1948, is founding member of Subjects of the Artist school, and makes *Ink Sketch (Elegy 1)*. Has retrospective at Bennington College in 1959, and at The Museum of Modern Art in 1965. Paints *Open No. 1* in 1967. In 1971 moves to Greenwich, Connecticut. In 1972 has collage retrospective at the Museum of Fine Arts, Houston, and finishes *A La Pintura* book of poetry and prints. Retrospective exhibitions shown in Düsseldorf, Venice, Paris, Edinburgh, and London in 1976-1978.

ROBERT MOTHERWELL:

The Elegies to the Spanish Republic

E. A. CARMEAN, JR.

"There is so much to be seen in a work of art, so much to say if one is concrete and accurate, that it is a relief to deal on occasion with a simple relation. Yet not even it, no more than any other relation in art, is so simple,"[1] wrote Robert Motherwell in a catalogue note for a 1950 group exhibition of pictures on the motif of black and white. Included in this exhibition was one of the first of his own large black and white paintings which came to be called "The Elegies to the Spanish Republic"; but in spite of his perception of "simplicity's complexity," little did Motherwell realize that the development of what earlier had begun as a minor design for a periodical illustration would become the persistent artistic focus of his career. The Elegies now number over 140 works,[2] stretching back in an unbroken lineage of multiple expressions over the past thirty years.

The Elegies are the most famous of Motherwell's paintings despite the fact that they actually constitute only a small percent of all of his important work in painting and collage. In looking back, it appears that in the early 1960s the general belief was that the Elegies were all that Motherwell ever painted; for example, H.H. Arnason, in his major study of the artist in 1966, referred to them as a kind of "signature" for the artist.[3] More recently, because of the attention paid to Motherwell's collages and his Open paintings (a series of large pictures of colored fields with drawing begun in 1967) the opposite conclusion may now be prevalent, namely that the Elegies stopped as a theme some years ago and that they belong to only an abstract-expressionist phase of the artist's career.[4] This latter view is incorrect, of course, because the artist continues to paint Elegies. Yet it does recognize an essential aspect of the series: that they began as, and continue to be, abstract-expressionist works in terms of their coloration, scale, and manner of invention, and also because of the nature of the subject matter itself.

In addition, there appear to be more Elegies than is actually the case. The sequential numbering by the artist includes both small oil sketches and numerous works subsequently destroyed; thus a major painting numbered, for example, 124 suggests there are 123 other major Elegies, when, in fact, there are perhaps only twenty or so, representing four very different periods: those tied to the invention of the format in the late 1940s, the works which represent the new direction developed in the following decade, the explosive painterly Elegies of the 1960s, and the more studied compositions of the recent years.

Interestingly, the Elegies to the Spanish Republic began as a simple ornamentation for a poem.[5] Like many other modern movements in this century, abstract expressionism during its developing years was discussed not only in contemporaneous journals like *The Partisan Review* or *The Nation* but was also accompanied by several small publications more directly related to it, such as *VVV*, *Dyn*, or the *Tiger's Eye*. In 1948 Wittenborn & Schultz published a new magazine, *Possibilities (An Occasional Review)*, with John Cage, Pierre Chareau, Harold Rosenberg, and Motherwell as the editors. Only one issue appeared, although another one was planned. For the latter edition Motherwell agreed to "illuminate" a poem by Harold Rosenberg, "The Bird for Every Bird," and decided to follow a style then popular in the French publication *Verve;* the artist wrote out the author's poem in his (the artist's) hand and added illustrations to it. Because they could not afford the cost of reproducing in colors, Motherwell restricted his palette to black and white.

The first page consisted only of the opening lines of the poem, handwritten by Motherwell. For the facing second page Motherwell conceived of the five final lines at the top, with the illustration below. In making the Rosenberg illustration (fig. 2), Motherwell started with one of the many surrealist automatic devices for initiating a picture; he used "linear automatism," making a doodle on a sheet of paper. The general practice of the surrealists would have then been to transform the doodle by "seeing things" in it—i.e. faces, landscapes, etc.—they would take something nonobjective, random, and work back toward a figurative presentation.[6] In the Rosenberg illustration, however, the clarification of the doodle depended upon exactly the opposite step—Motherwell structured the work by emphasizing abstract elements in the chaotic scribble. This was accomplished by accenting certain lines, adding other passages, and filling in areas with black ink. "Somewhere I read . . . some artist, possibly Picasso, said that one of the most beautiful means an artist has is juxtaposing straights with curves," Motherwell recalls. "And in the middle of making this I was desperate, and then at a certain moment I began to straighten some and curve some [of the forms], and found that I liked that."[7] This drawing was to become, in effect, the first Elegy image.

In the spring of 1976, while discussing his procedure for making the Rosenberg illustration, Motherwell repeated all of the steps involved for the first time since he had made the initial drawing. Unfortunately that recreation was not photographed sequentially. A diagrammatic recreation—though not by the artist's hand—is illustrated here (diag. A-C). It does not record

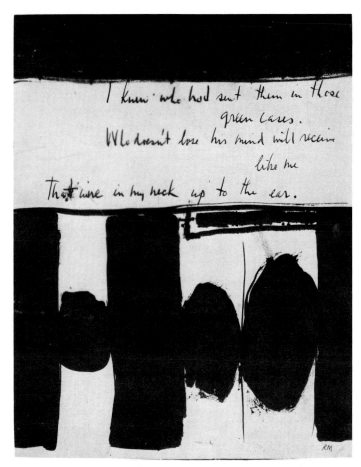

Figure 2. Robert Motherwell. *Ink Sketch (Elegy No. 1),* 1948. Ink on paper, 26.8 x 21.6 cm (10½ x 8½ in). Collection, Robert Motherwell, Greenwich, Conn. Cat. no. 1

the exact positions of all of the elements in the Rosenberg drawing, but it does show the procedure that was followed. In diagram A, linear automatism is used to cover a sheet of paper, creating an unarticulated "fabric" similar to the one Motherwell had made in 1948. The pen moved randomly over the surface, leaving a curvilinear network. In diagram B, the straights and curves come into action, as the artist emphasizes and picks up certain lines and begins to make shapes by blocking out and filling in areas within the linear pattern; at the same time he begins to add the rectangular passages superimposed on the linear scribble. Even at this very rough stage what eventually becomes the essential Elegy motif begins to emerge: a pattern of blackened oval forms contrasted to blackened vertical, rectangular panels. Diagram C represents the drawing near its final stage. Now the artist has filled in the forms, to create solid shapes, and—reading the leftover scribble areas as "white"—leaves smaller accents of thin black drawing to articulate the newly emerged image.

The thin linear elements were then added to the image, a vertical line between the touching ovals to the right and the enclosed horizontal bar in the upper right corner. These components serve to change the "pace" of the drawing and add a "handmade" touch—a detailing—which prevents the design from looking like a filled-in poster image woodcut. Motherwell

then added another horizontal black bar across the top of the page and wrote in the lines from the Rosenberg text.

This reconstruction of the invention of the Elegy format makes it clear how much indebted to, and also how finally different from, the surrealist standards of automatism this composition is.[8] The initial doodle is not only abstract but incoherent. However, rather than finding referential figures within this linear scribble as a surrealist would have done, Motherwell continued the abstraction, using automatism as a "plastic weapon with which to invent new forms."[9] Thus an abstract language is employed throughout the entire process of making the *Possibilities* sheet (the Rosenberg illustration)— uncontrolled, in the surrealist sense at the beginning, and consciously composed in the finish.

Motherwell had used automatism almost from the beginning of his work in 1941. But, as detailed study of his collages reveals, it often came in at the second stage in the evolution of the final pictorial image. Motherwell usually began with a quite generalized figural image (derived from certain of Picasso's works) and then allowed the automatic technique to determine the direction this initial structural schema would take.[10] The first Elegy drawing is distinct from Motherwell's earlier works in that both automatism and complete abstraction are present throughout the whole making of the work. Its origin and development remain apart from any "external" figuration, either as an initial compositional armature or as a final reference.

This is not to say, however, that the Elegies, or the Rosenberg illustration, are divorced from the artist's previous work. Indeed, while the contrast of straights and curves here originates within the fabric of linear automatism, this kind of compositional union is characteristic of much of Motherwell's earlier work. Certain key pictures of the early 1940s employ such juxtapositions. In *Pancho Villa, Dead and Alive,* 1943, for example, the two oval forms which comprise the trunk of the body in each section are placed between black vertical elements, which are further emphasized by the different textures. But if the use of ovals and straights is a common Motherwellian touch which appears in many works of the period, it is also usually combined with amazingly rich varieties of other shapes, as well as different placements, textures, and colors of the collaged papers. Set against Motherwell's other works of the 1940s, the Rosenberg illustration derives its arresting quality from the boldness and completeness with which it isolates the contrast of ovals and straights, one of the structural devices which recurs throughout the artist's work.

The reconstruction also makes clear—when we allow the artist's preference for straights and curves, verticals and ovals—how spontaneously generated was the initial Elegy image. Clearly it has no direct formal link with the Rosenberg text, even with the words which eventually appeared on the same page with it. "It has literally nothing to do with the poem—except perhaps for their both having brutal qualities—certainly not its images," says Motherwell.[11] "Certain critics [for example] have read the phrase 'wire in my neck' as being described by the line between the ovals. No wire or neck is there."

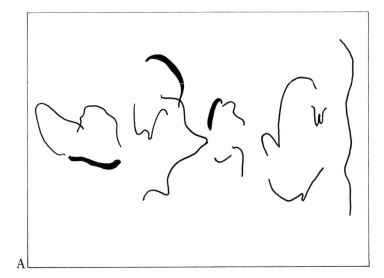

A

B

C

Diagrams A-C. These three drawings, not by the artist's hand, are a reconstruction of the stages of making *Ink Sketch (Elegy No. 1)*. Diagram A represents the "doodle," Diagram B represents the addition of "straights and curves," and Diagram C indicates the addition of black ink.

As fortune would have it, the second issue of *Possibilities* was canceled, and the drawing—in effect *Elegy to the Spanish Republic No. 1*—was put away in a drawer, the artist forgetting about it until he rediscovered it a year or so later when moving his studio. He was struck by the image, when he rediscovered it, and made a second version, in casein on board, entitled *At Five in the Afternoon* (fig. 3). "At one moment I was looking around for a generating idea, and thought well, I'll try another version, only larger and eliminating the written script. It was one of those times when I just wanted to paint for the act of painting."[12] In spite of the close resemblance between the Rosenberg illustration and this second version, significant changes have occurred, alterations which are probably responsible for the artist's later "discovery" of the subject of the picture, as well as his recognition of the expressive and monumental potentials of the format.

The primary change, of course, was the elimination of the Rosenberg text, thereby creating a painting in place of an illustration. To many who are familiar with the Elegies, suddenly to see them exhibited with the artist's handwriting blown up in large script on the wall above them would seem exceedingly novel; the reverse—the discovery of the format without the text—must have seemed equally revolutionary to the artist, if not more so. In making the painting Motherwell left certain edges quite ragged, loosely brushing them into the surrounding white ground. This touch captured in painting the softer edges in the drawing which there had been naturally produced where the ink bled into the paper. This touch is especially pronounced around all the edges of the right oval and at the bottoms of the other two. There, and on two of the left vertical panels as well, Motherwell left the runs of paint which had flowed out of the black areas when the picture was in a vertical position. This record of spontaneity and chance challenges the concept of "copying" in the enlargement and was kept by the artist. (The spontaneous touch shows up both in major and in detailing roles in subsequent Elegies [see Elegies 70 and 124, figs. 13 and 16, for example].) The feathered edge also keeps the Elegies from relating to Matisse's or Arp's tightly drawn shapes and, at least in the detailing, relates them to the general painterly look of abstract expressionism as a whole.

At the upper right of *At Five in the Afternoon* the artist introduced color in the form of a warm blue—"it was a challenge to see if I could add color to it and not have color interfere."[13] Much of the blue was then painted over, and only traces of it remain. The white areas also different from those of the drawing. Because the artist used thin white paint on a cardboard support, the taupe undercolor bled through in many places, giving here a more atmospheric tone to the ground than is present in the drawing.

But central to our understanding of the Elegies, more than learning these formal changes and prescriptions (which recur throughout the series) is that this enlarged and text-free version produced the general direction of the theme of the series. Motherwell, who often makes a point by creating an analogy, draws the following one for the Elegies at this critical point in

Figure 3. Robert Motherwell. *At Five in the Afternoon,* 1949. Casein on board, 38.1 x 50.8 cm (15 x 20 in). Private collection [photo: Peter A. Juley]. Cat. no. 2

their creation: "When I painted the larger version—*At Five in the Afternoon*—it was as if I discovered it [the image] was a temple, where Harold's [the *Possibilities* illustration] was a gazebo, so to speak. And when I recognized this [that the image was now a temple], I looked around for whom represented what the temple should be consecrated to, and that that was represented in the work of Lorca."[14] Lorca is Federico García Lorca, whose writings had deeply impressed Motherwell. His poem *Llanto Por Ignacio Sánchez Mejías,*[15] a lament for the bullfighter, with its constant refrain, "at five in the afternoon," supplied the appellation for this enlarged version.

But this particularization of title for the second version should not be read as a descriptive one. The artist states: "To be more concise [I would say] the 'temple' was consecrated to a Spanish sense of death, which I got most of from Lorca, but from other sources as well—my Mexican wife, bullfights, travel in Mexico, documentary photographs of the Mexican revolution, Goya, Santos, dark Hispanic interiors."[16]

The poem itself, especially Part One, "The Corrida and Death," offers interesting parallels to the painted forms of *At Five in the Afternoon.* As Robert Hobbs has pointed out in his study of the Elegies, Lorca's *Llanto Por Ignacio Sánchez Mejías* repeats the refrain "at five in the afternoon" *(a las cinco de la tarde)* thirty times in fifty-two lines of poetry. The poem builds to a high pitch of horror in the interposing lines, while the persistent pulse of "at five in the afternoon" continues. Hobbs observes:

By piling refrain upon refrain and interspersing between them lines that become expletives, Lorca creates a sustained climax that has a lot in common with Motherwell's painting—the refrain "at five in the afternoon" is an inevitable thrust, a continuing, overwhelming force that surrounds and compresses together the intervening lines in a manner very similar to the way that the ponderous verticals of the painting remain implacable, forcing the ovoids to remain suspended in an uneasy tension.[17]

The rhythm of Lorca's lament can be compared to that of a drum beat, and indeed Motherwell entitled two later Elegies *Spanish Drum Roll* and *Little Spanish Drum Roll*—in recognition of this quality. "I've always been spellbound by drum-rolls," he says, "the contrast between the clear rolling sound and the period of silence. The Elegies—in the pattern of the black forms against the white—have a similar feeling."[18]

It is also important to emphasize here that just as the illustration for the Rosenberg poem was not tied to that text, so the Elegies—and *At Five in the Afternoon* in particular—are neither directly nor causally linked to Lorca's lament. Indeed, as we have seen, the initial image was generated automatically and abstractly and was not intended to illustrate (as such) either poem. Rather, Motherwell recognized within an already existing format—the "Elegy" image itself—something recalling a sense of an existential "trial of nerves, a running the gauntlet"[19] that was especially Spanish and that was most closely approached in Lorca's poem.

In this regard it is pertinent to discuss the general titling practices of the abstract expressionists. Many works were titled after completion, either from lists of names drawn up by fellow artists, friends, and critics, or at "titling sessions" at the artist's studio, involving these same people. Motherwell has observed about his own titles that "their function was partly a negative one, that is to say, to mark off what can't be said about the picture. The cubists are quite literal in their titles—Picasso calls a painting of an apple and a pipe 'Apple and Pipe.' I thought about trying to be that literal in my own titles, but [realized that] my work is not specific in the cubist sense."[20] But Motherwell's referential title *At Five in the Afternoon* was too obscure in this instance. Motherwell recalls: "One reason I changed the name of the series as a whole to 'Elegy to the Spanish Republic' was that someone would come up to me and say 'I saw a marvelous picture by you—what was the name? Something to do with cocktails.'"[21]

GRANADA

The change of title direction toward the generic—Elegy to the Spanish Republic—began in 1950, with the exhibition of the first paintings in the series, at the Samuel Kootz Gallery in New York (November 14-December 4). In the catalogue for this exhibition Motherwell listed ten paintings under the series assignation "Elegies (to the Spanish Republic)." Among them was the first enlargement of the Rosenberg illustration, there entitled *At Five in the Afternoon Sketch* (Kootz cat. no. 4A), along with another larger and later version of the same image, there and subsequently called *At Five in the Afternoon* (Kootz cat. no. 5A; collection of Mrs. Wright Morris, Pacific Palisades, California). Among the other paintings grouped as Elegies was the third in the series, *Granada* (Kootz cat. no. 3A; our fig. 4). *Granada* is considerably bigger at 47 x 55½ inches, as opposed to the 15 x 20 measurements of the initial *At Five in the Afternoon*. It is the first of the larger Elegies and marks the proper beginning of the series as a whole.

Granada was painted in two eighteen-hour sessions in December 1948 along with another key work, *The Voyage* (fig. 6), which is not of the Elegy series. In spite of some similarities, the two differ significantly in their final effects in ways worthy of attention. While *The Voyage* shares the black

Figure 4. Robert Motherwell. *Granada*, 1949. Oil on paper over masonite, 119.4 x 141.0 cm (47 x 55½ in). Collection, Nelson A. Rockefeller. [photo: Charles Uht]. Not in exhibition

and white of *Granada* and the other Elegies, it employs "other" colors, ochre, green, and yellow, which also appear in subsequent Elegies. But in *The Voyage* these colors are more prominent than in their later use—especially the large center areas of ochre which dominate. *Granada*, by contrast, is black and white. While both works employ vertical panels, *The Voyage* has only one oval and this is in white reversed out against the black of the center rectangle. The sense of compression which marks each of the first three Elegies is missing from *The Voyage*, where it is replaced by complex spatial shiftings between black and white throughout the picture (these occur in earlier works by the artist as well). Finally, there is a very strong sense that *The Voyage* is constructed in a collagelike fashion and, as such, differs markedly from the rigid unity created by the simple black and white palette of the Elegies.

The collagelike structure of *The Voyage* also points to one of its sources, namely the découpages of Matisse which may also have influenced the Elegies, but less directly. Matisse's paper cutouts were gaining wide recognition at this time, and there is a strong resemblance to them in many of the forms in *The Voyage*, not just in the star-shaped black element to the right, but even in the staccato movement caused by the arrangement of the shades and the colored panels.[22]

Motherwell painted *Granada* concurrently with *The Voyage*. It is actually the third version—the second enlargement—of the Rosenberg illustration. "After I'd made Helen's (*At Five in the Afternoon*) I liked it so much better than Harold's, I thought I'd 'make it even bigger.'"[23] The actual size of *Granada* was determined by the material used for the support, a brown stencil paper which was torn unevenly from a roll. Indeed, the ragged and angular edge to the right is a result of this cutting. The proportions which were given by this sheet made *Granada* a much more vertical composition than the preceding versions. Because of this, the area of white between the two black panels is longer and thinner than the previous examples, and the black oval is also reduced in proportion to its surrounding field. Thus it is missing the sense of density found in the earlier versions. Nonetheless, this lengthening of the vertical panels gives the architectonic qualities a greater prominence, making *Granada* more monumental, even if it appears at first to be less expressive, than its two sources. This monumental quality appears in tandem with the increased scale: "Although [I know] it is now easel sized [when placed] in comparison with the later Elegies, I remember it looked enormous in my studio at the time. The monumental concept started with this picture,"[24] says the artist. This recognition gave Motherwell the idea of making the format into a group of pictures when he began in 1949.

SPAIN

Eight of these new works, along with the two earlier *At Five in the Afternoon* paintings, were gathered together in the 1950 Kootz exhibition and labeled as "Elegies (to the Spanish Republic)," the first use of the generic term. As we have seen, the two *At Five in the Afternoon* works recall the refrain from Lorca's poetry. Two of the eight other pictures also relate to Lorca, *Spanish Drum Roll* and *Little Spanish Drum Roll* (Kootz cat. nos. 9A and 10A), and suggest there is an analogy between the measured drumlike cadence of Lorca's poem and the measured procession of forms in the Elegies. The remaining six paintings bear as titles the names of towns in Spain: Sevilla, Málaga, Granada, Madrid, Barcelona, or in one case a region, Catalonia (Kootz cat. nos. 1A, 2A, 3A, 6A, 7A, 8A). With these ten pictures grouped as Elegies and named in various ways for Spanish "things," Motherwell made the aggregate shift from the abstract identity of the Rosenberg format to relating the design to particular Spanish qualities. Titles in Motherwell's works often have multiple meanings beyond their function of "marking off what cannot be said about the picture." The collective title of the series—The Elegies to the Spanish Republic—serves, in part, a function of recording the artist's biographical and "poetic" associations.[25] One of Motherwell's themes since the inception of his art had been about Spain or Mexico and, in more general terms, about a Mediterranean spirit, which he relates to his childhood in California. Motherwell had visited Mexico with Matta during the summer in 1941 and had stayed on through the fall (to talk with Wolfang Paalen). At this time he married a Mexican actress, Maria Emilia Ferreira y Moyers. He returned to Mexico again in 1943 and visited Florida in 1945 "because of its 'Southern light.'"[26] Drawn in part from these personal impressions, and from his interests in Picasso and Miró, many of Motherwell's key works of this early period have Spanish or Mexican themes. *Pancho Villa, Dead and Alive*, for example, is specifically about the Mexican revolutionary. In addition to its formal connection to the Elegy format, this 1943 collage is also indirectly linked to the series, for Motherwell described it in the Kootz catalogue as the first of the Capriccios, a set of companion paintings to the Elegies (also shown in the 1950 exhibition). Motherwell pointed out in his preface that he used the different

Figure 5. Robert Motherwell. *Spanish Prison (Window)*, 1943-1944. Oil on canvas, 132.7 x 107.4 cm (52¼ x 42¼ in). Collection, Mrs. H. Gates Lloyd III, Haverford, Pa. Not in exhibition

groupings of Elegies and Capriccios "in order to point out certain subtle differences among them, a difference in meaning that accounts for certain differences in form . . . these differences should not obscure the fact that the pictures are intimately connected."[27]

Motherwell made two other works during this early period which are also connected to Spain, the *Little Spanish Prison*, 1941-1944, and *Spanish Prison (Window)*, 1943-1944 (fig. 5). The latter is of special significance, for in the Kootz catalogue Motherwell lists it as "the first of the Spanish Elegies." Thus, the artist's identification of his work with Spanish themes exists throughout the 1940s, even if the earlier works were not specifically identified with the ostensible Elegies subject.

We can propose other reasons for this Spanish theme aside from the experiential ones. These are directly related to the Spanish Civil War—and the defeat of the Republic, which, after all, is explicity stated in the Elegies series title (and the implied subject of the earlier and related Spanish Prison series). E.C. Goosen has observed, "The Spanish Civil War was fought when Motherwell was in his early twenties. One may assume this was for him *that* War in which all young men participate either in reality or in spirit. It was the daily topic of his university and, later, his artistic circle. It was a war which suggested the virtue of Cause and the violence of men to a degree not even true of World War II."[28]

In her broader account of the scene in New York during this period Dore Ashton writes, "It would have been hard to find a writer or a painter who was not profoundly disturbed by the reports from Spain, or who did not have at least one friend who had volunteered for the International Brigade. Spain loomed large in everyone's thoughts, all the larger because it seemed so far away."[29] And there was the tremendous impact of Picasso's *Guernica*—the landmark painting about the Civil War—on the New York art world (although *Guernica* is not a formal source for the Elegies).[30] Part of Motherwell's choice for entitling the series "Elegies to the Spanish Republic" lies in his memory of the war; as he recounted to Bryan Robertson,

I suppose it was the first public event which I felt deeply emotionally involved in as did many artists and intellectuals of my generation; I suppose [it was] my first getting out of my own private narcissism into a sense of the drama of other people. It seemed to me something beautiful and marvelous died, at least temporarily, in that conflict, and if I were going to elegize something, since it is against my principles to elegize autobiographically, I preferred then to connect it with something that seemed to me of great consequence. . . .[31]

But, it is essential to remember that the Elegies were generated abstractly and in another context as well, and that it was only the feelings which the abstract schema produced that caused the artist to identify them—beginning with *Granada*—less with Lorca and more directly to the Spanish Republic. In this sense, although the Elegies record

private feelings [nevertheless they are] about a public event—and to me the event was political. It was a revelation (and especially so in England) that totalitarianism could reappear once a parliament had been established. Among the sense of the black and white contrasts, beyond general feelings of the contrast of life and death, was the 'Spanishness' [of the Elegy forms].[32]

THE NATURE OF THE SUBJECT

In view of Motherwell's feelings about the Spanish Civil War, it is appropriate here to consider what relationships, if any, exist between the Elegies and political/historical paintings. Indeed, their collective title—Elegies to the Spanish Republic—suggests that the artist intended them to be seen as part of the tradition of history paintings, which extends from the Renaissance and Alberti's concept of *istoria*, through the works of Delacroix and Goya.

By 1948 this tradition had lapsed, at least in terms of modern painters and the nature of their subjects. Yet, there are two significant exceptions to this statement: Picasso's *Guernica* (estate of the artist) and Miró's *Still Life with Old Shoe* (private collection, New Canaan, Connecticut). *Guernica* is often cited as a precedent for the New York School, not only because of its sheer physical size but also because of the larger context of its subject matter. And Miró's painting, which offered certain compositional lessons (as, for example, in the work of Gorky), was also addressed to a political statement.[33] Furthermore, both are about the Spanish Civil War, ostensibly the subject of Motherwell's Elegies as well.

Because *Guernica* and *Still Life with Old Shoe* do not directly portray events of the war, we might think them apart from the tradition of history painting. However, they hark back to earlier conventions of the tradition, which evaded a direct depiction of an historical event—because of problems of

costume, and so forth—and relied instead on symbolic presentations—paralleled in Picasso's situation of horror and Miró's punctured still-life object.

Nonetheless, though *Guernica* and *Still Life with Old Shoe* may be precedents for the Civil War as broad subject matter, Motherwell comments, "They simply exercised no influence, period [on the Elegies]."[34] Yet *Guernica* in particular is sometimes seen as a source for the Elegies. Some of this confusion may come from the fact that *Guernica* is often described as a black and white painting, when its actual palette is "shades of gray, varying from a completely neutral tint to slightly purplish and bluish grays at one extreme and brownish grays at the other."[35] Its effect is that of a grisaille. Furthermore, *Guernica*, with its use of an old master pedimented organization, is compositionally unrelated to the schema of the Elegies.[36]

Finally, given the more personal nature of the abstract-expressionist vocabulary in general and the clearly nonrepresentational role of Motherwell's forms in the Elegies in particular, the Elegies are too general to be seen as records—in either the descriptive or the symbolic sense, as in Picasso's and Miró's works—of the Spanish Civil War. We are mistaken, then, if we link the Elegies to the tradition of history painting, to which even *Guernica* and *Still Life with Old Shoe* can be joined. Motherwell indicates that the Elegies are "not Historical paintings of the Civil War— but [more] like a memorial to it, like a tomb."[37] This analogy recalls his statement, made in 1963: "The 'Spanish Elegies' are not 'political,' but my private insistence that a terrible death happened that should not be forgot."[38] This statement suggests three key considerations—the "terrible death [that] happened," the abstract-expressionist artist and "political" paintings, and finally the "private" nature of the expression.

The artist's feelings about the Spanish Civil War are quite clear:

It was [for me in the late 1940s and 1950s] the last time it was possible for one to feel total involvement. We all despised Hitler, of course, but World War II was more like a sequence in the continuing European drama of forming empires. Where in Spain, the Civil War represented the question of if Spain would enter the twentieth century. In that sense, it was unique because Liberal intellectuals felt about it as one man, throughout the world.[39]

But it is important to emphasize that the Elegies to the Spanish Republic are *elegies*, about a terrible death—that of the republic—which had "happened." They were not a protest about the current regime. This avoidance of a contemporaneous political statement is in keeping with abstract expressionism as a whole and with Motherwell's beliefs in particular.

The avoidance of the political context was seen as elementary to the development of the New York School by Harold Rosenberg. He wrote in 1966:

Action Painting solved no problems. On the contrary, it remained at its best faithful to the conviction in which it had originated: that the worst thing about the continuing crisis of art and society were the proposals for solving it. . . . The war and the collapse of the Left dissolved for the artist the drama of The Final Conflict (the only kind of conflict which, in the realm of the spirit, love or politics, might justify putting aside the conflicts of creation). The social crisis was to have no closing date and had to be accepted as the condition of the era. If it ever did end, nothing would be left as it was now. Thus art consisted only of the will to paint and the memory of paintings, and society so far as art was concerned consisted of the man who stood in front of the canvas.

The achievement of Action Painting lay in stating this issue with creative force. . . . The American painter discovered a new function for art as the action that belonged to himself.[40]

Motherwell had written as early as 1944 that the artist was left "without any vital connections to society, save that of opposition . . . [therefore he must] replace other social values with the strictly aesthetic."[41] Three years later Motherwell and Rosenberg came together in this opinion, in the statement for the first issue of *Possibilities,* signed by both. It indicates a clean break from the previous decade's belief in politically oriented painting:

Once the political choice has been made, art and literature ought of course to be given up. . . .

Political commitment in our time means logically—no art, no literature. . . .

If one is to continue to paint or write as the political trap seems to close upon him he must perhaps have extremist faith in sheer possibility.[42]

This emphatic rejection of the political paintings—dating so close to the development of the Elegy subject—underscores the lack of any relationship between the content of *Guernica,* a protest painting, and the Elegies. Rather, Motherwell's deep and passionate feelings about the terrible death of the republic are cast as an Elegy, "a poem of subjective character, sometimes reflective, but more often a lament."[43]

Thus the Elegies are "a private insistence . . . that [something] should not be forgot." They are autobiographical in nature and as such are more directly connected to other differing passions also held by the artist. They are not historical or political in the traditional meaning of these terms. We are perhaps closer to their subject if we propose that they are essentially about private feelings which are meaningfully expressed and which are made more "publicly available" by evoking a public or political subject, one of history.

As noted above, the listing as it appeared in 1950 of Spanish names—Granada, Sevilla, Málaga, Madrid, Barcelona, and Catalonia—as titles for Elegies is the first direct connection the artist made between the format and the Spanish Republic. While this roll call of cities (and a region) introduces a cadence recollecting the measure of Lorca's poetry, it has another, more biographical source directly tied to the civil war. In 1937 Motherwell heard André Malraux talk on the Spanish Civil War, a speech which made a deep impression on him. His use of the "roll call" of city names in 1950 probably comes from Motherwell's memory of Malraux's speech, for as Robert Paine noted of the event, Malraux "cast a spell upon the audience by reciting a litany of cities."[44] However, Motherwell soon abandoned the use of city titles for fear he would accidentally commemorate a Republican defeat and to avoid any suggested correspondence a viewer might project between an individual picture and an actual locale.[45] In 1951 Motherwell entitled another painting in this series *Spanish Elegy: García*

Lorca Series. As Hobbs has pointed out, this is the first appearance of the generic term Spanish Elegy as part of a specific title.[46] We should also point out that at this late date the artist continued to vary between his Elegy to the Spanish Republic reference and a more particular identification with Lorca, recalling Motherwell's initial decision to use *At Five in the Afternoon.* Soon after this, however, each painting began to bear as its title the generic Elegy to the Spanish Republic, followed by its own specific chronological number.

THE SUBJECT AS A WHOLE

As we have seen, after Motherwell painted three versions of the original Elegy schema, he then began to make variations upon its general arrangement of vertical panels and ovals, still predominantly in black and white. But in making these works, Motherwell only gradually gained an understanding of what the Elegy format was, both in formal terms as well as its essential subject. "In the early 1950s I painted some bad ones [Elegies]. They were not 'automatic' enough [because] I didn't realize the crucial role the doodle had played in the initial one. Even *Granada* is somewhat stiff because of this [absence]. In the next ones [1950-1953] the shapes went haywire."[47] This is not to say that the Elegies could only be successful with an abstract design underneath, but rather that at this time the artist was using the schema as only a flat design and that the sense of energy, of "battle between elements," is not present.

In the first drawing [the Rosenberg illustration] the ovals *press* against the vertical panels—and I say press because the automatic drawing gives a sense of energy underneath. That they would explode out unless something stopped them. . . . they were clusters of energy, or like oil on water, they wanted to spread out. In 1953-54 I saw what it [the Elegy schema] was—and [also] that it could slip out again. Only then I painted what I feel is one of the most important in the series, No. 34 at Buffalo [at the Albright-Knox Art Gallery; our fig. 8; see below for a discussion of this painting].[48]

If the artist was slow in fully grasping these essential formal and generative qualities of the schema, he was equally slow in comprehending the essential subject itself—what these black shapes against white ground were *really* about. "[It was only] after a period of painting them [the 1950-1953 pictures] I discovered Black as one of my subjects—and with black, the contrasting white, a sense of life and death which to me is Spanish. They are essentially the Spanish black of death contrasted with the dazzle of a Matisse-like sunlight."[49]

The sense of a struggle between life and death which pervades the Elegies may come as well from Motherwell's having asthma when a youth of fourteen. Due to its severity, he attended Moran Preparatory School, in Atascadero, California—an arid region with a climate that is helpful in treating the affliction—from 1929 to 1932. His attacks causing loss of breath were quite serious, and he recalls worrying when he went to sleep at night if he would live through until morning. "I remember the celebration of my twenty-first birthday—like that of my sixtieth—in joy that I had actually lived that long, when my mother was convinced I would not."[50] Thus death was understood by the artist as being constantly possible,

Figure 6. Robert Motherwell. *The Voyage*, 1949. Oil and tempera on paper mounted on composition board, 122.0 x 238.8 cm (48 x 94 in). The Museum of Modern Art, New York, Gift of Mrs. John D. Rockefeller 3rd. Not in exhibition

rather than as an abstract, philosophical concept. Furthermore, this feeling was developed with the dry, arid climate of California itself, especially the setting of Motherwell's school as a "background."

The artist feels that his youth in California is directly related to the feel of the Elegies.

Yes certain childhood impressions last a lifetime. What a burden! Sunlit, and high blue skies, green or blue ocean, sun-baked, yellow ochre inland. Both dry (except for foggy San Francisco) and sensual. Painting problem: dryness and sensuality both! Sharp edges, soot black shadows. Death is dessication there not wet rot, like garbage. . . . In a Southern clime, one would usually not be an atmospheric painter. In bright sunlight everything, even in the distance, is clear, with sharp shadows and sharp edges, as with the hill-towns of Italy, or mid-day Spain.[51]

The sources for the Elegies, then, are numerous and multiple: the artist's childhood, his travels and connections with Mexico, his "political" experience of the Spanish Civil War, his readings of Lorca, and his knowledge of Matisse, Miró, and Picasso. Yet none of these are "described" in the Elegies. Rather they correlate to the general feeling of the format and its suggested confrontation of life and death, in Spanish terms. Instead of the subject being a combination of various sources, it is as if the Elegies themselves created their subject, or as the artist says, "I recognized in them Black as one of my subjects."[52]

Within the general context of making the abstract-expressionist picture, certain choices of composition and coloration become more appropriate to the work than others. For Motherwell, these pictorial decisions—what he calls feelings in this instance—can be directly aligned with artisanal or artistically practical choices: "When the artistic mind is functioning in its medium, it is wholly empirical, dominated by structural necessities whose origin is in felt values . . . art does not have to find good or bad reasons to justify the feeling, art simply expresses the feeling. . . ."[53]

We have already seen this distancing when we examined the steps involved in the making of the first Elegy image. There the movements and decisions we can reconstruct appear to be decisions made entirely on the basis of what the design seemed to require. In the process of painting abstract pictures—in this abstract-expressionist manner—artisanal choices are made,

from whatever starting point, as part of the process itself and are judged "internally" against the particular composition, rather than being judged by any "external" programs or formulae. Confronted with the necessity to articulate the forms in an unfettered way, self-expression, we can propose, is a natural result of the operation. Self-expression is probably part of all art in the Western tradition. But what we are talking about here is not the *degree* of self-expression. The central distinction is that in the abstract-expressionist picture the references for expression are not given in general cultural terms, but rather are given in terms that are partial to the picture itself, although the disparate elements which combine to produce the expression are drawn from the artistic language of the modern tradition.

In effect, Motherwell's work and theories turn the common perception of expression on its head, so to speak. Rather than knowing what he wants to express, then finding an appropriate subject, and then properly painting it, the reverse is true: drawing from various formal "beginnings," Motherwell paints the Elegies, discovering in the process what the subject is, and then what his particular expression about that subject is in that particular painting. He states that when he makes an Elegy it is "not that I'm going to paint something I know, but through the act of painting I'm going to find out exactly how I feel. Sometimes it's like swimming for your life."[54]

Even if the forms are "felt" by the artist as he paints them, and if the structure is decided empirically with respect to the developing internal requirements of the picture itself, what remains to give the picture—or its developing structure—its meaning? Especially an abstract schema such as in the Elegies? Motherwell has observed:

I have continuously been aware that in painting I am always dealing with, and never not, a relational structure. Which in turn makes permission "to be abstract" no problem at all. All paintings are essentially relational structures whether figuration is present or not is not the real issue. So that I could apprehend, for example, at first sight, my first abstract art. For painters with either literary or art school backgrounds, at least in my time, to make a transition from figuration to abstraction was a threatening problem. . . . I understood too that "meaning" was the product of the relations among elements, so that I never had the then common anxiety as to whether an abstract painting had a given "meaning."[55]

What Motherwell's thesis proposes for his Elegies (as well as for his other works, and by implication, for those of other abstract expressionists) is that meaning lies within or arises from the structural conception and finish of the picture, whether the work is abstract or figurative. Thus, the meaning of a particular Elegy is not "referential" in the way that, for example, impressionist and fauve pictures express their "recording" of a figure (landscape, etc.), or that cubist works analyze or construct a figure, or that surrealism uses its automatic technique to induce a figure. Nor is it referential to a program of abstraction based on rules or procedures. Meaning derives—just as the foundation and the subject of the picture do—from the process of artisanal choices, made on grounds of feeling within the act of making the painting.

To understand this analysis we are bound to propose that

within the Elegies, form and subject are inextricably bound. Motherwell makes the following analogy:

These matters are not easy to be clear about if one has, in the background of one's mind, the traditional critical distinction between "form" and "content" as a valid and necessary distinction. To experience a work of art, as in making love, is to experience a human contact: and one can say equally well, the "content" is just the "form" involved, or the "form" is just the "content" involved. If we were to employ the old distinction, then the "content" of love-making is the human contact, and that the contact is made in such-and-such a way is its "form"; but it is at once evident that—in love-making—the specific human contact that is made is determined precisely by its form; that with a different form there would be a different human contact, that what the human contact is, is just the form of what is done—just as the form of what is done is determined by the human contact; that, in short, when we talk about "form" and "content" in the human contact that is making love, we are not talking about two different things, but about the same thing, felt structure, that is, the relations among feelings as they progress in time.[56]

This analogy suggests why, ultimately, the Spanish Elegies can express death only in "Spanish" terms, and why—to Motherwell—this sense of death can only be expressed in the Elegies.

This view also requires that we consider this kind of abstract-expressionist picture to have a more formal origin than has been recognized, because the loci of the picture's meanings lie within its structural qualities. Certainly our reconstruction of the invention and development of the initial Elegy would support this proposition. This approach, which Motherwell would call *structuralism* "rather than formalism,"[57] was in fact first advanced in his "The Public and the Modern Painter" of 1951:

The real content of a painting is the rhythms and the proportions on the canvas, just as a person is his own inner rhythms and proportions, not what he happens to say when you meet him on the corner. This inner life is a mysterious and elusive thing. Still it is there, but not on the surface, which is why modernist artists do not paint the surface of the world.[58]

THE MODERN LANGUAGE

In Motherwell's analogy, the markings on a surface, their arrangement, individual shapes, colors, tones, and so forth, can be said to parallel—not correspond to nor record nor depict—the proportions or felt rhythms or placements we experience abstractly in life. But at the same time a painting speaks in a given language, even if it is altering or extending that language as it speaks. Broader language is the formal and structural vocabulary of the modern tradition.[59] We have seen that the Elegy schema was discovered, within both the overall compositional makeup and the particular relationship between the panels and ovals. At the same time, the Elegies also draw firmly upon forms and sensibilities from the modern tradition. On the one hand the bold, graphic quality of the design derives not only from precedents in Matisse's *Verve* illustrations, but also from Matisse's découpages. Even the black and white filled-in shapes owe something to Matisse's ink drawings of this same period, which could be seen in New York galleries and in publications (fig. 7).[60] "They caused my realization that black

is a hue," recalls the artist. On the other hand the structure of these pictures, with their low bas-relief-like space and the frontality of the forms is clearly derived from that used by the cubists in their synthetic collages, which Motherwell knew thoroughly. But the "invented" schema of the Rosenberg illustration masks the immediate perception of these stylistic traits in the Elegies (by comparison, *The Voyage,* made during the same period, makes these same sources more openly perceptible, as we have seen). Nevertheless, however much the total as well as the individual elements in the Spanish Elegies were "invented," their essential characteristics are still those of a formal language drawn from the modern tradition. "We modern artists have no generally accepted subject matter, no inherited iconography,"[61] Motherwell wrote twenty-six years ago. He adds today, "Art always gets its moral support from a tradition—the church, governments, etc.—here [in abstract expressionism] it gets its support from itself, from the culture of modernism."[62]

Yet, however much the forms of the Elegy schema derive in part from the modern tradition's formal language, the subject matter itself is internally invented and does not belong to any tradition, save what we might say of what all men feel.

"There is an analogy to collage," comments Motherwell, "where I am working with ready made elements. In the Elegies the ovals and the vertical panels are *a priori* elements in my mind . . . and in that sense they are not very innovative."[63] Nor could they be, for, as we have seen, these *a priori* ovals and panels are precisely the generative basis for the Elegy subject itself. "In this sense," says the artist, "the Elegy I painted last month could have been painted twenty years ago . . . except that it also expresses how I feel at a given period in time."[64]

The final subject in each individual Elegy—its particular spirit, its separate meditation on life and death—is determined by the making of the picture out of its constituent parts. In this sense the Elegies (as a series) are fragmentary, although each is complete as a picture or as a speech. They correspond to our experience of the modern world, which we only partially know and not from a fixed point of view. "I learned that I can't say it all in one work," says the artist.[65]

Yet, as we have seen, the Elegies remain essentially a family group, with certain shared features and a common subject. "In the early days I remember I'd paint to see how far it could go and still be an Elegy. To me the question is still the mystery of how they can change—the slightest touch will produce a whole, a new felt tone—and yet they still remain Elegies. To me this raises a profound question: . . . [are these colors and shapes] an iconography or a tone of voice. I'd argue that the subject matter of all of the Elegies—of all abstract expressionism—is a tone of voice."[66]

We have seen, however, "the tone of voice" arises out of and continues to speak from the format of an invented schema. Within that schema itself—its black and white palette and bold forms—we can propose that particular structural properties are present which will allow a diversity of expressions.

104

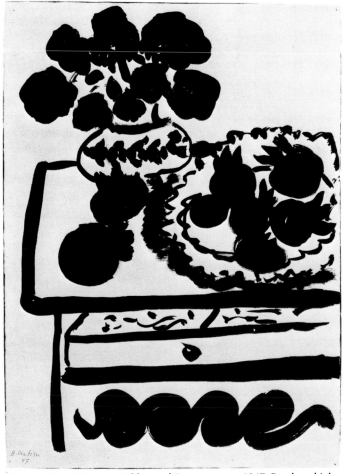

Figure 7. Henri Matisse. *Dahlias and Pomegranates,* 1947. Brush and ink, 76.5 x 56.5 cm (30⅛ x 22¼ in). The Museum of Modern Art, New York, Abby Aldrich Rockefeller Fund. Not in exhibition

THE PARTICULARITIES OF THE INVENTION

Along with the phenomenon of the appearance of larger scale, painterly abstraction both in Europe and America after the Second World War was the widespread making of pictures using a palette of only black and white. By 1948 it was current enough in Europe for the Galerie des Deux Iles to stage an exhibition—*Black and White*—with works by Fautrier, Hartung, Mathieu, Wols, and others. In New York in 1950 the Kootz Gallery held a show entitled *Black and White,* which featured both French and American artists. And, as we know, many American painters—among them de Kooning, Kline, Pollock, and Motherwell had begun making black and white pictures as early as 1947.

The reasons we can advance for this development in painting are multiple, ranging from de Kooning's doing monochromes because of the dictates of money shortage,[67] to what Lawrence Alloway calls "renunciations . . . [a] voluntary poverty, the mode of reduction which led to the discovery that art might not, after all, need either the multiple viewpoint or Freudian iconography."[68]

As we have seen, in the Kootz catalogue Motherwell identified this choice of palette with the need to "deal on occasion with a simple relation." Yet this dealing with simplicity had far-reaching effects in American art and was perhaps even a major factor in the development of abstract expressionism. As Alloway notes in his detailed study of this problem

By cutting down the number of colours, painters were able to increase their speed without losing their control. Black in large areas tends to read as a flat area, more so than other colours, and it has, when used in linear forms, an ineradicable connection with message making, either writing or drawing. Thus black was at the centre of the wide-spread post-war desire to invest abstract art with a momentous subject or, to put it the other way round, to have an expressive art not slowed down by the need to represent objects.[69]

Motherwell conceived of black as a color in and of itself rather than as part of a process of shading (as in de Kooning's black and white pictures), a lesson learned from Matisse's black drawings (fig. 7).[70] By limiting his palette for the most part to black and white, Motherwell can use white so that it accents the black or makes it stronger. In the Elegies black also has a Matisse-like intensity because its shapes are those of a continuous flat surface, similar to the surfaces in Matisse's paper cutouts.

The black elements in the Elegies are like those in Matisse's later works, in that they create a new kind of "edge." In Western painting, from the Renaissance to Manet, the edges of forms are indicated by shading, which marks the turning of a form into or from depth, or by use of sfumato, which downplays edges, slipping the figure into its surrounding space through gradations in tone. In the Elegies we might say the reverse of the traditional use of chiaroscuro takes place: "shading," that is to say, "black," takes over the entire form. Edge becomes one with the surface as the shapes read as flat silhouettes.

The shapes in the Elegies read as abstract, two-dimensional forms; they are flat. Because the edges are not modeled, they do not turn into depth along the profile, although certain of Motherwell's abstract shapes can indicate very shallow, optically felt, turnings on the surface plane. (Matisse took advantage of a similar property in his works to create figurations out of single, wholly saturated shapes of color.)

The Elegies thus bear resemblance to Matisse's découpages in the silhouetted forms but are different from the Matisse works in their absence of figuration. In addition the Elegies differ from the French master's work in another significant way, involving one of the key aspects of the Elegies. Not only is the palette of the major forms limited to one color, black, but while the composition allows the forms to read as individual shapes, nonetheless it brings them together by having them touch or lie tangent to one another on the surface. But rather than being layered atop one another, the forms read as continuous because the solid black surfaces fuse together on the same plane. The solidity which results from this fusion of shapes creates a kind of integral firmness to the whole Elegy image. It is this solidity along with the rigidity of the repeating vertical panels that gives the Elegies their feeling of monumentality. "The verticals also gauge the curving [of the oval forms] rather than just being a result of the drawing," observes the artist. "That's why the Elegies have a certain stiffness which Matisse doesn't [have in his work]—he can draw without reference."[71]

The Elegies also differ from the cutouts of Matisse in their use of painterly edge, rather than the sharply contoured one of the découpage elements. In this painterly quality the Elegies are linked with the works of the other abstract expressionists; indeed, it is the one common stylistic trait of the artists. Clement Greenberg wrote that "the grafting of painterliness onto a cubist structure was one of the great accomplishments of the abstract expressionists."[72] In the works of Gorky, Pollock, and de Kooning, the cubist structure is essentially that of analytical cubism. However, in the Elegies the flat shallow space and repeated verticals create a structure which is ultimately derived from synthetic, rather than analytic cubism. This structure—with its use of a language central to the modern tradition—implies that in many of the Elegies a gridlike organization is somewhere "in" the picture, both preserving and balancing the pressure of the oval shapes. Thus the power of the pressing shapes and the expressive drawing of the contours are counterpointed not only by the vertical panels themselves but by the sense of the continual grid beneath.

Motherwell's work has always ranged between two poles of expression—the active sensual picture and the work of restrained, classical elegance. What is so amazing about the invention of the Elegy schema is that it has allowed both of these artistic traits to function in the same picture, at varying extremes of emphasis and at varying levels. To begin with, on the one hand, the schema wants to be read as a preexisting form, an archetypical image, incapable of change. On the other hand, it offers endless possibilities of formal permutation and expression. On one level there is the simple contrast between the immobile vertical panels and the more malleable ovals. But in spite of their differences, both of these form groups are in black, and function in tandem against the white ground. It is astonishing to realize that the subject—"a black [shadow] of death contested with a Matisse-like sunlight"—remains the same throughout the series. The Elegies address us with divergent expressions, but the tone of voice is constant.

ABSTRACTION AND INTERPRETATION

The first major change of expression away from the restrictive starkness of *At Five in the Afternoon* and *Granada* occurs in *Elegy 34* of 1953-1954 (fig. 8). It has a new, stately presence, derived from a larger scale (80 x 100 inches) as well as a bannerlike composition with brilliant accents of color, which, because they are pure tones in oil, give an almost silklike finish to the surface. These characteristics introduce a more complex and finished treatment of the Elegy schema: "*No. 34* is . . . one of the half-dozen most realized of the Spanish Elegy Series."[73]

The "realization" of *Elegy 34* may come from the fact that the actual time spent on the completion of the work was considerable—over a year. Motherwell painted most of the work in 1953; but, unlike his previous pictures which were completed at a relatively rapid rate, he took over a year to make final adjustments in colors and to refine the black forms. "This was completed during the time I had a sort of 'painting block,'" he recalls, "and I was content to work on detail."[74]

The artist had lost touch with the Elegy schema following the 1950 exhibition. Between 1951 and the completion of *Elegy 34* no major Elegy pictures were made, although some important works tangential to the Spanish series—the *Wall Paintings* and *La Dance II*—were painted. Rather, Motherwell made only very small paintings using the Elegy schema. These are really Elegy studies; and although they are fascinating as notations of his thought, it is also clear none had the potential for enlargement because they do not convey a pictorial authority that could be sustained in the larger format. Nevertheless, certain qualities of these studies—and aspects of the companion *Wall Paintings* and *La Dance II*—were ultimately used in *Elegy 34*, particularly the more fluid shaping of the black ovals and the changing of the black panels into the curving, arabesquelike shapes.[75]

Elegy 34 has been the origin of persistent and wide-ranging interpretations of the essential forms. The most crucial interpretation is that the black forms are phallic, the first published discussion of which is E.C. Goosen's 1959 study of the artist, significantly subtitled "The Seriousness of Subject." The crucial portions of his text read:

The huge ovarian forms hang in heavy precariousness between broad male uprights; or perhaps it is the phallus and cojones of the sacrificial bull hung on the whitewashed wall.[76]

Yet, Goosen goes on to caution:

The sexual implication in Motherwell's work can always be found, if one is inclined to make interpretations of this sort. But I take sexual assertions in high art, even when discovered rather than obvious, as secondary to whatever is ultimately the inner secret the artist wishes to share but does not make explicit.[77]

Nevertheless, Goosen's text does two things. First, he implies that the Elegy forms are referential to a subject existing externally, apart from the picture; that is to say, that they are descriptive of "something" and the art historical problem is to pin that "something" down. Secondly, rather than a simple reading of the shapes as phallic, in Goosen's analysis they are transferred to a Spanish setting and become a Spanish subject, thus both suggesting a direct explanation of the title of the series and "legitimizing" the phallic interpretation. Because Goosen's projected imagery of phallus and *cojones* seemed so apt, it was accepted without question two years later by Irving Sandler, who refers to "Goosen's calling attention to the symbolic references in them [the Elegies], the phallus and *cojones*. . . ."[78] Moreover Sandler never mentions Goosen's other readings—"ovarian forms . . . [and the] male uprights," since the phallic identification, cast in Spanish terms, seems more particular and more explanatory of Motherwell's subject.

Three years later, Frank O'Hara writes in reference to this "symbolism":

Individual paintings of the series have been variously interpreted as male verticals and female ovoids, as bulls' tails and testicles hung side by side on the wall of the arena after the fight.[79]

And he adds:

The possibility of the schema's arousing such a broad range of associations, depending on the emotional vocabulary of the viewer, is a sign

Figure 8. Robert Motherwell. *Elegy to the Spanish Republic, No. 34*, 1953-1954. Oil on canvas, 203.2 x 254.0 cm (80 x 100 in). Albright-Knox Art Gallery, Buffalo, N.Y., Gift of Seymour H. Knox. Cat. no. 3, pl. 13

of its power to communicate human passion in a truly abstract way, while never losing its specific identity as a pictorial statement. The exposure is one of sensibility, rather than of literal imagistic intent, and therefore engages the viewer in its meaning rather than declaring it.[80]

H.H. Arnason, in a study of the artist written at the same time as O'Hara's, notes

The *Elegies* have frequently been interpreted as male and female sexual symbols. Although the artist has no recollection of any specific sexual symbolism in his first exploration of the *Elegy* theme, to him these paintings embody within their life and death starkness a high degree of Mediterranean sensuousness.[81]

Yet, in his discussion of *Elegy 34*, Arnason also writes, "All shapes . . . are more loose and organic. . . . the black verticals are now presented as freely phallic shapes alternating with familiar ovals."[82] Hobbs, writing eleven years later in the most recent study of the works, continues this reading, referring to "the black *cojones* of the Elegies."[83]

This reading of the forms in *Elegy 34* (and in subsequent paintings) as phallic shapes and the transferral of them to a Spanish bullfight context as "cojones hung on a white wall" is essentially a "projected iconography." Nothing in the painting *specifically* accounts for this reading, and indeed, on the contrary, careful analysis of its generation precludes it. This "projected iconography" is not only false, it serves to undercut our understanding of the structural expression achieved in the Elegies by substituting inventive images for the nonrepresentational shapes. Proposing the idea that Motherwell is painting phallic imagery can lead to speculation; but it tells us little about the pictures themselves. Moreover, such a reading introduces a different relationship among the Elegies. Arnason, for

example, proposes an artificial linkage between *Elegies 44* and *45* and *Pancho Villa, Dead and Alive* by suggesting that the paintings are "an enlargement and isolated reminiscence of Pancho Villa's genitals in the first (1943) suggestion of the motif."[84] In a similar manner, Hobbs writes of *La Dance II* not that its forms are one of several abstract shapings which were enrolled in *Elegy 34*, but that they "become a source for the genitalia. . . ."[85]

Faced with a record of projected iconography and a misalignment of pictures and sources, it is logical we would also find misinterpretations of artistic action based on these readings. For example, Arnason writes of the ovals in *Elegy 78* (fig. 15) that Motherwell "distorted their contours in order to emphasize their existence as living organisms rather than as simply color shapes."[86] Thus Arnason's reading of these shapes as "organic" forces him then to account for Motherwell's actions in traditional descriptive terms, rather than in terms of abstract nonreferential choices. In Hobbs' reading of *Elegy 34*, which he calls "the first work in which phallic associations, implicit in earlier paintings, become explicit,"[87] he discusses one of several preceding works as a "sketch" for *Elegy 34*. Hobbs accounts for the difference between the small impasto sketch and *Elegy 34* in terms of a kind of prudity on Motherwell's part:

[Comparison] with the sketch for it, *Tombs of Capitain* [sic] indicates how much the painter has refined his initial idea. Only the main movements of the black forms in the large painting are indicated in the sketch by a summary pushing of the thick impasto over the surface of the canvas board and barely hinting at the psychological interaction of verticals and ovoids. Because the painter made an overt reference to genitalia in this painting, he may have felt the need to refine his initial

107

outburst to the point that he created an emblem of mourning rather than an object that is only blatantly sexual and shocking.[88]

Hobbs' interpretation of the scale of *Elegy 34* becomes equally misplaced. He writes:

The interplay between intimacy and large scale, a type of hermeticism enlarged to the point that it is made into the form of public art, has become one of the unique characteristics of Abstract Expressionism. In the organic *Elegies* genitalia, or an abstraction of it, and shapes reminiscent of fruit hanging on a branch [see below] are conceived in Gargantuan terms, creating a fascinating interplay between what one considers public and private, bringing the private into the open and making it part of a public event. With these paintings the problem is that they monumentalize an autographic technique of drips and sketchy brushwork as well as intimate subject matter, genitalia, not that they are conceived in a picayune manner that is enlarged. The organic paintings achieve a dichotomy with interesting psychological ramifications, embodying in structural terms the essence of Motherwell's intention to attain the universal via the personal. And he chooses to do this by transforming something that is by its very nature intimate into a monumental emblem.[89]

Hobbs suggests that the artist paints more graphically explicit phallic sketches, then enlarges them—but at the same time in such a way as to make them "refined" not "blatantly sexual." Hobbs' central thesis is that Motherwell has deep within his motivation in painting the Elegies the desire to show in public his private subject matter and does so by increasing its size—but "fools" the public by hiding it. That this is clearly not the case we can see by reconstructing the steps which were involved in painting *Elegy 34*.

Although the forms in *Elegy 34* are presently fluid and arabesque, in its initial stage (in 1953) the painting was more similar in composition and feeling to *Granada;* indeed the ovals still retain a resemblance to those of *Granada*. Originally there was only a simple pattern (reading from left to right): rectangular band/oval/rectangular band/oval/narrow rectangular band. The two center rectangular bands were later partially painted over in white or in colors, but they are still visible as either pentimenti or as the left and right vertical limits of the color areas. The remaining portions serve as part of the black commalike shapes. These latter elements, in their final state, are reminiscent of forms used in certain of the preceding small Elegies, such as *Elegy 17 (Segura)* (fig. 9). But these earlier Elegy sketches lack the verticals which had been an essential aspect of contrast in the initial Elegy schema. In *Elegy 34* then, Motherwell began by returning to the first Elegy layout of three years earlier, and then altered the composition toward the direction of the preceding small oil works. This allowed him to retain the verticals, albeit now used in a secondary role. "*No. 34* is different from the others [Elegies], in that the rectangular structure is in the background, so to speak," he comments. "It reads as if the black is over the colors. This introduced a kind of special 'punning,' of positive and negative spaces between the panels and the shapes, which was further emphasized by the addition of color."[90]

But the addition of color came later. With the ovals largely set as we now see them, Motherwell began the "finishing" process by drawing in chalk upon the left black rectangular panel until he "got the left shape, which I loved."[91] Still using

Figure 9. Robert Motherwell. *Elegy to the Spanish Republic, No. 17 (Segura),* 1953. Oil on board, 22.9 x 30.5 cm (9 x 12 in). Collection, Mr. and Mrs. Burton G. Tremaine, Jr., Meriden, Conn. Not in exhibition

chalk, he then drew on the top of the right-hand panel a sweeping movement to the right which echoed that drawn in for the left-hand "comma."

The bottom portion of the right vertical panel was determined more by the ovals flanking it on either side than by the left comma. Thus the left profile of the right vertical begins with the vertical line of its initial panel edge, then suddenly turns to the right, following the general direction set by the oval above and to its left. This line continued into an arc, reaching back up under the right oval, ending in a ragged irregular shape—which is still visible under the white ground—similar to a shape to the right in *Elegy 17 (Segura)*.

Later in finishing the work, Motherwell abandoned this irregular shape, turning the profile upward and stopping it so as to echo the vertical bisection of the oval by the line atop the oval. The slight bump at the top of the comma records another detailing touch, namely returning in a reverse arc from the right profile of the right oval.

It is important to emphasize that at this stage *Elegy 34* still looked like *Granada*—black panels and ovals—and that the comma forms were only drawn in with chalk and charcoal. At this point Motherwell began to paint in areas of red and ochre at the bottom and blue at the top left. "Suddenly," he recalls, "I saw them as stripes and lined them up [with a ruler]."[92] These horizontal divisions of the surface are present in the resulting stripes of color, partially obscured by the white, and in black lines which continue through the white ground immediately above the black oval. Thus a subtle gridlike pattern was introduced into the work. As for the color, Motherwell notes that when adding it, "I ignored the Elegy as a whole, which is to say it has a whole separate system of color from the whole of the Elegy."[93] The closing step in the painting was painting in the black shapes following the drawing, and then making the final adjustments.

We can see that *Elegy 34* was the result of a set of differing structural choices and emphases, and that these are still visible,

Figure 10. Robert Motherwell. *Elegy to the Spanish Republic, No. 55*, 1955-1960. Oil on canvas, 177.8 x 193.3 cm (70 x 76⅛ in). Contemporary Collection of The Cleveland Museum of Art. Cat. no. 4

being overlaid in a complex manner. Rather than a directly painted composition, the image is a compound of isolated decisions, made in the yearlong process of finishing the picture. "It was made by lining up shapes and stripes. . . . I was looking [during the finishing] at compositional parts, working so close I didn't see the total image."[94] As the artist recalls, "Not long after this was painted someone pointed out that it looked phallic." But, he continues, "It was, of course, unintentional."[95] Indeed, as we have seen in our reconstruction the forms were determined by a series of disparately located selections, and the final shapes—as well as their arrangement—were determined on a structural basis, in a manner which precluded even a subconscious expression of phallic imagery. "I subsequently made one that was intended to be phallic," says the artist, "and it was unsuccessful. My intention in altering the shapes in *Elegy 34* [away from the panel/oval layout] was to make them more moving."[96]

ARCHITECTURE

If *Elegy 34* is the origin of the phallic interpretation, one of the next major Elegies completed, *Elegy 55* of 1955-1960 (fig. 10), is a central example in the alternative reading of the series: that they have affinities to architecture. It is certainly easy to see why these analogies are drawn for pictures like *Elegy 55,* as its emphatic vertical panels and horizontal planes suggest a basic post and lintel architecture. But, unlike the projection of the phallus and the *cojones* in *Elegy 34*, the discussion of *Elegy 55* and other works in architectural terms—keeping in mind they

are not descriptive of architecture—is revealing, both about the place of the Elegies in the larger context of Motherwell's work and in the analogies it suggests to the basic nature of his creative methods.

Curiously, the first Elegies exhibited were characterized in terms of architecture. In her review of the 1950 Kootz exhibition Belle Krasne wrote: "[These are] somber arrangements of black ovals crushed between massive black piers. . . ."[97]

The first discussion of particular elements as architectural components is that of Seitz, in 1955. He writes: "The horizontal band atop the widest division of certain of the 'Elegies' seems like an architectural enframement placed at some distance behind the picture surface. . . ."[98] Then, referring to the linear passage in the upper right corner of the Elegies, as in *At Five in the Afternoon,* Seitz observes it "suggests a window."[99] Both of these observations are repeated in subsequent discussions by other authors.

In his discussions of Motherwell's art, Arnason observed of the Elegies: "Individual examples also include suggestions of a horizontal window, roof, or floor structures. . . ."[100] He notes of *At Five in the Afternoon,* "As in most of the series, there is a strong architectural sense, of pilasters or doorways or intercolumnation . . ."; and following Seitz, "In the upper right hand corner . . . there is a horizontal, framed element, like the bottom of a window. . . ."[101] Of *Elegy 54* (1957-1961, Museum of Modern Art, New York) and *Elegy 55* he comments that "the architectural structure is accentuated further . . ." and later refers to the central rectangular panel of *Elegy 55* as a "column."[102] Furthermore, he notes "in the upper right corner [of *Elegy 55*] is an almost square rectangle that seems to be an abstraction of the earlier window edge—in this case a complete window." [103]

There is, of course, no window as such in the Elegies, nor an "abstraction" of one in *Elegy 55*. The paintings are endemically abstract; and while they may, as Edward Henning has written of *Elegy 55*, promote "some obvious suggestions based on common association," [104] these suggestions remain generalities. They are certainly not, as Arnason has written, meant to suggest or be read with "the monoliths as the architecture of a mausoleum [or] a chamber of death...." [105] We can determine this not only from the persistently nonreferential character of the entire series, but from our reconstructions of how they came to be as they are. In the same way these reconstructions preclude any external "formal" sources. [106]

But, unlike the issue of "phallic content," the question of architectural associations is not so easily closed. The artist himself frequently refers to the Elegies in metaphorical terms as having "a kind of Stonehenge-like quality" [107] and in 1965, observed:

I think it's [the meaning of the Elegies] deeper than what's obvious and I think it has something to do with the human but I also think it has something to do with architecture. I know a psychoanalyst who I play poker with, who collects German Expressionist painting. He is originally a German and he sent me from Greece one summer a photograph of some Greek columns, three Greek columns with the—what is it—the pediment across the top that had been taken at twilight so that the columns and the bar across the top appeared black against a kind of twilight whiteness and it looked very much like my pictures. [108]

In a classic study of Motherwell's Open paintings Arnason put forth the theory that a major aspect of all of Motherwell's work involves in one way or another architecture. "The wall and the window have played an important part in Motherwell's work since 1941," [109] he wrote, citing the window of *Little Spanish Prison* (1941, collection of the artist), and the wall of *Wall Painting with Stripes* (1944, Lennan collection, Chicago) as examples. And, as we have seen, Arnason identifies the upper right portion of *At Five in the Afternoon* and *Elegy 55* as "windows." He concludes by discussing the Opens in terms of walls (surface), windows (the drawn rectangle), and dados (the horizontal bands).

Motherwell himself has discussed his work in an architectural context. In the 1950 Kootz catalogue for the first exhibition of *Elegies* he divided the works into three groups—"Spanish Elegies, Capriccios, and Wall Paintings." He wrote that the Capriccios have as subjects "the classical ones of 20th-Century Parisian abstract paintings: figures, *interiors* and still lifes." [110] In contrast, Motherwell said of the Wall Paintings, "[They] are not conceived of as easel paintings, but as embracements of a wall." [111]

Curiously, the precedent work which Motherwell cites for each series is "architectural"—the *Spanish Prison* for the Elegies, *Pancho Villa, Dead and Alive* for the Capriccios, and *Wall Painting* for the first of the Wall Paintings. Furthermore, there is a stylistic relationship among the three series. We have already seen the relationship between *Granada* and *The Voyage*. The interior presented in *Room 8, Hotel Flora, Cannes,*

one of the Capriccios, partakes of features of the Elegies: the division of the surface into vertical bands, here with an oval figure placed between the central two.

In this manner we might suggest that the Elegies balance between two extremes: the French interiors—architectural spaces—of the Capriccios, and the more decorative abstraction of the Wall Paintings. Moreover, their structure and atmospheric touches recall the Capriccios, while their increasing scale and planar orientation comes closer to that of the Wall Paintings. They are not a depiction of architecture per se—nor a panel designed for it—but easel paintings (through 1950) which have affinities to each.

There is another reason why we sense architectural qualities in the Elegies, one which appears only in Seitz's study of the artist, though there only as a suggestion, not specifically addressed. Seitz writes that "a painting more closely resembles an 'object' [to Motherwell] than it does to the other [abstract-expressionist] painters." [112] Seitz identified the "materiality" of this "object"-ness as derived from the artist's work in collage, where forms are presented as actual materials, without the use of illusion. "Space is a product of material elements," [113] Seitz writes of the collages and the paintings; and for collage he notes, "Recession—although it far exceeds the actual physical separation of the materials—remains immediate and objective in its shallowness." [114] Because of this "object"-ness or the materiality of components, Seitz proposed that Motherwell "produces physically scaled [rather than illusionistic] works. With the special function of eliciting feeling, their physical existence and actual size refuse to dissolve into the aura. Even the murals and 'Wall Paintings' keep their one to one relationship to you." [115] These characteristics led Seitz to conclude that Motherwell "does not represent, but constructs." [116]

We have already seen that by isolating the rectangles and ovals as black forms the Elegies emphasize one of the artist's basic artistic touches, the contrast of straights and curves. This same isolation also allows them to be read as components which Motherwell then uses to construct the particular painting. Perhaps as much to emphasize the sense of "object"-ness of the elements as to create the final construction Motherwell avoids overlapping the components, aligning them as tangents to one another. These black forms—as solids—link into each other on the surface plane only flirting with different visual depths. We have, then, works made from components, all of the same "material," which are assembled—or constructed—into the Elegy composition, much as Stonehenge is a construction made out of stones. We must be careful here because it is finally this composition constructed from elements of the same material which more properly deserves the architectural references, even though the post and lintel design of *At Five in the Afternoon* or *Elegy 55* may resemble, indirectly, Stonehenge or a Greek temple.

This proposition must be weighed because these architectural qualities of construction and shared material are true of the most fluid and freely painted Elegies as well as the most geometric ones: this helps us to see how "composed"—in these terms—all these works actually are.

In the case of *Elegy 55*, its more impressive architectural

Figure 11. Wall in Motherwell's New York studio in spring 1960. *The Figure 4 on an Elegy* is at the top in the center row. [Photo: Peter A. Juley]

Figure 12. Robert Motherwell. *The Figure 4 on an Elegy*, 1960. Oil on paper, 58.4 x 73.7 cm (23 x 29). Collection, H. H. Arnason, New York [photo: Steve Sloman, courtesy Robert Motherwell]. Cat. no. 5, pl. 14

affinities are the result of a degree of emphasis. And even here the case is not so simple. As we can determine from a photograph of its earlier state, *Elegy 55* originally had another vertical band on the right, which was painted out in white before its completion.[117] This alteration lessens the rigid nature of the work, allowing more "atmospheric Matisse sunlight," and begins to change the graphic character of the work to correspond more with the delicately brushed surfaces of the black forms. (These surfaces, unfortunately, do not show up well in black and white photographs.)

ANOTHER DISCOVERED ELEGY

Motherwell's collages of 1957-1958 are distinguished by their use of rich patterns and bright colors and by their violently torn edges. And in 1958 in France, the artist began a series of small black and white gestural pictures, The Frontiers, notable for their meandering forms and the flowing quality of the paint. These works are much different from the measured presence of *Elegy 55,* also of this period, with its austere, rigid composition.

During the winter of 1959-1960 the artist continued in the more automatic direction set by The Frontiers. This unplanned, gestural-painting technique created such a vast variety of new compositional arrangements and shapes that the resultant oil-on-paper sheets can really only be linked to one another in their shared "scheme of ruthless movement and freely painted passages."[118]

In studying the small paintings and collages made from these works, one of them—visible at the center of the top row in the studio photograph (fig. 11)—was "determined" by the artist to be an Elegy. "Unlike the others [Elegy paintings] where I know I'm painting one before I start," Motherwell recalls, "this one was discovered after I painted it. For some time I had a question of whether or not it was an Elegy, simply because it was discovered."[119] This painting was subsequently entitled *The Figure 4 on an Elegy.* Its being "found" amidst the plethora of the other black and white compositions is reminiscent of Motherwell's discovery of the original Elegy schema twelve years earlier. And this parallel can be extended; for just as the *Possibilities* design generated the model for the Elegy compositions of the 1950s, so *The Figure 4 on an Elegy* is the determinant picture for many of the 1960s works in the series.

The key to the importance played by this second "discovered" Elegy lies in the improvisational nature of its gestural forms, strongly different from those of the highly structured *Elegy 55* which immediately precedes it. *Elegy 55* represents, perhaps, the ultimate statement of the essential construct of the Elegy schema. *The Figure 4 on an Elegy,* with its automatic derivation of shapes and composition, indicated to Motherwell a new manner in which he could continue to paint Elegies.

It is possible to see why the *Figure 4 on an Elegy* was recognized as part of the series, as its alternating pattern of ovals/long curving shape/oval/black vertical mass corresponds to earlier Elegy paintings. Yet, how different from the preceding works it is; none of its forms seems to follow the prescription. To the contrary, they read as if they merely flowed into their position—a characteristic underscored by the splashes of paint which were thrown off by the artist's brush as he made the picture.

The Figure 4 on an Elegy differs from the others, as well, in

111

Figure 13. Robert Motherwell. *Elegy to the Spanish Republic, No. 70*, 1961. Oil on canvas, 175.3 x 289.6 cm (69 x 114 in). The Metropolitan Museum of Art, New York. Cat. no. 6

its use of a painted element—the figure *4* in red—on a black shape. The symbolic or autobiographical importance of its being a *4* is downplayed by the artist:

The figure 4, which appears as early as 1942, i.e., during the first several years of my painting, has baffled curious iconographers. There is a long discussion of 4's significance by Jung, but whether his notions are relevant to me or not, I do not know.[120]

His reasons for the use of the *4* in this Elegy are principally structural: "I put in the figure *4* because without it the [black] shapes would read as paper thin. With it [the] black becomes more solid—sculptural."[121]

As we have seen for the earlier Rosenberg drawing, the pictorially rich aspects of the second discovered Elegy were only gradually employed in subsequent works. As he had previously done with the initial elegy schema, Motherwell decided to make an enlargement based on *The Figure 4 on an Elegy*, which resulted in two pictures, *Elegy 70* and *Elegy 78* (figs. 13, 14), and another partly indebted to it, *Elegy 77*. Motherwell utilized the procedure he had employed in making the drawings, the support placed horizontally and the paint applied from above. "*Nos. 70* and *78* were painted directly on the floor of my studio, like Pollock had done," recalls the artist. "Because of this [procedure] they were not seen [initially] as a whole. I used no sketches or studies; just the idea of *The Figure 4 [on an Elegy]*."[122]

Studying *Elegy 70*, especially the left portion, reveals how influential was the example of the automatism of the drawing, as found in the fluid character of the forms, the quite painterly treatment of the edges of individual shapes, and the far less rigorous structuring of the entire image. In spite of the artist's

disavowal of not using "sketches or studies," however, *The Figure 4 on an Elegy* clearly served as a *modello* for portions of the Metropolitan's *Elegy 70*. This is apparent in the similarity of shape between the left ovals, in the way the long central comma in each picture does not reach directly to the top, but rather jogs to the right and then touches the upper horizontal, and in the manner in which the central oval (to the right of the comma) overlaps the large black shape. Even one of the thin lines which connect the comma to the top is present in *Figure 4 on an Elegy*. The more geometric shape to the right in *Elegy 70*, bound by its vertical black line, might also have been suggested by the black ovals to the right in the Arnason sheet, and its cagelike structure derived from the linear quality of the superimposed *4*.

Elegy 70 also resembles *Figure 4 on an Elegy* in that it also includes the product of its rapid execution—the paint spraying outward from the black forms onto the adjacent white fields. But in *Elegy 70* the spray has been painted over in many areas, probably when Motherwell turned the picture vertically after he had painted the major shapes while the canvas was on the floor. At the left the overcoat of white is applied so it encloses the left-hand oval, producing a line running vertically through the connection between the oval and comma. This creates a subtle panel around the left oval, but one which is even more secondary—"in the background"—than the drawn ones of *Elegy 34*. Its repetition of the intense black line to the right structures the picture, but its ghostly presence does not interfere with the painterliness of the powerful black shapes. The initial splattered surface runs to the right of this line, under the comma, and ends in an irregular fashion, similar to that of the

Figure 14. Robert Motherwell. *Elegy to the Spanish Republic, No. 78* (final state), 1962. Oil and plastic on canvas, 180.4 x 335.9 cm (71 x 132¼ in). Yale University Art Gallery, New Haven, Gift of the Artist. Cat. no. 7

black linear elements which reach down and outward from the comma. Many splatters and drips are still present throughout the painting, but these appear on top of the white overpainting, and from their character are clearly part of runs created with the picture in an upright position.

The edges of the black shapes in *Elegy 70* are treated in a most painterly manner, with splatters left in some places and with the warmer shade of the initial ground showing through. A touch of yellow ochre is introduced next to the left oval. But the most painterly area is at the upper right where the traditional rectangle has been filled with white scumbled into black, generating numerous soft grays, with runs of color down onto the semioval form.

Elegy 70 differs dramatically from *The Figure 4 on an Elegy* in its use of black linear elements which structure the composition. Although the verticals and horizontals in the right-hand section are transposed from earlier Elegies, in *Elegy 70* they have been broadened to be shapes in and of themselves. At the long linear bar at the top, which descends from left to right and cuts off the top of the black comma, is a transposition from those earlier Elegies where two masses of black descending from each corner would meet near the center. In *Elegy 70* Motherwell has straightened these out and lightened their character. The artist himself refers to this line in architectural terms: "like the spot where the ceiling meets the wall."[123] If we recall the appearance of the windowlike form to the upper right in the early Elegies and compare Motherwell's French Interior pictures with the general feeling of the boxlike structure to the right, we can see that something architectural in tone is present. And certainly the shapes of the black forms can be likened to

those cast onto a white wall. But the painteriiness of *Elegy 70*, and its placement of black forms against such a large area of white wall, brings the "architecture" to a human scale rather than a monumental one. The powerful feeling engendered by *Elegy 70* derives from the scale of its forms and the energy they display of their making, not from any sense of a monolithic structure.

The left portion of *Elegy 70* so intrigued the artist that he made another version isolating those features: *Elegy 78*. A simple look from one elegy to another reveals how much of the left portion of the Metropolitan's painting was transposed to entirely make up the Yale version.

As was the case earlier, various writers have projected an iconography, and Motherwell's artistic decisions are characterized as having descriptive ends rather than being the result of structural choices. In his 1966 study of Motherwell's work Arnason writes of *Elegy 78* that Motherwell "increased the sense of organic life by suspending the three black ovals like fruit from a horizontal branch."[124] Hobbs, following this suggestion for *Elegy 70*, cites *Elegy 59* as the first example of "the motif of a branch on which ovoids hang like pieces of fruit."[125] While Hobbs' discussion cites the fruit motif as something "like" the oval forms, he nevertheless proposes that they have "as a source . . . Rilke's *Druid Elegies* . . . in particular number six in which life is the flower and death is the fruit . . . [it is] a direct precursor for Motherwell's allusion to it in his paintings."[126] Then, in his specific discussion of *Elegy 70* Hobbs merges his concept of phallic imagery with Arnason's fruit so that in his reading this painting "repeats the idea of genitals hanging on a branch like fruit."[127] Because of his identification

Figure 15. Robert Motherwell. *Elegy to the Spanish Republic, No. 78* (preliminary state). [Photo: Peter A. Juley]

of the black ovals as fruit, Arnason then accounts for other forms in descriptive terms. He writes of the "curving, vertical... [which] becomes . . . a twisting tree trunk."[128] Indeed Arnason's discussion of the painter's detail in this work is premised on illusionistic rather than formal grounds.

The extensive use of paint spattered out from the black form increases the sensation of a living organism in an actual state of growth, something to which the asymmetrical organization contributes, with the blacks massed to the right and flanked by a large, clear, if somewhat bespattered area to the left.[129]

Motherwell comments on these readings that "there is not fruit hanging in *Elegy 70* or *Elegy 78*."[130] The automatic method employed in the two paintings, combined with the careful structuring of the resultant forms further supports the argument that the "creation" of such fruit is only in the minds of a few viewers.

The Yale painting, like *Elegy 70,* was painted on the floor, and its black forms were also "haloed" by splatters of paint, as seen in a photograph of it in an early state (fig. 15). These were later covered with paint, lending slightly visible pentimenti to nuance the surface and yet making the overall contrast between the black forms and the white field much greater. This is crucial in *Elegy 78* as it is the most spare of the series. Indeed, the role of the empty field in this picture is perhaps more properly compared to the subsequent Open paintings (fig. 18) than to other Elegies, where the verticals break up the one continuing surface plane. The function of the horizontal black line in *Elegy 78* points forward to the *U* shape in the Opens. "This analogy is revealing," comments the artist, "[because] when I painted *Elegy 78* I remember thinking about that empty blue Miró . . . where there is just one line with red spots. And that's very much like the Opens. Where they [*Elegy 78* and the Opens] are alike is that for the first time in *Elegy 78* I wanted to cut into the whole format of the canvas—as if it were *whole*."[131]

REVISION

The taxing burden of the New York retrospective at the Museum of Modern Art in 1965, the failure of *Elegy 100,* and the advice of friends like Bryan Robertson to stop painting Elegies[132] derailed Motherwell from the series for several years.

With the "discovery" of the Open format in 1967 and the attention given to his collages in the early 1970s, Motherwell painted few Elegies during this period.

But among the small number of Elegies from this bleak period is the commanding *Elegy 124,* begun in 1971 and finished the following year. "It is one of the most complicated," states the artist. "I must have painted it a half a dozen times, changing it as many times."[133] It is also one of the most thoroughly documented in its various stages, the artist shown working on it in a preliminary state in a 1971 Blackwood film and on its middle state in a British Broadcasting Corporation film in 1972.

As we see in its first state (fig. 1), the painting was begun as a line drawing over a pink field, recalling the colored grounds which Motherwell was also employing for the start of the Opens. The general arrangement of the basic forms was largely set at this stage—the *L*-shaped panel to the left, the three ovals separated one to the left, two to the right, by a vertical panel ending as a comma shape. A vertical panel ends the composition on the right. Motherwell began by filling in the basic schema elements, and the ovals are almost finished at the preliminary point. The middle rectangular panel is painted in so as to be a keellike shape, with the comma endings—there are two of them—left as drawing. The bracketing *L* to the left, which ends with the keel, is not yet filled in.

By the second state (fig. 17) significant changes have occurred, making the work far more complex. The *L* shape has now been filled in with black and extends across the lower edge stopping at the center of the middle oval. The horizontal bar above the left oval has been filled with black, with the line drawing of the "window" above. Above the two right ovals, a dot and dash pattern in black and ochre has been added, in two lines running horizontally. But the major change is the overpainting of the ground in a warm gray, silhouetting the left oval and the right pair and extending the lower horizontal across the surface. This is further enhanced by the addition of passages of dark blue around the center oval. In subsequent—but unrecorded—states, the left oval was surrounded with red; and on the right, passages of rich yellow were added. (Traces of these colors still remain on the surface.)

The completed state of the painting makes it considerably different from its previous appearances. Now the artist has painted in the field with white—"I painted in so much color and suddenly realized that I needed more white"[134]—and extended the bands across the bottom of the canvas. A continuous ochre bar crosses above the ovals, loosely overpainted on black. Thick white lines are placed across the black vertical panels "because they hold the black on the picture plane."[135] Although *Elegy 124* is resolved toward a more standard black and white Elegy appearance, the artist kept many areas of color at points adjacent to the ovals, introducing small flickers of color into the juxtaposition of black forms and white ground. Moreover the black *L* shape and the lower horizontal serve to bracket the central forms, but in a manner which curiously avoids the kind of rigid structural approach found in *Elegy 55.*

Elegy 124 is probably the most complex work in the entire series in terms of its color detailing and its spatial organization.

Figure 16. Robert Motherwell. *Elegy to the Spanish Republic, No. 124*, 1971-1972. Acrylic on sized canvas, 260.4 x 444.5 cm (102½ x 175 in). Collection, Robert Motherwell, Greenwich. Conn.; on extended loan to the National Gallery of Art, Washington. Cat. no. 8 , pl. 15

Where its revisions and pentimenti of brilliant hues recall *Elegy 34*,[136] the complicated pattern of shapes, brackets, and detailing relate *Elegy 124* more to *The Voyage* than to any work properly within the Spanish series.

This similarity may derive from the fact that both works have a white center field which is bracketed or framed at the outside and across the bottom—partially in *The Voyage* and entirely in *Elegy 124*. Alternatively in *Elegy 124,* the black outside panels can be seen as part of the entire structure, so that here the Elegy schema is essentially three black verticals and three ovals. However, in *Elegy 124,* like *The Voyage,* certain elements pull away from the central design schema: for example, the ochre bar in *Elegy 124* seems divorced from the black verticals and the white field—much as the black horizontal bar in *The Voyage* reads as if it were "applied"—even though the ochre bar is compositionally enrolled by its alignment with the other horizontal markings. Its separation is reinforced by the several similar suggestions elsewhere in the design of one form overlapping another, as in the two comma endings of the center vertical or the manner in which the horizontal black "bracket" stops and then resumes its course. *The Voyage* is filled with this kind of layering, so much so that it is really much closer to reading as a collage than as a painting.

Yet the spatial quirks created by the overlapping remain peculiar to their separate areas of the surface. Overall, *Elegy 124* continues to read as an articulated plane (curiously, these spatial details read as more important when the painting is seen in a reproduction or a photograph). The complexity of *Elegy 124* and its final coherence suggest we look again at the series in terms of its spatial organization and its relationships to pictorial expression.

In a 1969 discussion of Motherwell's works Rosalind Krauss observed:

In the greatest of the *Elegies to the Spanish Republic* this fact—that depth was signalled only locally—was a source of expressive power. Because each black or white vertical band was felt to be frontal and synonymous with the wall surface, the eye read the difference in size between the contiguous black ovoids of the pictures as a shift in level.

Given the apparent continuity of the wall plane, this difference in level appeared simultaneously impossible and convulsive.[137]

As we have seen, the silhouetted forms within each Elegy gave Motherwell a schema of forms that would remain essentially flat. Then there is an arrangement of the individual units such that their uniform blackness would promote simultaneously a coherence into a single "architectonic" whole. Krauss' discussion demonstrates a third factor: the depth which each element may effect—but only locally. It is crucial to realize that these aspects of the Elegy schema remain consistently structural—that, for example, the "pressures" of one oval upon another, or their expansiveness against the verticals are not present in any illusioned manner. The tension one reads in the work—the separation of the basic three ovals/one vertical from the brackets in *Elegy 124,* or in the same work, the manner in which the central oval seems to drop back as well as the manner in which it is confronted—is cued to the "architectonic sense of black." In *Elegy 124* the schema remains endemically pictorial and abstract.

This formalism of the Elegies should not be seen as a way to deny their subject matter, but on the contrary, suggests a way to account for subject matter in works which are resolutely abstract. The black ovals and verticals are not signs: rather the artist's intention is that their structural qualities are present in such a way as to correspond to other experiences. In this manner, it is necessary that the subject matter of the Elegies as a whole—the contrast of black (and death) against the white (and life)—remain constant throughout the series. The ominous qualities of *Elegy 55* are properly felt because the painting is structurally resolved by the dominance of the black. It is not the amount of black in *Elegy 55* that gives it this sense of hermeticism, but rather the dominating role black plays in organizing this use of the schema. In *Elegy 78,* the sense of explosive tension derives not from a resemblance to "splitting fruit-like ovals," but rather from the strain of the architectonic unit to cohere the splayed-out placement of the forms against the increased amount of white ground. In *Elegy 124* it is the tension between the bracketed shapes, the detailing quirks of

Figure 17. Robert Motherwell painting *Elegy 124,* spring 1972. [Photo: Renate Ponsold]

Figure 18. Robert Motherwell. *Open No. 11 (in Raw Sienna with Gray),* 1968. Polymer, paint, and charcoal on canvas, 221.0 x 537.6 cm (87 x 210 in). San Francisco Museum of Modern Art, Anonymous gift in honor of Margaret H. Rosener. Not in exhibition

overlay against the schema, and the local drops into depth that gives the armature its looming, complex, and sonorous power.

REDISCOVERED ELEGIES

Where the previous Elegies had been painted in the artist's New York studios or on Cape Cod, *Elegy 124* was one of the first painted in Motherwell's Greenwich, Connecticut, studio. Having moved there early in 1971, he enlarged his studio in 1974, and it was soon after that he began eight Elegy paintings divided into four "pairs" one in black and white, the other in black and color. Begun either on white or on freely brushed colored grounds—derived from the Opens—each pair shared one of four designs drawn in with charcoal over the field, the patterns derived from previous works or from small studies. Of these eight works, only one, *Elegy 128,* was completed in 1974, the others remaining unfinished even in April of 1975. The artist underwent five serious operations in September and October of 1974, and these health difficulties and his continuing concentration upon collage (which required less purely physical effort) were contributing factors to the postponement of the remaining seven drawn Elegies. Yet, it is also possible that they were not being fully resolved—as a project—in the artist's mind. They were, perhaps, too "programmatic" for an artist whose work—whether simple and geometric or complex and painterly—had always depended upon spontaneous choices. It was a situation very much like that of the late 1950s, when the inventions of the automatic "splash" oil drawings—including the discovery of *The Figure 4 on an Elegy* in 1960—had suddenly released the artist to finish several paintings (*Elegy 54* dates from 1957 to 1961; *Elegy 55,* 1955 to 1960; and *Elegy 58,* 1957 to 1960). Such a "breakthrough" came in August of 1975 with the painting of *Spanish Death* (fig. 19). The next and

presently (1977) continuing phase of Elegies dates from this work.

Spanish Death, painted on August 30, 1975, can be considered the third of the discovered Elegies (along with the *Possibilities* sheet and *The Figure 4 on an Elegy*). Motherwell recalls:

I was at a party at Bob Friedman's, and decided to go home early, and go home to paint. It was one of the last days in the summer studio in Provincetown. As I was coming up the stairs to my studio I saw the Metropolitan picture [*Elegy 70*] on the Museum of Modern Art poster of my show. I suddenly thought—I can take a detail of it, the right portion—and make a picture out of it. There was a horizontal canvas in my studio, which had been prepared to paint an *Open.* I turned it vertically and began to paint *Spanish Death,* using one brush with white and another with black. The whole thing was finished in six hours.[138]

The resemblance between *Spanish Death* and the right portion of *Elegy 70* is quite apparent. Aside from the almost direct transfer of the basic black forms, the artist kept the loosely scumbled area at the upper right (traditionally the "window") as well as the horizontal diagonal crossing line, which in *Spanish Death* becomes a short passage out to the left side of the painting. But changes have also occurred: the central black forms have been slightly widened and are now aligned with the vertical edges of the canvas. The enclosed center oval "tips" at a greater angle, and the right-hand black panel is considerably broader.

Elegy 70 had been raided before, as we have seen, for *Elegy 78.* What Motherwell realized in looking at *Elegy 70* was that "the right portion was essentially an Elegy as well."[139] But a compressed one. Where other Elegies also have truncated black panels, squeezed ovals, and vertical elements which end as oval forms, none is as compact as *Spanish Death.* Nor is the white ground of any so beautifully painted; here subtle nuances of white over beige are consistently present.

Spanish Death is also the only vertical Elegy (*Elegy 55* at 70⅛ × 76⅛ is approximately square, and the closest precedent), which also accounts for its compressed character. This may explain why Motherwell had never seen the right portion as an Elegy, especially at the time when he had transferred the left portion.

Early in 1974, Motherwell began making collages at a much larger scale than he had previously used. Emphatically vertical, these works usually measure 72 × 36 inches. Using scumbled, painted grounds, the artist then pasted papers and pieces of painted cloth over the initial field. The structural organization

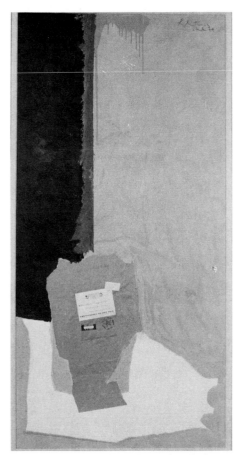

Figure 19. Robert Motherwell. *The Spanish Death*, 1975. Acrylic on oil-sized canvas, 243.9 x 198.1 cm (96 x 78 in). Collection, Robert Motherwell, Greenwich, Conn. [photo: Steve Sloman]. Cat. no. 9

Figure 20. Robert Motherwell. *Heidi and Claus,* 1974. Collage, 182.9 x 91.5 cm (72 x 36 in). Collection, Mr. and Mrs. Claus Colsman-Freyberger, New York [photo: Renate Ponsold]. Not in exhibition

and shapes of certain elements in many of them anticipate similar components in *Spanish Death* of the following year. In *Heidi and Claus* (1974, collection of Mr. and Mrs. Claus Colsman Freyberger, Tokyo; fig. 20), for example, a dark blue and black rectangular panel runs three quarters down the left side, similar to the panel on the right in *Spanish Death*. Equally similar is the manner in which the collaged white form at the bottom both cuts out an area and is overlapped by the brown mail cover. This is also true for the squared-off white field at the bottom center of the painting and the intrusion of the oval form into this region.

This is not to suggest that the collages are derived from a portion of *Elegy 70,* even unconsciously, as their metamorphosis from the Open collages of 1972 could be demonstrated. Rather it suggests that the vertical composition, with the isolated rectangular pattern and the complicated and intricate overlap of curving shapes, was already present in the artist's working vocabulary, and his recognition of *Spanish Death* was unconsciously prepared for with his collages. In speaking of influences upon his art in the late 1940s and early 1950s Motherwell noted that "it cannot be emphasized enough that my 'influences' are in the nature of 'after images', dimly remembered, rather than from deliberate analysis. . . ."[140] It is perhaps the "after image" here of his own collages that promoted the sudden recognition of *Spanish Death*.

The painting, with its stark palette and schematic coherence, differs drastically from the collages. Also particular to *Spanish Death* is its quality of self-containment. Unlike previous Elegies, the black form reads essentially as one unit, rather than an armature of comprised ovals and vertical panels. This relatively isolated character makes *Spanish Death* an especially poignant work. While its strength as a picture derives from the contrast of the form against the vertical field—indeed decisively so, for the proportions of *Spanish Death* at 96 × 77½ are not nearly so vertical as the image appears—nevertheless, of all the Elegies, the image is the one most capable of being lifted out of its context and remaining integral (the left portion of *Elegy 70* interestingly is changed dramatically in its effects from *Elegy 70* to *Elegy 78*). Proof of this is its role in the third stage of *Elegy 100*.

QUOTATION AND INVENTION

The next major work after *Elegies 70* and *78* was the monumental *Elegy 100* (fig. 23), which at 94 × 240 was the largest of the series. It was rushed to exhibition for the artist's 1965 retrospective at the Museum of Modern Art. Viewing it there, hung with the other Elegies (fig. 21), the artist was dissatisfied with the painting, and it was returned to the studio where it went through two complete revisions.

Elegy 100 differs from the others not only by virtue of its size

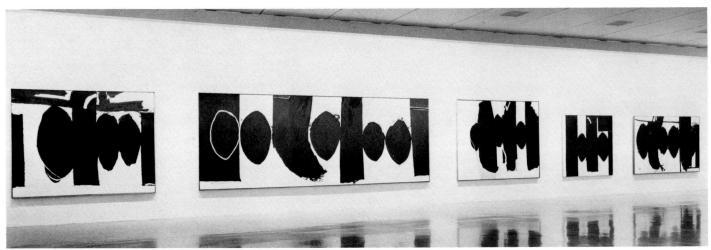

Figure 21. View of Motherwell's exhibition at The Museum of Modern Art, New York, 1965. [Photo: Rolf Petersen, courtesy of The Museum of Modern Art, New York]

but also in its proportions. The approximately three to one ratio of this canvas makes it a far more horizontal field than that of the conventional Spanish picture, which rarely exceeds one and a half to one. In meeting the long horizontal requirements of these proportions the artist stretched out the schema by adding more ovals and panels to the armature and placing them at greater distance from each other. Studying the painting in its original guise we can see why it was rejected by the artist (fig. 21). To begin with, the ovals are simply too small, in spite of their large physical size. Furthermore, aligned generally along the same horizontal axis, these diminutive shapes are strung out across the surface like apples on a table. Their regularity of shape and pattern, as well as the larger amount of surrounding white ground, makes them visibly "ping" like the perceptual shapes found in optical art. The reverse is true of the three rectangular elements: they remain inert, lifeless, and seem to merely fill in surface. Even the curvilinear passage at the center left is flaccid, despite the spray of paint at the bottom.

The central reason for the failure of this state is the spreading out of the forms. As we have observed, the tension produced in the best Elegies results from the contrast between the individual components and the manner in which the schema works *structurally* to organize the painting. In the initial stage of *Elegy 100* the forms are not only without much interest, they are not unified in any manner by the general Elegy schema; *Elegy 100* reads as if it is simply a pattern rather than the result of contending compositional components.

The second state of the painting overcorrected the problem; here the forms were so massive and solid as to deny any reading of contrast, either spatially—in terms of figure ground—or laterally. The painting as we know it today is drastically altered from its initial state.

The third state of *Elegy 100* is a compound drawn from two previously separate images. Within the composition may be seen, to the left, another version of *Spanish Death*, while on the right two-thirds of the long canvas is filled with an enlargement from a small oil work entitled *Mural Study* (fig. 22). This latter section is organized in a pattern of panel/oval/panel/oval/panel, which also repeats the general organization of the initial

Figure 22. Robert Motherwell. *Mural Study,* 1974. Oil on canvas board, 15.2 x 30.6 cm (6 x 12 in). Collection, Robert Motherwell, Greenwich, Conn.; on extended loan to the National Gallery of Art, Washington. Not in exhibition

schema of the Rosenberg sheet. The difference is that here the panels are rectangular and emphatically vertical and are set in greater contrast to the more freely painted ovals. Using the *Spanish Death* motif on the left means that for the first time the right edge of the motif does not coincide with the right edge of a canvas. Flanked now by white ground, the black forms read more as a strong vertical panel.

Motherwell's mastery of placement—often commented upon in regard to his collages—shows in the arrangement of these shapes with respect to the predominantly horizontal format. The center section of the entire work—the two vertical panels and the enclosed oval—is placed precisely at the middle of the field, so that not only the centered oval but its two adjacent vertical panel edges introduce a symmetrical balance. But in the flanking positions this is turned to asymmetry, with two ovals in the right third and the *Spanish Death* motif, which is basically a vertical black panel, in the left section. This asymmetrical contrast is present in detail as well, for the two ovals and their rectangular panels create a broad, spreading image, whereas the *Spanish Death* motif encases the oval forms into a compressed, self-centered image. Finally, the asymmetry is further enhanced by the color reversal at the outer vertical edges, white ground on the left and a black panel on the right.

Compositional balances of symmetry and asymmetry are

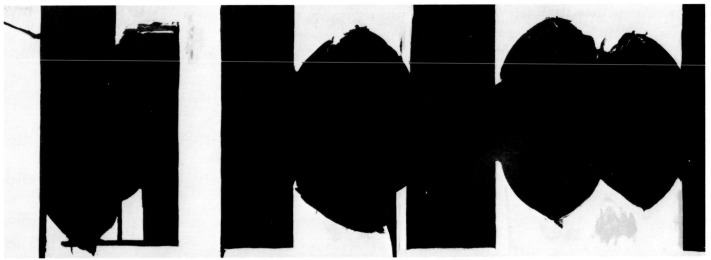

Figure 23. Robert Motherwell. *Elegy to the Spanish Republic, No. 100* (final state), 1965-1975. Acrylic on oil-sized canvas, 213.4 x 609.6 cm (84 x 240 in). Collection, Robert Motherwell, Greenwich, Conn. [photo: Steve Sloman]. Cat. no. 10

spelled out in another way in *Elegy 100*. Significantly the right edge of the *Spanish Death* motif abuts exactly the left quarter-mark division of the painting. This suggests that the painting is organized in a geometric pattern of four equal parts. The far left area is that between the left edge of the work and the right edges of *Spanish Death*; and the center left quarter, that area between *Spanish Death* and the center of the work (the center being the imagined vertical line around which the center oval and the vertical panels are organized). However, the third or center right quarter mark is not indicated by anything in the painting, suggesting that though the picture may well be divided into four parts, Motherwell chose to treat it as two units, one consisting of one quarter of the work and devoted to *Spanish Death*, and the other consisting of three quarters and containing the basic Elegy schema. But, within the right three-quarters unit—that is the picture from *Spanish Death* to the right edge of the whole canvas—Motherwell introduces another note of symmetry, for the black panel at the middle of this section is symmetrically placed with respect to the outer limits of this three-quarter division.

Thus symmetry is introduced in two ways in *Elegy 100:* at the center of the entire composition, marked by the oval and the vertical lines of the two adjacent panels; and at the center of the separate Elegy schema, here marked by the center black panel and the outward curve of its two adjacent ovals. These two arrangements are the reverse of each other: panel/oval/panel versus oval/panel/oval.

The subtlety and complexity of these divisions and alignments in *Elegy 100* match those of *Elegy 34* and *Elegy 124*. But the latter works are characterized by a complexity resulting from colors and spatial layerings where *Elegy 100*'s complexity is the result of placement and construction. The final, monumental quality of *Elegy 100* derives from the complexity of its construction held in tandem with the large physical scale and the attenuated length of the work itself. Of all of the Elegies it is the one where the black of death seems most assuredly in control of the work and so multifarious in its manner of achievement.

"THE BURDEN OF INTENTION"

Elegy 100 is also directly related to *The Figure 4 on an Elegy,* in spite of the considerable differences in their scale, vocabulary, and construction. If we look back over some of the major works—*At Five in the Afternoon, Elegy 34, Elegy 55, Elegy 70, Elegy 124, Spanish Death,* and *Elegy 100*—we see the vast range of individual expressions: starkness, pageantry, ominousness, expansion, sonority, compression, and monumentality. But we know each to be part of the Elegy series—because the Elegies are serial in their essential subject: "The Elegy I painted last month could have been painted twenty years ago." But, this does not mean that they are serial in their statements, because each Elegy is also particular: "it expresses how I feel at a given moment."

Within the concept of the Elegies lies a struggle between their individuality and their collective natures. O'Hara singled this out—and Motherwell's extraordinary achievement in the face of it—twelve years ago:

Motherwell from *At Five in the Afternoon* . . . on, is fighting an over-dominant and already clarified symbolic structure from which, through the years, he will wrench with astonishing energy some of the most powerful, self-exacerbating and brutally ominous works of our time, and some of the most coldly disdainful ones as well (emptying of Self). In this sense, Motherwell creates the structure that opposes him, the domination of which he must overcome to remain an artist. . . . In Motherwell the family of forms is a relatively small one and the plastic handling of them carries the burden of intention, whether passionate or subtle, whether buoyant or subdued. . . .[141]

We know from our experiences that when we encounter a death, we are suddenly burdened with how to say precisely what we feel, and our speech seems only to reiterate mundane clichés, entrapping private emotions—not so much in ceremony as in banality. For abstract painting the burden of communication is, perhaps, even greater than for representational art and (to be specific about a nuance of its subject) a most demanding task. In this regard, the Elegies—with their articulate speeches about death (and life)—stand as a remarkable achievement.

This analysis of The Elegies to the Spanish Republic would not have been possible without the generous assistance of Robert Motherwell. The discussion is based on numerous conversations with the artist about the Elegies over three years. These meetings were followed by sessions where earlier comments were transcribed as direct quotes from the artist, which were then approved at subsequent meetings. References to these sessions with the author will be made as follows: conversation May 6, 1976, conversation Aug. 17, 1977, conversation Oct. 9, 1977. Certain details were also discussed in telephone conversations with the author, and are referred to as conversation Sept. 23, 1977 and conversation Oct. 28, 1977. Notes from all conversations are on file in the Department of Twentieth-Century Art, National Gallery of Art.

1. Robert Motherwell, *Black and White*, exh. cat. (New York: Samuel Kootz Gallery, 1950), 9.

2. For a discussion of the problems of numbering see below. In this text the generic title, The Elegies to the Spanish Republic, will be abbreviated as Elegies. This term is not meant to include variants on the format, such as the *Irish Elegy* (1965; collection of Mr. and Mrs. Richard E. Long, Medina, Washington) or unrelated pictures such as the *New England Elegy* (1966; John F. Kennedy Federal Building, Boston). On the other hand it is meant to include certain pictures which do not bear a direct Elegy assignation as with *Spanish Death*, 1975 (fig. 19). Individual titles, as in *Elegy to the Spanish Republic No. 34* will be abbreviated in this essay as *Elegy 34*.

3. H. H. Arnason, "On Robert Motherwell and his Early Work," *Art International*, 10 (Jan. 1966): 35. Harold Rosenberg has referred to Motherwell "presenting variations on his established signatures: solid black ovals between vertical bars, with titles referring to Spain (the elegiac Motherwell)," in *The Anxious Object* (New York: Horizon Press, 1966), 101. This general idea—that a given artistic schema can be seen as a "signature" or a stylistic badge—has recently been given a different interpretation, however; J. P. Cooney in 1973 suggested that the Elegies were in fact an abstraction based on the artist's own signature ("Robert Burns Motherwell: A Study of the Development of Abstract Expressionism as Seen in His Works" [1973; on file at Whitney Museum of American Art, New York], p. 55). Robert Hobbs, in his 1975 study of the Elegies ("Motherwell's Concern with Death in Painting: An Investigation of his Elegies to the Spanish Republic, Including an Examination of his Philosophical and Methodological Considerations" [Ph.D. diss., University of North Carolina]) takes this suggestion to great interpretative lengths, based on his observation that "time after time in this series there is an interplay between three verticals and three ovals" (p. 167) which he sees as an abstraction of the artist's signature *Motherwell*. From this basis Hobbs proposes that Motherwell "makes his signature the basis for the Elegies" (p. 169), that "the three dominant verticals in the signature as well as the three oval shapes become basic elements that are shifted and readjusted in each work in the series" (p. 167), and that "Motherwell employs his own name as an 'essential word' in the Elegies" (p. 190). This leads to a comparison to Mallarmé's poetry based on the emphasis of each word, and Hobbs concludes that Motherwell "takes his own name and refashions it. . . . His abstraction upon the abstraction of one word as a vehicle for the entire content of his series shows how much he trusted the Frenchman's researches into the evocation of a single word" (p. 192). This author finds this a serious misinterpretation of the Elegies. Motherwell's own comment to Hobbs that he had never (even) noticed any resemblance between his signature and the Elegy schema should give us pause. Motherwell has subsequently dismissed any serious meaning to this literal interpretation (conversation, Aug. 17, 1977). Furthermore, the resemblance between Motherwell's signature and the Elegy schema is at best indirect, as one can demonstrate by taking this name and trying to make any known Elegy out of it. There are uncountable words which could be read—as Hobbs suggests—as a formal basis for the Elegies; even the word *elegy*, for example, can be seen as more directly related to the initial works than the word *Motherwell*. Finally, and perhaps most importantly, Hobbs' analysis proposes a formal source for the Elegies—an existing set of shapes made from the letters, M-O-T-H-E-R-W-E-L-L—which the artist abstracts and then moves around like chess pieces to make new Elegies: careful examination of the structured development of the Elegies (see below) shows not only that this interpretation is impossible in terms of how the paintings were made but that it suggests a serious misrepresentation of abstract-expressionist painting in general.

4. See H. H. Arnason, "Motherwell: The Wall and the Window," *Art News*, 68 (Summer 1969): 48-52, 61-68; and this author's *The Collages of Robert Motherwell*, exh. cat. (Houston: Museum of Fine Arts, 1972).

5. This author's preliminary study of this discovery was published in "Robert Motherwell's Spanish Elegies," *Arts, 50* (June 1976): 94-97.

6. For an excellent discussion of the surrealist use of automatism, see William Rubin, *Dada, Surrealism and their Heritage*, exh. cat. (New York: Museum of Modern Art, 1968).

7. Robert Motherwell in an interview with Princeton seminar students, Greenwich, Conn., Dec. 13, 1972 in *Robert Motherwell: Recent Work*, exh. cat. (Princeton: Princeton University Art Museum, 1973), 34.

8. "It is a question of using it for fantasy vs. the Sublime"; Motherwell, conversation, Oct. 9, 1977.

9. Robert Motherwell, "The Modern Painter's World," *DYN*, 6 (Nov. 1944): 13.

10. See this author's *Collages*, 15-18.

11. Conversation, Aug. 17, 1977.

12. Conversation, Aug. 17, 1977.

13. Conversation, Oct. 9, 1977.

14. Conversation, Aug. 17, 1977. On a subsequent conversation, Oct. 9, 1977, Motherwell added: "What I felt was that *At Five* was like a sacred structure as opposed to the drawing which was like a shelter, or a temporary improvised structure. *At Five* struck me like a monument."

15. Lorca's poem is reprinted in several places, the most accessible to the student of Motherwell's work being: H. H. Arnason, *Robert Motherwell* (New York: Abrams, 1977), opp. pl. 80.

16. Conversation, Aug. 17, 1977.

17. Hobbs, "Robert Motherwell's Elegies to the Spanish Republic" in *Robert Motherwell*, exh. cat. (Düsseldorf: Städtische Kunsthalle, 1976), 30.

18. Conversation, Aug. 17, 1977.

19. Conversation, Oct. 9, 1977.

20. Conversation, Aug. 17, 1977.

21. Robert Motherwell; quoted by Margaret Paul, "Robert Motherwell: A Conversation at Lunch" in *Robert Motherwell*, exh. cat. (Northampton, Mass.: Smith College, 1963), cat. no. 5.

22. "I remember I treasured the Matisse issue of *Verve*"; conversation, Oct. 9, 1977.

23. Conversation, Aug. 17, 1977.

24. Conversation, Aug. 17, 1977.

25. By "poetic" I mean Motherwell's own poetic sense. Hobbs, "Motherwell's Concern with Death," suggests in several places that Motherwell's work is directly related to the poetry of Rilke and Mallarmé, not to mention Lorca and Rosenberg.

26. Robert Motherwell; quoted by Kynaston McShine in "Chronology," in Frank O'Hara, *Robert Motherwell*, exh. cat. (New York: Museum of Modern Art, 1965), 74.

27. Robert Motherwell, *Motherwell*, exh. cat. (New York: Kootz Gallery, 1950), n.p.

28. E.C. Goosen, "Robert Motherwell and the Seriousness of Subject," *Art International*, 3 (Jan. 11, 1959): 34. Goosen's text is the first significant discussion of Motherwell's work and its relationship to subjects.

29. Dore Ashton, *The New York School* (New York: Viking Press, 1973), 102.

30. But Hobbs offers the following opinion: "His Spanish Elegies can be considered a critique of Picasso's work providing an interpretation of it in a more abstract format" ("Motherwell's Concern with Death," 233). Hobbs further suggests that when de Kooning, Motherwell, Newman, Pollock, Still,

Tomlin, and Kline "began to make black and white paintings on a large scale, each [was] attempting to make *Guernica* over in his own image" (p. 234). He concludes that "when Motherwell names his first Elegies after cities in Spain following the precedence of *Guernica,* he openly acknowledges his debt to Picasso" (p. 237). See below for a different interpretation of the Elegies and *Guernica* and comments on the origins of the city names.

31. Robert Motherwell in conversation with Bryan Robertson, "Art, N.Y.," TV broadcast produced by Colin Clark, New York, Channel 13, Dec. 15, 1964 [typescript in Motherwell papers, Greenwich, Conn.]; quoted by Hobbs, "Motherwell's Concern with Death," 176.

32. Conversation, Aug. 17, 1977.

33. See William Rubin, "Arshile Gorky, Surrealism and the New American Painting," *Art International, 7* (Feb. 1963): 27-38.

34. Conversation, Oct. 9, 1977.

35. Anthony Blunt, *Picasso's Guernica* (New York: Oxford, 1969), 13.

36. See William Rubin's discussion of *Guernica* in his "Jackson Pollock and the Modern Tradition, Part II," *Artforum, 5* (Mar. 1967): 34.

37. Conversation, Aug. 17, 1977

38. Quoted by Paul in *Robert Motherwell* (Smith College), cat. no. 16.

39. Conversation, Oct. 28, 1977.

40. Harold Rosenberg, *The Anxious Object,* 39.

41. Robert Motherwell, "The Modern Painters' World," 14.

42. Robert Motherwell and Harold Rosenberg, in *Possibilities 1;* William Seitz offers many insights into this issue in his "Abstract-Expressionist Painting in America: an Interpretation Based on the Work and Thought of Six Key Figures" (Ph.D. diss., Princeton University, 1955), esp. 298-301 and 381-385.

43. Second definition of *elegy,* in *Webster's New International Dictionary of the English Language,* 2nd ed.

44. Robert Paine, *A Portrait of André Malraux* (New Jersey: Prentice-Hall, 1970), 267.

45. Conversation, May 6, 1976.

46. Hobbs, "Motherwell's Concern with Death," 217.

47. Conversation, Aug. 17, 1977.

48. Conversation, Aug. 17, 1977.

49. Conversation, Aug. 17, 1977.

50. Conversation, Oct. 9, 1977.

51. Motherwell; quoted in Hobbs, "Motherwell's Concern with Death," 127.

52. Conversation Aug. 17, 1977. See Introduction to this catalogue for a discussion of "discovered subjects."

53. Robert Motherwell, unpublished note, cited in Hobbs, "Motherwell's Concern with Death," 15.

54. Robert Motherwell, interview with David Sylvester, "Painting as Existence," London, BBC, Oct. 22, 1960 [typescript in Greenwich, Conn.], in Hobbs, "Motherwell's Concern with Death," 49; and conversation, Oct. 9, 1977.

55. Motherwell; quoted in Hobbs, "Motherwell's Concern with Death," 24; Motherwell adds: "I realized some of this from Mondrian and his intensity of feeling about abstraction" (conversation, Sept. 23, 1977).

56. Robert Motherwell, unpublished note, cited in Hobbs, "Motherwell's Concern with Death," 33.

57. Conversation, Aug. 17, 1977.

58. Robert Motherwell, "The Public and the Modern Painter," *Catholic Art Quarterly, 14* (Easter 1951): 81.

59. See Rubin, "Jackson Pollock"; and this author's "Morris Louis and the Modern Tradition," *Arts, 51* (Sept.-Dec. 1976).

60. H. H. Arnason was the first to single out Matisse as a formal source for the Elegies, in "Robert Motherwell: 1948-1965," *Art International, 10* (Apr. 1966): 25.

61. Robert Motherwell, "Introduction to the Illustrations," *Modern Artists in America* (New York: Wittenborn, 1952), 20.

62. Conversation, Aug. 17, 1977.

63. Conversation, Aug. 17, 1977.

64. Conversation, Aug. 17, 1977.

65. Conversation, Aug. 17, 1977.

66. Conversation, Aug. 17, 1977.

67. See Thomas B. Hess, *Willem de Kooning,* exh. cat. (New York: Museum of Modern Art, 1968), 50-51.

68. Lawrence Alloway, "Sign and Surface: Notes on Black and White Painting in New York," *Quadrum, 9* (1960): 59.

69. Alloway, "Sign and Surface," 60.

70. The following discussion is adapted from this author's "Spanish Elegies," 95 (see n. 5 above).

71. Conversation, Sept. 23, 1977.

72. Clement Greenberg, "The 'Crisis' of Abstract Art," in *Arts Yearbook 7: New York: The Art World* (New York, 1964), 91.

73. Robert Motherwell quoted in *Contemporary Art 1942-72* (Buffalo: Albright-Knox, 1972), 39.

74. Conversation, Aug. 17, 1977.

75. See Hobbs, "Motherwell's Concern with Death," 220-224 for a discussion of this, and below.

76. Goosen, "The Seriousness of Subject," 34.

77. Goosen, "The Seriousness of Subject," 34.

78. Irving Sandler, "New York Letter," *Art International, 5* (June-Aug. 1961): 116.

79. O'Hara, *Motherwell,* 19.

80. O'Hara, *Motherwell,* 19.

81. Arnason, "Motherwell: 1948-1965," 26.

82. Arnason, "Motherwell: 1948-1965," 28-29.

83. Hobbs, "Motherwell's Concern with Death."

84. Arnason, "Motherwell: 1948-1965," 29.

85. Hobbs, "Motherwell's Concern with Death," 220.

86. Arnason, "Motherwell: 1948-1965," 30.

87. Hobbs, "Motherwell's Concern with Death."

88. Hobbs, "Motherwell's Concern with Death," 175. In his list of illustrations Hobbs identified the sketch for *Elegy 34* as *Tombs of Capitain* (1953) in the collection of the Munson-Williams-Proctor Institute, Utica, New York. There is a related work for *Elegy 34* in this collection, but it bears the title *The Tomb of Captain Ahab.*

89. Hobbs, "Motherwell's Concern with Death," 238-239.

90. Conversation, Aug. 17, 1977.

91. Conversation, Aug. 17, 1977.

92. Conversation, Aug. 17, 1977.

93. Conversation, Aug. 17, 1977.

94. Conversation, Aug. 17, 1977.

95. Conversation, Aug. 17, 1977.

96. Conversation, Aug. 17, 1977.

97. B[elle] K[rasne], "Fifty-Seventh Street in Review," *The Art Digest, 25,* no. 5 (Dec. 1, 1950): 17-18.

98. Seitz, "Abstract-Expressionist Painting," 138.

99. Seitz, "Abstract-Expressionist Painting," 158.

100. Arnason, "The Window and the Wall," 52.

101. Arnason, "The Window and the Wall," 52.

102. Arnason, "Motherwell: 1948-1965," 29.

103. Arnason, "The Window and the Wall," 60.

104. Edward B. Henning, "Language of Art," *Cleveland Museum Bulletin, 51* (Nov. 1964): 219.

105. Arnason, "Motherwell: 1948-1965," 26.

106. Hobbs proposes that the Elegies may be based on a photograph of a Greek temple published by A. A. Paalen in *Dyn I* in 1944 and republished in *Form and Sense* in 1945, in "Motherwell's Concern with Death," 254.

107. Conversation, Aug. 17, 1977.

108. Motherwell; quoted in Hobbs, "Motherwell's Concern with Death," 182.

109. Arnason, "The Window and The Wall," 51.

110. Emphasis mine. Motherwell, Kootz Gallery, 1950, n.p.

111. Motherwell, Kootz Gallery, 1950, n.p.

112. Seitz, "Abstract-Expressionist Painting," 229.

113. Seitz, "Abstract-Expressionist Painting," 137.

114. Seitz, "Abstract-Expressionist Painting," 136.

115. Seitz, "Abstract-Expressionist Painting," 229.

116. Seitz, "Abstract-Expressionist Painting," 136.

117. Illustrated in Henning, "Language of Art," 218.

118. Sam Hunter.

119. Conversation, Aug. 17, 1977.

120. Motherwell; quoted in Arnason, *Motherwell*, 126.

121. Conversation, Aug. 17, 1977.

122. Conversation, Aug. 17, 1977.

123. Conversation, Sept. 23, 1977.

124. Arnason, "Motherwell: 1948-1965," 30.

125. Hobbs, "Motherwell's Concern with Death," 241.

126. Hobbs, "Motherwell's Concern with Death," 241.

127. Hobbs, "Motherwell's Concern with Death," 260.

128. Arnason, "Motherwell: 1948-1965," 30.

129. Arnason, "Motherwell: 1948-1965," 30.

130. Conversation, Aug. 17, 1977.

131. Conversation, Aug. 17, 1977.

132. Bryan Robertson, "From a Notebook on Robert Motherwell," *Studio International,* 171 (Mar. 1966): 90.

133. Conversation, Oct. 28, 1977.

134. Conversation, Oct. 28, 1977.

135. Conversation, Oct. 28, 1977.

136. See Hobbs on this point as well, "Motherwell's Concern with Death," 280-282.

137. Rosalind Krauss, "Robert Motherwell's New Paintings," *Artforum,* 7 (May 1969): 29-30.

138. Conversation, Aug. 17, 1977.

139. Conversation, Aug. 17, 1977.

140. Motherwell; quoted in Carmean, *Collages,* 26.

141. O'Hara, *Motherwell,* 23.

JACKSON POLLOCK:
Classic Paintings of 1950

Figure 1. Jackson Pollock painting *Autumn Rhythm* in autumn, 1950. [Photo: Hans Namuth]

CHECKLIST

1. Number 1, 1950 (Lavender Mist)   1950
   oil, enamel, and aluminum paint on canvas
   221.0 × 299.7 cm (87× 118 in)
   Signed and dated lower left: Jackson Pollock '50
   National Gallery of Art, Washington, Ailsa Mellon Bruce
   Fund, 1976

2. Number 2, 1950   1950
   oil, lacquer, silver paint on canvas
   287.0 × 91.4 cm (113 × 36 in)
   Signed, upper right: Jackson Pollock
   Fogg Art Museum, Harvard University, Cambridge, Mass.; in part
   given and in part lent by Reginald and Charlotte Isaacs and family
   and friends, and in part purchased from the Contemporary Art
   Fund

3. Number 32, 1950   1950
   oil on canvas
   269.2 × 457.2 cm (106 × 180 in)
   Signed, back, upper left: Jackson Pollock
   Kunstsammlung Nordrhein-Westfalen, Düsseldorf

4. Number 31, 1950 (One)   1950
   oil and enamel on canvas
   270.0 × 535.0 cm (105⅞ × 209½ in)
   The Museum of Modern Art, New York, Gift of
   Sidney Janis, 1968.

5. Number 27, 1950   1950
   oil on canvas
   124.5 × 269.2 cm (49 × 106 in)
   Signed and dated, lower right corner: Jackson Pollock 50
   Whitney Museum of American Art, New York

BIOGRAPHY

Born in 1912 in Cody, Wyoming; is raised in Arizona and California. After studying painting at Manual Arts High School in Los Angeles, moves to New York and studies with Thomas Hart Benton at the Art Students League. In 1936 participates in Siqueiro's experimental workshop. Paints large *Mural* for Peggy Guggenheim during December 1943–January 1944. Marries Lee Krasner in 1945, and moves to Springs, Long Island. In 1947 begins to pour paint, and expresses interest in large paintings. Begins large classic pictures in spring 1950 with *Lavender Mist*. Exhibition of 1950 works November 28 to December 16 at Betty Parsons Gallery, New York. In 1951 begins black and white figural works. Paints two more large abstract paintings, *Convergence* and *Blue Poles*, in 1952. Dies in automobile accident in 1956.

JACKSON POLLOCK:
Classic Paintings of 1950

E. A. CARMEAN, JR.

Jackson Pollock's poured or drip paintings of 1947 to 1950 are judged by almost all accounts as his greatest works. Moreover, they are recognized as crucial to the development of abstract expressionism and its almost immediate international recognition, especially in Europe.[1] Their influence on subsequent painting has been cited repeatedly. When "Pollock broke the ice," to quote de Kooning, he did so in these works. They had the requisite authority to inaugurate the shift of the center of advanced painting from Paris to New York.

Despite the enthusiastic reception by fellow artists, Pollock's poured paintings received the opposite reaction among critics, who saw the works as disorganized, violent expressions. More recently these works, and especially those painted in 1950, have been referred to as "classic" or "classical."[2] Certainly this term is not employed to suggest that Pollock's work is "in accordance with ancient Greek or Roman models,"[3] and even the most cursory art-historical analysis of the period at the end of the 1940s would deny their "conforming to established taste or critical standards: [or] adhering to traditional forms." The dictionary's first definition of *classic*—"of the first or highest class or rank"—carries with it the sense of critical judgment that is being exercised when the term is employed. But for the 1950 paintings, there is also the sense that the term is used to denote those works where Pollock fully realized what his painting style could achieve. They are "classic" in their thorough use of the pouring application and the uncompromising unity which resulted.

By 1950 Pollock had been developing his pouring technique for three years, acquiring an extraordinary degree of control over a complex battery of touches. This is most evident in the only wall-sized pictures of the period, all from 1950: *Lavender Mist* (cat. no. 1), *Number 32, 1950* (cat. no. 3), *One* (cat. no. 4), and *Autumn Rhythm* (fig. 18), and in many of the medium-sized works from the same time, including the tall, vertical *Number 2, 1950* (cat. no. 2) and the exceptionally beautiful *Number 27, 1950* (cat. no. 5).

It should be made clear from the beginning that while they may be linked as "classic" Pollocks, these works do not form a series such as Gorky's Plow and the Song paintings or Motherwell's Elegies. Pollock's attention to a particular theme is not so confined and focused. Rather, they are joined in their being made during a remarkable period in Pollock's art, and each is a result of his touch at its most assured. But Pollock's technique is all the more significant with these works because their ultimate subject is inextricably linked to that technique;

and if technique is shared in particular ways among the works, so then is the ultimate subject from it. But because Pollock's technique develops through his work as a whole, the poured pictures all share, to some degree, a similar thematic concern. The thesis here is that particular formal emphases, which we call "classic" in certain works, make the subject more explicit.

The 1950 works are not divorced from Pollock's work of 1947-1950; all six of the classic 1950 Pollocks draw upon the artist's earlier poured paintings. But they attend to the corpus of previous works in separate ways, relating directly to different pictures. In a similar manner, the 1950 works have—as William Rubin has so thoroughly shown[4]—deep connections to the modern tradition, especially impressionism, the late Monet, cubism, and certain aspects of surrealism. While sharing to various degrees all aspects of this tradition, the six classic works each turns a differing face to it, and the correspondences change from painting to painting.

The relationship of the classic pictures to each other is thus complex, consistent in the level of touch and in their correspondence to both Pollock's earlier works and the modern tradition, and differing in their separate selections and emphases. Because of this the subject of these works and what it is drawn from are equally difficult to determine, given the multiple contexts, the interconnections, and the differences.

The key to all of this lies in comprehending Pollock's technique. This is not to suggest that the works are purely material. That Pollock emphasized the pouring style was clearly the result of certain expressive needs. Its use began in 1947 in order to say certain things, and stopped in 1951 when what Pollock wanted to say changed. Pollock's development of the pouring technique in turn produced his clearer understanding of its ultimate expressive abilities—and subject matter. As Robert Motherwell wrote of Pollock three years before the drip paintings began: "His principal problem is to discover what his true subject is. And since painting is his thought's medium, the resolution must grow out of the process of his painting itself."[5]

THE POURED TECHNIQUE

Scholarship has pretty well cleared up the major issues in the relationship between poured automatism as a technique and Pollock's own particular procedures. This relationship is a side issue anyway, as "it was not the dripping, pouring or spattering *per se*, but what Pollock *did* with them that counted."[6]

Figure 2. Jackson Pollock painting *Autumn Rhythm* in autumn, 1950.
[Photo: Hans Namuth]

in its completeness; the technique is not only generative but continuous: the painting is begun, carried on, and finished using this procedure. This description might suggest that Pollock began his works in a manner extrapolated from the work of Masson—doodling paint on the surface in a random pattern—but that, unlike Masson, Pollock kept it up, adding different colors and layers, until the surface was covered. A crude description of this form of painting was attached to Pollock by Alonzo Lansford in 1951:

Pollock's current method seems to be a sort of automatism; apparently, while staring steadily up into the sky, he lets go a loaded brush on the canvas, rapidly swirling and looping and wriggling till the paint runs out. Then he repeats the procedure with another color, and another, till the canvas is covered.[8]

That this was not the case we know from studying the works themselves, Pollock's statements, and the photographic records of him at work. Rather a different view of Pollock's procedure is now generally held, namely that he began his works "automatically" but then continued and finished them with greater control. The picture is thus an accumulation of responses to the initial random layer and, then, to each subsequent application. Pollock's 1948 statement in *Possibilities* clearly defines just this procedure:

When I am *in* my painting, I'm not aware of what I'm doing. It is only after a sort of "get acquainted" period that I see what I have been about. I have no fears about making changes, destroying the image, etc., because the painting has a life of its own. I try to let it come through. It is only when I lose contact with the painting that the result is a mess. Otherwise there is pure harmony, an easy give and take, and the painting comes out well.[9]

A note of clarification must be introduced here, for in talking about automatism and accidental or random markings we are dealing with the issue on two different levels. At one level is the large automatic pattern which Pollock used to initiate the painting, or what we might call a random doodle image. At another are the random markings, necessarily produced by his technique at all times throughout the making of the work; it is what we might call the accidental detailing of puddles, spots, lines. Thus if the work was begun by using a random or uncomposed pouring of paint and finished in a more controlled manner, that finishing still involved a degree of accident. Frank O'Hara pointed out in 1959:

There has never been enough said about Pollock's draftsmanship, that amazing ability to quicken a line by thinning it, to slow it by flooding, to elaborate that simplest of elements, the line—to change, to reinvigorate, to extend, to build up an embarrassment of riches in the mass by drawing alone.[10]

But, as William Rubin observed, this control must be understood in a particular way:

Yet even a cursory glance at a drip Pollock shows that *on a purely operational level* this was not entirely true despite the remarkable virtuosity he developed in his technique. There are numerous small spots and puddlings which were manifestly not one hundred percent controlled *as they happened*. But they are accidental only then; in the final work they have been transmuted into esthetic decision.[11]

In the same way, our use of the concepts "doodle" or "random pattern" to describe Pollock's initial application must be

As Rubin has shown, the use of poured paint is precedented in the works of Picabia, Miró, Masson, Onslow Ford, and Paalen, all of which Pollock may have known.[7] Pollock's direct exposure to experimental uses of the technique came not later than 1936, when it was one of various procedures being explored in Siquerio's workshop. With Motherwell, Pollock saw Ernst's rather mechanical poured pictures in 1942 and may have known Hans Hofmann's 1943-1944 pictures which used poured lines in a more painterly manner. Pollock's own works using dripped paint began in 1943 or 1944. But in all of these works—including Pollock's, until 1947—the use of poured paint is only one of several techniques employed to make the picture.

The exemplary use of poured paint in surrealist pictures is to be found in the work of Masson, where the paint was applied "automatically," or like a doodle. This doodle was then changed into recognizable images, often suggested by the abstract, random patterns. In Pollock's 1943-1945 work the opposite often took place: the poured lines are on top and function with previously established patterns or areas (Hofmann's do as well). In the later *Moon Vessel* of 1945 (collection of Lydia Winston Malbin, New York), where the lines are more independent, they are still seen in the context of other kinds of application (and with figuration).

Pollock's use of the pouring technique in later paintings—especially the 1950 pictures—differs from previous examples

The 1950 works were not preplanned and then executed, but they are more consistently directed than the preceding works. And it is important to realize that this change in the 1950 works developed out of his most complete final command of the drip technique itself.

CLASSIC PAINTINGS

If the 1950 works differ from the previous poured paintings in terms of their manner of initiation and completion, they are connected to them in sharing certain characteristics of style. This is to be expected, given the nature of the evolution of Pollock's art. As Lawrence Alloway has emphasized:

The longer one looks at the succession of periods the more one realises that Pollock's changes were not like Masson's (as one or two critics rashly said as exhibitions of both artists coincided). Masson, in each new period, knows no more than he did in the last one; each phase is just another shot in the arm to keep his art going. Pollock, on the contrary, in his changes, would do what he had not yet done but without losing the substantial knowledge of where he had been.[12]

No work is more revealing of this relationship than *Lavender Mist* (fig. 4). Of the paintings from 1950, *Lavender Mist* is the most complex. Its passages and skeins of paint far outnumber those of any previous or subsequent picture. Just the sheer balancing of these disparate elements would be remarkable in any work, but their fusion into the delicate and unified surface of *Lavender Mist* is virtually incredible.

Lavender Mist is also a unique work in Pollock's oeuvre because it relates directly to a previous painting, namely *Number 1, 1948* (fig. 5). It does so in several ways, including scale, pattern, touch, detailing, and finally effect. At 5 2/3 × 8 2/3 feet, *Number 1, 1948* was the largest poured painting Pollock had made until painting *Lavender Mist* in the late spring or early summer of 1950. These are the only two pictures which attained his goal of "large pictures which will function between the easel and the mural."[13] *Number 1, 1948* and *Lavender Mist* also correspond in terms of a general compositional pattern—or, more precisely, within the composition of *Lavender Mist* we find aspects of layout which are, among Pollock's poured pictures, precedented only in *Number 1, 1948*. Within its horizontal field *Number 1, 1948* is organized by the black lines into left and right sections that slightly overlap in the center. Far from being a run-on surface, the painted web in *Number 1, 1948* avoids the edge of the canvas on all four sides, and indeed turns inward in a V-like depression along the center of each side, forming a butterflylike image. This arrangement is challenged, but not overcome, by the subsequent layers of paint.

Turning to *Lavender Mist*, it seems at first too unified or allover a surface to relate to the more palpable field of *Number 1, 1948*. And indeed it is, given the number of layers and multiple directions of the linear elements. But part of *Lavender Mist*'s layout involves two ovals, shapes tilted left and right and tangent in the center. This creates a deep V-like depression in the center, which is filled with other painted elements, including portions of the initial black layer. Within the context of a similar physical size, the layout of each work might require

Figure 3. Jackson Pollock standing outside of his studio in summer, 1950. *Lavender Mist* is to the right, next to the door. [Photo: Harvey Weber]

qualified, for in most cases it involved a linear weblike composition which bears at least an indirect resemblance to the finished painting. Indeed, as Pollock's poured pictures developed, this initial layer or pattern seems increasingly related to the final composition.

Pollock's statement of 1948 and Rubin's analysis of Pollock's procedures (written to apply to all of the poured pictures) clearly fit the 1947-1949 paintings. But the classic works of 1950 seem distinct on one key point: the degree of automatism present in their beginning pattern. It is proposed here that rather than being divided, as in the 1947-1949 works (and even here the division is not sharp), into a "doodle" and then corrections—or a time of "not aware of what I'm doing," a "get acquainted period," followed by a period of completing the work—the execution of many of the 1950 works was continual, without a change either in the general touch or the direction of the final composition. Pollock here was aware of what he was doing—in that he used what we identify as his finishing control—from the beginning of the work. The automatism of his method was thus narrowed more to those accidental elements which resulted from his technique. Of course Pollock still faced the choices and responses that occurred within the development of the picture, and thus the painting still evolved "automatically." But even this was in a much more limited fashion, especially given how much more controlled and understood Pollock's technique had become since 1947.

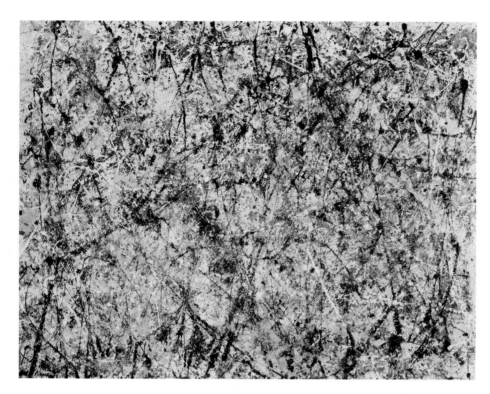

Figure 4. Jackson Pollock. *Number 1, 1950 (Lavender Mist)*, 1950. Oil, enamel, and aluminum paint on canvas, 221.0 × 299.7 cm (87 × 118 in). National Gallery of Art, Washington, Ailsa Mellon Bruce Fund, 1976. Cat. no. 1, pl. 17

other similarities because of the demands established by the size, especially given Pollock's manner of working; all works of this size—in theory—might have to look like this. This proposal—if correct—would also account for their related uses of long looping passages of paint which would have been needed to cover such an enormous surface. And while *Lavender Mist* and *Number 1, 1948* have, as detailing elements, broader areas of color—not lines—they share this feature with a number of other poured pictures.

Thus we might account for the similarities between the two works as sheer coincidence, or as practical coincidence produced by the artist working at a larger scale. However, both *Number 1, 1948* and *Lavender Mist* share a curious feature of detailing, Pollock's use of handprints. Of all of Pollock's major works, these are the only two paintings which incorporate the artist's handprints, made by Pollock slapping or pressing his left hand against the canvas surface. Even more significantly, the prints occur in each picture in the same general location, along the left vertical edge of the canvas and in the upper right horizontal edge. In both works they serve as secondary elements in the transition between the painted web and the more spare reserve of canvas which surrounds it.

The presence of these relationships in size, detailing, and composition makes plausible the idea that in painting his second large poured painting, *Lavender Mist,* Pollock would have taken into account his first large poured painting, *Number 1, 1948*—not in the sense of replication, but in a more general fashion, as a mark of what he had previously achieved at this scale. Furthermore, *Number 1, 1948* would have been on Pollock's mind in another sense during the spring and summer of 1950, as it was the major work of three by Pollock included in the Venice XXV Biennale. Alfred Barr, in the *Art News* issue of summer 1950 singled out *Number 1, 1948* as "his master-

piece."[14] Finally, and perhaps more importantly, *Number 1, 1948* was acquired by the Museum of Modern Art on January 27, 1950.

Even if the earlier *Number 1, 1948* served as a general concept for *Lavender Mist,* the 1950 work is drastically different in the end. While certain passages in *Lavender Mist* have the broad, spreading qualities of other poured works, many of the lines can be characterized as extremely thin and exquisite. The delicacy of this tracery is compounded by the sheer number of crisscrossings enrolled within the allover fabric of paint. The intersecting and fragmenting of the skeins of paint produces a molecularization of the surface as we see in the majority of densely poured works. But in *Lavender Mist* this fragmenting creates a pulverization of the allover fabric. This powdery quality is further complemented by the effusive tone of the work, created out of pinks, blues, and silver aluminum paint and the interspersion of off-white pigment, which echoes the color of the canvas ground and introduces a sense of transparency. Of all of Pollock's works, *Lavender Mist* is the most delicate in terms of touch and coloration.

These characteristics set it clearly apart from the thicker and more blunt passages of *Number 1, 1948*. But the relationship which does exist between the two suggests that Pollock did consider the earlier picture when he began *Lavender Mist.* The realization of the 1950 work's complex layering results in part from Pollock's having a sort of preconceived characterization, however much the initial layer and subsequent applications of paint differ drastically in terms of number, location, or touch. Thus, in painting *Lavender Mist* Pollock did not start with a random doodle, which was then painted into a picture, but rather began with at least a general conception—the precedent, *Number 1, 1948*—which he could begin and complete using a greater and more constant degree of refined control and touch.

Figure 5. Jackson Pollock. *Number 1, 1948*, 1948. Oil on canvas, 172.8 × 264.2 cm (68 × 104 in). The Museum of Modern Art, New York. Not in exhibition

If this proposes a new basis for the 1950 pictures, a use of previous works as a kind of underpattern, that is not the case. Indeed the correspondences between these two large paintings—as limited as they are—are apparently unique to these two. Nonetheless, it does propose a way of accounting for the incredibly even control which *Lavender Mist* evidences. And it is this issue of continuous control which is crucial in the 1950 works.

VERTICAL STRUCTURES

The numerical titles which Pollock assigned to his 1950 works do not necessarily correspond to their order of execution. Thus there is no secure reason to assume that *Number 2, 1950* (fig. 6) followed *Number 1, 1950* or *Lavender Mist*. The exact sequence may well have been the reverse, or several paintings could have been made between the creation of the two. However, some features of *Number 2, 1950*—its more delicate drawing and the silver and pink of its palette—do suggest that it dates very near *Lavender Mist*. While it is a considerably smaller work in terms of total surface area, its towering verticality also invites comparison with the domineering scale of *Lavender Mist*.

There are no elements in *Number 2, 1950*—such as the handprints or butterfly pattern of *Lavender Mist*—to cause us to link it directly with any previous work. However, by virtue of its vertical format and composition it is automatically a part of a subset of allover pictures.

The majority of Pollock's important poured paintings are in a horizontal format which stays within what we might call traditional proportions (not actual size) of the easel picture, though other horizontal works are quite extended into a scroll-like composition. And there are several decidedly vertical compositions, for example *Cathedral* (fig. 7; 1947) and *Full Fathom Five* (Museum of Modern Art, New York). Of these vertical works, *Number 2, 1950* is closer in style and composition to *Cathedral* than any of the others. The initial layer of black in each is composed of more tightly closed curving

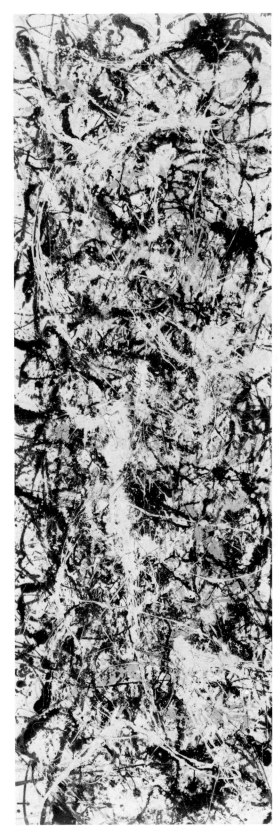

Figure 6. Jackson Pollock. *Number 2, 1950*, 1950. Oil, lacquer, silver paint on canvas, 287.0 x 91.4 cm (113 x 36 in). Fogg Art Museum, Harvard University, Cambridge, Mass.; in part given and in part lent by Reginald and Charlotte Isaacs and family and friends, and in part purchased from the Contemporary Art Fund Cat. no. 2, pl. 18

Figure 7. Jackson Pollock. *Cathedral*, 1947. Enamel and aluminum paint on canvas, 181.6 × 99.0 cm (71½ × 35⅟₁₆ in). Dallas Museum of Fine Arts, Gift of Mr. and Mrs. Bernard J. Reis, New York. Not in exhibition

Figure 8. Claude Monet. *Rouen Cathedral, West Façade,* 1894. Oil on canvas, 100.4 × 66.0 cm (39½ × 26 in). National Gallery of Art, Washington, Chester Dale Collection, 1962. Not in exhibition

shapes. In both works there is a pattern of ovals, stacked one above the other along each of the outer vertical sides of the picture, forming a pictorial structure. The use of these stacked ovals occurs to a lesser extent in other vertical compositions—and not at all in some—as well as being suggested in a few horizontal works. It is nowhere as consistent nor as obvious as it is in *Cathedral* and *Number 2, 1950.*

By its very title, *Cathedral* suggests comparison with the *Rouen Cathedral* paintings of Monet (fig. 8). Leaving aside those formal correspondences—of touch, color distribution, and so forth—which exist in general between most of Pollock's poured work and impressionism as a whole, there are aspects of compositional structures which are shared, in particular, by *Cathedral* and Monet's series. Of primary importance is Pollock's use of long straight vertical elements running through the field, to the inside of the ovals, not unlike the vertical lines created in Monet's towers and the cathedral's façade. Pollock's use of "patches" of aluminum paint within the structure of his more fragmentary web recalls Monet's distribution of the purple and blue areas of shading in the architecture of the façade. Rubin has observed that Mondrian made a connection between cubist painting and Gothic architecture:

[The] upward narrowing and dematerialization [of cubist structure] has always seemed to me something akin to Gothic architecture despite the fact that Picasso and Braque discovered these scaffoldings primarily in motifs of figures and still-life objects (which only confirms the remarkable autonomy of Cubist structure). I am convinced, however, that Mondrian perceived this analogy to the Gothic and that it is reflected in his frequent use of cathedral façades as motifs precisely at the moment he was recapitulating this phase of Analytic Cubism (that is, in 1912).[15]

Pollock's *Cathedral* suggests strongly that he was aware of similar analogies—to the *Rouen Cathedral,* cubism, and Mondrian's façades—in his own work at this crucial point of development. Indeed *Cathedral* may be based on Monet's work, or the artist may have simply named the work in reference to the Monet because he recognized—*post facto*—the correspondences to the painterly architecture.

Number 2, 1950, by virtue of its more emphatic vertical shape, does not suggest any direct connection to Monet's Rouen paintings. But beyond sharing those aspects of detail which are found in the vertical *Cathedral,* it also shares the latter's sense of being a vertical structure. As Harry Rand has written:

In *Number 2, 1950,* color is more precisely contrived than simply exuberant or articulate of mood, and this precision of piquant consonances lends to the vertical architecture a severe but distinct personality. Viewed as a possible horizontal painting, the very architecture which so clearly excites under the tension of the vertical format, with its allusive implications of the stress of erecting a mass in air, devolves into a massive repose. The decision for the vertical is amply justified.[16]

The traditional opinion regarding Pollock's "decision for the vertical" is that the 1950 works were painted without reference to what was top, side, or bottom, and that decisions about orientation were made after the works were completed. But the stacked ovals in *Cathedral* would "roll" in a horizontal work, suggesting that it was conceived as a vertical painting. In a similar manner the vertical passages create a center section to the work that broadens as it recedes. If turned horizontally, *Cathedral* would simply fail to be an allover picture, due to the introduction of a vector to one side of the work.

In *Number 2, 1950* similar features of detail and of the general buoyancy of the composition suggest that if it is not based on *Cathedral,* it employs parallel compositional factors. As these factors are part of the initial black layer of *Number 2, 1950,* moreover, it is possible that Pollock's decision for verticality was made at the time of painting the black layer—whether drawn from *Cathedral* or not.

It is tempting to suggest that the larger patches of aluminum paint on the web of *Number 2, 1950* are directly related to those of the 1947 work. But in the later work these areas are applied in broad strokes and have a clear identity as commas and hooks, which sets them apart from the patches in the earlier work. What they do relate to is a touch Pollock used later in 1950 in such works as *Autumn Rhythm* or *Number 27, 1950.* This would propose that though Pollock finished *Number 2, 1950* near the time of *Lavender Mist* in late spring or early summer, he added the broader strokes later, in September or October. Pollock had added touches or reworked pictures before: *Out of the Web* (Staatsgalerie, Stuttgart), for example, was stretched as a completed work before Pollock decided to cut out the broader flat shapes.[17] *Number 2, 1950* may have been altered later in the year to accord with subsequent developments in Pollock's battery of strokes; that in the 1950 exhibition (November 28-December 16, Betty Parsons Gallery, New York) it was hung side by side with *Number*

27, 1950, with which it shares a great many features, would suggest this idea.

THREE PAINTINGS

In the summer of 1950 Pollock painted three large and extraordinary paintings—*Number 30* or *One; Number 31* or *Autumn Rhythm;* and *Number 32, 1950.* By coincidence, all three of these works were photographed during part of the process of their being painted, by Rudolph Burckhardt in a session in July or August,[18] and by Hans Namuth in sessions from September to late October. These photographic records provide important clues to understanding Pollock's art during this phase of his "classical" period, and especially to understanding the relationship of these three works to one another.

While Namuth's photographs are well known—more so than Burckhardt's—they have received little scrutiny as to what they can tell us about the sequences of the works and the situation in which each was painted. Those which Namuth took in his initial session (fig. 14) show Pollock painting *One* placed on the studio floor with *Number 32* already completed and hung at one end of the studio. Namuth's later photographs (fig. 17) show Pollock painting *Autumn Rhythm,* the canvas spread on the floor. Here *One* and *Number 32* are both completed; significantly they are hung at opposite ends of the studio (see diag. A). This photographic sequence led B. H. Friedman to conclude that *Number 32, 1950* preceded *Number 30* [*One*] and *Number 31* [*Autumn Rhythm*].[19] However, what they may actually reveal is the finishing of *One,* not its beginning. Namuth recalls:

The day before I was to come to his studio (Summer 1950) he had promised that he would start a new painting for me and perhaps finish it while I was still there. When I arrived, however, he shrugged his shoulders and told me it was too late, the painting was done; we could not take any pictures.

I was disappointed; I also was aware of his reluctance to have anyone present while he was at work. Hesitantly, I suggested going into his studio.

An enormous painting covered almost the entire surface of the floor. Dripping wet paint, white, black, maroon; the painting was finished.

There was complete silence. (He never communicated much, verbally.) I looked aimlessly through the ground glass of my Rollei. He examined the painting. Suddenly (he must have decided then that there was more work to be done) he took hold of a paint can and a brush and began to re-do the entire painting, his movements, slow at first, gradually becoming faster and almost dancelike. . . .[20]

Pollock often painted one or two layers and then stopped, so he could study the picture, at whatever stage it was in, for a significant period of time. It is important to note that this was with the work in an upright and vertical position. Pollock would then return it to the prone position on the floor and add any additional layers of paint. The procedure of stopping and studying might be repeated many times during the making of a work. His wife, Lee Krasner Pollock, recently recalled of these study periods:

How well I remember when Pollock would want to study one of those big canvases up on the wall. He'd attach the top edge to a long piece of 2 × 4, and together we'd lift it up—do you know how much one of

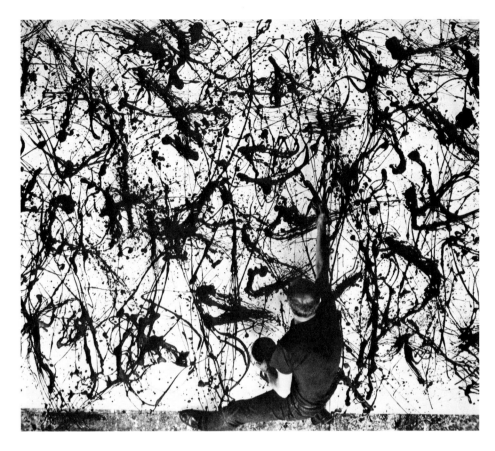

Figure 9. Jackson Pollock painting *Number 32,*
1950 in summer, 1950.
[Photo: Rudolph Burckhardt]

Figure 10. Jackson Pollock painting *Number 32,*
1950 in summer, 1950.
[Photo: Rudolph Burckhardt]

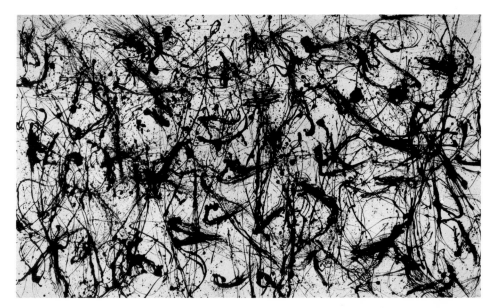

Figure 11. Jackson Pollock. *Number 32, 1950,* 1950. Oil on canvas, 269.2 × 457.2 cm (106 × 180 in). Kunstsammlung Nordrhein-Westfalen, Düsseldorf. Cat. no. 3

those big pictures with all that paint weighed? We'd take it to the wall, and lift it up ladders, and just nail the ends of the 2 × 4—which stuck out—into the studio wall.[21]

Knowing the enormous effort involved in moving big paintings to an upright position, we can sense how important the study of their progressive states was to Pollock. However, Burckhardt recalls that *Number 32, 1950* was painted in one session. And Namuth's account of *One*—that it was begun only the day before and was still wet when Pollock finished it—notes two changes in procedure: Pollock's time period was considerably shorter—one day for the first "finish"—and no trial hanging. If *One* was wet, Pollock could not have studied it upright, as the paint would have run. This suggests there was a more preconceived idea of the work, at least throughout its initial finished state, which Pollock then altered in the second session. But it is still possible that only some of the colors were wet and other layers—the initial black pattern for example—had been finished earlier. Examination of *One* indicates few of the puddles which often resulted when Pollock painted into wet paint.

Namuth's photographs taken at later sessions reveal that *Autumn Rhythm* was begun after the finish of *Number 32* and *One*. And, that *Autumn Rhythm* was painted on the floor of the studio with *Number 32* and *One* hung at opposite ends of the room (diag. A). The first pictures indicate that Pollock began by unrolling the bare canvas across the studio floor, starting at the *Number 32* end of the room (fig. 17). But after crossing the studio floor—to the *One* end of the room (fig. 20), the canvas roll was not cut off, but merely left at the end of the picture (the double line in the diagram indicates this).

Namuth's photographs taken at the end of Pollock's painting *Autumn Rhythm* indicate that the canvas sheet of the painting had still not been cut from the roll. Because of the difficulty of lifting an attached roll of canvas, this indicates that like the previous two works, *One* and *Number 32, Autumn Rhythm* was probably never raised to a vertical position for study. While Lee Krasner Pollock does not recall whether or

not *Autumn Rhythm* in particular was ever lifted off the studio floor, she does note that to do so and not cover the other works would have required covering up the studio window, and she does not recall—nor believe—Pollock would have allowed that to happen.[22] This further supports our thesis that the 1950 works in general—and here the three large paintings in particular—were more thoroughly understood by the artist from beginning to completion.

Harvey Weber's photograph of another part of the painting barn from this same period (fig. 3) indicates that the fourth of the large canvases, *Lavender Mist,* was also present, although not hung in the studio proper, but placed upright in the smaller, adjacent lean-to, which was really a sort of foyer to the studio itself. We can see this arrangement in diagram A, which indicates the studio/barn at the time *Autumn Rhythm* was painted.

BLACK PATTERNS

Given the physical proximity of these works to one another in the studio and that the larger three—*One, Autumn Rhythm* and *Number 32*—were painted during the late summer and early fall, we might have reason to expect some relationships among them. However, each picture is decidedly different from the others. *Number 32*'s black and white palette and spare markings set it apart from the cool tones and peppered surface of *One;* in turn, both are different from the counterpointed composition and the russet colors and dappled areas of *Autumn Rhythm.* The works are alike only in each having black as the initial base or, in the case of *Number 32,* as the only layer. This fact is not significant in and of itself: many of Pollock's poured works began with a black pattern. What is important about the black pattern, as distinct from its use in other Pollock works, is that in these three it shares certain characteristics of style and application.

One stands apart from the other two in the more curvilinear character of its black pattern, and the weaving nature of its first layer is carried on in the subsequent applications of colors, turns. In both, the stroke itself is broader than the tracery of *One,* and this is made more graphic by the greater presence of unpainted surface.

Significantly, however, *One* was considered finished by Pollock when it had less paint on the surface, as Namuth has recalled. Thus at one point *One* must have had a more open character, like that subsequently used in *Autumn Rhythm,* even if the paint was more even in dosage and applied in a more consistently curvilinear style. Furthermore, Namuth's account of the initial state of *One* mentions only three colors—black, white, and maroon—the latter a brownish tone. These are the dominant shades of *Autumn Rhythm;* and the colors which were added to *One* later in the second stage—blue, green-gray, and more black, brown, and white—are those which make it different from *Autumn Rhythm* in both dosage and color. Or, to put it another way, *Autumn Rhythm* bears a resemblance—on this issue—to the earlier state of *One.*

These two paintings are also related in that they are almost identical in size, *Autumn Rhythm* at 8 5/6 × 17 2/3 feet and *One* at 8 5/6 × 17 5/12 feet, a small difference at this scale. However, we should note that given Pollock's need to walk around the painting—he "worked from all sides"—this size (approximately 9 × 17½ feet) was the maximum surface that he could have painted in his studio. In this sense, *Autumn Rhythm* and *One* clearly represented the largest pictures he could have undertaken in his studio. *Number 32,* probably painted first, comes close in size at 8 5/6 × 15 feet.

Thus despite their very real differences, a relationship does exist between these three works: certain aspects of the black pattern for all three, elements of stroke between *Number 32* and *Autumn Rhythm,* and palette and colored field between *One*'s initial state and *Autumn Rhythm.* If recollections of *Number 1, 1948* played a role in the creation of *Lavender Mist,* then a comparable situation may have been present here. The fact of the placement and sequence of these works—*Number 32* hanging while *One* was painted, and both of them up while *Autumn Rhythm* was made—suggest the artist had a point of departure for the work, especially in *Autumn Rhythm (Number 32,* as the initiator of the set, is independent). As argued earlier with *Lavender Mist,* this suggests a revised concept of Pollock's procedures in 1950 and accounts for his exercise of continuous control in his paintings of that year.

Pollock himself gave some verbal evidence to this theory in a radio interview taped at the exact time he was painting these large works. He was asked by William Wright,

Then, you don't actually have a preconceived image of a canvas in your mind?
[Pollock replied] Well, not exactly—no—because it hasn't been created, you see. Something new—it's quite different from working, say, from a still life where you set up objects and work directly from them. I do have a general notion of what I'm about and what the results will be.[23]

It is the "not exactly" which causes pause, along with Pollock's statement—in reference to beginning the work—"I do have a general notion of what I'm about—and what the results will be." When this is contrasted to the earlier, 1947-1948 comments ("When I am *in* my painting, I'm not aware of what I'm

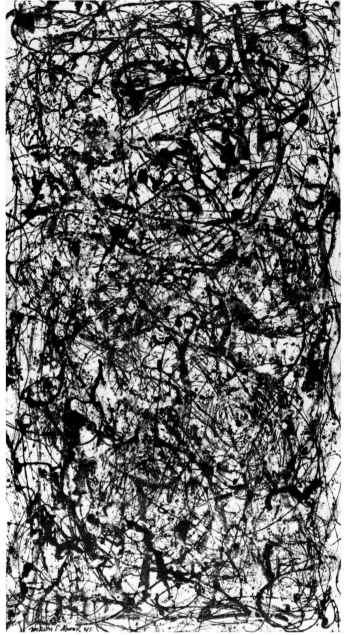

Figure 12. Jackson Pollock. *Number 26A, 1948: Black and White,* 1948. Duco on canvas, 208.0 × 121.7 cm (81⅞ × 47⅞ in). Collection, Lee Krasner Pollock, New York [photo: Otto Nelson]. Not in exhibition

which twist in and out of the black pattern. However, all of *One*'s colors save two—both green-grays—are shared with *Autumn Rhythm.* But the dosage of colors in *One* is fairly uniform in both placement and amount, whereas *Autumn Rhythm* is not so balanced and the brown tone and the black pattern dominate graphically and tonally.

The more densely painted surface of *One* is a pictorial characteristic which relates it, along with its curvilinear nature, more to works of 1947-1949, than to those of 1950. *Autumn Rhythm,* by contrast, is more open, with distinct areas of white ground showing through the web, and is thus closer to *Number 32.* And in the latter two, the pattern is composed of passages which are less curvilinear, given more to hooks and *V*-shaped doing. It is only after a sort of 'get acquainted' period that I see what I have been about"), it becomes clear a change has taken place.[24] The "general notion" can coincide with our understanding of *Lavender Mist*'s relationship to *Number 1, 1948*, or the interrelationship among the larger works for the late summer and fall. Pollock did "not exactly" have a preconceived image in his mind, but in beginning *Lavender Mist, One*, and *Autumn Rhythm* on premises established by previous works, he "had a general notion . . . of what the results would be." This is not to say—as Pollock did not—that the works were preconceived: they still required his extraordinary exercise of control and judgment, made in tandem and sequentially in the process; successes or failures still depended upon Pollock's contact with the developing picture. Thus the idea that a black pattern was shared (generally) by all three works and that the later two works are variations upon a matrix means a shift from the previous notion about more automatic procedures.

Pollock did few drawings during the period of the poured pictures, and these are only generally related to the larger paintings. In this regard, it is significant that these drawings give strong evidence of the artist's new desire for a shared starting point among several works. Bernice Rose writes of these sheets:

In 1951 Pollock made several "pairs" of drawings by placing one sheet of absorbent rice paper over another so that the poured ink from the top sheet would soak through to produce a ghost image on the second sheet, deliberately inducing a new kind of controlled accident—perhaps fascinated with the possibility of another chance at the same work. He then reworked the ghost image with additions of line and color (or . . . with . . . white gouache).[25]

Any possible connection to the large works has been ignored because these drawings have usually been assigned to 1951 on the basis of an inscription on an untitled work in the collection of Mr. and Mrs. J. O. Lambert. It reads: "For Clem 1951 / Jan 16 / Jackson / Pollock." But this date, January 16, 1951, most likely does not refer to the date of execution of the sheet, but rather to the time of its being given to Clement Greenberg for his birthday, which is January 16. Even if the drawings were done on Greenberg's birthday, the date provides a *terminus ad quem* for the sheet and separates it from Pollock's black and white pictures which followed later in the year.

A *terminus post quem* can also be established for the work on the basis of its being executed on rice paper. Tony Smith recalls giving Pollock a booklet or pad of rice paper, in a long scroll-like format on September 26, 1950. Pollock liked the paper and visited Chinatown "about a week later" and purchased larger pads of rice paper and began making ink drawings.[26] Thus the "paired" drawings could date as early as October 7, 1950, and some were certainly made before the following January 16. If we date the "pair" drawings to October 1950—as is quite feasible—then they shed further light on the "pairing" of *Number 32, One*, and *Autumn Rhythm*—especially the latter two which were painted at this time. The fact that these drawings begin with a black pattern and were then worked in both colors and white—which corresponds to Pollock's manner of making *Number 32, One*, and *Autumn Rhythm*—is significant.

Figure 13. Jackson and Lee Krasner Pollock walking on flat marshland behind the studio in Springs, Long Island, 1949. [Photo: Martha Holmes, Life Magazine © 1949 Time Inc.]

If this is the case—that *Lavender Mist* began as a recollection of *Number 1, 1948*, that even *Number 2, 1950* does consider *Cathedral*, and that *Number 32, One*, and *Autumn Rhythm* are variations on a general idea (but not a schema) of a black pattern—it sheds new light on the black and white stained paintings of the following year. As Pollock wrote Alfonso Ossorio of these pictures, "I've had a period of drawing on canvas in black—with some of my early images coming thru,"[27] they are related to the artist's previous drawings of the early 1940s. This return has usually been explained in terms of a psychological need or a release from the pressure of the abstraction of the 1947-1950 paintings.[28] We can now propose an alternative theory: that the return in 1951 to earlier drawings was a more considered step in an established direction involving the artist's use of his previous work.

"ABSOLUTE ORIGINAL"

These interrelationships should not blind us to the independence of each of the larger paintings. When an interviewer commented on Pollock's 1950 work—"Well, actually every one of your paintings, your finished canvases, is an absolute original"—the artist replied, "Well—yes—they're all direct paintings. There is only one."[29] Among all of the poured paintings, *Number 32, 1950* is the work with the fewest connections to formal precedents. To be sure, it does join the others in being a poured painting, but Pollock's use of only black in such an open and dramatic composition is unparalleled. Pollock had done black and white pictures before, many of which date from 1948 (fig. 12); and while on the small side, they are among his most lyrical works of that period. *Number 32, 1950* does share

Figure 14. Jackson Pollock painting *One*. [Photo: Hans Namuth]

Lavender Mist, the issue is resolved by covering the surface almost completely with multiple crisscrossings which pulverize any dominant pattern or patterns and/or by using white paint to suggest transparency. But other solutions were pursued. In the 1948 black and white works (there are also a few using muted colors) Pollock melded the poured line into the surface by applying it directly into wet gesso, which allowed the paint to sink physically into the field. A similar effect is reintroduced in the 1950 works, especially *Number 32, 1950* and *Autumn Rhythm* (but also *Number 27* and *One* as well), because Pollock thinned the black paint and allowed it to soak into the unprimed cotton duck support. This identification of paint with surface—as *in* the surface—appears in its most emphasized form in the graphic display of *Number 32, 1950*.

ONE

In many ways *One* is the most curious of the four large works of 1950. It shares with *Autumn Rhythm* some features of the black pattern of *Number 32, 1950*, especially its openness against the surface; and both have a tendency to be divisible into sections. Yet *One*'s vocabulary is more linear and given to more closely curved passages, avoiding the bunchings and straighter, angular markings of the other two.

One is related to *Lavender Mist* in that both are compounds of multiple layers of paint crossing the surface. But the surface density is far greater in *Lavender Mist;* in this sense *One* stands midway between the first large picture, *Lavender Mist,* and the later *Autumn Rhythm.* But because of its curvilinear design, its "graspable" interweaving of tracery (as opposed to *Lavender Mist*'s powdery, not so palpable forms), and its even dosages of colors, *One* really has much more in common with the poured pictures of 1947 to 1949 than with contemporaneous works of 1950.[30]

Among the works from the earlier period, the relatively large *Number 1, 1949* (fig. 16) seems especially pertinent. While this work is far more dense in its application of layers, uses more colors—such as yellows and pinks—and has broader patches of paint, it does correspond to *One* in using a peculiar blue in detailing over the entire canvas, and in the generous use of white as one of the final layer colors. This tends not only to fragment the other colors but also to unify the surface with a less emphatic pattern. Thus the use of any other color tone would shift the coloration of the picture to that tone; i.e. a green layer on top would make a green-toned picture. White is a neutral shade and not only avoids coloration but also correlates to the white of the canvas ground.

Finally, the paint used in both *Number 1, 1949* and *One* must have been fairly thin, and the application more rapid, as both are replete with small dots of color—splatterings—given off by the pouring, though these dots are present in other works as well, *Autumn Rhythm,* for example, but in lesser numbers or prominence. Nonetheless these two works are distinct in being so "pointillist." The relationships between *One* and *Number 1, 1949* are more direct than coincidental. As Namuth's photographs reveal (figs. 17, 20), *Number 1, 1949* was out in the studio when *Autumn Rhythm* was being painted and presum-

two characteristics with the 1948 paintings: the balance between drawing and painting and an identity of the paint with the surface.

The 1948 works were made by pouring black Duco onto a surface of wet gesso. Because of their linearity and the reduction to simple black and white palette, these paintings have a quality more like that of a traditional drawing, and this flavor is carried over into the few larger black and white paintings of the same year, done using the same technique. *Number 32, 1950,* while also lacking subsequent layers of colors, does not read like a sketch but more like an extension or further complication of the underpattern or initial layer of automatic drawings.

Given its palette *Number 32, 1950* has often been linked to the black and white pictures of the following year. That it was not directly transitional to the subsequent figural and abstract works we know by studying the sequence of the works (see also the discussion of *Number 27, 1950* below). Nevertheless, in its dramatic layout of clusters of broad rhythms and stark directness on this scale, *Number 32* is more a part of them than it is of the polychrome works of 1950.

Number 32, 1950 also relates to the earlier and later black and white works on the question of surface facture and ground. From the beginning of making the poured works Pollock appears to have been concerned with the relationship between the paint web and the canvas support. In certain pictures, such as

Figure 15. Jackson Pollock. *Number 31, 1950 (One)*, 1950. Oil and enamel on canvas, 270.0 × 535.0 cm (105⅞ × 209½ in). The Museum of Modern Art, New York, Gift of Sidney Janis, 1968. Cat. no. 4, pl. 21

ably was present when *One* was made. Namuth's photographs of *One* being finished do not record that section of the studio where *Number 1, 1949* subsequently was. Thus *One* may join *Lavender Mist* in having a possible correspondence with a key earlier work that provides aspects of style to be enrolled in a larger new work.

WEIGHTED SKEINS

As with *Lavender Mist* we must caution that this view of Pollock's *One* does not propose that he copied or made another version of an extant picture. The classic 1950 paintings differ in many ways from the preceding poured pictures, and this is true of *One* as well, however much the artist's touch and patterning are recollective. One of the most crucial distinctions involves the skeins of paint in certain 1950 works, including *One* and *Autumn Rhythm,* where the overlayering gives a certain visual weight to the paint.

Pollock's poured pictures of 1947 through 1950 are usually characterized by the term *allover.* As Rubin observes of this term, it "combines remarkably delicate variations in texture, drawing, color, etc."

[Thus] it is crucial here not to be misled by the term "all-over." It is also important not to judge the pictures on the basis of reproductions, as certain of Pollock's critics have done. The term "all-over" is a *relative* one.[31]

And,

The poured web—quite to the contrary of being a "run-on" fabric— usually *stops short of the edge (or "frame") of the picture,* frequently by doubling back on itself. . . . This recession from the frame, [is] virtually standard from 1948 through 1950. . . .[32]

Rubin's definition is a general one, broad enough to be true of the 1947-1949 works and many of those from 1950 as well. But it does not fit certain paintings done in 1950. Both *One* and *Autumn Rhythm* (and *Number 27, 1950*) stand apart precisely because they do not follow this description; rather in each case there is an increase in the density of the interweaving across the entire bottom section of the work; conversely, the upper portions in each are much lighter. Both works—and especially *Autumn Rhythm*—have a sense of weight built up by the skeins

of paint, which is contrasted to the linear elements across the surface, which are, in turn, made more emphatic in the sparser zone across the top. Simple inversion of these two works reveals how much pictorial weight is present or how distinct they are from being allover in the sense of the preceding poured works. *Lavender Mist,* which in time is closer to the earlier allover works, seems to balance between an evenness and the suggestion of weight to one side, which, given its delicate qualities, is extremely slight.

This weight means that *One* and *Autumn Rhythm* have a top and a bottom edge which are evident from the design of the picture. We have seen—in Namuth's photographs—that Pollock's procedure was to work from all four sides of the canvas, and that the traditional view of the works in progress is that any edge could be the top, bottom, or lateral edge at any given moment in the evolution. And the allover characteristics of the 1947-1949 works generally bear this out. In theory the decision as to the orientation of the work was then made on the basis of what worked best, on straight aesthetic grounds. And this choice could be quite narrow. Lee Krasner Pollock recalls of the later 1951 works,

Sometimes he'd ask, "Should I cut it here? Should this be the bottom." He'd have long sessions of cutting and editing, some of which I was in on, but the final decisions were always his. Working around the canvas—in "the arena" as he called it—there really was no absolute top or bottom. And leaving space between paintings, there was no absolute "frame" the way there is working on a pre-stretched canvas. Those were difficult sessions. His signing the canvases was even worse. I'd think everything was settled—tops, bottoms, margins— and then he'd have last-minute thoughts and doubts. He hated signing. There's something so final about a signature. . . .[33]

But this is clearly not the case for *One* and *Autumn Rhythm.* Here only the black layer is fairly evenly distributed, at least in terms of vertical weight, as it is in *Number 32, 1950* (indeed, this supports formal connections to *Number 32, 1950* as a source for *One* and *Autumn Rhythm,* in light of the differences in style in their color layers); the other layers were applied in such a manner that they are denser at the bottom. This means Pollock knew at that point the orientation of the work. This observation can be supported by a study of the Namuth and Burckhardt photos, which show that the works' placement on

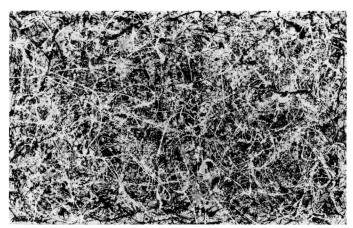

Figure 16. Jackson Pollock. *Number 1, 1949*, 1949. Duco and aluminum paint on canvas, 160.3 × 259.0 cm (63⅛ × 102⅛ in). Collection, Mrs. Taft Schreiber, Beverly Hills, Calif. Not in exhibition

the studio floor was consistently in the same alignment—the top edge always to the door side of the room. (We should note, as well, that a similar density is present in *Number 27, 1950* and *Number 29, 1950,* thus establishing certain alignments for the works at an early point.)

AUTUMN RHYTHM

Autumn Rhythm is an extraordinary example of what this new control could achieve. Pollock worked "contrapuntally," each application changing or reinforcing preceding marks. If, as has been suggested, *Autumn Rhythm* was painted with more conscious direction, drawn from the idea of the black pattern of *Number 32* and recollective of an earlier state of *One*, with a known sense of weighted design and thus orientation, Pollock still had to make the painting cohere in the face of numerous choices, some of them given simply by the accidental nature of his method.

While the black pattern of *Number 32* advised the pattern of *Autumn Rhythm,* it did not determine it. Unlike the more allover characteristics of *Number 32*'s design, the massing of crisscrossings in black pattern in *Autumn Rhythm* clearly divides into three side-by-side elements, creating a kind of triptych portioning to the work, most visible along the upper edge. This division is then challenged by other elements of the black pattern which tend toward the allover qualities of the previous works. The many thicker, straighter passages and hooks of *Number 32* are here made more emphatic as Pollock turned them into semigeometric intersections of black. It is this aspect which he then pulled out for the general touch of the brown tones, creating bronze "hinges," especially across the top. This created a kind of visual rhyming between the black pattern and the active bronze tone. As Rubin observes, making order

meant that within the diverse local accents, Pollock would have to *multiply analogies,* finding common denominators in the patterns. These analogies are developed not only on the level of the smaller units but the larger; in the angular rust-brown "joints" of *Autumn Rhythm* and as well as in the black and white "hooks" in *Mural on Indian Red Ground.*[34]

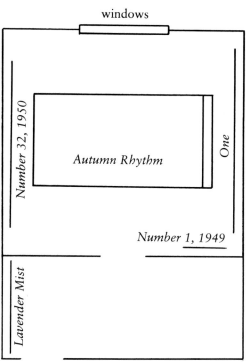

Diagram A. Represents Pollock's studio in the autumn of 1950 when he was painting *Autumn Rhythm*. *Number 32, 1950* is hanging to the left and *One* is hanging to the right, with *Autumn Rhythm* on the studio floor between them. *Lavender Mist* is hanging in the adjacent room.

All classic works involve to one degree or another a kind of visual rhythm. In the 1947 works it is generally a question of pairing similar vocabulary elements which occur in different areas, but earlier such pairing is often subdued by the more pressing task of establishing the allover field. When the pairing of elements does appear obvious, to the contrary, it often dominates the work (this is true as well of those pictures with shapes in them, such as *White Cockatoo*; collection of Lee Krasner Pollock, New York). Pollock seems to have first resolved the issue of balance, between the interspersion of elements and the maintenance of an allover surface, by extending the scale of the picture in the long friezelike compositions of 1949 (such as *Number 2, 1949*; fig. 22) and in certain works of 1950, including *Number 7, 1950* (collection of Joseph Slifka, New York). Here Pollock established a rhythm in broad strokes of paint in the underpatterns, which is then counterpointed by more delicate passages of varying colors in subsequent applications. The long horizontal format tends visually to stretch out, while the rhythmic stops and starts of the varying patterns brake against this movement, thus unifying the surface field.

Of the four large works from 1950 *Autumn Rhythm* is the only one to parallel fully this form of poetic composition, in the dialogue between the black pattern and the bronze and white layers. And unlike the earlier frieze compositions, *Autumn Rhythm*'s vertical weight, which allows the thinner tracery of paint to form a greater presence above, adds yet a third element to its visual poetry. *Autumn Rhythm*'s varying voices—light and dark, heavy and light, straight and curved—can be found in other works as well, but never so emphatically stated.

Figure 17. Jackson Pollock painting *Autumn Rhythm*. [Photo: Hans Namuth]

INTERLACED

A similar kind of visual rhythm can be seen in the more traditionally sized *Number 27, 1950* (fig. 23), which probably dates after *Autumn Rhythm*. But unlike *Autumn Rhythm,* with its open and airy surface, *Number 27* is densely painted and more complexly interlaced.

The palette of *Number 27* is quite brilliant, with sharp tones of yellow, black, white, pink, bronze, and aluminum. Interestingly, with the exception of the black—which is covered over a great deal—all of the other tones are closely valued toward the light end of the scale. Because of this evening out of values, the colors are more emphatic as colors, and their shapings or their graphic qualities—which our eye often reads in terms of value contrast—are of secondary importance. Furthermore, like the classic Pollocks such as *Lavender Mist* (which is also close valued), the colors in *Number 27* are applied in an evenly distributed fashion. This tends to even out both the shading and the color, as no one color shape can command any major area of the surface.

But the color application varies significantly. Aluminum and white, the most effusive tones, are put down using the broader sweeping strokes that appear in *Number 32* and *Autumn Rhythm.* The white, especially in some areas, is surrounded by splatters, or has long traces or "tails" attached to it. Pink appears throughout but is applied in straight lines and in one "hinge," which recalls the upper bronze passages of *Autumn Rhythm.* The yellow and bronze markings—and at times those of the other colors as well—are characterized by thinner curvilinear hooks and loops.

Curiously the close valuing of color in *Number 27* allows Pollock actually to treat the colors more as shapes—or as passages which enjoy a particular stylistic identity—because the work is not interlaced in the traditional fashion. No continuous (or seemingly so) web is in *Number 27.* Thus *Number 27* is curiously more figurative—given to individual shapes—and, simultaneously, as allover as previous pictures.

The question of figuration in *Number 27* was first addressed to Stephen C. Foster's analysis of it and Pollock's *Mural* of 1943-1944 (fig. 24), his first large paintings. Foster proposes

Mural as a kind of precedent. In *Number 27* . . . the quality of the figuration and its rhythm across the canvas are strikingly similar. Although the line is less discernible as a contour, and less differentiated from the field in terms of value, the figures again represent something different in nature from the field they occupy.[35]

From the context of his argument it seems clear that Foster's use of *figure* is parallel to the use of *shape* employed above to describe passages with particular characteristics of style. And he suggests that the figural qualities were employed by Pollock to introduce a more "graspable" message. He writes:

From 1947 to 1950, the absence of a figure was the rule, but by 1950 Pollock expressed a sense of insecurity about the communicability of his procedure in the drip paintings which finally accounted for his gradual return to more explicit figuration by 1950. . . . *Mural* and *Number 27* represent two peaks of Pollock's creativity. *Mural* represents the problem's initial statement and *Number 27* its nearly definitive solution.[36]

But Pollock took several steps in *Number 27* precisely to put its figuration—or passage shapings—on a secondary level and to place the work as clearly a part of allover compositions. The use of distinctive shapings for the passages indicates another manner of introducing a visible poetic scansion. Its differences from the other classic works suggests not disenchantment with them, but rather that Pollock continued throughout the allover

Figure 18. Jackson Pollock. *Autumn Rhythm*, 1950. Oil on canvas, 266.8 × 550.0 cm (105 × 207 in). The Metropolitan Museum of Art, New York, George A. Hearn Fund, 1957. Pl. 20

works of 1950 to press out into a new direction, no matter how fecund his painting had become. Furthermore, while the color passages read as shapes, they are still knitted together in an impressionist manner that is radically different from the silhouetting effects of figuration in Pollock's 1951-1952 compositions.

In this regard, the black pattern of *Number 27* is worthy of note. Unlike the initial layer of other allover works, in this picture black covers far more of the surface, reading (if one could remove the other subsequent layers of color) as if the white ground were holes or openings in a far more dense surface. In this regard it is closer to the black and white paintings of the following years, especially such densely painted horizontal works as *Number 14, 1951* (fig. 25). The comparison might be fortuitous were it not for the fact that the black layer of *Number 27* is soaked into the canvas in a manner like that used in the later works. It is this aspect—rather than the shaping of the color strokes—which ties *Number 27* to Pollock's next period.

MYTHS AND IMAGES

Pollock's art is surrounded by myths, about him as an artist and person, and about the pictures he made. Indeed a significant portion of the serious Pollock literature is devoted to discussion of the origins of these misunderstandings, what needs they served, Pollock's own role in generating them, and what is true within the mythology. Specific discussion of mythology itself—as opposed to simply corrections of the myths—begins with Hilton Kramer's article "Jackson Pollock and Nicolas de Stael: Two Painters and their Myths" in 1959, and is followed with discussions by Harold Rosenberg (February 1961), Greenberg (April 1961), Thomas Hess (January 1964), Rubin (February 1967), and, most recently, Brian O'Doherty (1973).[37]

Because of our inquiry—the subjects of the 1950 works— and in light of Foster's more complex discussion of "figuration" in *Number 27, 1950,* it is important to examine one of the most persistent myths in the literature—namely that the allover poured pictures have "hidden images" in them, that

there exists a clearly descriptive figuration somewhere within the allover works which Pollock presumably hid by painting over it with the dense skeins of paint. This reading has, in fact, been supported by a quote attributed to Pollock—in his 1956 conversation with Sheldon Rodman, Pollock is recorded as saying: "I don't care for [the term] 'abstract expressionism'... and it's certainly not 'nonobjective,' and not 'nonrepresentational' either. I'm very representational some of the time, and a little all of the time."[38] Critically, Sam Hunter was the first to indicate directly that "the labyrinthian coils of his 'drips' and whipped lines in the paintings of 1947-1950 seem to heave and bulge, as if some invisible beast, trapped within their depths, were seeking desperately to free itself."[39]

Writing in 1968, Rubin suggested of Pollock's "hidden images,"

Nevertheless, as Pollock relaxed his drip style in the black-and-white paintings of 1951, fragments of anatomies—some monstrous and deformed, others more literal—surfaced again, as if the fearful presences in his work of the early forties had remained as informing spirits beneath the fabric of the "all-over" pictures.[40]

But the most extended discussion of images being hidden within the allover web of paint has recently been published by Charles F. Stuckey. Based on an analysis of *Number 1, 1948,* and especially its handprints, Stuckey suggests that Pollock's works involved "secrets" or "some alien code," and that central to understanding this "code," is that Pollock's allover works have sides, a fact he finds announced in the use of handprints:

Do the handprints in *Number One* testify to pressure cast upon the surface from without (as they should, since Pollock made them in that way), or do they "represent" the palms of hands? Can we imagine them exerting pressure from within and being limited by the painting's surface from extending out into the space of the spectator? Are they the prints of left hands attempting to penetrate the canvas, or are they representations of right hands trying to escape it?[41]

This unusual notion of Pollock behind his picture trying to "get out," is taken a step farther by Stuckey, suggesting that Pollock drew inspiration from André Breton's quotation of Diderot's *Letter on the Blind* in 1942:

Pollock's most intense flirtation with Surrealist ideologies was during his association with the Art of this Century Gallery, from late 1942

142

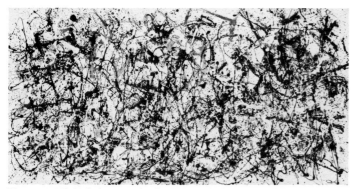

Figure 19. Filtered photograph of *Autumn Rhythm* stressing the pattern formed by the black paint

until 1947. Under the circumstances do the handprints in *Number One* signify the groping of the blind? The hand that hides the object from sight in the Diderot quotation could buttress Pollock's notion of images hidden . . . if we recall again Krasner's description of Pollock's work procedure.[42]

The Lee Krasner Pollock description, cited by Stuckey, is worth repeating here. She observed to B. H. Friedman in 1969:

I saw his paintings evolve. Many of them, many of the most abstract, began with more or less recognizable imagery—heads, parts of the body, fantastic creatures. Once I asked Jackson why he didn't stop the painting when a given image was exposed. He said, "I choose to veil the imagery." Well, that was that painting. With the black-and-whites he chose mostly to expose the imagery. I can't say why. I wonder if he could have.[43]

But Lee Krasner Pollock's discussion of Pollock's "veiling the imagery" is not, as Stuckey writes, "a description of Pollock's work procedure." It is, more precisely, a description of how *some* of the works *from 1951*, were made; it is not a description of Pollock's methods in painting the allover works of 1947 to 1950. Furthermore, Lee Krasner Pollock's description of Pollock "veiling" images in 1951 should cause no surprise, exactly because many works from that year are figural and in the initial layer; but it in no way suggests that Pollock veiled the images in the allover works of the preceding years.

More importantly, no one has been able to point to any evidence of a figure hidden behind the skeins of paint in any of the poured pictures and those few which do have figuration—the figure in *Cut Out*, 1949 (Martha Jackson Gallery, New York) or the suggested bird at the center of *White Cockatoo*, 1948 (collection of Lee Krasner Pollock), for example—are distinguished by precisely the opposite condition, namely that the figuration is emphatically present; it is certainly not hidden or "veiled."

Motherwell has written of this issue:

With convulsive violence, Pollock then splashed out, or struck out his human image. Then I think a time came when he abandoned the original human image, realizing that his negative striking-out was image enough.[44]

Pollock accomplished this by "inventing" his poured line and the interwoven pattern. Michael Fried writes of Pollock's works:

Thus an examination of *Number One*, or of any of Pollock's finest paintings of these years, reveals that his all-over line does not give rise to positive and negative areas: we are not made to feel that one part of the canvas demands to be read as figure, whether abstract or representational, against another part of the canvas read as ground. There is no inside or outside to Pollock's line or to the space through which it moves. . . . Pollock's line bounds and delimits nothing. . . .[45]

We can see this distinction clearly by comparing *Number 32, 1950* with one of the black and white paintings and drawings of the following year (fig. 25). *Number 32, 1950* employs small hooks and closures similar to those which are used in the later pictures, but in the classic poured painting Pollock also uses longer sweeps of thin tracery across the surface. This extends the rhythm and scansion to a much larger scale and then makes the hooks function like detailing—almost a secondary poetic patterning which remains subservient to the larger rhythm. In the later works the reverse is true; either the larger interconnected rhythm is ignored, or it is painted in such a way as to tie in the hooks and closures as part of the primary image. Comparative scansion of these later works reveals that the figural suggestions of Pollock's drawing have in fact been promoted so they read almost as a silhouette (as in Matisse's paper cutout figures)[46]—or as a flat image, since, given Pollock's vocabulary, all parts must read as equally flat to cohere integrally. The black and white figural works clearly indicate that Pollock could paint in a figural style and still stay within the broader range of his technical procedures—if he chose to do so. But there is no evidence in the 1947-1950 works that a similar kind of figure construction was present, which Pollock then chose in 1951 to "unveil."

Pollock's decision to paint figural compositions after the allover works has been ascribed to various reasons, as we have seen: as an "escape" from the pressure of allover abstraction which was foreign to his nature, as an indication of his decline into a state of psychological imbalance, combined with drinking, or as an "unveiling" of images he never did get rid of. An alternative reason for this figuration is suggested here, namely that Pollock considered them as ideas (if not direct studies) for windows of a church which Alfonso Ossorio and Tony Smith had proposed to him in the fall of 1950.[47] From this point of view Pollock did not reject or abandon his allover works so much as he must have seen the introduction of figuration as an integral requirement for the nature of this proposed commission. This interpretation also accounts for the presence of Crucifixion, Lamentation, and Descent images among the black and white paintings.[48] By implication, this also proposes that Pollock's concept of this project involved a narrower conception of thematic matter which he felt the broader range of his subject in the allover works could not directly accommodate. Thus Pollock's figural works of 1951 do not show him returning to figuration, so much as turning to it because it was required.

With this in mind, we can see, furthermore, that any analysis of Pollock's art which ascribes "hidden images" to his work proposes a different motivation to his earlier, classic, poured pictures, and a different kind of subject matter. Rather, the nature of Pollock's subject matter is complex and it cannot be explained in terms of its being hidden. If we desire to understand it, we must deal with what Pollock put there—and that is

Figure 20. Jackson Pollock painting *Autumn Rhythm*. [Photo: Hans Namuth]

his allover pictorial fabric. The allover pictures are *endemically abstract*—"concrete" Pollock called them in 1950; and our understanding of Pollock's motivation in painting them this way requires realizing that for Pollock his subjects were only possible in this manner. Or, as we proposed earlier, the subject is inextricably tied to technique.

THEMES, TRADITIONS, AND SOURCES

When Pollock's unconventional technique was joined to his biography it created the myths about him as a "cowboy twirling his lariat of color."[49] This legend was to cast Pollock as an inarticulate, "savagelike" painter. Even with correction of this image, a certain doubt probably still exists about the range and

depth of Pollock's knowledge—and uses—of the history of modern art. They were, to put it briefly, full and profound. Pollock was certainly no novice cowboy. As Phillip Pavia remarks, "How significant at this point to recall Jackson Pollock's intense schooling, spanning seven years, of almost constant attendance at the Art Students League."[50] Clement Greenberg, the critic who knew Pollock best, observes:

He was one of the people least likely not to know that art was impossible without the observance of norms and conventions. No one had ever worked harder than he to learn the norms and conventions, and to master the skills they implied.[51]

Moreover we know from various testimony that Pollock was constantly studying works of art, in journals and books, and attending a wide range of exhibitions.[52]

But, more importantly, this knowledge of modern art was put to work in his pictures. Pollock's "instincts for what was usable were faultless . . . ," writes Brian O'Doherty.[53] And as Rubin has thoroughly demonstrated in his study *Jackson Pollock and the Modern Tradition*, Pollock was capable of attending to a wide range of practical ideas and enrolling them in a complex and noncopyist manner. Central to understanding Pollock's art is comprehending his connections to the modern tradition joined with other observations about Pollock's works, technique, environment, and his other interests, especially with respect to the 1950 paintings. These elements, when fused, form the historical basis for his subject.

ANALYTICAL CUBISM AND STRUCTURE

Cubism was the dominant stylistic force in modern art until the mid-century. Especially in its synthetic guise, it provided an underpinning of pictorial design as crucial to modern art as perspective had been to Renaissance painting. If Pollock's career is "haunted" by the works of one artist, it is the Picasso of the synthetic and surrealist-cubist phase. From the late 1930s through his early major works of the 1940s, Pollock's visual language is drawn primarily from Picasso; and when he turned to religious imagery in 1951, Pollock again turned to Picasso.

But the poured paintings, and especially the classic works of 1950, do not show an interest in the synthetic style or its surrealist variant. Rather, as Clement Greenberg and William Rubin have shown, they correspond with the earlier analytical style of the movement, albeit in a most indirect way.

Pollock had turned his attention to analytical cubism earlier in his career. His oval painting *Interior with Figures,* c. 1937 (collection of Lee Krasner Pollock, New York), is based directly on works by Picasso and Braque of 1911-1912, and his later *Gothic* of 1944 (collection of Lee Krasner Pollock) seems to derive from Picasso's paintings of the *Three Women* series from 1908. But in these earlier works the relationship to Picasso's work is one of quotation or transfer and alteration: in the classic poured work the correspondence is far more amalgamated into the larger aims of the style.

Greenberg's analysis of the connection of the allover pictures to the higher analytical style was written in 1961:

By means of his interlaced trickles and spatters, Pollock created an oscillation between an emphatic surface—and an illusion of indeterminate but somehow definitely shallow depth that reminds me of what Picasso and Braque arrived at thirty-odd years before, with the facet-planes of their Analytical Cubism. I do not think it exaggerated to say that Pollock's 1946-50 manner really took up Analytical Cubism from the point at which Picasso and Braque had left it when, in their collages of 1912 and 1913, they drew back from the utter abstractness to which Analytical Cubism seemed headed. There is a curious logic in the fact that it was only at this same point in his own stylistic evolution that Pollock himself became consistently and utterly abstract.

The interstitial spots and areas left by Pollock's webs of paint answer Picasso's and Braque's original facet-planes, and create an analogously ambiguous illusion of shallow depth. This is played off, however, against a far more emphatic surface, and Pollock can open

Figure 21. Pablo Picasso. *Nude Woman,* 1910. Oil on canvas, 187.3 × 61.0 cm (73¾ × 24 in). National Gallery of Art, Washington, Ailsa Mellon Bruce Fund, 1972. Not in exhibition

145

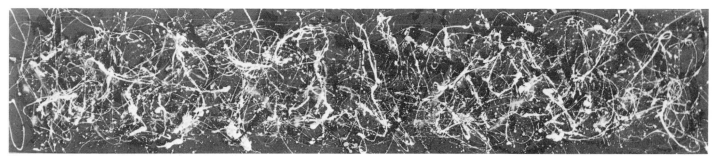

Figure 22. Jackson Pollock. *Number Two, 1949,* 1949. Oil, duco, and metallic paint on unsized canvas, 96.9 × 481.3 cm (38⅛ × 189½ in). Munson-Williams-Proctor Institute, Utica, N.Y. Not in exhibition

and close his webs with much greater freedom because they do not have to follow a model in nature.[54]

While Rubin cautioned,

I want to make clear at the outset that I do not accept Greenberg's contention that the drip pictures "have an almost completely Cubist basis." The reader will not be surprised that I consider Impressionism extremely important for him as well. (And Surrealism—though here more in the methodology and poetic spirit than in the plastic structure of the finished works.)

He goes on to note,

Nevertheless, Greenberg's thesis seems to me to contain a profound truth, however much he may overemphasize it and however little he has ever explicated or developed it. . . .[55]

Rubin's discussion of this issue in Pollock's work (as well as his discussions of other aspects) is too detailed to repeat here. And part of Rubin's analysis involves Mondrian's work of 1913-1914, which we will discuss below in another context. But two salient points of Rubin's discussion should be reviewed. The first is Rubin's thesis that Cézanne's simulation of a bas-relief in his pictures was transferred into the cubist grid pattern which allowed

the possibility of solid, monumental forms with the gravity and solidity of architecture but still readily assimilable to the two-dimensional plane of the canvas in a way that monumental Old Master painting rarely was. They somewhat weakened Cézanne's conception of composition, however, by so frequently "standing" their scaffoldings on the bottom of the frame. The Cézannesque conception was more sophisticated, and involved all sorts of distributions, such as compositions that "spill" downwards (and still paradoxically have the weight of architecture). Of course the Cubists had by 1911 dissolved the sculpturesque solidity inherited from Cézanne into a less tactile, more painterly composition (but this, too, was at least anticipated in the work of Cézanne's last years).[56]

From this Rubin writes,

Pollock showed that by accepting the challenge of wholly liberating his line, he could reincorporate the essence of Cubist architecture in a new way, *at the end of his process,* i.e., as the web filled out and the freely meandering lines became locked in an architecture of their own making.[57]

Rubin's other central observation, based on Greenberg's comments, concerns the nature of Pollock's allover pattern and its relationship to Mondrian's work:

In the crucial Mondrians of late 1913, like the Guggenheim Museum's *Composition No. 7,* the dissolution of the scaffolding near the edge is *consistently carried out on all four sides,* as it is in the classic

Pollock. Moreover, Mondrian's "floating" of his now more filigree structure in the *lateral as well as the shallow recessional space of the composition* gives it a lightness and less allusively architectural appearance more akin to Pollock than are the 1911-12 Picassos and Braques.[58]

As Rubin has shown, this fading on only the upper three sides—or conversely, the cubists' " 'standing' their scaffoldings on the bottom of the frame,"—was derived from the widening out of Cézanne's composition as it moved to the bottom of the picture. And it is this aspect which distinguishes the allover pattern of the 1947 to 1950 works (which was Rubin's subject).

But, as we have seen above, three of the classic works from 1950—*Lavender Mist, Autumn Rhythm,* and *One*—differ from the other works precisely along these lines. Like the other allover works, these paintings do fade along the outer edge on all four sides, "floating" the web in a manner which differs from the "standing" of the cubist grid. But within the allover field of *Autumn Rhythm* and *One,* and to a far lesser extent, *Lavendar Mist,* the density of the painted web does fade at the top and, however challenged by the allover rhythm of the picture, nevertheless provides a new sense of pictorial weight or gravity to the painted scaffolding.

This weight, new in Pollock's work, goes, as we have reviewed, back to Cézanne. The up and down of linear movements within Pollock's web is also like Cézanne. Pollock's correspondence with it may not be coincidence, especially given the similar palette of browns, blues, and white in *One* and *Autumn Rhythm.* Interestingly, Cézanne represents the transitional point between impressionism and cubism, the two stylistic currents which are fused in Pollock's art. Tony Smith suggests this perception was foremost in Pollock's mind:

I remember that Cliff Still and Barney [Newman] and Mark [Rothko] were interested in Monet and the Impressionists. We were too, but Jackson and I were always more interested in Cézanne. I think it's the structural aspect which interested us."[59]

Certainly the manner in which Pollock opens and closes the surface, by massing areas and then lessening the dosages and crisscrossings in the 1950 works, *Autumn Rhythm* in particular, is closer to the inflections of Cézanne's *passage* planes (and the cubist structure) than to the evenly dosed "mosaic" pattern of the impressionist works.

But this should not dissuade us from Pollock's direct relationship to high analytical cubism, which other writers have suggested it parallels along different lines. Robert Goodnough,

146

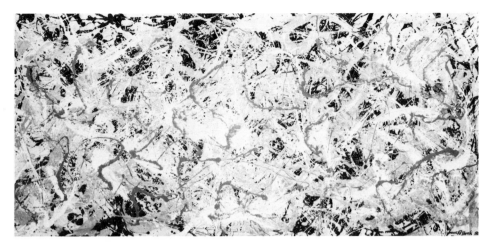

Figure 23. Jackson Pollock. *Number 27, 1950, 1950.* Oil on canvas, 124.5 × 269.2 cm (49 × 106 in). Whitney Museum of American Art, New York [photo: Geoffrey Clements]. Cat. no. 5, pl. 19

for example, speaks of a "glow of light" which emanates from *Autumn Rhythm,* a quality not dissimilar from that of the inner, spectral illumination of 1911 cubist works.

There are also details in the allover works which are analogous to the aspects of the cubist works of 1911-1912. For example, the handprints in *Lavender Mist* not only serve the same pictorial function as the letters in Picasso's *Ma Jolie*—two dimensional "printed" forms which identify the surface plane at the perimeter of the allover pattern—but they also introduce a parallel element of autobiographical imagery into the work.

Yet in the final analysis the subjects of Pollock's classical poured paintings are not (directly) those of the cubist assemblages drawn from landscape, still lifes, and portraits. While Pollock's works do correspond to cubism in a most formal way, the rhythms of *Number 2, 1950* or *One* do not recall, in any fashion, the fractured interpretations of guitars, faces, and so forth in Picasso's work. Pollock's rhythms are more internal in their requirements. Nevertheless, we should keep in mind that Pollock's organization and cubist composition—like that of the impressionist picture to which we now turn—are the products of a sophisticated, urban art.

IMPRESSIONISM AND NATURE

The literature on Pollock contains several references to Pollock's work and nature, as well as indirect connections to impressionism. While certain formal observations about his work could be seen as proposing aspects parallel to impressionist painting, not until 1967 and Rubin's discussion "Impressionism and the Classic Pollock" were the many connections spelled out with depth and precision. If Rubin's total analysis of Pollock's work remains the standard for discussion of the allover pictures, it is the impressionist text which is the most crucial.

Rubin's observations are divided into two portions: stylistic affinities and its expressive and social character. We will consider the former here.

Rubin's analysis is so tightly argued it can only be quoted at length.

No one has yet observed the importance of the Impressionist innovations for his earlier, classic all-over pictures. The insistent materiality of Pollock's surfaces which nevertheless end by scintillating in an essentially optic way (in this connection consider the implication of the title of the transitional *Shimmering Substance)*, the molecularization of shapes into myriad small sensations (by criss-crossing the variously colored lines), and the approximately even distribution of these pigment-sensations over the whole surface of the canvas are all features common to the most advanced Impressionist paintings.

Moreover, like the Impressionists, Pollock did his best to fragment and widely distribute the color sensations so that *they would not constitute a shape of color.* When dealing with large shapes of a single local color (the roof of the house in Renoir's *Duck Pond,* for example) the Impressionists atomized them by juxtaposing complementaries and picking up reflected lights from adjacent objects. (In this period and, indeed, in general, the Impressionists tended to avoid subjects and vistas that confronted them with dominant fields of a single color.) But the Impressionists—despite their considerable though little remarked editing back at the studio—were hampered by their primary commitment to the visual field before them. Pollock was able to bring some of their plastic ideas to a perfect and more natural fulfillment by rendering them wholly consistent *from within.*

The degree to which particular drip Pollocks relate to Impressionism—an art of color spots, not of line—is measured by the extent to which the density of the lines in them, hence the frequency of their intersection, *isolates their segments as spots,* and also by the extent to which their linearity is otherwise modified by patching and puddling (effects present in all classic Pollocks). *Number I* (1948), *One* and *Lavender Mist* (both 1950) strongly reflect these practices. *Autumn Rhythm* and *Number 32* (also both 1950), owing to their greater openness, remain more linear. The former three, along with such pictures as *Number 8, Number 27* and *Three* (all of 1950), show Pollock at his most "painterly" and thus at his closest to Impressionism.[60]

If, as Rubin suggests, the title of the transitional *Shimmering Substance* implies a connection with the optical vibrations of the impressionist facture, Pollock's later titles repeatedly suggest connections with natural phenomena. In his exhibition of the 1946 transitional works Pollock grouped the paintings under two "headings," entitled *Sounds in the Grass* and *Accabonac Creek,* the latter, as Ellen Johnson has pointed out, named for the actual creek on Pollock's property.[61] Of interest to our discussion are the following titles: from the *Sounds in the Grass* series, *Croaking Movement* (a "sound in the grass"), *Shimmering Substance* (cited by Rubin), and *Earth Worms;* and from the *Accabonac Creek* grouping, *Constellation.*

In 1948 or early 1949 Pollock began to discard the use of

Figure 24. Jackson Pollock standing before his *Mural*, 1943-1944, now in the collection of the Museum of Art, University of Iowa, Iowa City. [Photo: Herbert Matter, c.1947, courtesy of Lee Krasner Pollock]

word titles, preferring instead to simply number the works. However, even here certain pictures were given subtitles. Of interest are two works from 1948, *Number 2*, subtitled *Shadows*, and *Number 9*, identified as *Summertime*.

Pollock's 1949 works all bear numerical titles, save two, and in both cases the word title is descriptive of a detail of the work. He continued this practice in 1950 except for four works included here, *Number 1* as *Lavender Mist*, *Number 2* as *Shadows*, *Number 30* as *Autumn Rhythm*, and *Number 31* as *One*, although the latter—if related to nature—is more metaphorical, in its references to a kind of pantheistic unity.[62]

In her brief study of some of these titles Johnson reports that although Pollock sometimes got help from others in the difficult task of naming paintings, Lee Pollock says that even so he never accepted a suggestion unless it fitted in with his own ideas; and in any case the *Sounds in the Grass* and *Accabonac Creek* titles were entirely his own.[63]

It is equally important to realize what other titles Pollock used during this period. From the 1947 works the following titles joined those listed above: *Cathedral, Lucifer, Unfounded, Gothic, Magic Lantern,* and *Alchemy*. For the 1948 works, if we eliminate titles that are either descriptive—such as *Black and Red,* or that are descriptive of a single element in the work itself, as in *The Wooden Horse* and *White Cockatoo,* only one title not referring directly to nature—*Arabesque*—remains. The 1949 works include two with word titles—*Out of the Web* and *Bird of Paradise,* descriptive of elements in the work. The four titles from 1950 all refer to nature. Leaving aside *Cathedral* and *Gothic*—which may be special "references"—out of the twenty-two "abstract" word titles used by Pollock for the allover pictures, seventeen or over three quarters suggest nature or natural phenomena.

Interpreting works of art which are endemically abstract by their descriptive titles is a most unsure enterprise. To propose, as Johnson does, that

From the incessant buzzing of the insects in the grass by his studio to the nebulae floating in outer space and, above all, the everlasting rhythm of the ocean—whether roaring in anger, sullen in its cold grey depths, or twinkling through the gossamer veils of *Lavender Mist*—the nature he loved is in Pollock's paintings[64]

is to engage in an effort that is similar to the erroneous pursuit for "hidden imagery." While the title *Lavendar Mist* does suggest a condition found in nature, the work itself was nonetheless titled by Greenberg, not Pollock.[65] The important point is not that Pollock named or accepted the name for any particular work, but rather that the preponderance of his "abstractly" worded titles do refer to natural phenomena. Any single title—by itself—will not lead to sure analysis; but, that there is such a large proportion of such titles does suggest that Pollock viewed the allover works as connected with nature in some manner.

Even here interpretation of groups of titles is difficult. For example, three of the 1947 works, *Shooting Star, Comet,* and *Reflections of the Big Dipper,* joined by a fourth, *Constellation,* a transitional work of the previous year, suggest stars. They may be merely reflective of Pollock's interests. As early as 1950, from his visit with Pollock in the summer, Goodnough had recorded: "His work may be thought of as coming from landscape and even the movement of the stars—with which he seems almost intimate at times. . . ."[66] Frank O'Hara included in his poem *Digression on November 1, 1948* (1959) the line "Stars are out," and Tony Smith recalls:

Jackson loved the landscape out on the island, anything beyond Riverhead. He would take me for rides to show me building sites, or just to places that he liked. Sometimes we would just sit and look and not say anything. On clear nights we would get out of the car and look at the stars.[67]

But, there are no stars present in the allover works, and the rhythmic pattern of *One* and *Number 27* is present from inner pictorial needs, not as records or as memories of celestial motions.

But as Rubin and Greenberg have argued, it is precisely the distillation of cubist space that is important. While certain Pollocks of the earlier period are capable of being "read" as though the layers of paint extended backward to "infinity," in

148

Figure 25. Jackson Pollock. *Number 14, 1951*, 1951. Duco on canvas, 146.4 × 269.2 cm (57⅞ × 106 in). Collection, Lee Krasner Pollock, New York [photo: Otto Nelson]. Not in exhibition

the 1950 works Pollock undertook measures exactly to deny this reading, by introducing a compositional weight at the bottom of the web or by staining the layers into the surface or by both—thus identifying the web with the flat support.

A more specific landscape source has been suggested for other allover pictures, especially *Number 32, 1950;* this would be the trees of Pollock's Long Island environment. Again in his early article on Pollock, based on a visit to the studio when this work, *Number 32, 1950,* was painted, Goodnough described Pollock's living "in the tiny village of Springs, with the ocean as background and in close contact with open, tree-studded fields where cattle graze peacefully. . . ."[68] But more directly, in a 1969 interview, B. H. Friedman asked Lee Krasner Pollock:

Several writers have connected the black-and-white paintings, and some of the coloured ones also, with the feel of the East Hampton landscape, particularly in winter: the look of bare trees against the sky and flat land moving out toward the sea.
[She replied] Jackson was pretty explicit about that in the *Arts & Architecture* questionnaire. ('. . . I have a definite feeling for the West: the vast horizontality of the land, for instance; here only the Atlantic Ocean gives you that.') Then (1944) he emphasized the West, but by the time of the black-and-white show, after living in Springs for six years, I think he would have given just as much emphasis to this Eastern Long Island landscape—and seascape. They were part of his consciousness: the horizontality he speaks of, and the sense of endless space, and the freedom. . . .[69]

We can reconstruct a semblance of this landscape at the time of Pollock's work on the allover pictures through photographs taken outside of the studio in 1949. One of them in particular (fig. 13) shows the Pollocks walking under a large bare tree, which is contrasted to the low flat horizon of the landscape. But comparing this image with the black and white painting of the following year, *Number 32, 1950,* we can project only the most general of connections between the organic forms of the tree and the abstractedly structural patterns of the canvas. If the bare trees in winter on Long Island served as an inspiration for *Number 32, 1950,* it was only in the sense of a distilled memory of a particular rhythmic shaping—especially so in this instance as *Number 32, 1950* was painted in July or August, the high point of summer foliage.

Both Goodnough and Lee Krasner Pollock refer to the ocean as part of Pollock's environment, as have other writers. Pollock's 1944 statement on his work reads in full:

Living is keener, more demanding, more intense and expansive in New York than in the West; the stimulating influences are more numerous and rewarding. At the same time, I have a definite feeling for the West: the vast horizontality of the land, for instance; here only the Atlantic ocean gives you that.[70]

We know that Pollock was interested in Melville's *Moby Dick,* and certain early allover pictures carry titles referring to the ocean: *Sea Change, Full Fathom Five,* and *Watery Paths* (and perhaps *Reflections of the Big Dipper*). These have lead Robert Rosenblum to write:

In *Number 1, 1948,* we are as immediately plunged into divine fury as we are drenched in Turner's sea; in neither case can our minds provide systems of navigation. Again, sheer magnitude can help produce the Sublime. Here, the very size of the Pollock—68 by 104 inches—permits no pause before the engulfing; we are almost physically lost in this boundless web of inexhaustible energy. To be sure, Pollock's generally abstract vocabulary allows multiple readings of its mood and imagery, although occasional titles *(Full Fathom Five, Ocean Greyness, The Deep, Greyed Rainbow)* may indicate a more explicit region of nature. But whether achieved by the most blinding of blizzards or the most gentle of winds and rains, Pollock invariably evokes the sublime mysteries of nature's untamable forces. Like the awesome vistas of telescope and microscope, his pictures leave us dazzled before the imponderables of galaxy and atom.[71]

But Rosenblum is careful to state that Pollock's works of this period "evoke" these sensations. Nothing in them is descriptive of the ocean, nor is the "rhythm of the ocean . . . twinkling through the gossamer veils of *Lavender Mist. . . .*" Nothing is depicted—or depicted and hidden in *Lavender Mist;* Pollock's connections to the ocean are by a pictorial parallel, not by translation.

But there is something in the environment of the ocean and the flat landscape which may have played a role in determining the directions of Pollock's art. His works move toward and then become allover pictures, bearing titles with references to nature, related to the impressionists' and Cézanne's pictures (and to the late Monets, see below) only after his move to Long

Island in 1945. But it is difficult to chart these changes in Pollock's work—in stylistic terms—because of his rapid assimilation of varying formal and thematic ideas. *Shimmering Substance* with its thickly painted commas of pigment is readily identifiable with the impressionist pictures, but *Cathedral* (fig. 7) of the following year, because it alludes both to the scaffolding of the cubist works and to Monet's Rouen cathedral compositions (fig. 8), is less direct in any connections.

As we have seen above, Rubin also points to a parallel fusion of cubism and impressionism in Mondrian's art, which led then to his allover paintings of 1915-1917, which were based on seascapes.

Rubin also recounts his conversation with Tony Smith, wherein the latter recalls the interest Pollock had shown in these "plus-and-minus" Mondrian works.[72] Smith has more recently indicated how Pollock was also interested in Mondrian's earlier church façade pictures and Pollock's comments about how they connected—as did more fully the "plus-and-minus" works they also studied—with the allover works which he was then painting.[73] Pollock must certainly have been aware not only of the formal similarities between developments from impressionism to cubism and cubism to the allover in Mondrian's work but also of the roles that the parallel "sources" played following his own move to a landscape and seascape environment.

POETIC REFERENCES

While there are interesting parallels between the art of Mondrian and Pollock, there are significant differences in the way that each developed. Mondrian's art was evolutionary, as he shed impressionism for cubism, and then drove this style— still keeping certain aspects of the impressionist allover composition—to the plus-and-minus works and then into the band-and-block style of his mature work. Pollock's art, to the contrary, is characterized by the manner in which he enrolled impressionism, cubism, surrealism, and, in 1950, a sense of Cézannian/cubist weight and compositional movement into his paintings to form a confluent whole.

There is another stylistic affinity in Pollock's poured works, which is, perhaps, more pronounced in the paintings of 1950 as a whole than in the earlier poured pictures—to the late works of Monet. Again, Rubin was the first to fully address this connection. He writes that the Monets are

closer to Pollock in the poetic and visionary character that such "distance" from the motif made possible. Like Pollock, the late Monet digests nature but recasts it poetically. But Pollock opened up the distance between nature and the retina even further, which allowed his exquisite allusions to it—as in *Lavender Mist, One* and *Autumn Rhythm*—to simultaneously comprehend other metaphoric levels. The Impressionists—given their naturalistic commitment to the external visual world—had to choose between the landscape and cityscape; Pollock was able to fuse them—with other allusions—in a single image.

The spirit of landscape in Pollock is carried primarily by the *atmospheric tonalities* and *large size* of the pictures (since they are not *illusions* of nature they are free to communicate its *qualities* in this more direct way).[74]

As Rubin rightly points out, the affinities in Pollock's works to those of Monet's late period are probably coincidental, as almost nothing was seen of the French master's "symbolist" paintings in New York during this period at the end of the 1940s.[75] What these stylistic affinities underscore in the 1950 paintings in particular is their poetic nature, or the manner in which they suggest atmosphere through their coloration and dominant scale.

SUBJECTS

However, Pollock's 1950 paintings are unlike the late works of Monet in the way in which they so openly display the physical energies that went into their making. While Pollock's works do have connections to the modern tradition and speak in a language which is part and parcel of that tradition, they were not made by drawing on that tradition's technical procedures, save for those of the automatic procedures of surrealism, and these, as we have seen, were greatly transformed in Pollock's hands. Pollock developed a style which allowed him to speak through the formal language of a tradition and thus make his works historical and comprehensible even though that style required the most demanding of painterly and even athletic skills; this simultaneous combination of tradition and invention is the final clue to the subjects of his classic pictures.

Just as the vocabulary of the modern tradition carries within it certain figures of speech which are linked to our comprehension of the modern world, so Pollock's development of the poured style linked his work to that tradition in a manner which was more direct and revealing. More than simply taking the accidental in his work as a point of departure—as did Miró or Masson—or as a curious form of detailing, Pollock openly courted its presence in his work and in such a manner that the accidental had to be continually dominated, especially in the 1950 works, which were intended as more consciously controlled. Indeed it is the emphasis on control in these very works which is evidence of Pollock's deepest intentions. The balance which resulted out of the combination of accident and control was precisely the manner in which Pollock could introduce the modern world—contemporary life—into his painting. And the poured technique not only meant that he avoided any copying of previous art—as he had done in his works from the early 1940s, often after Picasso's creations—but it allowed him to include, though with more allusive results, stylistic affinities to widely differing faces and foundations within the very traditions to which he so deeply wanted to align his art. These affinities permit his subject to become part of an historical context.

Greenberg observed this aspect in Pollock's paintings in 1947. He wrote:

For all its Gothic quality, Pollock's art is still an attempt to cope with urban life; it dwells entirely in the lonely jungle of immediate sensations, impulses and notions, therefore is positivist, concrete.[76]

Pollock's art may have been one of "immediate sensation, impulses and notions" when he began the poured pictures in 1947, but in the classic works of 1950, as he moved his art to a greater scale—he also recognized that he could exercise more conscious control and still explore the boundaries of his theme. Perhaps the lesson of *Lavendar Mist* was that the possibility of accident would always be part of his pouring technique, and that if he wanted to paint on a larger scale, which would demand even greater control, he could do so by introducing decision in other ways: he would still face the potential of accident and its resolution in the process of painting.

The subject of the classic paintings is this balance of control and chaos. It is directly a part of Pollock's technique and not a function of any hidden imagery; indeed, Pollock's subject demanded that it be unequivocally present. Beyond any stylistic affinities to impressionism, cubism, and surrealism, it is this subject which Pollock shares with the modern tradition. As Rubin writes:

Those crowds *are* there somewhere in the poetic allusiveness of Pollock's drip pictures. But like the real crowd, whose collective image is the sum total of purposeful movements, they are not milling undirectedly. Pollock's image is not, of course, a *picture* of a crowd, or anything else, but it is no less engaged with the feeling and pulse of such contemporary experiences. Like the pictures of life in older art (except at its most corrupt, as in Victorian realism) which were not images of the way life really was but the way it might ideally exist, Pollock accepts the challenges of the molecularity and *prima facie* confusion of modern life and transcends them, endowing them with a comprehensive order. His image is an equilibrated and ordered structure of modern experiences which as *art* provides symbolically precisely the unity, equilibrium and absolute completeness which life lacks.

As a closed and fixed system, a picture is able to show life whole—from the outside—in a way that man, "inside" life, can never experience directly. If we see only a piece of Pollock—in effect, the way we experience life—no matter how much richness is involved, we miss its essential structure, its monistic simultaneity.[77]

Chaos was clearly the one thing that Pollock did not want seen in his art. In 1950 the Italian critic Bruno Alfieri wrote of Pollock:

It is easy to detect the following things in all of his paintings:
—chaos
—absolute lack of harmony
— complete lack of structural organization
— total absence of technique, however rudimentary
— once again, chaos. . . .[78]

This discussion appeared in *Time* magazine on November 20; Pollock sent his only reply to any published criticism of his work. The telegram read "NO CHAOS, DAMN IT."[79] What Pollock was about was the ordering of chaos. Among Pollock's notes is the following analysis of his aims:

            Technic is the result of a need————————
new needs demand new technics————————
            total control————————————denial of
the accident————————
            states of order————————
organic intensity————————
            energy and motion
made visible————————
            memories arrested in space,
human needs and motives————————
    acceptance————————[80]

Pouring allowed Pollock's art not only to have formal affinities to the modern tradition, but also to share aspects of the essential subject matter of this tradition—modern urban life; and it did so in a manner which is metaphorical on one hand—as it is in the impressionist cityscape and the cubist fractured objects—and constantly, physically present as a painting, on the other. "I paint it, I don't illustrate it," Pollock is quoted as saying.[81] Pouring paint constantly courted disaster, but left a record of Pollock's control over it. It was the only way Pollock could directly state his subject. It was an extraordinary decision to come to terms with the modern tradition in this way, and one that made unmatched demands upon the artist. Robert Motherwell has observed:

But I would suspect . . . that Pollock was an essentially passive man, who occasionally, at an emotional price that it frightens me to contemplate, overcame his passivity through a convulsion of activity that became transcendant when coupled with his sensitivity to painting as a medium.[82]

"I AM NATURE"

Discussion of Pollock's subject matter often involves reference to nature, as we have seen, and frequently mentions Lee Krasner Pollock's remembrance of her late husband's meeting with Hofmann. She states:

I brought Hofmann up to meet Pollock for the first time and Hofmann said, after looking at his work, "You do not work from Nature." Pollock's answer was, "I am nature."[83]

This meeting took place in the early 1940s, and Pollock's statement can only make sense in psychological terms, or in reference to Pollock's holding the surrealists' view of nature as being derived from the inner self, rather than as an external, in the traditional view, as something outside of oneself which the artist could work from, like an apple. But Pollock did not abandon this viewpoint in the classic paintings so much as he transformed it into part of his subject. Importantly Lee Krasner Pollock goes on in her recollection of Pollock's reply to Hofmann to state:

I think this statement articulates an important difference between French painting and what followed. It breaks once and for all the concept that was still more or less present in Cubist derived painting, that one sits and observes nature that is out there. Rather, it claims a oneness.[84]

Ultimately it is Pollock's oneness with his technique that is meaningful—or that is made meaningful in the paintings. Pollock is nature—or a benevolent view of nature—in his making order out of chaos as he does in *Lavender Mist, One, Autumn Rhythm*. The classic quality of the 1950 pictures is the thoroughness with which the artist explored this subject, through means which directly express it. Order is realized in the physical presence of the work, and even its art-historical and metaphorical references depend upon this cohesion. Pollock achieved this order only at the end of one of the most creatively demanding tasks that any painter has set for himself.

NOTES

After this essay was set in type, *Number 32, 1950* was examined. Along the bottom of this picture are small areas of brown, teal blue, and white, which are surely splashes of paint from the execution of *One* and *Autumn Rhythm* when they were painted on the floor next to the hanging *Number 32*. The splashes are identical to the colors used in the subsequent two large pictures. Also found on the lower surface of *Number 32* are small splashes of pink, which are identical to the color used in *Number 27, 1950*. This supports the theory, advanced above, that *Number 27* was painted after *Number 32* and, in fact, was made on the floor directly under it.

1. This is not to say the acceptance of abstract expressionism, but rather the acknowledgment that painting in New York was of interest. Certain critics view Pollock's great work as extending through his subsequent Black and White pictures. For example, see Michael Fried's discussion of them in his *Morris Louis* (New York: Abrams, 1971), 21-25. Hilton Kramer argues a differing view, namely that Pollock's allover palette knife works of 1946—he cites *Shimmering Substance* (collection of Lee Krasner Pollock, New York)—as superior to the later poured paintings; see "The Jackson Pollock Myth," in *The Age of the Avant-Garde* (New York: Farrar, Straus and Giroux, 1973), 337.

2. See William Rubin's "Jackson Pollock and the Modern Tradition, Part I: 1. The Myths and the Paintings," *Artforum*, 5 (Feb. 1967): 14-17, or Lawrence Alloway, *Jackson Pollock*, exh. cat. (London: Marlborough Fine Art Ltd., 1961), 52: "The group of large drip paintings . . . constituted a classical point in Pollock's drip paintings."

3. These and definitions below from *classic* and *classical, American College Dictionary* (New York: Random House, 1970), 222-223.

4. Rubin, "Myths and Paintings," as well as "Jackson Pollock and the Modern Tradition, Part I: 2. The All-over Compositions and the Drip Technique" (Feb. 1967); "Part II: 3. Impressionism and the Classic Pollock; 4. Color and Scale; Affinities with the Late Monet" (Mar. 1967); "Part III: 5. Cubism and the Later Evolution of the All-over Style," (Apr. 1967); "Part IV: 6. An Aspect of Automatism" (May 1967), *Artforum*, vol. *5*.

5. Robert Motherwell, review in *Partisan Review*, winter 1944; quoted in Francis O'Connor, *Jackson Pollock*, exh. cat. (New York: Museum of Modern Art, 1967): 31.

6. Rubin, "An Aspect," 28.

7. Rubin, "An Aspect," 28-33.

8. Alonzo Lansford; quoted in O'Connor, *Jackson Pollock*, 43.

9. Pollock; quoted in O'Connor, *Jackson Pollock*, 40.

10. Frank O'Hara, *Jackson Pollock* (New York: George Braziller, 1959), 26.

11. Rubin, "Cubism," 31.

12. Lawrence Alloway, "London Chronicle," *Art International*, 2 (Dec. 1958): 34.

13. Pollock on an application for a Guggenheim Fellowship; quoted in O'Connor, *Jackson Pollock*, 39.

14. Alfred H. Barr; quoted in O'Connor, *Jackson Pollock*, 53.

15. Rubin, "Cubism," 21.

16. Harry Rand, *American Art at Harvard*, exh. cat. (Cambridge: Fogg Art Museum, 1972): cat. no. 157.

17. This is visible in a photograph taken in Pollock's studio in 1949, in O'Connor, *Jackson Pollock*, 50.

18. Rudolph Burckhardt, in conversation with Trinkett Clark, Jan. 1978 (on file in the Department of Twentieth-Century Art, National Gallery of Art).

19. B. H. Friedman, *Jackson Pollock: Energy Made Visible* (New York: McGraw-Hill, 1972), 166.

20. Hans Namuth; quoted by Friedman, *Energy Made Visible*, 161.

21. Lee Krasner Pollock, in conversation with the author, New York, Dec. 1, 1977 (on file in the Department of Twentieth-Century Art, National Gallery).

22. Conversation with the author, Dec. 1, 1977.

23. William Wright interview with Pollock, summer 1950; quoted in O'Connor, *Jackson Pollock*, 81.

24. Clement Greenberg refers to this statement which he calls a "qualification," in "The Jackson Pollock Market Soars," *New York Times Magazine*, Apr. 16, 1961, 42; when asked by Selden Rodman in 1956 "do you have any preconceived visual image in mind . . .", Pollock replied, "I have and I haven't"; in Rodman, *Conversations with Artists* (New York: Devin-Adair, 1957), 82.

25. Bernice Rose, *Jackson Pollock: Works on Paper*, exh. cat. (New York: Museum of Modern Art, 1969 [published in association with the Drawing Society, Inc., distributed by New York Graphic Society, Ltd., Greenwich, Conn.]), 90. Certain of these drawings may date from early 1951; see an untitled sheet in the collection of Mr. and Mrs. Jacob Kainen, Chevy Chase, Md., for example, which is inscribed "Jackson Pollock 51."

26. Tony Smith, in conversation with the author, Jan. 16, 1978, and Feb. 11, 1978 (on file in the Department of Twentieth-Century Art, National Gallery of Art).

27. Pollock correspondence of June 7, 1951; quoted in Friedman, *Energy Made Visible*, 174.

28. See, for example, Fried, *Morris Louis*, 21.

29. Write interview, in O'Connor, *Jackson Pollock*, 79-81.

30. Rubin mentioned this characteristic in correspondence, Aug. 25, 1977 (on file in the Department of Twentieth-Century Art, National Gallery of Art).

31. Rubin, "The All-over Compositions," 19.

32. Rubin, "Cubism," 21.

33. Lee Krasner Pollock in interview with B. H. Friedman, in *Jackson Pollock: Black and White*, exh. cat. (New York: Marlborough-Gerson Gallery Inc., 1969), 10.

34. Rubin, "The All-over Compositions," 20.

35. Stephen C. Foster, "Turning Points in Pollock's Early Imagery," *University of Iowa Museum of Art Bulletin*, 1 (Spring 1976): 34.

36. Foster, "Turning Points in Pollock's Early Imagery," 34.

37. Hilton Kramer, "Jackson Pollock and Nicolas de Staël: Two Painters and their Myths," *Arts Yearbook*, 3 (1959): 53-60; Harold Rosenberg, "Review," *Art News*, 59 (Feb. 1961): 35; Clement Greenberg, "Pollock Market Soars"; Thomas Hess, "Pollock: The Art of a Myth," *Art News*, 62 (Jan. 1964): 39; and Brian O'Doherty, "Pollock's Myth," in *American Masters: The Voice and the Myth* (New York: Random House, 1973), 82-111.

38. Pollock; quoted by Rodman, *Conversations with Artists*, 82.

39. Sam Hunter, "The United States," in *Art Since 1945* (New York: Abrams, 1958), 277.

40. Rubin, *Dada, Surrealism and their Heritage*, exh. cat. (New York: Museum of Modern Art, 1968), 178.

41. Charles F. Stuckey, "Another Side of Jackson Pollock," *Art in America*, 65 (Nov. 1977): 86. Stuckey suggests that a possible source for Pollock's handprints was Val Telberg's cover illustration for Louise Varèse's translation of Rimbaud's *A Season in Hell*, published in 1945, based on Pollock's reading Lee Krasner Pollock's copy. However, Lee Krasner Pollock has recently commented that she did not own this translation, but rather an earlier one by Delmar Schwartz. Thus, *Number 1, 1948* is not, as Stuckey suggests, "a recollection of this powerful image [of the Telberg cover]"—nor is *Lavender Mist*.

42. Stuckey, "Another Side of Jackson Pollock."

43. Lee Krasner Pollock, in Friedman, *Black and White*, 9.

44. Robert Motherwell, "Jackson Pollock: An Artists' Symposium, Part 1," *Art News*, 66 (Apr. 1967): 66.

45. Fried; quoted by Stuckey, "Another Side of Jackson Pollock," 82.

46. On this point see the author's "Robert Motherwell's Spanish Elegies," *Arts*, 50 (June 1976): 94-97, and n. 3, p. 97.

47. The proposed Pollock church was discussed by the author with Ossorio on June 7, 1975, and with Tony Smith on Jan. 16, 1978.

48. The *Black and White Painting*, 1951 (pri-

vate collection, New York), for example, suggests crucifixion imagery. Among Pollock's 1951 drawings is *Untitled* (collection of Mrs. Penelope S. Porter, Amagansett, New York; illustrated in Rose, *Works on Paper*, 89) which is a crucifixion based directly on Picasso's *Crucifixion* of 1930 (estate of the artist, Paris).

49. Hunter, *Art Since 1945*, 278.

50. Phillip Pavia, "Jackson Pollock: An Artists' Symposium," *Art News*, 66 (Apr. 1967): 61.

51. Greenberg, "Pollock Market Soars."

52. Lee Krasner Pollock has repeatedly made this point. See, for example, "Who Was Jackson Pollock?" *Art in America*, 55 (May 1967): 48-58.

53. O'Doherty, *American Masters*, 84.

54. Greenberg; quoted by Rubin, "Cubism," 19.

55. Rubin, "Cubism," 19.

56. Rubin, "Cubism," 24.

57. Rubin, "Cubism," 25.

58. Rubin, "Cubism," 21.

59. Tony Smith, in conversation with the author, Feb. 12, 1978.

60. Rubin, "Impressionism," 28-29.

61. Ellen Johnson, *Modern Art and the Object* (London: Thames and Hudson, 1976), 114.

62. The lists of works exhibited in 1947-1950 is taken from O'Connor, *Jackson Pollock*, 40, 42-43, 45, 48, 56.

63. Johnson, *Modern Art*, 114.

64. Johnson, *Modern Art*, 118.

65. Greenberg, in conversation with the author, May 1976 (on file in the Department of Twentieth-Century Art, National Gallery of Art).

66. Robert Goodnough, "Pollock Paints a Picture," *Art News*, 60 (May 1951): 60.

67. Tony Smith in "Who was Jackson Pollock?," 59.

68. Goodnough, "Pollock Paints," 38.

69. Lee Krasner Pollock; quoted in Friedman, *Black and White*, 8.

70. Pollock; quoted in O'Connor, *Jackson Pollock*, 32.

71. Robert Rosenblum, "The Abstract Sublime," *Art News*, 59 (Feb. 1961): 41.

72. Rubin, "Cubism," 23.

73. Tony Smith, in conversation with the author, Feb. 12, 1978.

74. Rubin, "Color and Scale," 33.

75. Morris Louis' 1953 *Trellis*, for example, appears to be based on Monet's late wisteria paintings, but these Monet works were not accessible to Louis. See the author's "Morris Louis and the Modern Tradition, Part III: Impressionism," *Arts*, 51 (Oct. 1976): 116-117.

76. Greenberg; quoted in O'Connor, *Jackson Pollock*, 42.

77. Rubin, "Impressionism," 30.

78. Bruno Alfieri; quoted in O'Connor, *Jackson Pollock*, 54.

79. Pollock; quoted in Friedman, *Energy Made Visible*, 160.

80. Pollock; quoted in Friedman, *Energy Made Visible*, 158.

81. Lee Krasner Pollock, in conversation with the author, Dec. 1, 1977.

82. Motherwell, "An Artists' Symposium," 66.

83. Lee Krasner Pollock in Bruce Glaser's "Jackson Pollock: An Interview with Lee Krasner," *Arts*, 41 (Apr. 1967): 38.

84. Lee Krasner Pollock in Glaser, "Jackson Pollock," 38.

85. Ossorio, in conversation with the author, June 7, 1975.

WILLEM DE KOONING:

The Women

Figure 1. De Kooning at work on drawing preliminary to *Woman I,* June 1950. [Photo: Rudolph Burckhardt]

CHECKLIST

1. Woman I   1950-1952
   oil on canvas
   192.8 x 147.3 cm (75⅞ x 58 in)
   The Museum of Modern Art, New York, Purchase, 1953

2. Woman II   1952
   oil on canvas
   148.9 x 109.2 cm (59 x 43 in)
   Signed, lower right: de Kooning
   The Museum of Modern Art, New York,
   Gift of Mrs. John D. Rockefeller 3rd, 1955

3. Woman III   1951-1952
   oil on canvas
   170.5 x 122.2 cm (67⅛ x 48⅛ in)
   Signed, lower right: de Kooning
   Tehran Museum of Contemporary Art

4. Woman IV   1952-1953
   oil on canvas
   149.9 x 117.5 cm (59 x 46¼ in)
   Signed, lower left: de Kooning
   Nelson Gallery-Atkins Museum, Kansas City, Mo.,
   Gift of Mr. William Inge

5. Woman V   1952-1953
   oil and charcoal on canvas
   154.8 x 113.8 cm (60⅞ x 44¾ in)
   Signed, lower left: de Kooning
   Australian National Gallery, Canberra

6. Woman VI   1953
   oil on canvas
   174.0 x 148.6 cm (68½ x 58½ in)
   Signed, lower right: de Kooning
   Museum of Art, Carnegie Institute, Pittsburgh

BIOGRAPHY

Born in 1904 in Rotterdam. Studies at the Academy of Fine Arts and Techniques between 1916 and 1925. In 1926 emigrates to New York where he comes to know John Graham, Stuart Davis, and Arshile Gorky, sharing a studio with the latter in the late 1930s. In early 1940s begins series of Women, turning to abstract compositions in 1945, concluding with *Excavation* in 1950, which wins the purchase prize of the Art Institute of Chicago. In June 1950 begins *Woman I* in New York studio, finishing this and *Woman II, III,* and *IV* in fall of 1952 after a summer of pastel drawing in East Hampton, Long Island. Paints *Woman V* and *VI* in winter 1952-1953, showing all six at Sidney Janis Gallery in March 1953. In 1955 returns to abstraction in series of cityscapes, then in 1957, landscapes. In 1963 moves to Springs, Long Island, and begins the new series, Women. In 1969 he makes first sculpture. Continues to live and work in Springs, Long Island.

WILLEM DE KOONING:

The Women

E. A. CARMEAN, JR.

In 1950 Willem de Kooning began the first of six large paintings on the theme of woman—a series which he would complete by March 1953. The theme was certainly not a new one to the history of art, nor was it even new to de Kooning, who had turned his attention to the subject in his works of the early 1940s and again in a few smaller paintings and drawings in 1948 and 1949 immediately before the Women series. However, when the six canvases of women were shown in 1953, they received varying critical attention.

De Kooning was painting abstract works at the end of the 1940s and, indeed, had gained his fame for a large abstraction, *Excavation* (fig. 15), which had won the purchase prize of the Art Institute of Chicago in 1950. In view of his position, certain artists felt that de Kooning had committed a crime in returning to the theme of the human figure, that in doing so he was in effect denying the validity of abstraction.[1] Others, however, felt that the real crime which de Kooning had committed was his attack upon the human form. And there is something curious in this: namely that de Kooning's painting style itself was not attacked. Whereas to one group, it was merely the presence of human figuration rather than the manner of its presentation which was to the discredit of the paintings, to another, de Kooning's abilities to draw the human figure were not seen as an issue; rather, from this point of view, de Kooning had simply painted a series of monsters.

One thing is certain about the paintings, the subject is clearly a woman. In the context of abstract-expressionist painting at mid-century, de Kooning in these works presents a clearly identifiable theme. As de Kooning himself has commented,

Certain artists and critics attacked me for painting the *Women*, but I felt that this was their problem, not mine. I don't really feel like a non-objective painter at all. Today, some artists feel they have to go back to the figure, and that word "figure" becomes such a ridiculous omen—if you pick up some paint with your brush and make somebody's nose with it, this is rather ridiculous when you think of it, theoretically or philosophically. It's really absurd to make an image, like a human image, with paint, today, when you think about it, since we have this problem of doing or not doing it. But then all of a sudden it was even more absurd not to do it. So I fear that I have to follow my desires.[2]

Although the six women constitute a clear series, the context which surrounds them has never been fully examined. While the artist has said "The *Women* have to do with the female painted through all the ages, all those idols . . . ,"[3] the way this idea fits into the exact statements made by these particular six

paintings remains unexplored. Save for Thomas Hess' more general studies of the paintings,[4] the very seeming obviousness of this subject may have prevented an exegesis of the broader themes which the series may embrace.

The abstract-expressionist work represents a confluence of quite separate formal and thematic traditions, and the Women series is no exception in this regard. The Women paintings involve three different aspects of de Kooning's art: first, the profound change in de Kooning's entire idea of his work, a change which occurs between 1950 and 1953; second, the combined aspects of invention and style, both of de Kooning's own making and from the works of other artists; and, finally, the subject of the works, what they are, and how they allow de Kooning to connect his works to much broader thematic concerns. In addition two other issues are tangential here: the exact chronology of the paintings, and the identity of the artist's sources, his drawings, as well as other influences for each separate *Woman*. The drawings in particular need sorting out, both as to the role which they played in the generation of the paintings themselves as well as in the formation of the theme of the series itself.[5]

PREPARATION

Woman I (fig. 2) is an almost legendary work because of the time it took to paint the picture—over two years. In its final guise it seems quite separate from de Kooning's previous work, and, indeed, it is, being the result of numerous and dramatic shifts and inventions in his style. But this should not blind us to the fact that in its original state and in the ideas which were present at its conception, *Woman I* was much more connected to the artist's work of the preceding decade. Indeed, generally, it would not be wrong to propose that the changes which normally take place in an artist's work over a three-year period—his development of new forms and new vocabulary—took place in de Kooning's case within this one painting.

Before he began painting *Woman I* de Kooning made two very large drawings of standing female figures, on sheets of paper pinned to the studio wall (fig. 1). If we consider these two sheets as actually comprising one composition, then we can link the composite to a series of smaller oil on paper works which the artist had made the previous year, including *Two Women on a Wharf*. Sharing aspects of figural construction as well as theme with the earlier works, the two large drawings indicate that up to the beginning of *Woman I*, de Kooning was

Figure 2. Willem de Kooning. *Woman I*, 1950-1952. Oil on canvas, 192.8 x 147.3 cm (75⅞ x 58 in). The Museum of Modern Art, New York, Purchase, 1953. Cat. no. 1, pl. 7

continuing to develop ideas that had originated in the late 1940s. The relationship of these two large drawings—either as separate sheets or as one composition—to the immediately following *Woman I* is, nonetheless, unclear. Perhaps they were intended as a "cartoon" for a painting which was not carried out but rather changed into *Woman I;* or they may be independent. At any rate, from its first stages *Woman I* was conceived of as a singular figure, seated in the middle of the composition.

De Kooning began the work in early June 1950, with the canvas not stretched but rather attached to the wall as the drawings had been (fig. 3). He continued working on the painting for eighteen months or so, until January or February 1952, when the painting was abandoned, unfinished. Soon after this the art historian Meyer Schapiro, upon seeing the work, encouraged de Kooning about the painting, and the artist again began to work on it. According to Thomas Hess in

1953, the painting was near its finish in mid-June 1952, although some changes were subsequently made. However, more recently Hess has proposed that the painting was not actually finished until November of that year when de Kooning accepted it as complete.[6] As we will see below, it will be proposed here that the painting was not finished at least until part of the summer of 1952 had passed.

One final change was made to the work probably in January of 1953, when de Kooning decided to restore a few inches of surface to the picture, which he had cropped off in his initial decision about its size.[7] This restored area is plainly visible as the aluminum painted band which runs along the vertical right side of the picture.

Fortunately we can follow the development of *Woman I* from near its initiation to its completion, because six photographs showing its progress between summer 1950 and its abandonment in winter 1952 were taken by Rudolph

Figure 3. De Kooning's studio in summer 1950. The first state of *Woman I* is shown attached to the wall at the upper right. [Photo: Rudolph Burckhardt]

Burckhardt and Walter Auerbach. Together with the final version of the painting, these photographs record, at least partially, the major shift in de Kooning's art from a 1940s figural conception to the much richer and more fully integrated *Woman I*.

STATE ONE

Photographed on de Kooning's studio wall by Burckhardt in the summer of 1950, state one of *Woman I* (fig. 4) reveals the artist's original intentions in the painting. Seated slightly to the left of center in the composition, the figure is placed before what is presumably an interior wall, with a window behind her to the right, indicated by a rectangle which is divided into four panes of glass. Over her other shoulder is another squared-off element, indicating perhaps something hanging on the wall. The figure itself is made up of sweeping, disconnected curves which stand for parts of the legs, arms, and torso, while other aspects of the figure and of the surrounding space are given to sharp, angular markings.

These characteristics, both of subject and style, are greatly different from the final image and vocabulary of *Woman I*. However, they do reveal how firmly the painting in its initiation was directly connected to the artist's work of the 1940s. For example, *Woman* of 1948 (fig. 5) shares many of the traits of subject and style with state one (1950), from an "object" being located over the figure's left side to the U-shaping of the breasts and its echo in the figure's left arm. Other figures painted by de Kooning during this period reveal similar thematic and compositional concerns. Furthermore, these works in turn reflect de Kooning's paintings at the beginning of the 1940s and those he made in 1948-1949 (fig. 5), where again his

Figure 4. State one of *Woman I*, 1950. [Photo: Rudolph Burckhardt]

art was focused on the theme of the seated female figure. De Kooning often contrasted a three-quarter view of the figure with a parallel back plane that included a window or color rectangle, located in the upper right corner of the picture. These early works even have the disconnected and disparately scaled limbs which are more fully apparent in state one (1950).

The shared traits of this linkage from 1940 to *Woman I* also reveals a source for the subject and aspects of its formal presentation, namely the seated figures of Picasso from the 1930s. Certain of these paintings (fig. 6)[8] share not only the same specific subject but also elements of detail, such as the window/rectangle/picture/mirror on the wall in the upper right corner, and they treat the figure as being composed from separate elements which are marked by their fluid curves in contrast to more angular passages of subordinate areas. Other paintings by Picasso on this theme are more given to surrealist distortions, such as *The Nude in an Armchair* of 1929 (estate of the artist).

State one of *Woman I*, coming as it does at the end of the linkage, is somewhat removed from more overt connections to the Picasso works. And de Kooning's process of collaging parts of the composition while painting makes certain comparisons seem more like grotesque parodies or extrapolations. Certainly the far-flung definition of the body and the double head with four eyes reads as a parody of Picasso's surrealist works, until we realize that this is in fact only a working state of the painting, not its final image, and that its disparate qualities are more representative of de Kooning's experiments in determining the figure than of its intended completed appearance.

Figure 5. Willem de Kooning. *Woman*, 1948. Oil and enamel on board, 135.9 x 113.0 cm (53½ x 44½ in). Hirshhorn Museum and Sculpture Garden, Smithsonian Institution, Washington. Not in exhibition.

Curiously state one seems focused around the mouth of the figure, which was in fact cut out by the artist from a magazine advertisement. This was a constant feature of the painting as it evolved through its various states. As de Kooning recalls,

I cut out a lot of mouths. First of all, I thought everything ought to have a mouth. Maybe it was like a pun. Maybe it's sexual. But whatever it is, I used to cut out a lot of mouths and then I painted those figures and then I put the mouth more or less in the place where it was supposed to be. It always turned out to be very beautiful and it helped me immensely to have this rare thing. I don't know why I did it with the mouth. Maybe the grin—it's rather like the Mesopotamian idols, they always stand up straight, looking to the sky with this smile, like they were just astonished about the forces of nature you feel, not about problems they had with one another. That I was very conscious of—the smile was something to hang onto.[9]

State one also reveals de Kooning's rapid and rather fluid execution of the painting, the overlays of collaged elements upon the surface, the piling of paint strokes in various areas, and the runs of paint down the surface, the latter especially visible along the bottom edges of the painting. Although these aspects can be found in many of the artist's previous paintings, especially the abstract compositions, but including some of the figural works as well, never had they acquired or been left in such an apparent state. This "evidence" of the artist's craft is not only retained in the final state of the painting, but will come to play an essential role in determining de Kooning's new pictorial structure.

STATE TWO

State two (fig. 7) also taken by Burckhardt, probably shows the painting near to state one, thus dating in summer 1950. Many elements around the figure, for example, are unchanged: the right side of the painting and the section running across the bottom, as well as the area of the painting at the upper left. Other elements of the work, such as the figure's left leg, which had been part of state one as a collaged piece of paper, are now painted into the painting itself.

But major changes have also taken place. The image of the figure seated in the space has now become more clearly focused, and the elements of anatomy seem less tentative and less disparate. The figure reaches out rather precisely with her left hand and arm, and on the right holds her hand upright, arm on the chair bent at the elbow. The window to the right is now more clearly defined, as is the face of the figure, turned upward; for the eyes the artist used the strange diamond and triangle shapes only suggested in state one.

Other elements in the work which were only suggested by state one are here made part of the painting. The left leg and the V-shape of the skirt above were part of a collage paper pinned to the surface in state one, whereas in state two these components have now been painted into the work, although traces of the collage overlay still remain in the seams which run across the work below the knees of the figure.

Throughout the development of *Woman I* de Kooning used collagelike overlays of new or previously used parts of the figure to introduce new ideas in the working out of the composition. This is a device taken from de Kooning's drawings of the period which were often the result of cutting various sheets of studies of female figures into half and making new juxtapositions out of different combinations. Studying these sheets would then lead to new ideas in subsequent drawings. In making the paintings in the Women series de Kooning extended this technique to introduce separate but whole elements of the body, such as the arm pinned to the surface in state two, which then could be moved around the composition and tried in various places. If the use of the collaged mouth gave the painting an element "to hang onto," the use of collaged parts of the figure allowed de Kooning other options in working out the woman's figure. He recalls:

The *Woman* became compulsive in the sense of not being able to get hold of it—it really is very funny to get stuck with a woman's knees, for instance. You say, "What the hell am I going to do with that now?"; it's really ridiculous. . . .

I wouldn't know what to do with the rest, with the hands, maybe, or some gesture. . . .[10]

State two continues the same loose and brushy quality in the areas around the figure, including here the head as well, as it is made more precise. And for the first time on top of the head is the suggestion of a hat with a brim sticking out to either side which is found in subsequent states (and in drawings), as well as the sense that the head itself is curiously encased by rather loose brushstrokes.

Figure 6. Pablo Picasso. *Woman with a Book,* 1932. Oil on canvas, 129.6 x 96.5 cm (51 x 38 in). The Norton Simon Foundation, Los Angeles. Not in exhibition.

STATE THREE

In state three (fig. 8), from 1951, while the bottom portion of the painting is virtually the same as it was in state two, the upper areas of the work have been changed both in the figure and the setting. Here the window to the upper right has been overpainted and replaced by a paper or cutout which indicates perhaps some kind of structure drawn in perspective. At the upper left of the work more loose brushwork is present, but three rather sharply defined vertical elements have been introduced.

For the figure itself major shifts have taken place. The woman's left hand, extended outward by collage in state two, has now been painted so as to rest at the waist, the arm turned in at the elbow. The right arm has become almost indistinguishable due to the multiple layerings of paint in that portion of the work. The torso of the figure has also changed.

But the major alteration in state three is the head. Even more than state two, de Kooning has now begun to focus upon the face, and it has acquired an almost conventional character. The blocking in of an area around the head continues.

Figure 7. State two of *Woman I,* 1950. [Photo: Rudolph Burckhardt]

STATE FOUR

In spite of the inventions and changes in the first three stages of *Woman I,* by state three the canvas still bore little relationship to the final image. State four (fig. 9) presumably dates near state three, as again the lower portion of the work is unchanged. But significant alterations have been made at the top of the picture, and for the first time some hint of the final appearance of *Woman I* is visible.

This is most apparent in the face of state four: the diamond shaping of the eyes with vertical, oval pupils, the sharp nose with large nostrils, and the rather pointed chin are all features of *Woman I*'s face. This is not surprising, as this face was "saved" by de Kooning during the painting of state four by his making a tracing of the face in charcoal on thin paper (fig. 10), to which he returned when finishing the painting.

In turn this face in state four, as Thomas Hess has pointed out, is taken from the face on a full-length figure drawing, presumably dating from the year before.[11] This drawing even shares with the face of state four (and the tracing) the placement of a wide-brimmed hat atop the figure's head, subsequently reduced to a suggested cap or scarf in *Woman I.*

The use of transfers in making *Woman I* is important. As we will see, the face of the figure (and the body as well) in states five and six depart greatly from the physiognomy presented in state four, though they return in the finished painting. Indeed,

Figure 8. State three of *Woman I,* 1950. [Photo: Walter Auerbach, courtesy of The Museum of Modern Art, New York]

Figure 9. State four of *Woman I,* 1950-1952. [Photo: Walter Auerbach, courtesy of The Museum of Modern Art, New York]

when Meyer Schapiro encouraged de Kooning about *Woman I,* he saw it near the appearance of state six, and it is important to note that in continuing the work de Kooning actually returned to an earlier state, four. Even in earlier drawings, *Woman I* went through uncounted changes and inventions, and only the use of tracings and drawings could allow de Kooning to recover previous appearances.

State four also relates to the final painting in the way in which the upper torso is defined. The breasts have become large and round, encased in a low-cut dress with straps. The arms, while more disconnected from the body than in the completed picture, are flatly painted and placed frontally, far apart from the body, swinging outward on the figure's incredibly broad shoulders. Both the manner in which these elements are painted—in broad, flat strokes—and the general placement of the figure in the pictorial space, as parallel to the picture surface, underscore the increasing two-dimensionality of de Kooning's style.

Other areas of state four reveal oddities. A window (or a picture) is now at the upper right, but at the center is a Gorky-like shape attached to an upright element. To the immediate left of this area the surface is blocked by a rectangular plane which is actually a sheet of paper attached to the surface. To the far left the three vertical elements are present, but they have now been given a more architectural or structural presence, shaded as solid forms and joined by a horizontal crossbar.

STATES FIVE AND SIX

From state one through state four there is developed a greater separation of the figure from the background. In state four very few elements of ground break through and penetrate the contour of the figure, although the contour itself is not continuous. This isolating trait is emphasized even more in state five (fig. 11).

A significant period of time must have elapsed between states four and five. For the first time since the beginning of the work we see major changes in the lower portion of the canvas—basically a painting out of this area with broad, nondescriptive areas. The same is true of the upper background as well, save for the windowlike form which is still to the upper right. The figure, to the contrary, while broadly painted, is outlined in such a way as to detach itself from the background—indeed so much so that it seems almost buoyant in its placement.

After seeing the direct connections between the face of state four and that of *Woman I,* state five seems at first unrelated to the final image. But here the contrapposto of the seated figure now comes into being—the upper torso turned full face, with the legs turned off to the figure's left, crossing the surface. Indeed the shift of the woman's left leg is near to its final position, and the arrangement of the skirt as in the completed work is already indicated. Other connections can be made as

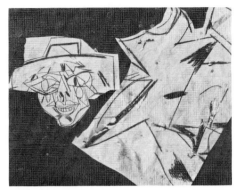

Figure 10. Willem de Kooning. Tracing of *Woman I* (charcoal on paper). Executed while *Woman I* was in progress, this drawing has since been destroyed. [Photo: reproduced from Thomas Hess, *Willem de Kooning: Drawings* (Greenwich, Conn., 1972)].

well: not only the large round breasts but the arc about them and the horizontal markings beneath the chin are present. De Kooning was still experimenting with the figure's arms in state five: the figure's left arm is turned out, palm up, while the right arm trails down the side of the figure. But in spite of these "unresolved" areas, the figure of state five looms large and unified.

It is in this sense that state six (fig. 12) comes as a surprise. The solidity and the continual surface of state five's figure is here replaced by a much more textural construction made of angular units, broken contours, and dissolving parts. This more active breaking up of the figure extends to the background as well, while de Kooning employs more freely brushed passages all around the figure. Some of these traits are carried over to the final painting, but state six is still a distance from the final image of *Woman I*. If we turn back to state one we can see how drastic have been the changes in de Kooning's art between 1950 and early 1952 (state six); more changes and the "realization" of all of them come in the painting of *Woman I* between spring and summer/fall of 1952 (below). These will reveal how dramatic the shift in de Kooning's art during this time was and bring into focus how these changes occurred in the process of painting *Woman I*.

But in January or February of 1952 de Kooning stopped work on *Woman I*, leaving it appearing probably much like state six. This abandonment of a painting—leaving it in an unfinished condition—was not unusual in de Kooning's work. Many of his paintings from the 1930s and 1940s were left unresolved, and de Kooning even enjoyed a reputation as a genius who could never finish his paintings. Perhaps more to the point, however, is that de Kooning expected this situation to occur. He notes:

And then in the end I failed. But it didn't bother me because I had, in the end, given it up; I felt it was really an accomplishment. I took the attitude that I was going to succeed, and I also knew that this was just an illusion. I never was interested in how to make a good painting. For many years I was not interested in making a good painting—as one might say, "Now this is really a good painting" or a "perfect work." I didn't want to pin it down at all. I was interested in that before, but I found out it was not my nature. I didn't work on it with the idea of

Figure 11. State five of *Woman I*, 1950-1952. [Photo: Walter Auerbach, courtesy of The Museum of Modern Art, New York]

perfection, but to see how far one could go—but not with the idea of really doing it. [12]

What is central to realize in de Kooning's invention of his new figural style in *Woman I* is that it allowed him to avoid precisely the very problems—of balance and relationship of parts—which had plagued his earlier works.

But at this point—late winter of 1951/1952—de Kooning did not abandon in despair his goal of painting a woman; he merely put aside its then present realization and embarked on three more paintings of women. These works eventually became *Woman II, III,* and *IV.* Thus the next three works were actually begun not following *Woman I*—which was finished in the summer or fall of 1952—but following the incomplete state six of the work. If de Kooning did not begin to make major revisions to *Woman I* until summer of that year, and *Woman II, III,* and *IV* were painted—at least in part—earlier in the spring, then questions of chronological ordering become important. Indeed, as we will see below, both *Woman II* and *Woman III* are closer in style to state six in many ways than they are to *Woman I*.

WOMAN I

Woman I has a powerful presence. Following the contraposto of states five and six, her large body is placed, with the upper torso, full face—parallel to the picture plane—and her legs swing to her left. The sharply defined face and head is placed,

Figure 12. State six of *Woman I, 1950-1952.* [Photo: Walter Auerbach, courtesy of The Museum of Modern Art, New York]

Figure 13. Willem de Kooning. *Woman* (two assembled drawings), 1950-1951. Pencil, 43.1 x 34.2 cm (17 x 13½ in). Present location unknown. [Photo: reproduced from Thomas Hess, *Willem de Kooning: Drawings* (Greenwich, Conn., 1972).] Not in exhibition

again as it had been in earlier states, to the left, thus elongating the figure's left shoulder. Both arms now rest beside the body, turned inward at the elbows with the hands placed in her lap. The large breasts are still present, covered in white while the red straps of the figure's dress cross over her shoulders. The skirt of the figure is also red, which contrasts with the strong passages of green and blue filling the lower portion of the painting.

Both the turn of the woman's body and the layered colors bring up the question of what role drawings and pastels played in the creation of the painting. De Kooning did hundreds of drawings of women during the period 1950 to 1952, though many are no longer extant. Among those which we have, some are clearly related to *Woman I,* while others—as well as other parts of the same sheets—correspond to *Woman II, III,* and *IV.* Furthermore, of those which relate to *Woman I* some of them date before the summer of 1952 on characteristics of style and correspondences to earlier states of the picture. Other relevant sheets, especially a series of pastel and charcoal works, date from the summer of 1952, when de Kooning turned to this medium in East Hampton. Although some of these may reflect the completed image of *Woman I*—and variants after it—other sheets are more plausibly viewed as studies or ideas for the painting. This being the case, the completion date of *Woman I* would be some time later in the summer than mid-June 1952.

As Philip Larson has written, "Drawing was always central to de Kooning's art."[13] During the early 1940s de Kooning concentrated on two kinds of drawings, highly refined studies for oil paintings of seated figures, and more academic sheets done in the manner of Ingres and Picasso's 1925-1940 works. With his move to abstraction in 1946, de Kooning changed his concept of drawing. Again Larson:

In the late 1940s de Kooning considered drawings to be essentially "warm-up" probing exercises for painting in oils. He began with charcoal drawings on paper, which were then torn and juxtaposed with fragments of other drawings and oil sketches. These composites were adhered to canvas and, thus, preliminary sketches became the visible history of the painting. The unitary drawing, independent of painting, reemerged in de Kooning's work around 1950. Imagistically, these were basically spin-offs from previous paintings. Executed in ink or black enamel on paper, these crucial drawings were variations on the quasi-anatomical forms outlined in his Abstract Expressionist oils. Some of the enamel drawings are characterized by dripped paint in loose, curvilinear forms; others are improvisations on interlocking Cubist forms.[14]

But with the beginning of the Women series in 1950, de Kooning again began to consider his drawings as exploratory in purpose. In 1956, when he turned to landscape following the female subjects, de Kooning's drawings consisted of both small, rather finished pastel studies as well as torn and collaged pieces which are relevant basically as ideas. The landscapes were also accompanied by small—12 x 12 inch—oil sketches, although it is unclear whether these were meant to be studies or records.

Thus drawings have played a direct role in de Kooning's art, either as highly developed "cartoons" for paintings or as more casually conceived jottings that eventually sparked ideas for paintings. Curiously, those surviving works which were involved in the long campaign to paint the Women series involve

164

aspects of each, thus making dating and relationship much more difficult to determine. The problem is further compounded by de Kooning joining together drawings from different dates. For example, the *Woman* drawing of 1950-1951 (fig. 13) joins together two previously separate sheets, an earlier drawing for the upper torso, and a slightly later drawing for the lower portion of the figure. Identified first by Hess as a preliminary design for *Woman I*, this drawing combines, by juxtaposing two images, the two parts of the essential contraposto pose of *Woman I*. It was perhaps among the studies which led de Kooning to alter the more frontal position of the figure we see in states one through four. Again its exact date in 1951 is difficult to determine, although another drawing, probably early in 1951, appears to derive its contraposto position from this juxtaposed sheet. As certain stylistic characteristics of this sheet, especially the fluid composition, seem related to state two of 1950, it would indicate that the invention of the pose in the *Woman* drawing would date near this time—late 1950 to early 1951—and that de Kooning set them aside until later in 1951 when he turned to the bottom portion of the *Woman I* painting.

COLLAGE

Collaged drawings played an important role in the development of the Women series. Although he did not use collage as such, de Kooning's works of the 1930s and early 1940s often treated the parts of the body as separate elements to be maneuvered into position in the work. Beginning with the simple biomorphic shapes around 1945 through the complex assemblages of the large abstract works of 1950, de Kooning treated these elements as movable units, changing their positions and, finally, overlapping them in the later works. But the cut drawings of the Women series add something new: a figure that is complete but not continuously designed. As Hess observes:

But the dislocation has the effect of elongating and flattening the figure, and, most of all, of enabling the artist to study three figures where before he had only two. The method is one which invokes contingency—chance occurrences and accidents; it keeps the forms off balance, so to speak, and permits the artist to elude definitions and dead ends. It also adds a mysterious zip of speed across the place where the image is cut, reinforcing the "object-quality" of the image by drastically unsettling our normal expectations from a drawing on paper. The surface now contains a high-speed jump, like the flick of an eye.[15]

De Kooning's cut and collaged drawings may derive from a surrealist technique of making drawings and collages called the *Cadavre Exquis*. Here the works were made by different artists each making one section of the body—head, trunk, etc.—to create a compound image. But as William Rubin has noted,

Based on an old parlor game, it was . . . adapted to the possibilities of drawing and even collage by assigning a section of the body to each player, though the Surrealist principle of metaphoric displacement led to images that only vaguely resembled the human form.[16]

In de Kooning's case the image was more unified since it was by the same hand, his own, and generally of the same subject, the female figure. Nonetheless the juxtaposition of whole sections

Figure 14. Willem de Kooning. *Woman,* c. 1952. Pastel, pencil, collage (showing face that was subsequently removed), 42.5 x 35.5 cm (16¾ x 14 in). Los Angeles County Museum of Art, Museum Purchase [photo: reproduced from Thomas Hess, *Willem de Kooning: Drawings* (Greenwich, Conn., 1972).] Not in exhibition

of previously separate images, as in the early *Woman* sheet, led to new formal and thematic inventions.

As we have seen, in states one, two, and three, de Kooning worked by attaching drawn parts of the body to the composition, moving them around to try various positions. This continued with state four, but the components—here the head—are larger and more definite. Thus the collage technique within the paintings was used in tandem with separate drawings to determine the final image of *Woman I*. Furthermore, the idea of whole anatomical sections being joined together as complete figuration, as first established in the drawings, was then transferred to the paintings; in the latter instance de Kooning painted some areas of the picture with adjacent sections masked off from view. This is especially apparent in *Woman II*.

FINAL DRAWINGS

Along with the tall full-length drawing from 1950, part of which was used for the face, and the *Woman* collage of 1951, both cited by Hess as important to the development of *Woman I*,[17] another sheet is here identified as crucial, a seated *Woman* (fig. 14) of 1952, done in pastel, pencil, and collage. If the full-length figure's head corresponds to the final face used in *Woman I*, in the 1952 drawing the connections can be extended to include much of the upper torso—both the general shape and the pulling around to the frontal plane of each arm

165

are remarkably similar, as is the position of the figure's fore-arms and hands placed in the lap. Other, more abstract elements are also related; to the left, the horizontal lines, at shoulder level in the painting, are raised higher in the pastel, and in both, the lines are surmounted by a triangular-shaped unit. In each work de Kooning suggests—as he had repeatedly in the early states of the painting—a semigeometric tone behind the figure, encasing the head. Finally the most striking connection between the works is the face itself, recalling both that of the full-length drawing and that of the tracing of state four, as well as the face of *Woman I.*

These correspondences might lead us to think that the *Woman* pastel was a record or study made after *Woman I* was finished. But certain areas are unresolved, such as the figure's left arm and hip, or the left shoulder, or the vertical lines running through the left arm—all of which would suggest that the work is preliminary. Other parts of the composition, the straight horizontal line through the left shoulder in particular, suggest that de Kooning actually masked off parts of the surface while making the work. Finally, and perhaps most importantly, the face which corresponds so strongly to that of *Woman I* is collaged onto the pastel, attached by two pieces of tape to either side. With this addition removed, the face below bears little resemblance to *Woman I;* in fact it is covered by rather freely drawn, almost automatic curving lines (the start of these lines is visible in the loops immediately above the figure's right breast, and they emerge on the other side of the enlarged face, then rise above the forehead).

Thus, if the pastel *Woman* dates before—or even during—the finishing of *Woman I,* it played an "advisory" role in the final appearance of the work. And its collaged face suggests that de Kooning drew the torso, based in part on the general arrangement of state six or some later stage of the oil; then satisfied with the figure he added the face which had been preserved in the full figure drawing as well as the transfer sheet of state four. That the *Woman* pastel was important to de Kooning there can be little doubt, for it also influenced parts of *Woman II,* and de Kooning had it pinned to his studio wall the following summer in 1953 (fig. 19).

Another drawing closely related to the *Woman* pastel and *Woman I* is the bust-length *Woman* from this same time. As with the *Woman* pastel discussed above, this bust-length drawing is so close to the final *Woman I* oil as to be a study after the work. Here the correspondences involve particular aspects of the face, including not only the eyes, but the black markings on the left side and under the chin, as well as the wide passage of black on the lower right side of the figure's head, possibly indicating hair. Still differences exist between the drawing and painting, including the blue and green passage above the head in the drawing and the sharply drawn curved plane which extends from the right eye there. Moreover, elements of dress—design and coloration—are different.

Given the lack of precise dating and sequence, the exact relationship between the pastels from the summer of 1952 and *Woman I*—and all the Women paintings—still remains a puzzle. These correspondences to the paintings suggest at the minimum that, if the drawings predate the finish of *Woman I,*

they belong together as a rather tight group intended quite specifically for this oil.

They also bear another, direct relationship to *Woman I* in the palette and the touch used in painting the work. Central to understanding this relationship is understanding de Kooning's particular use of the pastel medium. As Larson has observed:

In de Kooning's "woman" drawings, conventional techniques are ignored for a more immediate handling of chalk and charcoal. Traditional pastel application often calls for a layer by layer application, beginning with the darkest hues and working towards the lightest, with periodic fixing of colors. De Kooning prefers to blur his colors into each other; preliminary outlines in charcoal fuse with paper surface and gray the tonality of the colored chalks. Rubbing and erasing, the artist dematerializes his "woman" images. . . .[18]

De Kooning's use of blurred black outlines and brushed-over color occurs in his earlier abstractions of 1945-1950 but in a far less pronounced or continuous fashion. Significantly these early works were also accompanied by cut-paper studies and pastel sheets. In *Woman I* and the subsequent paintings, however, de Kooning's use of strong black outlines around the figure, the semitransparent overlays of tones of blue and green, or red, white, and yellow, and the spontaneity of the stroke all indicate a direct and concrete relationship to his pastels. This connection, furthermore, suggests that the conflict in de Kooning's earlier art between drawing and painting was resolved in the Women by adapting the sketchy touch of his pastels directly to his wide, turbulent brushstrokes.

CUBISM

"A major problem for de Kooning throughout his career was his relation to Cubism," wrote Irving Sandler in his study of abstract expressionism.[19] And it remains an art-historical problem in terms of understanding de Kooning's paintings, especially the Women. As we might expect there are different, even opposite, opinions about this issue. Thomas Hess, for example, writes that de Kooning abandoned cubism in 1945, in the last of the biomorphic abstract pictures.[20] To the contrary, Clement Greenberg, writing in 1956, described de Kooning as fully a late-cubist artist. Greenberg's discussion is of particular interest:

These savage dissections were carved out, were patently Cubist. De Kooning is, in fact, the only painter I am aware of at this moment who continues Cubism without repeating it. In certain of his latest *Women* . . . the brilliance of the success achieved demonstrates what resources that tradition has left when used by an artist of genius.[21]

Greenberg's description must be tempered, for de Kooning's Women are certainly influenced by other stylistic tendencies besides those of cubism; his discoveries made through the *Cadavre Exquis* cut drawings certainly owe something to surrealism, and his painterly qualities derive from his pastels as well as from a whole range of expressionist works and from Cézanne.

Nevertheless, Greenberg's statement contains within it a sense of accuracy: as de Kooning himself said in 1951, exactly in the middle of painting *Woman I,*

Of all movements, I like Cubism most. It had that wonderful unsure atmosphere of reflection—a poetic frame where something could be possible, where an artist could practise his intuition. It didn't want to get rid of what went before. Instead it added something to it. The parts that I can appreciate in other movements came out of Cubism.[22]

If de Kooning's art is related to cubism, it is important to realize that it enrolls aspects of cubism in diverse manners, and furthermore it draws from varying periods and styles within cubism itself. Sandler has observed that de Kooning "had been reared in it [cubism] and could not deny its insistence on flatness and firm pictorial structure. At the same time, he desired a form that was more ambiguous, dynamic, and evocative of his own impulsive creative action."[23]

As we have seen, de Kooning's paintings of seated female figures from the early and very late 1940s, as well as the early states of *Woman I*, are indebted stylistically and thematically to Picasso's late cubist/surrealist works on the same subject. Around 1944, de Kooning began a group of abstractions, using biomorphic shapes (and probably influenced by Arshile Gorky), which nevertheless combine compositional elements in a manner more directly derived from late synthetic cubism. Beginning with *Labrinth*, 1946 (collection of Allan Stone, New York), and a series of black and white pictures, these abstractions grew increasingly complex. Sandler has accurately noted that in these works

areas interpenetrate to form a continuous surface; their planarity calls to mind Synthetic Cubism, but they are more equivocal, closer in a way to Analytic Cubism . . . or to Duchamp's Futurist variant. . . . Much as the planes in Picasso's and Braque's canvases of 1909 to 1912 are shuffled, they are composed along horizontal and vertical axes into measured scaffolds. De Kooning's organic areas are, by contrast, ceaselessly shifting; images and backgrounds interchange, so that "parts do not exist. . . . It is impossible to tell what is 'on top of' what. . . ."[24]

If de Kooning's art at this point, 1947, employed a vocabulary of shapes drawn from synthetic cubism—with biomorphic variations—the general thrust of his composition as it grew more complex was increasing toward analytical cubism. At the same time, de Kooning's style was growing increasingly painterly, and again cubism, in its 1910-1911 style, represented one of the great periods of painterly pictures.

In this tendency de Kooning was not alone. Greenberg has observed that "the grafting of painterliness on a cubist infra-structure was, and will remain, the great and original achievement of the first generation of Painterly Abstraction [or abstract expressionism]."[25]

Robert Motherwell has referred to the aesthetic idea of abstract expressionism as "a looser form of 1911 cubism."[26] Indeed, not only Motherwell's 1948-1949 works in collages, but the paintings of Pollock, Bradley Walker Tomlin, and others reveal a general shift toward the pictorial structures and/or painterly touches of the high analytical cubist works of Braque and Picasso.

As de Kooning's art moved from the 1948 black and white paintings into large abstractions, such as *Attic*, 1949 (collection of Muriel Newman, Chicago, Illinois), and then *Excavation*, 1950 (fig. 15), the number of individual units increased

Figure 15. Willem de Kooning. *Excavation*, 1950. Oil and enamel on canvas, 203.5 x 254.3 cm (80⅛ x 100⅛ in). The Art Institute of Chicago, Mr. and Mrs. F. G. Logan Prize; Gift of Mr. Edgar Kauffman, Jr., and Mr. and Mrs. Noah Goldowsky. Not in exhibition

Figure 16. Paul Cézanne. *Le Château Noir*, 1900/1904. Oil on canvas, 73.7 x 96.6 cm (29 x 38 in). National Gallery of Art, Washington, Gift of Eugene and Agnes Meyer. Not in exhibition

while their size diminished. The density of the picture—the overlapping of forms and their relationship to the ground—grew so great as to practically obscure any clear rendering of figure/ground in the works. Clearly the distribution of parts and of light and dark balances throughout in these pictures, and the combination of the painterly and the linear corresponds to 1911 cubist works. Furthermore, lines or the drawn scaffolding in cubist works had served both to demonstrate the edge of a solid form as well as to indicate the surface of a plane which was transparent. De Kooning's elements in *Excavation* in particular have similar qualities.

In her discussion of the relationship between these works and analytical cubism Rosalind Krauss observes that in the 1949-1950 works, since line could be made to appear to bound everything on either side of it, de Kooning's line was able to serve as the contour for every available area within the painting. The question of what was figure and what was ground, what was bounded and what was unbounded, was mooted by the capacity of de Kooning's line to corporealize every part of the painting's surface. And this capacity seemed, at least in part, to be a function of scale. Like the canvases of Analytic Cubism, de Kooning's early paintings had confined themselves to still lifes in which objects retained their actual size, or full-scale portrait heads. After his line had become the descriptor for abstract shapes, de Kooning maintained the sense of scale-parity that one finds both in his own earlier work and that of Early Cubism, so that once again the framing edge did not seem to signal the beginning of the illusionistic envelope. Because the abstract shapes bounded by his line also did not seem to intimate that they "really" existed at a different scale from the actual planes which abutted and turned against each other on the real surface of the picture, every part of that surface seemed to be created and made measurable by de Kooning's line.[27]

We have dwelt on these connections to cubism in de Kooning's 1949-1950 works—which he shared with other artists—because when we turn to the Women these formal relationships appear to diminish: these pictures seem to bear far fewer overt correspondences to cubism, in either its synthetic or analytic styles. But if, as Sandler suggests, de Kooning "had been reared" in cubism, and his works preceding the Women evidence his clear command of the possibilities of the style, then it is probably correct to expect the Women to continue this inclination, albeit in a radically different—and even more erudite—manner.

COLLAGE, PAINTERLINESS, SUBSTANCE

To understand the relationship of the Women to cubism, we must examine the Women with respect to three aspects: collage, painterliness, and substance. As we have seen, the disparity of relative scale among the parts of the woman's figure derives from de Kooning's cut-drawing collages and their adaptation of this technique to his painting. Elaine de Kooning first noted the result of these overlayed areas:

"Impossible" passages often appear: a torrent of color will suddenly disappear into strokes of other hues running at right angles. Some of these effects are deliberately produced by masking—i.e., placing paper over the surface adjacent to the one being painted and running the strokes over the paper, which is then removed, leaving a clean edge. More of them—and more important—have a sort of montage effect, a jump in focus, as if someone had abruptly changed the lens through which you were looking.[28]

As Hess records,

The record of a shift in a unit's position is retained in perceptible but unaccountable shifts of plane. Here the masking is not in paint, but in ideas. The effect, however, is similar, and gives an illusion of shallow space in which edges flicker up and down the surface—as they do in some Cubist painting.[29]

While the surrealist *Cadavre Exquis* is the formal and thematic precedent for this technique in de Kooning's works, the results in surrealist art—given the nature of the movement—are often fragmentary; and even created with reference to the figure the

surrealist works lack the sort of unity which de Kooning's Women enjoy.

The precedent for—indeed the invention of—this shift in levels of focus within a unified organization is the cubist collage, in the way that Braque, Gris, or Picasso could divide the surfaces of a violin, for example, and shift the elements to various levels, yet maintaining the allover sense of the subject. Furthermore, the cubist collage often employed actual objects—labels, wall paper—pasted into the work as a compositional focus, again a precedent for the women's mouths made from advertisements. These provide "a focus of realist detail" in de Kooning's collages and in the early states of the painting of *Woman I*.

But cubist collages and synthetic paintings are characterized by a tendency toward crisply drawn, somewhat geometric shapes that underscore a "neat" surface, all qualities not found in the Women. Rather the painterliness of the Women series recalls more the 1911 cubist paintings discussed above with regard to de Kooning's 1949-1950 works. Unlike his earlier works, however, de Kooning's Women, with their broad passages and areas of focus, do not recall the evenly distributed scaffolding and planes of high analytical cubism. But their richly layered and impastoed passages and their broken contours of black do directly relate to the painterly strokes and the discontinuous grid of 1911 cubism. Indeed by sweeping paint from one surface onto another, and thus slipping together differing planes (and ultimately levels of focus), de Kooning reenacts with more bravura and less structural restraint the spatial turnings and mergings of the cubist facets. Yet even so, the cubist style of 1911 results ultimately in works of the most delicate poise and balance; these qualities cannot be applied to any of the Women, as they are characterized by their impressive solidity and scale.

SUBSTANCE

If de Kooning's Women relate in their montage shifts of focus to synthetic cubism, and in their painterliness and broken contour drawing to its analytic phase, their particular sense of mass and corporeality corresponds to cubism in its earlier phases, or to such proto-cubist works as Picasso's *Gertrude Stein* (fig. 20) of 1905 or even this work's ancestors in Cézanne's portraits. These precedents are distinguished precisely by the manner in which they bring together areas of differing focus while maintaining a continual sense of figural surface.

There are three levels of operation in de Kooning's Women which must be examined before comparing his work with early cubist compositions—or especially *Woman I* with Cézanne's works. First, certain areas of the figure of *Woman I*—the head, the chest, or the legs, for example—are clearly recognizable in both their descriptive forms and their relative figural scale. But as we have seen, the focus shifts from one area to another—the montage effect—thus requiring a visual readjustment. The seams between these different visual levels are either prominantly left in place, as in the transition from shoulder to left arm, or are smoothed over by broad, loosely painted passages, as in the neck or right hip. The background—or foreground—of

Figure 17. Willem de Kooning. *Woman II*, 1952.
Oil on canvas, 148.9 x 109.2 cm (59 x 43 in). The
Museum of Modern Art, New York, Gift of Mrs.
John D. Rockefeller 3rd, 1955. Cat. no. 2, pl. 8

Woman I is quite painterly, though nondescriptive, thus avoiding the question of another shift in focus; but it is the very painterly quality of the ground which isolates the more flatly painted figure, thus giving it a sense of continuity and solidity as surface.

Secondly, de Kooning's art is more subtle than the simple description above suggests; for the figure itself, if more broadly composed, nevertheless remains on this side of painterliness. Indeed, as we have seen, the adherence of separate focus depends upon this. Such sharing of inner and outer painterliness allows de Kooning to structure *Woman I* by drawing both direct as well as fractional analogies between figure and ground. In this sense he is able to structure the work by extending—indeed magnifying—its images into the ground.

Thus the figure is one with its atmosphere, while cohering as a single form both against its ground and within itself.

At the same time the balancing of these compositional forces have a third effect, that of orienting the image back to the picture plane. Because there is disparity between visual levels, our eye reads the parts as located within visual planes, thus flattening and spreading out each particular area (this accounts more for why the figure reads so broadly). Both the disembodied painterly passages and the broken contours of the figure again suggest a visual fragmenting; and rather than turning continuously into depth, they pull back from it toward the surface. Finally, because structure runs through the figure into the ground, it also makes the pictorial fabric more continuous and planar.

Figure 18. Willem de Kooning, Study for *Woman II*, c. 1952. Charcoal, pastel, and collage on paper, 65 x 47.5 cm (26 x 19 in). Collection, Dr. and Mrs. Martin L. Gecht, Chicago [photo: courtesy of Harold Diamond]. Not in exhibition

The combination in the Women of shifting points of view, rich painterly areas, and an intermingled rather than proscribed structure all suggest comparison not with cubism, but with its source—the works of Cézanne. De Kooning has spoken directly to this question: "I don't want to defend myself but I am said to be Cubist-influenced. I am really much more influenced by Cézanne than by the Cubists because they were stuck with the armature." "They [the cubists] made a superstructure . . . [where] Cézanne said every brushstroke had its own perspective. He didn't mean it in the sense of Renaissance perspective, but that every brushstroke had its own point of view."[30]

In both Cézanne's and de Kooning's work, the central problem is to cohere visual fragments into one continual surface. Cézanne's solution was either to slip the surfaces together by softening the edges between planes, his *passage,* or to treat the planes of his surfaces as distinct blocks and abut the edges in a sharp manner, giving a clear sense of spatial stepping. Weaving together his picture in this fashion, Cézanne's works could unify because of the *passage* areas—and from the similarity in the size of his planes—while the more crisply joined elements could indicate clear spatial contouring. Nevertheless Cézanne's works remained more emphatically two dimensional, and the indications of surface and depth have the characteristics of a bas-relief.

De Kooning joined his disparate views in two ways, either by very broad and quite loosely painted seams or by simply leaving the sharp split between them, creating the spatial jump. Certainly de Kooning's painterly seams can be paralleled to Cézanne's *passage,* in the way they slip the eye across the

distortions of surface, while his use of masked disconnections can be related to the sharper contouring of Cézanne's planes.

Because of the scale of the elements in de Kooning's Women, his compositions do not create a bas-relief surface like that of Cézanne's: rather they remain far more two dimensional and oriented to the surface. And furthermore these figures do enjoy a distinction between figure and ground, as we have seen. But toward the end of the six Women, and especially in *Woman VI,* these differences between de Kooning's system and that of Cézanne are less pronounced; indeed, the greater fragmenting of surface and the merging of the figure with its landscape in *Woman VI* suggest viewing them in even more Cézannesque terms, as if the formal properties of Cézanne's landscapes actually increase its influences.

There are two other aspects in de Kooning's works which suggest discussion with respect to Cézanne: the formal "pairings" of shapes and the intermingled structure. Because his method could "guarantee" cohesion, Cézanne was able to introduce visual rhythms into his work which often key the picture to effect a sense of balance and gravity; the tradition of impressionism and old masters is combined in this fashion. De Kooning's Women also have visual passages of repeated shapes and details; but unlike Cézanne's work, in de Kooning's they serve the function of cohering the work across the pictorial field by introducing emphatic surface markings. Cézanne's structure was not fully preexistent but could be adjusted and modified to the requirements of the subject. De Kooning's work evokes a similar freedom. In de Kooning's Women the various fragments of the figure are not made to fit a structure but rather are structured by painterly joinings or juxtaposed overlays.

De Kooning's distinction between the cubist superstructure or armature and Cézanne's more independent brushstrokes is thus revealing. It suggests that in spite of its differences from traditional illusionistic systems, de Kooning saw cubism as a compositional style which indicated a proper location for his pictorial elements, and thus not a solution for his particular problem of joining separated views of the figure. But being able to create a unified system internally in the Women—which was either drawn from Cézanne, or discovered in the drawings and then seen as parallel—allowed de Kooning to "finish" the work according to needs which he could find within them. That is to say, de Kooning's structure did not exist a priori in the Women, but was the end product of them. It was, in this sense, found.

EARLY ASPECTS OF WOMAN II AND WOMAN III

When de Kooning took to finishing *Woman I* in the summer of 1952 it was, at the urging of Schapiro, a return to a previously abandoned painting. During the conclusion of *Woman I* three other paintings were present, *Woman II, III,* and *IV,* and these had been initiated after the sixth state, and before the final changes, of *Woman I.* If we take *Woman I* as the point of radical change in de Kooning's art, two of the "later" Women—*II* and *III*—are rooted more deeply in previous ideas

about pictorial presentation and capitalize upon the inventions of *Woman I*.

Woman II (fig. 17) is the closest—in iconographic terms—of the subsequent work to *Woman I*, or to state six of this picture. Again we have a seated figure, turned full face, with large breasts. But there are differences: the hands do not fold into her lap; rather the left one is placed to the side, with a hint that it rests upon an overturned book (an element found as well in Picasso's 1930s paintings). *Woman II*'s lower torso now turns to her right; but here it is incomplete for the legs are cut off at mid-calf (it is also a smaller canvas). The face, which recalls that of *Woman I* in the general characteristics of large diamond eyes and sharp features, not to mention the crown or cap behind the head, is nevertheless different in its quite clear suggestion of a three-quarter profile.

But where *Woman II* differs most from *Woman I* is in its stylistic treatment of the figure and the background. In the former work, the parts of the body are clearly more disparate, and while the seams are covered over with de Kooning's use of wide painterly strokes, nevertheless the parts maintain a sense of greater individuality, derived in part from their more volumetric qualities. This reading of *Woman II*—that the elements are more like the fitting together of elements of a doll—relates the work more to state six of *Woman I* and to de Kooning's works of the late 1940s than to the finished *Woman I*. *Woman II* lacks the masterful qualities of transitional elision

Figure 21. Willem de Kooning. *Woman III*, 1951-1952. Oil on canvas, 170.5 x 122.2 cm (67⅛ x 48⅛ in). Tehran Museum of Contemporary Art. Cat. no. 3, pl. 9

found in its "predecessor"—although it derives much of its character precisely from the formal qualities of the earlier state of the latter. The clarity of component construction prevents the figure of *Woman II* from fully merging with the ground, again a characteristic of de Kooning's earlier style.

In *Woman III* (fig. 21) we encounter the first major change in the Women series: the figure is standing. Again while certain aspects of the figure are clearly indebted to *Woman I*—such as the facial type, the "crown," and the squaring off and extension of the figure's left shoulder—and thus postdate its realization, nevertheless, other stylistic traits suggest that *Woman III* is in part, more *retardataire* than *Woman I*.

It is pertinent to recall here that the full-scale drawings de

Kooning made before beginning *Woman I* were of full-length figures and that these sheets were connected to earlier works such as *Two Women on a Wharf*. Some traits from these works remain evident in *Woman III*, especially the narrowing of the figure's thighs to form a V-like shape above the knees. And again like *Woman II*, and unlike *Woman I*, anatomical parts of *Woman III* do not fully merge with the remaining figure or with the ground but retain their probable origin as independent elements. This separateness is especially pronounced in the figure's left arm which recalls the collaged arm of state three of *Woman I*.

Woman III has other features which relate it to de Kooning's earlier states of *Woman I*. Primary among these are the three

172

Figure 22. Willem de Kooning. *Woman*, 1952. Pastel and pencil, 53.3 x 35.6 cm (21 x 14 in). Mr. and Mrs. Stephen D. Paine, Boston [photo: Barney Burstein]. Not in exhibition

Figure 23. Willem de Kooning. Two Women, 1952. Pastel on paper, 45.7 x 53.3 cm (18 x 21 in). Collection, Mr. and Mrs. John C. Denman [photo: reproduced from Thomas Hess, *Willem de Kooning: Drawings* (Greenwich, Conn., 1972)]. Not in exhibition

Figure 24. Pablo Picasso. *Les Demoiselles d'Avignon,* 1907. Oil on canvas, 243.9 x 233.7 cm (96 x 92 in). The Museum of Modern Art, New York, Acquired through the Lillie P. Bliss Bequest. Not in exhibition

parallel vertical lines to the left of the head, recalling similar elements in state three, and the squared-off area to the upper right, suggesting a window on the plane behind the figure. Finally, there is the unpainted ground at the bottom of the work—crossed with vertical runs of paint—which suggests both the earlier states of *Woman I* and de Kooning's method, as well as the idea that this canvas received few changes and overlayerings of ideas.

Woman IV, which was also begun before *Woman I* was finished, bears far fewer connections to the earlier period of de Kooning's art and thus was probably fully painted after *Woman I* through *III*. This is not to suggest, however, that *Woman II* and *Woman III* predate *Woman I* in realization. As we have seen, they share a number of traits which are accountable only to the precedent of a finished *Woman I*. Furthermore, like that canvas, they raise the question of the role of the summer 1952 drawings as well.

WOMAN II

Woman II as a seated figure is the sister image of *Woman I,* sharing facial features and the general carriage of the body. But

Figure 25. Willem de Kooning. *Woman IV,*
1952-1953. Oil on canvas, 149.9 x 117.5 cm (59
x 46¼ in). Nelson Gallery-Atkins Museum,
Kansas City, Mo., Gift of Mr. William Inge.
Cat. no. 4, pl. 10

Woman II is in many ways more aggressive, her face at a much
greater scale, her shoulders of an enormous width and mass,
and her hands given to clawlike fingers, reminiscent of a hand
rake. The suggested book, opened and turned face down on her
lap, is another difference from *Woman I*. But the two initial
Women paintings are related in that they each correspond to
the collaged *Woman* pastel of 1952 discussed above. Indeed if
the top part of this drawing relates to *Woman I*, the entire
page—and especially the turn of the figure to her right—
corresponds with *Woman II*.

As with *Woman I*, there are other sketches which relate to
Woman II, again suggesting that a process of invention and
refinement surrounds the actual painting. *Study for Woman II*
(fig. 18), for example, is far more tentative than the twice-used
collage pastel. Nevertheless, this drawing is clearly related to
Woman II, with the scale of the upper torso and the more
dominant head, the indication of a red book held on the lap,

and the spikey hand—held downward here—on the left of the
sheet. *Study for Woman II* is a collaged work, made by
superimposing the lighter element of hand and book over an
already existing figure. This base sheet may date earlier than
1952, as the window to the upper right corner suggests. As he
had with *Woman I* de Kooning here probably made numerous
drawings and collages—some "finished" as in the collage pastel described above, and others more exploratory as in *Study
for Woman II*.

More than any of the other Women, *Woman II* reveals how
de Kooning adapted his montage drawing inventions into
paintings. The masking off of the painting's surface can be seen
at its most evident in the line which crosses horizontally immediately above the figure's breasts. Examination of the surface
reveals built-up paint along the once taped-off edge. Another
clearly masked-off edge is found in the face, immediately below
the nose. The resulting juxtaposition in these slices indicates de

174

Figure 26. Willem de Kooning. *Woman*, here dated 1952. Pencil, 30.1 x 24.1 cm (11⅞ x 9½ in). Collection, Allan Stone, New York [photo: reproduced from Thomas Hess, *Willem de Kooning: Drawings* (Greenwich, Conn., 1972)]. Not in exhibition

edges of the figure. Furthermore, Krauss has observed·that in these works Picasso and Braque often made the figures (and objects) comparable to actual life size, introducing a one-to-one, or less fictive, relationship, and that this sense of actual size was carried on by de Kooning in his large abstract pictures, including *Excavation*. If de Kooning carried over into the Women certain principles of cubism, as is argued here, he did not continue this scale relationship; rather, the figures in the Women are—in size—larger than life, but their formal presentation is geared to actual figural size. "But if I make a big painting," says de Kooning, "I want it to be intimate. I want to separate it from the mural. I want it to stay an easel painting."[32] The Women do—in formal prescriptions—but the figural size looms bigger, and this accounts, in part, for their almost gigantic presence. They are literally monstrous, whereas the drawings, by comparison, employ the same figural and facial displacements, but their fictive scale keeps them fictitious.

WOMAN III

Woman III (fig. 21) is the most *retardataire* of the entire series in terms of its stylistic connections to de Kooning's late 1940s concerns. The Women series was initiated by large drawings of a standing figure—or a single drawing of two figures, related to the 1949 *Woman on a Wharf*. It is important to realize that although the seated figure of *Woman I* occupied de Kooning's paintings from June 1950 to February 1952, during this period he continued to make drawings of standing figures. Among these earlier works is a rather automatic study in the Tishman collection, *Woman* (collection of Mr. and Mrs. Paul Tishman, New York), which unlike the vast majority of de Kooning's works—is dated: 1951. This locates the drawing—before *Woman III* was begun in February 1952—and, as it is stylistically relevant, provides a linkage between the 1940s and *Woman III*, indicating the painting was clearly an extension of de Kooning's ideas rather than a renewal of a previous theme.

As with the second *Woman* canvas, *Woman III* was also influenced by *Woman I* and by the pastel and charcoal drawings of the summer of 1952. In this regard, a sheet in the Paine collection, *Woman* (fig. 22), is relevant, as it relates to *Woman III* not only in the figural style but in details of the background—vertical stripes to the upper left and, here, a building with a window to the right.

Woman III also foreshadows the canvases of the subsequent Women, which, as in this instance, are also standing. The black lines, which had played a secondary role in *Woman I* and *II*, here take on increased authority, and in parts of the work—to the left of the head in particular—they cover the surface in a rather automatic and nondescript fashion. Here de Kooning also begins to pinch and pull the planes of the figural surface—for example the left side of the face—and then to extend the schematic pattern of the shapes into analogous markings nearby.

The palette of *Woman III*, her chalky orange hair, pink (and blue) skin, and pale yellow swimming suit, again connects the painting to the pastel drawings. Indeed, the standing, bikini-

Kooning's continuing use of changes in focus. The shoulders, for example, are much closer to us in scale, and this increases their massiveness. The same is true for the upper facial register, now propelling the already large eyes forward, with the mouth and chin twisting to the left and dropped to a lower level. These changes in scale and spatial location, more pronounced in the face, again suggest comparison to Picasso's *Gertrude Stein* portrait (fig. 20), which de Kooning surely knew. He himself associates the Women with Stein, though in terms of her literary characters, and not with the Metropolitan portrait:

When I was painting those figures, I was thinking about Gertrude Stein, as if they were ladies of Gertrude Stein—as if one of them would say, "How do you like me?" Then I could sustain this thing all the time because it could change all the time; she could almost get upside down, or not be there, or come back again, she could be any size. Because this content could take care of almost anything that could happen.[31]

The effect of these changes in size brings to attention the question of scale in the Women series as a whole. Although Cézanne's works and those of Picasso from 1906 to 1909 are composed with a continual sense of the surface, the figures within these works remain in their own perspective or fictive scale. But as cubism moved to greater distortion and an increased two-dimensionality (and a sense of transparency in 1910-1911), the relationship between figure and ground was established through the lessening of pictorial incidents at the

Figure 27. Willem de Kooning. *Woman V,* 1952-1953. Oil and charcoal on canvas, 154.8 x 113.8 cm (60⅞ x 44¾ in). Australian National Gallery, Canberra. Cat. no. 5, pl. 11

clad figure is present but usually in pairs in many of the richest drawings from 1952. While these drawings are only generally related to *Woman III,* it is worthwhile to single out two of them for their formal connections (thematic concerns will be discussed below). The drawings present nude or bikini-clad figures standing before a structure, buildings or piers, which record summertime activities and recall the *Two Women on a Wharf* precedent. Of special interest is a pastel, *Two Women* (fig. 23), which has two figures, one standing with hand on hip, the other squatting, her buttocks forming a strong *W* shape. To this we can join the Weisman drawing, *Two Women with Still Life* (collection, Mr. and Mrs. Frederick Weisman, Beverly Hills, Calif.) of two standing figures, with a pier behind them; on the beach at their feet is a triangular table with a still life of clams and hamburgers.[33] The subject elements themselves, as

well as the formal treatment, of these two works point to another picture which must be cited as a source, perhaps remembered rather than studied over: Picasso's *Les Desmoiselles d'Avignon* (fig. 24). This quintet of women—surely the most famous of modern art—thus came into consideration in de Kooning's Women, if only by influence upon the *Two Women* pastels.

WOMAN IV

Woman IV (fig. 25) was started in February 1952 along with the other two canvases. Yet it bears little relationship to de Kooning's works of the 1940s, or to state six of *Woman I,* or even to *Woman II* and *III*—save the spikey right hand—requiring us to propose that its original image was scraped off or painted out. It does find precedent in *Woman I,* and the

176

Figure 28. Rembrandt van Ryn. *A Woman Bathing in a Stream*, 1655. Oil on panel, 61.8 x 47.0 cm (24 5/16 x 18½ in). National Gallery, London, Holwell Carr Bequest [photo: Anderson, courtesy of Alinari, Florence]. Not in exhibition

undulating curve of her arm is paralleled by the sweep of the figure's full contour. Even the plane which is placed above the left arm and shaded on top with blue is present in the drawing and modeled in a similar fashion. The converging lines on *Woman IV*'s breast are echoed in the girderlike bands beneath the breasts in the drawing. Finally the oval shape in the lower right of the painting is found at the middle left of the drawing; unfortunately they presently escape identification. The drawing confirms what the coloration of the painting suggests: that the rich blue across the bottom of the work is water, and that the figure is standing in it. The flat opaque manner in which it is presented predicts the similar handling de Kooning gives to landscape elements in his later Parkways series.

WOMAN V AND VI AND REMBRANDT

De Kooning stopped painting *Woman I* at least by the end of the summer of 1952—during or after the period of pastels, leaving the picture until November, when he decided it was finished. Presumably *Woman II* and *III* were completed during the summer as well, whereas *Woman IV* might have extended into the fall, because it reflects later stylistic traits; indeed, work upon it might have continued into 1953. This completed the quartet of Women paintings which had existed in various states since February 1952. De Kooning began a new painting, *Woman V* (fig. 27), in the fall and initiated the last of the paintings, *Woman VI* (fig. 29), sometime after the beginning of 1953; both were finished by the March exhibition. We can date *Woman V* to the fall because like the winter *Woman VI* the palette of the picture is a shade darker than the previous works, and for both of them, none of the summer pastels seem directly related to their particular composition.

Woman V and *VI* are related generally to *Woman IV*, all being three-quarter-length figures standing symmetrically in the compositional field. "I put it in the center of the canvas," says de Kooning, "because there was no reason to put it a bit on the side." Throughout the series this reasoning also governed the "traditional" aspects of the head: "So I thought I might as well stick to the idea that it got two eyes, a nose and mouth and neck."[34]

Both works relate to *Woman IV* as well, where the figure stands "in" something, with a blue-green-yellow glaze covering the legs of *Woman V*, and the blue field surrounding the legs of *Woman VI*. As they are not summer pictures and are not drawn from pastels, they do not share earlier thematic directions with *Woman IV*. A more speculative source, especially for *Woman V* and *Woman VI*, is a variant, to be found in Rembrandt's *Woman Bathing* of 1654.[35] Beyond the similar gesture of the figure holding up her skirt (in *Woman V* the hands were later moved upward to clasp in the center) in *Woman V* the legs are covered with translucent greens, suggestive not of sea water, but the water of an inland stream, as in the Rembrandt. De Kooning could have come across this painting in an article by H. Richardson entitled "Discoveries Beneath the Paint of Masters" published in *Art News* in February 1952.[36] This essay, about cleaning paintings at the National Gallery in London, was illustrated with greatly enlarged details of old master

pentimenti of the originally crossed hands and the red skirt suggest it was originally a seated figure, and therefore much closer to the first canvas.

It is more proper to date *Women IV* to the end of the summer 1952 works because of its rich layering of chalky colors and its more automatically drawn and positioned figure. In the painting the pinching and pulling out of surface planes is quite pronounced, as in the figure's right shoulder and waist. The parts of the woman's anatomy are more separate and independent; the figure's left arm is virtually detached. Yet here the seaming effect of de Kooning's painterly connections is most productive.

As with the other three pictures, *Woman IV* has a related pastel. This sheet, *Women* (fig. 27), shows a woman standing in the water before a fence (or boardwalk?), with horizon line indicated and the suggestion of a house in the distance. While the figure is rather freely drawn, we can still identify the strands of hair blown over her left shoulder, while over her right the side view of her scarf is now visible.

Where the plane of the woman's right shoulder in the painting is gathered to a projected point, in the drawing only a small arrow indicates any shift of level. On the woman's left side the

Figure 29. Willem de Kooning. *Woman VI*, 1953. Oil on canvas, 174.0 x 148.6 cm (68½ x 58½ in). Museum of Art, Carnegie Institute, Pittsburgh. Cat. No. 6, pl. 12

paintings, a photographic technique parallel to the way de Kooning had previously studied details in works. The caption on the Rembrandt, labeled "Improvisation," speaks of his "thick bold strokes" and his "translucent halftones," both stylistic features of de Kooning's Women series.

If *Woman Bathing* did advise *Woman V* and *VI*—especially in terms of theme—they still remain within the confines of the Women series. Indeed, *Woman V* like *Woman IV* makes use of pinched and pulled planes and rhythmic echoings of the curvilinear designs. Only in the later work they have become more freely painted and begun to acquire a greater independence of the figure proper (see for example the bowed curve over the arm on the right, or the "rings" of arrows to the left of the head).

WOMAN VI AND LANDSCAPE

If *Woman II* stands apart from the series because of its affinities with de Kooning's earlier style, *Woman VI* announces the next series, landscapes. Of all of the works, it is the most abstract, the components of the woman's figure identifiable more from location than any descriptive connotations. Like *Woman V*, she reaches down to lift her skirt but does so in rigid symmetry. This rigid quality is maintained in the black drawing which is now thicker and more blunt and is applied predominantly in horizontal and vertical patterns. This is continued into the hard ground of the work, even including the strict horizontal line above the green and a red rectangle on the far right. Only the upper register of the painting—as in the other works—receives loosely brushed, wandering strokes, and these are interrupted by triangular patches.

Unlike the other works, in *Woman VI* there is far less contrast between figure and ground in terms of broadly painted areas and passage connections. Here the figure—denied any space suggesting contraposto—begins to merge with the landscape. After painting *Woman VI*, de Kooning made the analogy of "woman as landscape" in a drawing done in Washington, D.C., in 1953, where the nose is the Washington Monument and the left breast is the Jefferson Memorial.[37] Two years later he painted *Woman as Landscape* (private collection), further emphasizing the thematic correspondences set loose in *Woman VI*. Finally, in *Police Gazette* (private collec-

178

Figure 30. Willem de Kooning. *Suburb in Havana,* 1958. Oil on canvas, 203.2 x 177.8 cm (80 x 70 in). Collection, Mr. and Mrs. Lee V. Eastman, New York [photo: Eric Pollitzer, courtesy of The Solomon R. Guggenheim Museum, New York]. Not in exhibition

tion), also of 1955, de Kooning turned a woman figure upside down and the first of his landscapes properly begins.

As de Kooning's art evolved through the Women series, its Cézannesque and cubist aspects allowed him to enroll landscape into his art. But in the works of Cézanne and the cubists, painting touch and composition could shift between subjects and still remain consistent. As de Kooning's art turned this initial Cézannesque and improvisational structure to landscape, it also changed into a different style. The Women series, which began with a seated figure in a studio with a window, ended with a figure molded into the broad vistas of the out-of-doors.

WOMEN AS BATHERS

The works which comprise the Women series are linked together by their formal heritage in the inventions of *Woman I,* primarily found in the artist's ability to combine disparate focuses through the use of automatically generated *passage* and its resultant structure.

The Women are linked by a simple fact of theme—they are all women. But beyond this, we can connect the six works—and delve deeper into de Kooning's goal in them—by reference to what the Women are doing. To be concise, *Woman I* through *IV,* drawn from de Kooning's summer pastels, are bathers of one sort or another, and *Woman V* and *VI,* made in

reference to Rembrandt's *Woman Bathing,* repeat this theme but have shifted slightly in context.

Woman I and *II* are in fact sunbathing; this accounts for their costume of halter blouse, bare arms, and scarf on the head. As the drawings for *Woman I* reveal, the vertical mark above the triangular area to the right of the figure's shoulder is a boat; in the bust-length drawing it is plainly visible at the upper right and becomes more abstracted in the collaged, seated figure sheet. Viewing the Women as standing before a horizon line which runs through the figure below the shoulder (except for *Woman III,* where the suggestion of architecture is present; again this work, as argued here, is more dependent upon state six for aspects of its foundation) allows us to account for the more painterly markings in the upper register behind the head as indications of atmosphere and deeper space—seascape in *Woman I, II,* and *III*—which, being abstracted and fragmented, do not punch a "hole" into de Kooning's overall pictorial surface. De Kooning had often put a window in the upper portion of the work, as an indication of spatial release; in *Woman III* it is replaced by a more two-dimensional indication of the landscape vista. That the depth and surface could be acknowledged simultaneously in this manner is probably the motivation behind the woman becoming landscape, finally giving over to such works as *Suburb in Havana* (fig. 30).

If *Woman I* is positioned before the sea, she also has water at her feet indicated by the blue (indeed there was originally much more of it, now overpainted by greens and yellows). Certainly a woman seated by the water—here sunbathing—is what de Kooning has painted. He recalls:

Woman I, for instance, reminded me very much of my childhood, being in Holland near all that water. Nobody saw that particularly, except Joop Sanders. He started singing a little Dutch song. I said, "Why do you sing that song?" Then he said, "Well, it looks like she is sitting there." The song had to do with a brook. It was a gag and he was laughing, but he could see it. Then I said, "That's very funny, because that's kind of what I am doing." He said, "That's what I thought."
Rosenberg: You mean you had the water feeling even in New York?
De Kooning: Yes, because I was painting those women, and it came maybe by association, and I said, "It's just like she is sitting on one of those canals there in the countryside." In Rotterdam you could walk for about 20 minutes and be in the open country.[38]

Woman II joins this theme, here looking up at us from her book.

Woman III is ambiguous in her location, in- or out-of-doors, although her costume of a bikini (after all, a bathing suit) and her ancestry in the *Two Women on a Wharf* and the *Two Women* (before a pier?) series of drawings would argue for her location to be near the water. The palette of bright, sun-filled color would confirm this as well. *Woman IV* isn't by the water, but rather in it, as we can see by the areas of blue which surround the lower portions of her body. Indeed, even the positioning of her legs hints at a figure striding in the water. This is confirmed by the object located at the upper right, a schematic rendering of a house, with peaked roof. *Woman IV* is offshore and we are here looking back at the beach.

Figure 31. Jean-Auguste-Dominique Ingres. *Madame Moitessier Seated*, 1851. Oil on canvas, 146.7 x 100.3 cm (57¾ x 39½ in). National Gallery, London. Not in exhibition

It is this thematic device of *Woman IV* standing in the water which so strongly supports the idea that *Woman V*—and from it *Woman VI*—are drawn from Rembrandt's *Woman Bathing*. Rembrandt's picture offers a compatible theme to link the two latter works with the series, especially in light of de Kooning's absence from the seashore in winter and the absence of summer pastel drawings to work out the pictures. In the final analysis, all six are bathers of various sorts.

As de Kooning has said of the series,

The *Women* had to do with the female painted through all the ages, all those idols. . . .

Painting the *Women* is a thing in art that has been done over and over—the idol, Venus, the nude. . . .

It became a problem of picture painting, because the very fact that it had words connected with it—"figure of a woman"—made it more precise.[39]

By adopting as his theme "women as bathers" de Kooning could then link up his works more directly with grand traditions in the history of art, but without denying the modernity of their appearance—or even their origin.

And this broader fabric of subject allowed de Kooning to consciously or unconsciously paint attitudes—or more precisely, some of his attitudes about women—into the works, but in such a way that they were not illustrations:

Figure 32. Willem de Kooning. *Woman,* c. 1951. Pencil, pastel on paper, 21.6 x 28.6 cm (8½ x 11¼ in). National Gallery of Art, Washington, Andrew W. Mellon Purchase Fund 1978 [photo: courtesy of Xavier Fourcade, Inc.]. Not in exhibition

I wasn't concerned to get a particular kind of feeling. I look at them now and they seem vociferous and ferocious. I think it had to do with the idea of the idol, the oracle, and above all the hilariousness of it. I do think that if I don't look upon life that way, I won't know how to keep on being around.

I imagine that Cézanne, when he painted a ginger pot and apples and ordinary everyday wine bottles, must have been very grotesque in his day, because a still-life was something set up of beautiful things.

I feel now if I think of it, it will come out in the painting. In other words, if I want to make the whole painting look like a bottle, like a lot of bottles, for instance—maybe the end of the day, when everything is very light, but not in sunlight necessarily—and so if I have this image of this bottle and if I really think about it, it will come out in the painting. That doesn't mean that people notice a bottle, but I know when I succeed in it—then the painting would have this.[40]

As with Picasso's inscription of "Ma Jolie" on his works as a message of love for Eva, cubism offered a rough parallel to de Kooning's inclusion of personal images in a grander theme. But the wide-ranging and often monstrous views of women expressed in de Kooning's art is really precedented by Picasso's *Les Desmoiselles d'Avignon,* which advised the drawings from 1952; its thematic undertakings were probably equally important to de Kooning's ambitions.

The formal and thematic inventions of the Women allowed de Kooning to connect his art with Cézanne and even with Ingres, whose combination of unified drawing and psychological observation had previously eluded de Kooning. If *Woman I* can be linked with Ingres' *Madame Moitessier Seated* (National Gallery, London) on formal grounds, through Cézanne and the Picasso of the 1930s, it is the revelation of personality in both that is equally arresting, startling in the case of de Kooning's monsters (see, for example, figs. 31, 32).

Shortly after the appearance of the Women, Greenberg wrote of de Kooning:

He enjoys both the advantages and the liabilities of an aspiration larger, perhaps, than that of any other living artist. De Kooning's apparent aim is a synthesis of tradition and modernism that would grant him more flexibility within the confines of the Late Cubist canon of design. The dream of a grand style hovers over all this—the dream of an obviously grand and an obviously heroic style.

. . . No more than Picasso can de Kooning tear himself away from the figure and that modeling of it for which his sense of contour and chiaroscuro so well equip him. And there is perhaps even more Luciferian pride behind de Kooning's ambition than there is behind Picasso's: were he to realize all his aims, all other ambitious painting would have to stop for a generation since he would have set both its forward and its backward limits.[41]

Certainly de Kooning was not attempting to revive figural painting as much as to continue it within the context of abstract expressionism; this is the final "grandeur" of de Kooning's Women series. The ambition behind his theme of historical linkage—the subject of his Women series—connects de Kooning firmly to his colleagues.

NOTES

This essay on the Women would not have been possible without the generous assistance and shared insights of Xavier Fourcade, Thomas Hess, and Lee V. Eastman.

1. That de Kooning had returned to figuration at the end of the 1940s in the midst of his abstract works before beginning the Women series in 1950 was ignored in light of the revelations of the 1953 exhibition.

2. De Kooning; quoted in Thomas Hess, *Willem de Kooning* (New York: Museum of Modern Art, 1969), 148 (excerpts from an interview with David Sylvester for the BBC; reprinted from *Location, 1*, Spring 1963).

3. De Kooning; quoted in Hess, *De Kooning* (1969), 148.

4. Thomas B. Hess, "De Kooning paints a picture," *Art News, 52* (Mar. 1953): 30 ff.; as well as his *Willem de Kooning* (New York: George Braziller, 1959); *De Kooning* (1969); and *Willem de Kooning: Drawings* (Greenwich, Conn.: New York Graphic Society Ltd., 1972).

5. Hess' discussion, in *Drawings*, relates them only to *Woman I*, but as is shown below, these sheets also influenced other Women pictures as well.

6. Hess, in *Drawings*, revises the time of "finishing" to November 1952. A photo caption in his earlier *Art News* article gives June 1952 as the date.

7. The *Art News* illustration of *Woman I*, in "De Kooning paints a picture," 31, shows the picture as cropped. The caption notes that "after the photograph for the colorplate was made and the picture ready for stretching, the artist decided to extend it about 8 inches at the right side." Given the lead time necessary for printing color, this would put the "finish" of *Woman I* sometime between November 1952 and January 1953.

8. In spite of the similarities to this Picasso, there is a question of de Kooning's knowing the Simon picture, as it was generally unknown until recently; see Robert Rosenblum, "Picasso's 'Woman with a Book,'" *Arts, 51* (Jan. 1977): 100.

9. De Kooning; quoted in Hess, *De Kooning* (1969), 149.

10. De Kooning; quoted in Hess, *De Kooning* (1969), 149.

11. Hess, *Drawings,* 42.

12. De Kooning; quoted in Hess, *De Kooning* (1969), 149.

13. Philip Larson [and Peter Schjeldahl], *De Kooning: Drawings/Sculptures,* exh. cat., Walker Art Center, Minneapolis (New York: E. P. Dutton & Co., Inc. 1974), n.p.

14. Larson, *Drawings/Sculptures.*

15. Hess, *Drawings,* 43.

16. William S. Rubin, *Dada, Surrealism, and Their Heritage* (New York: Museum of Modern Art, 1968), 83.

17. Hess, *Drawings,* 42-43.

18. Larson, *Drawings/Sculptures.*

19. Irving Sandler, *The Triumph of American Painting: A History of Abstract Expressionism* (New York, Washington: Praeger Publishers, 1970), 128.

20. Hess, *Drawings,* 31. Hess states of *Abstraction* (collection of Allan Stone, New York): "a new post-Cubist space is emphasized."

21. Clement Greenberg, "American-type Painting," *Partisan Review* (Spring 1955), 184.

22. De Kooning; quoted in Hess, *De Kooning* (1969), 149.

23. Sandler, *The Triumph of American Painting,* 128.

24. Sandler, *The Triumph of American Painting,* 128.

25. E. A. Carmean, Jr., *The Collages of Robert Motherwell,* exh. cat. (Houston: Museum of Fine Arts, 1972) [Clement Greenberg, "The 'Crisis' of Abstract Art," *Arts Yearbook 7: New York: The Art World* (New York, 1964), p. 91.]

26. Robert Motherwell; quoted in Carmean, *Collages,* 94.

27. Rosalind Krauss, "The New de Koonings," *Artforum, 6* (Jan. 1966): 47.

28. Hess, "De Kooning paints a picture," 65.

29. Hess, "De Kooning paints a picture," 65-66.

30. De Kooning; in an interview in Harold Rosenberg, *De Kooning* (New York: Harry N. Abrams, Inc., 1973), 40.

31. De Kooning; quoted in Hess, *De Kooning* (1969), 148.

32. De Kooning; quoted in Rosenberg, *De Kooning,* 43.

33. Hess, *Drawings,* 46.

34. De Kooning; quoted in Hess, *De Kooning* (1969), 148.

35. Thomas Hess kindly pointed out this reference in conversation with the author, Dec. 1977 (on file in the Department of Twentieth-Century Art, National Gallery of Art).

36. H. Richardson, "Discoveries beneath the paint of masters," *Art News, 50* (Feb. 1952): 34, 54-55.

37. Hess, *Drawings,* 45.

38. Rosenberg, *De Kooning,* 49.

39. De Kooning; quoted in Hess, *De Kooning* (1969), 148.

40. Hess, *De Kooning* (1969), 149-150.

41. Clement Greenberg, *Art and Culture* (Boston: Beacon Press, 1961), 213-214.

BARNETT NEWMAN:

The Stations of the Cross - Lema Sabachthani

Figure 1. Barnett Newman in his library in New York, 1965. To the right is the *First Station* (cat. no. 1). [Photo: Ugo Mulas, courtesy of Annalee Newman]

CHECKLIST

1. First Station 1958
   magna on canvas
   198.1 x 152.4 cm (78 x 60 in)
   Signed and dated, lower right: Barnett Newman 1958
   Collection, Annalee Newman, New York

2. Second Station 1958
   magna on canvas
   198.1 x 152.4 cm (78 x 60 in)
   Signed and dated, lower right: Barnett Newman 1958
   Collection, Annalee Newman, New York

3. Third Station 1960
   oil on canvas
   198.1 x 152.4 cm (78 x 60 in)
   Signed and dated, lower right: Barnett Newman 1960
   Collection, Annalee Newman, New York

4. Fourth Station 1960
   oil on canvas
   198.1 x 152.4 cm (78 x 60 in)
   Signed and dated, lower right: Barnett Newman 1960
   Collection, Annalee Newman, New York

5. Fifth Station 1962
   oil on canvas
   198.1 x 152.4 cm (78 x 60 in)
   Signed and dated, lower left: Barnett Newman 1962
   Collection, Annalee Newman, New York

6. Sixth Station 1962
   oil on canvas
   198.1 x 152.4 cm (78 x 60 in)
   Signed and dated, lower right: Barnett Newman 1962
   Collection, Annalee Newman, New York

7. Seventh Station 1964
   oil on canvas
   198.1 x 152.4 cm (78 x 60 in)
   Signed and dated, lower left: Barnett Newman 1964
   Collection, Annalee Newman, New York

8. Eighth Station 1964
   oil on canvas
   198.1 x 152.4 cm (78 x 60 in)
   Signed and dated, lower right: Barnett Newman 1964
   Collection, Annalee Newman, New York

9. Ninth Station 1964
   acrylic on canvas
   198.1 x 152.4 cm (78 x 60 in)
   Signed and dated, lower right: Barnett Newman 1964
   Collection, Annalee Newman, New York

10. Tenth Station 1965
    magna on canvas
    198.1 x 152.4 cm (78 x 60 in)
    Signed and dated, lower left: Barnett Newman 1965
    Collection, Annalee Newman, New York

11. Eleventh Station 1965
    acrylic on canvas
    198.1 x 152.4 cm (78 x 60 in)
    Signed and dated, lower right: Barnett Newman 1965
    Collection, Annalee Newman, New York

12. Twelfth Station 1965
    acrylic on canvas
    198.1 x 152.4 cm (78 x 60 in)
    Signed and dated, lower right: Barnett Newman 1965
    Collection, Annalee Newman, New York

13. Thirteenth Station 1965-1966
    acrylic on canvas
    198.1 x 152.4 cm (78 x 60 in)
    Signed and dated, lower left: Barnett Newman/1966
    Collection, Annalee Newman, New York

14. Fourteenth Station 1965-1966
    acrylic and duco on canvas
    198.1 x 152.4 cm (78 x 60 in)
    Signed and dated, lower left: Barnett Newman 1966
    Collection, Annalee Newman, New York

15. Be II 1961-1964
    acrylic and oil on canvas
    203.2 x 182.9 cm (80 x 72 in)
    Signed and dated, lower right: Barnett Newman '61+64
    Collection, Annalee Newman, New York

BIOGRAPHY

Born in New York in 1905. Studies at the Art Students League and at City College, New York (B.A. in 1927), with graduate work at Cornell University in 1941. 1946 marks his first works using vertical elements. In 1948 is founding member of the Subjects of the Artist school, for which he provides the title. Paints two enormous canvases, *Vir Heroicus Sublimis* and *Cathedra* in 1951. Begins two paintings in February 1958 which eventually become the first Stations of the Cross. In 1960 paints two more works, and then decides to expand the series to the fourteen Stations. In 1966 the series is completed with *Be II,* painted earlier, added as the culminating work. *The Stations of the Cross* are exhibited at the Solomon R. Guggenheim Museum in 1966 and in the Newman retrospective at the Museum of Modern Art in 1971. In 1966 he begins another series of paintings, *Who's Afraid of Red, Yellow and Blue,* and the following year he finishes his major sculpture, the *Broken Obelisk.* On July 4, 1970, Newman dies in New York.

BARNETT NEWMAN:

The Stations of the Cross-Lema Sabachthani

THOMAS B. HESS

PREFACE

The text that follows was written in the spring of 1971 as the penultimate chapter of the Barnett Newman book which accompanied the retrospective for the artist which opened at the Museum of Modern Art that autumn. In other words, it was finished almost exactly a year after the artist's death on July 4, 1970.

His Stations of the Cross canvases were fresh in my mind at the time, from both exhibition and study in the reserves at the Guggenheim Museum. I've not seen them since the retrospective, seven years ago. Therefore it's impossible for me to revise in any significant manner—much less rewrite—the chapter. It's always dangerous to work from photos and other *aide-memoires*, and it's especially risky in works of such elusive yet evident sensuous appeal as Newman's Stations. Obviously a system informs them. I don't know precisely what it is—although I make a guess. Nor do I know precisely how important it is to an understanding of the works. (For example, you don't have to know much about Mme. Blavatsky and Theosophy to comprehend certain Kandinskys—but it helps; on the other hand, if you don't know the New Testament, you can't even see the Isenheim Altarpiece.) I believe that a close study of photographs of the Stations easily might suggest answers that easily could be wrong.

A few points did occur to me after writing the text and seeing the exhibition (that catalogues are written before the exhibits can be viewed under proper conditions is one of the paradoxes of the museum-al condition). The sculpture, *Here, 1*, 1950 (fig. 2), it seems to me, is crucial to an understanding of the Stations. It is the first major statement in Newman's work in which a sharp, dry, hard edge is confronted with a soft, viscous, active one ("the he and the she of it," to use Joyce's phrase). The motif first is stated in *The Promise*—that well-titled painting. *Here 1*, however, could be considered a noble, three-dimensional overture to the Stations.

Outcry, 1958, Newman's first work before beginning on the Stations, could be considered a revision in painting of *Here 1*; it has the soft, active, smeary, slablike shape, confined by (instead of confronted with) the crisp edges of a framing rectangle. *Outcry*, it seems to me, is not so much a repeat of the thin vertical canvases that led to *The Wild*, 1950 (fig. 2), as a double mirror set at a critical time in Newman's life—facing backward to his first sculpture and facing ahead to the vigorous new life that was opening before him.

I look forward to reading about the Stations now that they

once more will become available—about their link to the drawings made around the same time (it seems to be a vague connection to me); the place of related works to the series, such as *The Station*, 1963; the high significance Newman attached to black paint on bare canvas (the ultimate creative binary complement); and other interpretations and explications of these works that can repay decades of study and appreciation.

T.B.H.
New York, N.Y., March 1978

A hundred cares, a tithe of troubles and is there one who understands me? One in a thousand of years of the nights? All me life I have been lived among them but now they are becoming lothed to me. And I am lothing their little warm tricks. And lothing their mean cosy turns. And all the greedy gushes out through their small souls. And all the lazy leaks down over their brash bodies. How small it's all! And me letting on to meself always. And lilting all the time. . . .
—James Joyce, Finnegans Wake

The whole New York underground art world, just about, came to Newman's opening at the Betty Parsons Gallery, January 23, 1950. That evening there was a party for him at the Artists' Club on Eighth Street; the main decoration consisted of about a dozen card-table tops put against the walls with stripes made out of old feathers tied down their centers. It was a light-hearted, mischievous reconstruction of the show. When Newman saw the effect his pictures had made on his friends, tears came to his eyes. Did he realize they were poking fun at him? Or was he flattered, as he told the artists that evening, to see that his particular insignia had been recognized?

Years later, Newman implied that both interpretations are true. An artist who was then considered one of the spokesmen for the New York School came up to him at the opening and said: "I thought you were one of us, but I see you're a threat to us all." He overheard two artists' wives chatting. "What will Barney do next year?" said one. "Easy," was the answer, "he'll just hang the pictures sideways."

Aline Louchheim (now Saarinen), who had recently left *Art News* to write criticism for the *New York Times*, was stunned at the preview by the colors and scale of the pictures; she interviewed Newman and, she says, "I went back to the typewriter and wrote it as I think he told it." It was the only favorable review he would receive for years.

The whole of the New York art world, just about, stayed away from the opening of Newman's second one-man exhibition at the Betty Parsons Gallery, April 23, 1951 [fig. 2].

Figure 2. Barnett Newman at his exhibition at the Betty Parsons Gallery, which ran from April 23 to May 12, 1951. To the left is his plaster sculpture *Here 1*, 1950, and on the adjacent wall is *The Wild*, 1950. [Photo: Hans Namuth]

It is easy to account for the official, public hostility to Newman's work. The late 1940s and early 1950s were a period of ugly reaction in the arts, made even more vicious than usual by a mask of *bien-pensant* liberalism. Part of it came as a backwash from the hyperpatriotism of the war. Such spokesmen as the poet Archibald MacLeish, the publisher Henry Luce, the director of the Metropolitan Museum Francis Henry Taylor, and many others attacked modern art in all its forms as irrelevant to Great Human Needs and International Causes. Such men were not illiterate philistines, but rather smug intellectuals who had looked at Picasso, Matisse, de Chirico and even Mondrian, and who had "seen through" them to their "arid" inner meanings, and now they called for a renewal of realism, humanism and even allegorical and religious painting. They attacked the new American artists as pranksters trying to fool the public, as a self-promoting clique, as delinquents, and they phrased their attacks with all the well-used epithets that savage misunderstanding and fearfulness can evoke. It was a deplorable official cultural milieu. Poets and essayists—such as William Carlos Williams, Robert Lowell and Randall Jarrell, to name only the best—either looked to Europe for signs of a new modernism, or they ignored art completely, or they viewed it with a backwoodsman's suspicion. Not since the early days of the Impressionists, I believe, had artists been faced with such meanness and vicious disdain. The curtain of official hostility surrounding the art world seems to have had an effect similar to

that on the Impressionists. It drew the artists closer together, created a community where art was considered all-important, where it could be talked about endlessly, seen in studios and hunted down in the corners of galleries and museums. Even a café life was created by the artists, and they supported their own friends in other mediums—dancers, composers, poets, philosophers, many of whom later became famous: Merce Cunningham, John Cage, Paul Goodman, Buckminster Fuller.

You had the feeling that there was an "inside" and an "outside." Outside, Truman would attack all modern art in the person of Kuniyoshi (of all mild bêtes noires); Eisenhower would equate art with painting by the numbers; a congressman would spend hours in the Well of the House reciting lists of artists and critics who had worked for "subversive" organizations; the Institute of Modern Art in Boston changed its name to the Institute of Contemporary Art because, its director said in a manifesto, the adjective "modern" represented a degenerate tendency; *Life* magazine published screeching editorials denouncing Dubuffet. It was rather as if, in losing the war, cultural hegemony had been won by Mussolini—if not Hitler. That was the noise outside. Inside, as Harold Rosenberg wrote later, it was like living in a stockade. Everyone was united against a common enemy. Each individual's triumph helped a common cause.

Newman's favorable review in the *New York Times* was a freak thing—a bit of welcome sympathy from an unexpected quarter. But his hostile reception among the artists—inside the stockade—was even more unexpected. It hurt him deeply. He was, after all, very much a part of the artists' community in which the mutual aid of encouragement and congratulations was an unspoken rule.

It is instructive to examine some of the reasons for this reaction. First of all, there is the paradox of Newman as the integrated, self-confident citizen in an alien's milieu. He was, par excellence, the native New Yorker, connoisseur of cast-iron façades and of out-of-the-way restaurants, bars and little theaters; he was the cosmopolitan American who felt at home in any part of his country; he had warm deep affection for his family, a perfect marriage; he was as proud of his Jewish background as the du Ponts are of the French or the Kennedys of the Irish. The New York artists' world, however, in the late 1940s and early 1950s, had a peculiar coloration of exile and losses. The day of the American-American artists—pioneer types such as Edward Hopper, Stuart Davis, John Marin, Thomas Hart Benton; aristocrats such as George L. K. Morris and A. E. Gallatin—was passing. Most of the new leaders were "displaced persons"—de Kooning from Holland, Gorky from Armenian Russia, Pollock, Still, Rothko and Guston from the West, and Franz Kline and Baziotes from the Pennsylvania coal country. The city was strange to them and they were strangers in it—Pollock often talked about how lost and lonely he felt when he hit town, and how he wanted to catch the first freight and travel back to the plains. These artists loved the city with the passion of strangers. There was a hint of romance about them and of deep alienation from their roots. They were like princes in disguise, scarred by combats in distant lands, or like Indians who swoop in from the desert to pillage the water hole.

Among these men, Newman's frank, open nature, the ease with which he moved through his surroundings and the pleasure he took from them, his very evenness, made him seem odd. There must be something wrong with him—he could not be an artist.

Furthermore, as Newman said, "I paid a severe price for not being on the [government arts] project with the other guys; in their eyes I wasn't a painter; I didn't have the label."

Indeed, much of the substructure of the New York art community was based on friendships made while the artists worked together on the various mural and easel projects of the 1930s. Because Newman had been conspicuously absent from the scene, and because it was known that he had made his living as a teacher, it was assumed that he was some sort of an intellectual, a theoretician and, as far as painting was concerned, an upstart.

Newman himself, in his effort to encourage the development of an art world in New York, gave a certain credence to this image. In various writings and statements, he appeared as a spokesman, polemicist and philosopher for certain kinds of abstract painting, and from the middle 1940s, he had supported the work of Gottlieb, Rothko, Still, Pollock and a few others. From this it was deduced that he was an ideologue or a propagandist—brilliant, surely, but noncreative.

This at least was the general impression held among many of the "downtown" artists, the ones who might be called "bohemians," as against the uptown "intellectuals" (I suggest these labels for convenience's sake only—some of the "bohemians" were ultraintellectual and some of the "intellectuals" thoroughly happy as "bohemians"). Among the former were artists such as Gorky, de Kooning, Pollock, Kline, David Smith. They had gone through the disciplines of art schools and academies, not to universities. Their social life was centered around Greenwich Village. They wore workmen's clothes (the traditional European artist's uniform), talked about art and life in colorfully Delphic terms; they enjoyed the feeling of independence that comes from supporting yourself with odd jobs plus a little private teaching, from informal domestic arrangements and living in studio-lofts which they remodeled with the patience and tact of shipwrights. Among the "intellectuals" were Newman, Rothko, Still, Motherwell, Reinhardt and, by temperament if not with a college diploma, Gottlieb. Their social life gravitated uptown. They lived in apartments. When talking and writing about art, their language was clearer, more analytical. Many of them, and their wives, had taught in established schools.

The "bohemians" tended to show at the Egan Gallery; the "intellectuals" with Betty Parsons; Sam Kootz's gallery was in between. It was a vague, indistinct separation, but nonetheless a real one.

Although the "bohemians" knew Newman and liked him as a friend, enjoying his warm personality, his wit, and his enthusiasm for art, they did not understand him as well as the "intellectuals" and had no particular grasp of his intentions. Newman had exhibited in group shows at the Betty Parsons Gallery in 1946, 1947, 1948 and 1949, but the works were relatively modest and, to a casual observer, fitted in more or less neatly with the mythographic abstract style of the period.

When he suddenly burst forth with his 1950 exhibition, followed by the even larger and more astounding 1951 pictures, the "bohemians" decided that he was merely employing shock tactics—still acting as the spokesman. After all, it was well known that he had helped to build up the Betty Parsons Gallery (organizing shows of primitive art there, urging Mrs. Parsons to take on such artists as Hofmann and Pollock) and had introduced such artists as de Kooning to the pages of *Tiger's Eye* magazine. His paintings seemed to be visual diagrams, didactic attacks on establishment esthetics, proddings to his fellow artists to be more daring and more avant garde—as Picabia and Duchamp had prodded the Dadas in the World War I generation. For the emerging Abstract Expressionists, however, art had a high intellectual seriousness. It was no longer an anti-middle-class game, as it had been for the antiart masters. Art was the grail, and the artist, a tortured hero attempting the impossible task of reaching it. Newman used tapes to execute his zips (as Mondrian had done); this seemed an overt connection with the masking devices of commercial art. Newman left tapes exposed (in *Onement 1* and *Concord*) as if to mock the serious nature of modern techniques. Such, in brief and oversimplified form, was the initial reaction to Newman's exhibitions by his artist-friends who knew him least. Later, as they became more familiar with his work, they recognized him as an artist, but some still misinterpreted his work by attributing an ideological point of view to it. They felt that Newman was a doctrinaire abstractionist, a man who elevated the picture plane and the straight line into fanatical dogma (as the Neo-Plastic artists had done a generation before). Thus while such men as de Kooning and Kline were trying to open up new possibilities—to enlarge the expressivity and content of modern art—Newman, on the contrary, seemed to be trying to reinstate old formalist taboos. This opinion was reinforced by inferences from his writings and statements in which he seemed to be attempting to bring back to life the old concept of avant-garde art. Many of the first-generation Abstract Expressionists held as a fundamental tenet of their revolution against the Paris esthetic of the 1920s and 1930s that the whole idea of a vanguard in painting, and its corollaries of "progressive" movements and "isms," had to be discarded as irrelevant. They felt that no styles were "dead," that no approaches were invalid, that nothing should be excluded from art except the very idea of exclusivity. Pollock, de Kooning and Hofmann, for example, moved freely between abstract and figural shapes and resented any doctrinaire criticism that might tend to hamper this liberty. Newman, it seemed, had taken such a stance. But it was a snap judgment, proving mainly that they had neither read him nor looked at his pictures carefully. Of course Newman's work was not easy to see, and it should be emphasized that his hostile reception among the downtown artists and their friends (including this writer) ultimately was based on an impersonal esthetic argument. That Newman's friends among the "intellectuals" were equally hostile to his pictures is more difficult to understand.

In the early 1950s, he was attacked from most—then, from all—quarters, and there was no defending thunder from Motherwell or Still, no open letters circulated by Reinhardt or

Rothko. In those days, when an artist was misunderstood, his friends usually gathered around to applaud and support him and explain him to other artists. (Philip Pavia, sculptor and leading member of the Artists' Club, used to defend Newman, saying in cryptic tones, "Barney found a line to cut color," and Pollock, after 1951, also claimed that Newman was a great and misunderstood artist; but usually both were dismissed on the grounds that they were indulging in their favorite game of teasing de Kooning.) On the whole, silence surrounded Newman's work. And mockery.

In the 1950s, there was an anecdote about Newman that became an anthology piece: Franz Kline and Elaine de Kooning were sitting at the Cedar Bar when a collector Franz knew came up to them in a state of fury. He had just come from Newman's first one-man show. "How simple can an artist be and get away with it?" he sputtered. "There was nothing, absolutely nothing there!"

"Nothing?" asked Franz, beaming. "How many canvases were in the show?"

"Oh, maybe ten or twelve—but all exactly the same—just one stripe down the center, that's all!"

"All the same size?" Franz asked.

"Well, no; there were different sizes; you know, from about three to seven feet."

"Oh, three to seven feet, I see; and all the same color?" Franz went on.

"No, different colors, you know; red and yellow and green . . . but each picture painted one flat color—you know, like a house painter would do it, and then this stripe down the center."

"All the stripes the same color?"

"No."

"Were they the same width?"

The man began to think a little. "Let's see. No. I guess not. Some were maybe an inch wide and some maybe four inches, and some in between."

"And all upright pictures?"

"Oh, no; there were some horizontals."

"With vertical stripes?"

"Uh, no, I think there were some horizontal stripes, maybe."

"And were the stripes darker or lighter than the background?"

"Well, I guess they were darker, but there was one white stripe, or maybe more. . . ."

"Was the stripe painted on top of the background color or was the background color painted around the stripe?"

The man began to get a bit uneasy. "I'm not sure," he said, "I think it might have been done either way, or both ways maybe. . . ."

"Well, I don't know," said Franz. "It all sounds damned complicated to me."

The story made people laugh at Kline's good nature, but also at the ingeniousness with which he made Something out of Nothing to put in his place an intruder who had no right to call anything Nothing—even if it was.

History has a sense of humor, too. Only fourteen years later, in 1964, Don Judd, then emerging as an important sculptor in the Minimal style, wrote an article on Newman (published in *Studio International* in 1970) in which he describes among other works *Shining Forth (To George)* [fig. 20]:

It's nine and a half feet high and fourteen and a half long. The rectangle is unprimed cotton canvas except for two stripes and the edges of a third. Slightly to the left of the centre there is a vertical black stripe three inches wide. All of the stripes run to the upper and lower edges. Slightly less than a foot in from the left edge there is a black stripe an inch wide. This hasn't been painted directly and evenly like the central stripe, but has been laid in between two stripes of masking tape. The paint has run under the tape some, making the stripe a little rough. A foot in from the right edge there is another stripe an inch wide, but this is one of reserved canvas, made by scraping black paint across a strip of masking tape and then removing it. There isn't much paint on either side of the white stripe; the two edges are sharp just against the stripe and break into sharp palette knife marks just away from it. Some of the marks have been lightly brushed. The three stripes are fairly sharp but none are perfectly even and straight. It's a complex painting.[1]

It is appropriate that both the jibe of 1951 and the praise of 1964 make a point of the complexity underlying Newman's artist image and the difficulty of finding its source.

It is this real difficulty, I believe, that so dramatically silenced Newman's artist friends. There is no doubt that he expected them to come to his help, to defend by explaining his work. They probably could not.

The impact of symmetry, the tough, uncompromising head-on image, seemed to baffle all observers. American painters had been working at breaking up composition, but essentially their procedure was to smash the Cubists' armature, flatten it, pull it apart to expose voids, or cover it over with a rain of paint. The act of breaking up composition, and the intellectual and ethical pressures that informed it, remained on the picture as a kind of testimony to a newly gained freedom. There was plenty of evidence of the struggle: spatters of paint became signs of anguish; fragmentary shapes and knots of line were strewn across a picture plane that often looked a bit like a battlefield. Newman, in a gesture, did away with the whole problem. And who was Newman—a Johnny-come-lately, a former teacher, writer, polemicist, painter of gentle mythographies—to sweep the issue away in one lordly (arrogant?) gesture? In his pictures, the "background" presses forward to the surface, and the surface itself is materialized into the actuality of paint—coats of paint, which do not suggest thickness or wall-like stability, but an even, consistent layer of color. Matisse had made a similar move in such 1910-1911 paintings as *Music* and *The Red Studio*, although Newman never saw the former and viewed the latter only in 1949, when it was acquired by The Museum of Modern Art (the way Matisse pushed the red-brown background walls of the studio in front of the objects in the room might well have bolstered decisions Newman had made in *Onement 1* the year before). There is a "touch" to Newman's paint surface, but it does not have the hypersensitivity of Mondrian's patted whites or the latent calligraphy in Matisse's evenly stroked areas of saturated color. Newman's is a uniform handling which gets his effect of a ground of color through careful, steady brushing. It is obvi-

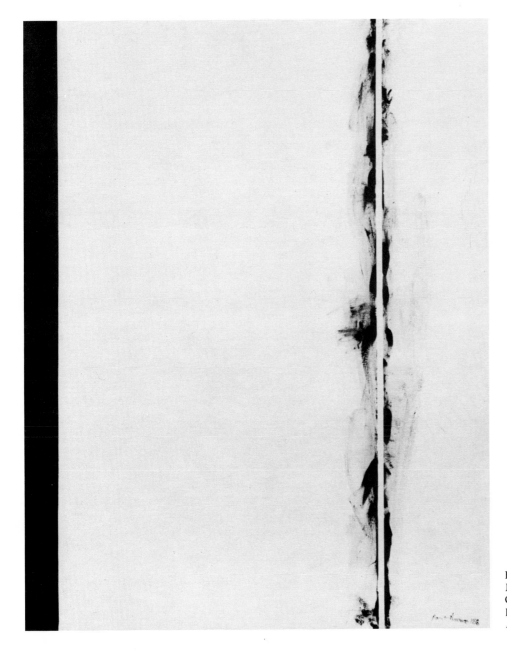

Figure 3. Barnett Newman. *First Station,* 1958.
Magna on canvas, 198.1 x 152.4 cm (78 x 60 in).
Collection, Annalee Newman, New York [photo:
Robert E. Mates and Paul Katz, courtesy of
Annalee Newman]. Cat. no. 1

ously man-made; autograph Newman. He never went back over his paintings to mask a touch or to pretend an impersonalized or manufactured look. The elegance of the method comes from its radical efficiency. The zip is treated in a similar manner: it is tidy where it is supposed to cut clean down the picture, ragged where Newman decided to give his mark a more emphatic plastic nature. There is no fuss or struggle, no symptoms of Existentialist doubt: it is art without anguish. The whole underlying development of Newman's search is given a shape and a finality that seems self-contained and seamless.

This is how the pictures looked, and why they seemed so shocking to Newman's uptown artist-friends who had followed his struggles and who thought they understood his exalted aims. The second one-man show was even more unnerving, as Newman carried his pictures to the radical extremes of the white-on-white paintings, the eighteen-foot stretch of

Vir Heroicus Sublimis and, in the center of the gallery, the gaunt plaster verticals of *Here I,* two poles stuck in plaster mud, the white substance running down the sides of a milk-bottle crate. It was evident he was serious, but was he intent on creating an image or on destroying the assumptions of others? Those who could not understand the work read it as mockery and aggression.

Some of Newman's friends, however, did begin to see what he was getting at. It is no coincidence, I believe, that Rothko's images quickly became larger and contained fewer and fewer forms after his exposure to Newman's paintings. Indeed, Rothko's horizontal rectangular shapes divided by horizontal passages of contrasting color are very close to Newman's vertical format placed on its side. Reinhardt's reduction of shapes to simple monochrome squares also was clued by Newman, and Still's mighty black wall of a painting, which dominated his

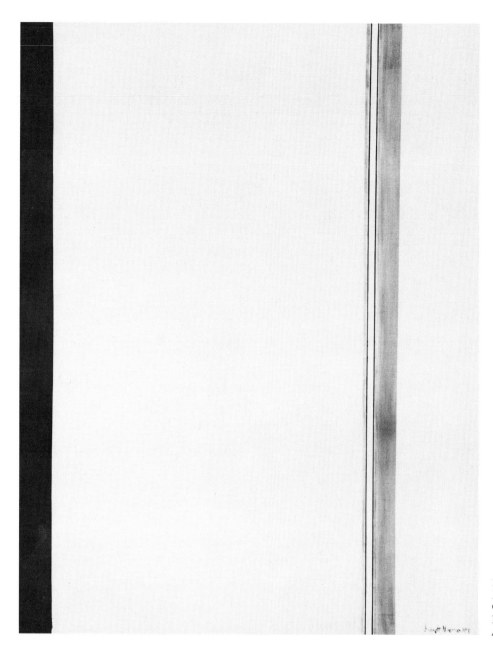

Figure 4. Barnett Newman. *Second Station*, 1958. Magna on canvas. 198.1 x 152.4 cm (78 x 60 in). Collection, Annalee Newman, New York [photo: Robert E. Mates and Paul Katz, courtesy of Annalee Newman]. Cat. no. 2

room at The Museum of Modern Art's "Fifteen Americans" show in 1952, seems a response to the equally majestic assertion of Newman's *Cathedra*. There was, however, still no general acceptance of Newman's paintings inside the stockade, and his omission from the "Fifteen Americans" hurt him deeply; he felt he had been excluded with the consent if not the advice of his friends: he had been betrayed.

As we have noted, he removed his paintings from the gallery in 1951, although he remained good friends with Betty Parsons. In 1952, he did the three pictures with Greek titles and loosened up his technique to approach the Abstract Expressionist gestures of de Kooning and Pollock, although he kept well within the limits of his own vision. In 1953 and 1954, probably pursuing ideas he had set off in *Cathedra*, he concentrated on blue pictures, the color becoming lighter and lighter as it contrasted with deep red-browns and black, culminating

in the eighteen-foot-wide *Uriel* of 1955. He still worked with "secret symmetries," disguising the center division of *The Gate* by setting up divisions in tenths, moving across the canvas (from right to left) as $\frac{1}{10}$-$\frac{4}{10}$-$\frac{5}{10}$ in respectively, black, pale blue and deep red-brown verticals. The halfway point seems to shift optically between the blue and the brown as the dark colors pull at each other across the central blue, making the image seem to read in thirds or sixths. In *The Word II*, the central axis is disguised by a parallel zip and by breaking up one half of the image into four elements which make the single element on the left seem larger than one-half. Here again, quarters and halves tend to read as thirds. *Uriel* also has its symmetry, but an asymmetrical force is in command—with a wide sweeping sleek milky blue meeting an eight-foot-high trisection of black, blue and deep red (like one of the vertical paintings leading up to *The Wild*), and ending in a feather-edged deep red (the blue showing through at the passage). *Uriel* is the only work Newman painted in 1955. In a way it is a résumé of the previous four years' experience.

Newman was more and more disheartened with his rejection by the art world. In 1955, he had his fiftieth birthday. He felt he could no longer let Annalee support him; he would have to make money on his own. Selling pictures was impossible. In a blithe bittersweet mood, he decided to beat the racetrack. He evolved a system for betting on horses, studying the morning forms and plotting numbers on a graph (he even found that a class was offered in this specialty at the Great Northern Hotel). The system worked for a while; but after a few months, it let him down badly, perhaps because he loved horseracing. He tried minor speculation—loans and counterloans. But his situation only grew worse; 1955 and 1956, Newman said, were "the blackest years." When they were first married, he had told Annalee that he had to be an artist or he could not live; now he told her that he was going to get a job as a fitter with a tailor; he had a fantasy of "chalking up" John Hay Whitney—making a drawing on the body of the president of The Museum of Modern Art, an institution that was supposed to help living artists, but which had helped to force him out of the art world. Annalee firmly vetoed the project and canceled his appointment at the shop.

Ten years later, Newman learned that his friend Jasper Johns had bought the building where the pawn shop had been where he and Annalee used to go with their wristwatches and binoculars, and that Johns had made it into a studio. Newman said laughing: "I heard it was for sale; I thought I might buy it, take down the sign that said 'PROVIDENT LOANS' and put up one reading 'BARNETT NEWMAN, REDEEMER.'"

If the 1930s and early 1940s were "limbo" for him, 1955 through 1960 was his inferno. The Abstract Expressionists had become well known to a relatively wide public; with color reproductions in mass magazines, their works the subject of serious debate among critics and historians, they were even beginning to sell. Newman felt more than ever that he was locked out—and by the men he had helped advance. Pollock, the artist to whom he felt closest, died in 1956. His other close friend, Tony Smith, was frequently away. The Newmans were evicted from their apartment on Nineteenth Street (it was taken over by a synagogue to Newman's indignation, and he considered suing the temple on the grounds that its rights of eminent domain as a religious institution were void because it was, in fact, mainly devoted to bingo), and they moved across the bridge to Brooklyn Heights, a few minutes from his studio on Front Street (next to Manhattan's Fulton Fish Market). But, as everyone knows, the East River separates you from the center of things as decisively as the Rocky Mountains.

He felt more and more isolated, left out—a dark Dostoevsky cloud from *The Insulted and the Injured* seemed to descend upon him.

This, more or less, is how he later told the story of those years, never directly, but in hints and fragments. To put all the blame for those "blackest years" on forces outside the artist suggests a curious anomaly. Newman was, after all, the totally convinced, independent, highly integrated man; he was a fighter, stood up for his rights, believed in himself as an artist so completely that he did not shrink from drawing the most radical conclusion from his art. Nor did he bother to explain his motives and goals, except in general, elusive, usually negative terms (it's not this, it's not that). He was the man of *semper idem*, of self-assertion against circumstances. Why then should he suddenly have cared so much about what other people thought and how other artists and outside institutions treated him?

Furthermore, things had been looking up a bit. Clement Greenberg included him prominently in an essay surveying "American-Type Painting," which appeared in *Partisan Review* in the spring of 1955. In 1952, Greenberg had noted that the general animosity aroused by Newman's one-man shows probably indicated that the artist was up to something worthwhile; he called him a "major" painter and suggested that Newman's use of color merited serious attention. In 1955, he used Newman to help demonstrate his developing thesis that "modernist" painting—like all modernist forms—was under the irresistible pressure of history to purify its medium, which for Greenberg meant that it necessarily was heading toward a pure color experience, uncontaminated by drawing, composition, surface textures (the "painterly") or anything else that might distract from the sensation of chroma. This must have been gratifying to Newman in terms of a positive reception, instead of the usual jibes and dismissals, although he objected strongly to Greenberg's formalist interpretation and to his reduction of art to a pawn in the dialectical chess of historical necessities. He also objected to Greenberg's insistence on yoking him to Rothko and Still—"as if we were in bed together" —and to the inference that he, Newman, had been influenced by Still's first exhibition, and finally to Greenberg's description of his paintings as if they were Rothko's, with the paint floated and stained into the canvas so that the colors were an apparent part of the weave itself. He wrote Greenberg a polite letter —overcoming an urge to write a polemical one for publication in the magazine—pointing out, among other things, that: (1) he did not invent the phrase "buckeye painting," which Greenberg had attributed to him, but rather, it was a time-honored epithet for, among other things, restaurant murals, as he had once tried to explain to the critic; (2) he had never applied the phrase "buckeye" to Still's work: that connection was Greenberg's own; (3) he could not have been influenced by Still's paintings, as the organic development of his own pictures from 1946 to 1948 demonstrates; and, finally, (4) that he had never "dyed" color on canvas in his life and never would. Nevertheless, Newman must have welcomed Greenberg's enthusiasm and especially his acceptance of the fact that Newman "belonged" at the forefront of the new American painting.

In 1956, a young New York collector named Ben Heller met Newman (through Pollock); he studied carefully—almost worshipfully—the paintings in the studio, and in 1957, he bought two of them, *Adam* (later sold to The Tate Gallery, London) and *Queen of the Night I*.[2]

These two events may have been slim pickings, compared with the acclaim that was greeting Rothko and de Kooning, Gottlieb and Kline, in the mid-1950s, but compared to

Figure 5. Barnett Newman talking in his apartment in New York, 1965. To the right is the *Third Station* (cat. no. 3). [Photo: Ugo Mulas, courtesy of Annalee Newman]

Newman's situation in 1954, things seemed to be improving.

Therefore, I believe, it is possible to conclude that the "blackest years" were almost unbearable to Newman not only because of the weight of outside hostility and rejection, but also because he had come to a serious problem in his painting.

Uriel, as has been suggested, is a culminating picture. Its theme is developed in *The Gate, The Word II, Primordial Light, White Fire I, Right Here,* a group of paintings in which blues become paler and paler, but more and more intense as they contrast with black and deep red-browns. The titles, as has been noted, refer to the act of creation (*Primordial Light*—the aspect of the world before Genesis; *White Fire*—the aspect of the Torah before Genesis) and to the mystical ascent of man to a place before the Throne (*The Gate* through which he must pass; *Right Here*, the place where he stands, *Makom*). *Uriel* recapitulates these themes on a grand, monumental scale, and it also, in a sense, recapitulates Newman's two other epic paintings, *Vir Heroicus Sublimis* and *Cathedra*. The former refers to man who, in working to reestablish the unity and harmony of a universe coexistent with God, acts as God in the here and now and aids in the coming of the ultimate reunion. *Cathedra*, the radiant Throne, is man's ultimate vision. In *Uriel*, the two

elements are conjoined. The shining pale blue, materialized in layer after layer of paint, stands next to the mud-blood color, which is more thinly painted, allowing the white ground to shine through. The metaphysical presence is opaque; the physical one is translucent. One is eternal, the other transient. One is man's vision—solid, real. The other, his identity—marked by doubts and equivocations. The blue is separated by a black zip from the brown—the last gate? the last guardian? But it pushes through, defining a brown zip (as the light of *Tsimtsum* discovered primordial man), and finally the two colors meet at a soft, lyrical edge. The pale blue dominates, but does not overwhelm, the red-brown (as it would have had Newman kept to the deeper blue of *Cathedra*). This is a vision of the ultimate meeting, the final reconciliation, the first day of the end of the world. Then what happens? What comes next? What is the color of the Day after the Last Day?

For Newman, I believe, his personal dilemma was acutely paralleled by a pictorial one. His next moves, in terms of recombination and variation, must have seemed too easy. His impetus toward a breakthrough had stopped. He had, in de Kooning's phrase, "painted himself out of the picture."

He had loved moving from the studio into the life of the art

194

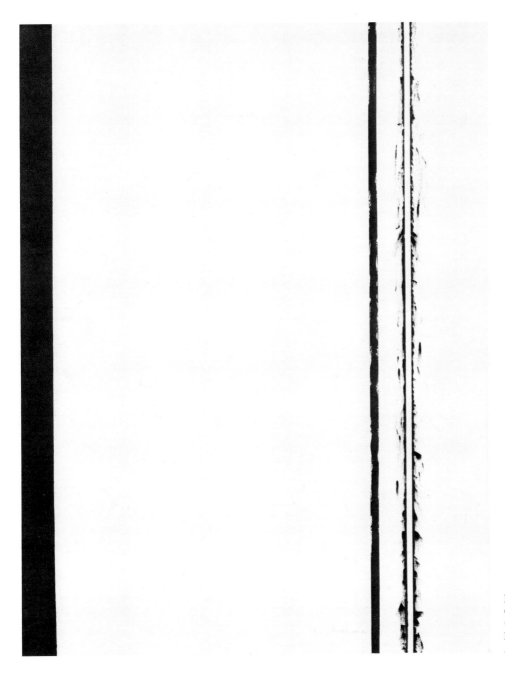

Figure 6. Barnett Newman. *Third Station*, 1960. Oil on canvas, 198.1 x 152.4 cm (78 x 60 in). Collection, Annalee Newman, New York [photo: Robert E. Mates and Paul Katz, courtesy of Annalee Newman]. Cat. no. 3

world and back again, getting recharged from each experience. Now both sides of life had begun to drain his energy.

He painted no pictures in 1956 or in 1957. On November 30, 1957, he went to a party at the house of his friends Jeanne Reynal and Thomas Sills. He left the room and did not come back; Sills noticed his absence, went upstairs and found Newman sitting down, in pain. An ambulance took him to the hospital. He had had a heart attack.

A heart attack, Newman said, "is like instant psycho-analysis." After six weeks in the hospital, he went back to his apartment in Brooklyn Heights. He took care of himself, went for walks along the waterfront. Later, Annalee Newman arranged for the basketball team from the high school where she was teaching to carry Newman up the three flights of stairs to his Front Street studio. It was a dramatic sight, and not without

an air of high triumph—the hero's return—as well as of low comedy, which Newman enjoyed enormously.

His first painting was done at the apartment, a narrow, vertical canvas related to the pictures which had led him to *The Wild*. It is a heavily smeared green and dark blue form—the action of the paint is emphatic, although the pigment itself is thin, and the gesture is rigidly contained in the tight, viselike format. He called it *Outcry*. A shout of despair? A call for help? A protest? The title would be explained by his next works.

Around February 1958, he picked out two canvases, stretched to six and one-half by five feet; and without even bothering to prepare the cotton duck with glue, started to work. He chose Magna paint—much easier to use in an apartment because it dries so fast—and restricted himself to black. Black is what an artist uses, he said, when he is trying to break

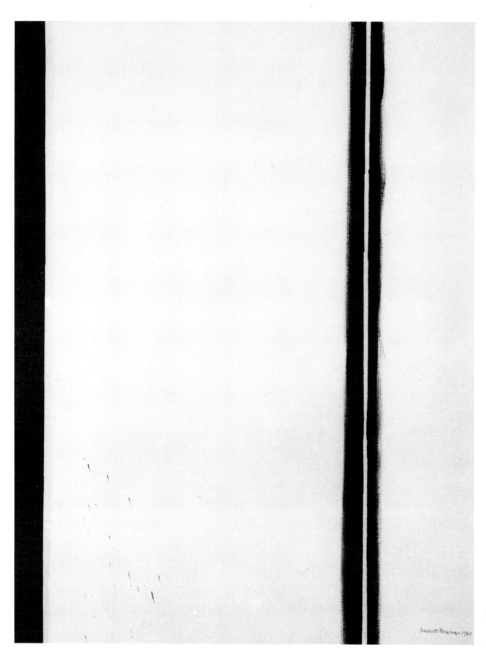

Figure 7. Barnett Newman. *Fourth Station*, 1960. Oil on canvas, 198.1 x 152.4 cm (78 x 60 in). Collection, Annalee Newman, New York [photo: Robert E. Mates and Paul Katz, courtesy of Annalee Newman]. Cat. no. 4

into something new, when he is clearing the decks for experiment, when he wants to find a new way to his image and a way out of the restrictions his old paintings have imposed. *Uriel*, as we have seen, was such an impasse. Using only black, then, he began to divide his canvas into a new set of relationships.

He had generally relied on halves, quarters, eighths and the like, as these are the intervals which can be extrapolated most simply and elegantly from the basic concept of symmetry. He had trisected some pictures, such as *The Way*, but even here the sections were ¼-½-¼. Now, perhaps using a reversal of *The Gate* as a hint to the image, and the trisection of *The Way* as a clue for the system, he began to work with thirds and with the duo-decimal procedure which thirds suggest. He had arrived at a very human sort of calculus, not unlike the twelve-tone scale in music, which allows the greatest freedom to the artist but

still structures his work in ways that increase the pressure on the imagination while increasing the number of options open to it. The first picture [figs. 1, 3] was laid out in divisions that placed two-thirds of the canvas, largely blank, in the left-center area of the image; one-twelfth painted black, to the left; one-fourth to the right, also largely blank white canvas.[3] The two white areas are separated by a negative zip, that is, a three-quarter-inch band of masking tape applied to the surface, over which Newman painted in rough slashes and feathery dry-brushings, and then removed the tape, leaving a white line of reserved canvas. Thus, you have a sharp black band at the left leading to an expanse of white, cut by the presence of a white vertical defined by blacks, which seem to dance from its edges. In the second painting [fig. 4], the format is the same; the black band remains, like a sentinel, at the left. But now the white zip

Figure 8. Barnett Newman. *Fifth Station*, 1962. Oil on canvas, 198.1 x 152.4 cm (78 x 60 in). Collection, Annalee Newman, New York [photo: Robert E. Mates and Paul Katz, courtesy of Annalee Newman]. Cat. no. 5

is outlined by sharp black lines which in turn rest against sharply edged columns of feathery black (which acts as gray)—a narrow wash of black to the left of the zip, a wider one to the right. The first painting has a lyrical, sensual quality. The white zip seems to gleam within the scumbles and smears that embody it; it seems to be a whiter white than the rest of the canvas, a more tightly focused light. The second painting seems to organize the effect; controls seem to have been established (although in fact the duo-decimal substructure is more clearly articulated in the first image; in the second one, the gray that demarks the white zip shifts in a kind of trompe l'oeil emphatically to the right, masking the location of the vertical).[4]

Why did he paint two works, one right after the other, same size, same format, same black and white medium, and in such a hurry that he did not wait to prepare the canvas (untreated duck is as fragile as spun glass; any fingermark embeds dirt so deeply in the weave that it takes a professional conservator to remove it)? He had done pictures using the same dimensions before—*Vir Heroicus Sublimis, Cathedra, Uriel,* for example, and *Adam* and *Achilles* and *Ulysses* and *Prometheus Bound* —but this was usually a sign that the image would drastically shift. In *The Voice* and *The Name II,* identical dimensions are used, but widths and heights are swapped. He also had used similar images, but usually in drastically changed scale, color and dimensions.

I suggest the answer lies in Newman's understanding that, using his new triadic system, the only way to reestablish a secret symmetry and with it the frontal, big-impact, epic quality to which he felt his art must aspire, would be to work in some sort of series. The separate pictures, repeating and varying his

Figure 9. Barnett Newman. *Sixth Station*, 1962. Oil on canvas, 198.1 x 152.4 cm. (78 x 60 in). Collection, Annalee Newman, New York [photo: Robert E. Mates and Paul Katz, courtesy of Annalee Newman]. Cat. no. 6

shapes, establish a larger unity and a heightened scale. They are secretly symmetrical in the sense that they echo each other in time—the time taken to see one, then the other, then both, then to recognize that one repeats the other. With only two paintings, however, the division of thirds breaks up the larger image by insistently implying a narrative sequence, moving from left to right, even though the right-hand element of the pair (the white on gray zip in the second painting) was given a firm anchoring or braking shape. Newman studied both paintings for months and decided that he would have to make at least two more.

He still had to be careful about working or playing too hard, however; furthermore, the remainder of 1958 was filled with distractions—probably very welcome ones, but they kept him from painting. (Or maybe he still had not decided how to break

out of the impasse; as I have mentioned, for all his daring and radical ideas, Newman's approach was cautious, modest, slow; and, as Annalee has said, "Barney always acted as if he had all the time in the world, as if life is eternal, and he would live forever.")

In the spring of 1958, four of Newman's pictures were chosen by The Museum of Modern Art for representation in its "New American Painting" exhibition, along with (alphabetically) Baziotes, Brooks, Sam Francis, Gorky, Gottlieb, Guston, Hartigan, Kline, de Kooning, Motherwell, Pollock, Rothko, Stamos, Still, Tomlin and Tworkov. The show toured Europe for two years, to Milan, Madrid and Brussels, and with a Pollock retrospective to Basel, Berlin, Paris, Amsterdam and London. During the same months that the show was being selected, he was invited to have a retrospective at Bennington

Figure 10. Barnett Newman. *Seventh Station*, 1964. Oil on canvas, 198.1 x 152.4 cm (78 x 60 in). Collection, Annalee Newman, New York [photo: Robert E. Mates and Paul Katz, courtesy of Annalee Newman]. Cat. no. 7

College. His friends Tony Smith and the painter Paul Feeley were teaching there, and they urged the head of the art program, Eugene Goossen, to give Newman a one-man show in May as part of an annual series that already had included Pollock and Hofmann. Goossen asked for eight to ten pictures, but Newman decided to gamble on a more ambitious affair and sent up eighteen (Hai), including a group of early works, as well as *Onement I, Vir Heroicus Sublimis* and *Day before One,* 1951 (shown for the first time). Greenberg wrote a generous, eloquent foreword, in his customary aggressive tone, and Newman probably was only slightly pained to notice that the critic still insisted on describing his paintings as if they were Rothkos—stained colors, with the weave of the canvas integrated into the plane. One can almost hear him grumbling sotto voce, "Goddamn batik!"

In March 1959, most of the paintings from the Bennington show were exhibited as the opening event of the new French & Co., Inc., galleries, which had been remodeled into airy, elegant space by Tony Smith, and for which Clement Greenberg was acting as artistic adviser. Greenberg asked Newman to inaugurate the Madison Avenue quarters; Newman agreed to show, but only works completed before The Museum of Modern Art's "Fifteen Americans" selection; perhaps he felt that the art world, which had turned him down so brutally in 1952, did not deserve to see his later work; more probably, he felt that he almost had been forgotten and that the public would have to start seeing him as if from scratch.

The exhibition was a revelation to many artists and critics. The general tendency in the late 1950s toward larger, more simple forms and toward a quieter, more objective surface

Figure 11. Barnett Newman. *Eighth Station*, 1964. Oil on canvas, 198.1 x 152.4 cm (78 x 60 in). Collection, Annalee Newman, New York [photo: Robert E. Mates and Paul Katz, courtesy of Annalee Newman]. Cat. no. 8

suddenly was confirmed and in a sense defined in ten-year-old paintings. The flat, clean, objective look of the 1960s was established even before the decade opened. The cool, tight-lipped aspects of Pop Art found a basis in Newman's apparently matter-of-fact presentation of extraordinary inventions. The surgical objectivity of later color-field abstraction also found sanction. The bands in Jasper Johns's flags, in Frank Stella's "pin-stripes" and in Kenneth Noland's layered pictures are based on hypotheses far removed from Newman's introspections on radiance and presence, and that distance is a function of the younger artists' originality. But Newman's work was a firm precedent for them; it opened doors which seemed to have been locked by Mondrian and the Constructivists and painted over by Abstract Expressionism.

After 1959, Newman was increasingly represented in group exhibitions—national and international. His paintings began to sell. The Oeffentliche Kunstsammlung, Basel, bought *Day before One* (in 1958); The Museum of Modern Art bought *Abraham* (in 1959); Betty Parsons took her commission from the sale of *Abraham*, doubled it and bought *Concord* (now in The Metropolitan Museum of Art); Jeanne Reynal bought *Horizon Light*. (It might be noted parenthetically that it took a little time for Newman's prices to catch up with those of his colleagues; $5,000 was the price of *Abraham*; in 1959, comparable paintings by Pollock were selling for about $40,000; by de Kooning for about $20,000; by Kline for about $10,000.)

In 1960, Newman went back to work with an energy he had not been able to tap since 1954. He did a series of twenty-two drawings in ink on ten-by-fourteen- and nine-by-twelve-inch

Figure 12. Barnett Newman. *Ninth Station*, 1964.
Acrylic on canvas, 198.1 x 152.4 cm (78 x 60 in).
Collection, Annalee Newman, New York [photo:
Robert E. Mates and Paul Katz, courtesy of
Annalee Newman]. Cat. no. 9

pads; they are meditations on the possibilities of his new-found duodecimal calculus and on the potentials of black as a color. There are areas of black neatly masked and trued; there are cutting strokes like a fencer's lunges; there are heavy deep washes and areas of staccato dapple. Elements are combined and recombined to make a black mass confront a gray quiver, or white contract and expand as its black borders are adjusted. These are not studies for paintings, nor simple warming-up exercises—they are far more finished and expertly controlled. Rather, they seem to be a series within the larger series, undertaken in order to experience a radical shift of scale, being able to cover the span of an image in a stroke and to have it change as rapidly as one could work, as Newman had gone from *Vir Heroicus Sublimis* to *The Wild*.

He returned to his two paintings begun in 1958, adding two

more [figs. 5, 6, 7]; after studying them, he decided to expand the number to fourteen and title them "The Stations of the Cross." "It was after the fourth that he realized the number and meaning of the work on which he was engaged," wrote Lawrence Alloway, in his important and penetrating essay in the catalogue of the exhibition of the Stations at the Guggenheim Museum in 1966. "In December 1961 what is still the first painting of the Stations was exhibited as a single work under the title of *Station*. The work was subsequently reproduced as *The Series, I* [and another, independent painting, done in 1963 was titled *Station*], but there can be no doubt that the Stations theme was now a definite project in Newman's mind."[5]

It is possible to interpret the series as an autobiographical metaphor of Newman's "blackest years" of neglect and de-

Figure 13. Barnett Newman. *Tenth Station*, 1965. Magna on canvas, 198.1 x 152.4 cm (78 x 60 in). Collection, Annalee Newman, New York [photo: Robert E. Mates and Paul Katz, courtesy of Annalee Newman]. Cat. no. 10

spair, of his heart attack and confrontation with death. It would also follow logically that this artist, who had made Genesis and the creative act his subject matter, would now turn to resurrection, to life after death—for what else, after all, is the subject of the Stations, which begin with Christ condemned to death and end with the Entombment? Indeed, in 1961, Newman painted a larger picture (eighty by seventy-two inches) which had been labeled "Resurrection." And in his statement accompanying the Guggenheim exhibition, Newman subtitled the series *Lema Sabachthani:*

Lema Sabachthani—why? Why did you forsake me? Why forsake me? To what purpose? Why?

This is the Passion. This outcry of Jesus. Not the terrible walk up the Via Dolorosa, but the question that has no answer.

This overwhelming question that does not complain, makes today's

talk of alienation, as if alienation were a modern invention, an embarrassment. This question that has no answer has been with us so long—since Jesus—since Abraham—since Adam—the original question.

Lema? To what purpose—is the unanswerable question of human suffering.

Can the Passion be expressed by a series of anecdotes, by fourteen sentimental illustrations? Do not the Stations tell of one event? *

No doubt the critic Barbara Reise is accurate in her response to the *First Station:*

The skinny un-primed zip at the right seems to screech like fingernails up and down a blackboard of dry-brushed edges, as if in terror of the

---

* See Appendix A.

Figure 14. Barnett Newman. *Eleventh Station*, 1965. Acrylic on canvas, 198.1 x 152.4 cm (78 x 60 in). Collection, Annalee Newman, New York [photo: Robert E. Mates and Paul Katz, courtesy of Annalee Newman]. Cat. no. 11

solid vertical band which seems to move with ominous slowness into the painting's space. This painting almost shrieks vital terror in the face of death as an inevitable absolute. . . .[6]

Art is not quite so single-minded, however, nor is Newman ever simple. He never used his painting simply to relay a message to the viewer. Nor did he ever illustrate an idea or paint an allegory. Certainly the Passion and the vision of death is there in the Stations, but what else?

First of all, there is the concept of the series. He saw that the secret symmetry, which had been a key to his earlier paintings, would not apply to his new triadic divisions of the image, neither in one painting, nor in a pair, nor in four pictures. The action kept moving in one direction, at first from left to right, and simply to balance it with compositional devices would be to apply an academic esthetic solution—the kind of "har-mony" he had fought all his life. At this point, I believe, he decided to make a large series, large enough to contain the flow of pictorial actions, to modulate and inflect some so that other individual images could offer violent gestures, but all would be given coherence and definite impact as they became echoed and canceled and reechoed across the sequence.

The Stations is not an open-ended series like Monet's Hay-stacks, for example, or Warhol's Marilyn Monroes, which apparently the artists kept painting until the drive behind the idea was exhausted. As Alloway pointed out, the number four-teen "embodies an order inseparable from the meaning of the work." This is probably one reason that Newman chose the Stations as his subject.

He wanted to be concerned with the idea of the Passion—of pain and suffering—and with the outcry of despair. In a "Con-

Figure 15. Barnett Newman. *Twelfth Station*, 1965. Acrylic on canvas, 198.1 x 152.4 cm (78 x 60 in). Collection, Annalee Newman, New York [photo: Robert E. Mates and Paul Katz, courtesy of Annalee Newman]. Cat. no. 12

versation" (May 1, 1966) held with this writer at the Guggenheim Museum at the time of the exhibition, Newman said:

I was trying to call attention to that part of the Passion which I have always felt was ignored and which has always affected me and that was the cry of *Lema Sabachthani*, which I don't think is a complaint, but which Jesus makes. And I always was struck by the paradox that he says to those who persecuted Him and crucified Him, "Forgive them for they know not what they do." But to God, and Jesus is projected as the Son of God, He says, "What's the idea!"

Later in our "Conversation":

I felt that to the extent that Jesus was crucified and did physically say *Lema Sabachthani* in relation to that drama, that it was more appropriate for me to be concerned with the Sabachthani (. . . forsaken me). Also since there is a tradition of Stations, as a painter I felt I could make the point more viable within that framework. . . .

Hess: It's like doing a sonnet, a given number of lines, and you fit into that form?

Newman: Well, to the extent that a sonnet is an arbitrary poem,[7] and to the extent that the Stations form an arbitrary [number of] paintings, I felt that it was appropriate to do it. . . .

In other words, Newman purposefully chose a rigid framework on which to present those two slipperiest of modern ideas—the sense of anguished despair (that rock upon which so many Expressionist ships have foundered) and the serial form (which tends to produce *peintures-fleuve* of the most banal variety). He applied severe disciplines to the Expressionist content of the Stations, as we shall see, but it is important to note that in limiting his series and tying its number so inextricably to the subject matter, he got rid of the antiart implications of serial mode. A group of more or less identical paintings

Figure 16. Barnett Newman. *Thirteenth Station*, 1965-1966. Acrylic on canvas, 198.1 x 152.4 cm (78 x 60 in). Collection, Annalee Newman, New York [photo: Robert E. Mates and Paul Katz, courtesy of Annalee Newman]. Cat. no. 13

usually implies that the particular quality of any individual picture in the series is irrelevant. It is the whole effort that counts; each part reinforces and adds new qualities to the others. In an open-ended series, you receive a total impression, a cumulative experience which in turn increases the value of each dependent unit. By limiting his series, Newman forces himself to give each work its independence. He wrote in *Art News* (May 1966): "The Passion is not a protest but a declaration. I had to explore its emotional complexity. That is, each painting is total and complete by itself yet only the fourteen together make clear the single event."*

He worked on the Stations for eight years, on and off, using the series as a source for other paintings, and coming back to it as a touchstone. He did the pictures in pairs. Using their con-

ventional titles (whose meanings Newman completely ignored), they date:

First Station (Christ Condemned to Death), *Second Station* (Christ Carrying the Cross), 1958.

Third Station (The First Fall), *Fourth Station* (Christ Meets Mary), 1960.

Fifth Station (Simon Helps Carry the Cross), *Sixth Station* (Veronica Wipes the Face of Christ), 1962.

Seventh Station (The Second Fall), *Eighth Station* (He Comforts the Women of Jerusalem), 1964.

Ninth Station (The Third Fall), *Tenth Station* (He Is Stripped of His Garments), winter 1964–1965 (the Ninth in 1964, the Tenth in 1964–1965).

Eleventh Station (The Crucifixion), *Twelth Station* (The Death of Christ), 1965.

*See Appendix B.

205

Figure 17. Barnett Newman. *Fourteenth Station*, 1965-1966. Acrylic and duco on canvas, 198.1 x 152.4 cm (78 x 60 in). Collection, Annalee Newman, New York [photo: Robert E. Mates and Paul Katz, courtesy of Annalee Newman]. Cat. no. 14

Thirteenth Station (The Deposition), *Fourteenth Station* (The Entombment), winter 1965–1966.
[*Fifth* through *Fourteenth Stations,* figs. 7-17.]

Newman's is a version of serial art from which practically all the autobiographical, informal, subjective nature of the approach has been eliminated, to be replaced by an intellectual architecture which alone could contain the emotional quality Newman wanted to project, and the impact he had sustained in his early symmetrical paintings.

Just as the number fourteen of the Stations perfectly meshed with Newman's pictorial demand for a long but finite series, so his decision to restrict his palette to raw canvas and black (and, in three Stations, white) paint answered both his pictorial and emotional demands. Black is the stark "color" of tragedy. In our "Conversation," Newman said:

In a large tragic theme of this kind, when Picasso does *Guernica*, he cannot do it in color. He does it in black and white and gray. I couldn't make a green Passion or a red one. I mean you wouldn't want me to make a purple Jesus or something like that? It had to be black and white—I was compelled to work this way. . . . Could I get the living quality of color without using color?

But black paint, as we have noted, is the material of the artist who seeks a maximum freedom for experimentation and range of expression. It is not only the substance of tragedy, but also of release, joyous release. Behind the image in Newman's Stations, you may recognize the cold sweat of agony and the blood of pain in the black paint. Behind it, too, is the artist happily at work, moving ahead, delighted by his relationship with the medium.

The raw canvas also met physical and pictorial as well as emotional needs.

206

Figure 18. Newman's apartment in New York in 1965. Hanging on the walls, from the left: *Fifth Station* (cat. no. 5), *Eighth Station* (cat. no. 8), *Seventh Station* (cat. no. 7), *Be II* (cat. no. 15). [Photo: Ugo Mulas, courtesy of Annalee Newman]

In his eagerness to start the first two Stations, to begin again after a long silence, Newman went directly to the canvas he had stretched in his apartment. The raw duck being there, while he was still too weak to work in his studio, filled a direct physical need.

After the series was finished, he wrote in *Art News:*

Raw canvas is not a recent invention. Pollock used it. Miró used it. Manet used it. I found that I needed to use it here not as a color among colors, not as if it were paper against which I would make a graphic image, or as colored cloth—batik—but that I had to make the material itself into a true color—as white light—yellow light—black light. That was my "problem."

The white flash is the same raw canvas as the rest of the canvas. The yellow light is the same raw canvas as the other canvas.

In other words, the "passionate," or "poor," or "rough" look of the raw duck might be perfectly appropriate to Newman's stark presentation of despair—*Lema Sabachthani*—but it was also a logical function of his decision as a painter to use only black.

Furthermore, raw canvas had a special sensuous attraction for Newman. From his years of work for his father, he had become expert in textiles; he knew all about weaving and mills, how the stuff was made, how it should be treated. He was as intimate with canvas as a whittler is with his stick of wood. He was a connoisseur of duck, just as he was a connoisseur of various kinds of black paint—he used at least three types in the Stations (acrylic resins, oils, acrylic polymers), possibly more.

Finally, in the dynamics of the paintings themselves, in exploring his triadic structure, Newman found an extraordinary number of new opportunities and resonances. ("It is as I work that the work itself begins to have an effect on me," he wrote in *Art News,* "just as I affect the canvas, so does the canvas affect me."⁹) He established a dialectic between the clean-cut, sharp-edged element and the one with fluid, vibrating or plumed definitions—coming back to the hard versus soft theme he had announced in the sculpture *Here I,* and in *Dionysius*

and *The Promise,* 1949. The width of the black areas varies, although their placement is relatively fixed, and they all stretch from top to bottom of the canvas. Their changing weights exert changing pulls and pushes across the surface. There is a dance-like quality to this action as it shifts from Station to Station. Sharp black zips emphasize the smudges and spatters that sometimes face them, sometimes replace them, and sometimes define them. In places, the medium from the oil paint bleeds into the canvas, making a "shadow" on the white. Where the black dry-brushing and smears define a narrow white vertical, the canvas gleams blue-white, like an icicle. Where the span of white canvas lies next to heavy black areas, the duck acquires a golden sunny glow. In certain divisions, Newman seems to have made a field for accidents, a place where he invites chance, spontaneous effects, the "quick crazy stroke" as the Zen swordsmen call it, or *sprezzatura* in Castiglione's famous phrase—"the masterful gesture of carelessness." In other divisions, the black moves with a precision that suggests fatality—inevitable, measured.

Culminating the Stations is a fifteenth picture, larger than those in the series, with an impastoed cadmium red light edge to the left of the canvas and a black, hard one to the right, and, in between, white paint replacing the bare canvas. At first it was nicknamed (not titled), at the suggestion of Tony Smith, "Resurrection."¹⁰ Newman began it in 1961 and added some finishing coats of paint in 1964. He also gave it his own title, *Be II* [figs. 18, 19].

There is an important key here, I believe, to an understanding of the Stations. It has been said, and it may be true, that the Stations are Newman's confrontation with death, and that to him the meaning of the Passion is Resurrection: life triumphant over death. I think that even if Newman had such an idea at the beginning (and this is doubtful), he changed his mind later. *Be* is the imperative of God of the Jews. Man should *be;* he should work in the Lord's ways in order to be able to stand before Him—as a man, in a place *(Makom),* just as the orange

Figure 19. Barnett Newman. *Be II,* 1961-1964. Acrylic and oil on canvas, 203.2 x 182.9 cm (80 x 72 in). Collection, Annalee Newman, New York [photo: Robert E. Mates and Paul Katz, courtesy of Annalee Newman]. Cat. no. 15, pl. 16

stripe—the color which for Newman represented man since *Onement I,* 1948—stands across the white field from its severe counterpart in black.

The large vertical center-left area of the Stations—which generally takes up three-fourths of the image—contracts and expands slightly from picture to picture, as if suggesting Luria's image of the *Tsimtsum* (it contracts most sharply in the *Seventh* and *Ninth Stations*). The *Tenth* and *Twelth Stations* are flooded with light, as the universe was after *Tsimtsum,* in the moment of creation. One could apply Kabbalist parallels even more closely here, but the crucial element is the command *Be,* which is both Jehovah's "let there *be* . . ." and the Kabbalah's admonition to *Be.*

Thus, Christ for Newman in the Stations is not the Messiah, nor is the Passion a ritual fourteen steps on the road to Resurrection. Rather, Christ is man; prototypical man born to suffering. He has lived from the beginning of the world until now. He suffers the torments of the artist, for "the first man was an artist," and the goal for all men is to be artists. He forgives enemies, but after life's humiliations and pains have become unbearable, he asks God the unanswerable question—*Lema Sabachthani?*

And God replies: *Be!*

Earlier in this text, I quoted the first paragraphs of Newman's Statement for his exhibition of the Stations at the Guggenheim Museum. Here is the rest of it:

The first pilgrims walked the Via Dolorosa to identify themselves with the original moment, not to reduce it to a pious legend; nor even to worship the story of one man and his agony, but to stand witness to the story of each man's agony; the agony that is single, constant, unrelenting, willed—world without end.

The ones who are born are to die
Against thy will art thou formed
Against thy will art thou born
Against thy will dost thou live
Against thy will die.

Jesus surely heard these words from the *Pirke Abot,* "The Wisdom of the Fathers."

No one gets anybody's permission to be born. No one asks to live. Who can say he has more permission than anybody else?

It seems evident here that Newman distinguishes sharply between the messianic Jesus, Son of God, and the historical Jesus. It is the historical figure who would have studied the *Pirke Abot* (or *Avot*), one of the sixty-three tractates of the

Figure 20. Barnett Newman. *Shining Forth (To George)*, 1961. Oil on canvas, 289.6 x 441.9 cm (114 x 174 in). Collection, Annalee Newman, New York [photo: Eric Pollitzer, courtesy of Annalee Newman]. Not in exhibition

Mishna, the pre-Talmudic corpus of laws and ethical principles compiled between the fourth century B.C. and the second century A.D. (*Pirke Abot* is usually translated "Ethics of the Fathers"—but Newman was his own scholar and did his own translations from the Hebrew). The messianic Jesus did not study the *Mishna,* but even as a child instructed rabbis; He was Himself the Word.

Furthermore, what "first pilgrims" on the Via Dolorosa would not have identified with Christ, with one Man and His agony, "but stand witness to the story of each man's agony?" They could only be the Jews who had followed Jesus' teachings as a prophet and a king, but not as the Messiah. Christians, on the other hand, would concentrate on the ultimate, informing nature of the Resurrection throughout their passage through the Stations.

Finally, there is one man who can say he has "more permission to be born" than anybody else: the Messiah. Newman is telling us that He is yet to come.

This, I believe, is the ultimate daring in Newman's Stations. He raises them to a philosophic enquiry on the nature of agony, on the nature of his art and on the life of man-as-an-artist. Fused with the pictorial structure of the black paint and the raw canvas and the serial nature of the image is the symbolic structure of his subject matter, which contains—secretly, although Newman always leaves hints and clues—his own ontological insight, with its parallels to (or metaphors from) the spiritual visions of the great Kabbalists.

In 1960, he finished two paintings outside of his work on the Stations, but both of them relate closely to it. One is a small painting in which dark green paint over two masking tapes divides the raw canvas surface into three equal parts. It is as if he wanted to make an evident materialization of his trisection concept. He titled the picture *Treble,* and in later titles he would refer insistently to this new calculus: *The Third* (1962), *The Three* (1962), *Tertia* (1964), *Triad* (1965). Even the fa-

mous *Who's Afraid of Red, Yellow and Blue* pictures carry in their titles the mark of "three."

The other picture, much more ambitious, is titled *White Fire II,* as if to indicate that, even while committed to the Christian iconography of the Stations of the Cross, he would keep his allusions to the Kabbalah and to its vision of Genesis of the Torah. In Gershom G. Scholem's paraphrase of the *Book Bahir* (one of the earliest books of the Kabbalists), the unknown author interprets

... the fiery organism of the Torah, which burned before God in black fire on white fire, as follows: the white fire is the written Torah, in which the form of the letters is not yet explicit, for the form of the consonants and vowel points was first conferred by the power of the black fire, which is the oral Torah. This black fire is like the ink on the parchment. "And so the written Torah can take on corporal form only through the power of the oral Torah, that is to say without the oral Torah it cannot be understood." Essentially only Moses, master of all the Prophets, penetrated in unbroken contemplation to that mystical written Torah, which in reality is still hidden in the invisible form of white light. . . .

The form of the written Torah is that of the colors of white fire, and the form of the oral Torah has colored forms as of black fire. And all these engravings [inner-most forms] and the not yet unfolded Torah existed potentially, perceptible neither to a spiritual nor to a sensory eye, until the will [of God] inspired the idea of activating them by means of primordial wisdom and hidden knowledge.

White Fire II can be considered a transplantation of elements from the triadic Stations to the symmetrical calculus of Newman's work in the early 1950s. It is black paint on raw canvas, but the height is increased to eight feet (as in *Vir Heroicus Sublimis*), and the format is narrower than the Stations; its verticality is accentuated by the wide black bands on both edges, and braked by their slightly curved, blotted "freehand" contours. The central sections of the raw canvas look golden compared with the negative zip formed by black

Figure 21. Barnett Newman at the exhibition of *The Stations of the Cross* at the Solomon R. Guggenheim Museum in New York, April 1966. [Photo: Bernard Gotfryd, courtesy of Annalee Newman]

plumes which seem to spray off to the sides, leaving an ice-white, dead-center band.

Noon-Light, 1961, nine and one-half feet high, puts full emphasis on the tawny "color" of white (raw) canvas set off, symmetrically, by a thin black band at the left edge, a thin ruled zip to the right. *Black Fire I*, of the same year, has the same dimensions, but is divided on the duodecimal scale, the center hidden and the raw canvas dominated by a wide, heavy, knife-edged black. These oversize, paired antinomes are closely tied into the experience of the Stations, and also provide a clue to Newman's most ambitious and astonishing work of the year, *Shining Forth (To George)* [fig. 20]. The ground, again, is raw canvas—it could be the sackcloth of mourning or a glittering cope of sun-flecked snow—or simply cotton duck prepared with a colorless, transparent, plastic medium, depending on how you see it. The format is symmetrical, with a wide black vertical in the center, a black stripe to the far left, a negative stripe defined by foaming, pulsing strokes of dry-brushed black at the right. Its horizontal format (nine and one-half by four-teen and one-half feet), marks one of the very few works by Newman to approach the Golden Section—that magical academic formula for achieving classical repose and grace.[11] Like almost all modern artists, Newman avoided that proportion, in which one axis of the painting is larger than, but does not dominate, the other axis. He preferred either to give his rectangles emphatic articulation, as vertical or horizontal fields, or to relate them to the square. In this picture, however, the format and proportions have the harmonious underpinning of a Greek temple. The stark blackness and whiteness make an even more vivid effect in this lucid context, adding a tragic, vulnerable dimension to the elegiac mood.

The painting is dedicated to Newman's brother George, to whom he had always been very close, and who died in February 1961. George's Hebrew name was Zerach, which derives from the verb "to shine," and which Newman translated as "shining forth."

Alloway, in his Guggenheim catalogue, cites the painting as Newman's testimony of his confrontation with death. But "shining forth" also describes perfectly what the light is doing in the painting; it seems to pour from behind the quivering negative zip and intensify even more brightly at the edges of the severe black cuts.

The picture was executed in unusual circumstances. Newman had had lunch with a friend one day, and in the afternoon, whether because of their conversation, or the food and the vodka, or the psychic climate—who can tell—he went to a second studio he had rented at Carnegie Hall, and in a burst of creative energy he finished the painting in an afternoon. He could not find his glasses, so he did the whole thing with the monocle that always hung from a black ribbon around his neck. (The reason for the monocle was that he often forgot his glasses, and Annalee kept spares for him in the apartment and in the studio, but in this "emergency" none could be found.)

He had thought about the painting for months. It was accomplished in a spurt of creativity that, afterwards, amazed him.

Thus there are three things in *Shining Forth (To George)*—three levels if you will. There is the tragedy of death, and of "being," living in the face of death. There is the conceptual struggle of the artist, the intellectual and emotional decisions which he confronts in the canvas. And there is the joy and exaltation of working and accomplishing, of reaching the vision. *Vir heroicus sublimis!*

It is this passion—it is such a trinity—I believe, that informs the Stations of the Cross.

Appendix A

Appendix B

The following statement was written by Newman for the 1966 exhibition of The Stations of the Cross at the Solomon R. Guggenheim Museum, New York.

STATEMENT

Lema Sabachthani—why? Why did you forsake me? Why forsake me? To what purpose? Why?

This is the Passion. This outcry of Jesus. Not the terrible walk up the Via Dolorosa, but the question that has no answer.

This overwhelming question that does not complain, makes today's talk of alienation, as if alienation were a modern invention, an embarrassment. This question that has no answer has been with us so long—since Jesus—since Abraham—since Adam—the original question.

Lema? To what purpose—is the unanswerable question of human suffering.

Can the Passion be expressed by a series of anecdotes, by fourteen sentimental illustrations? Do not the Stations tell of one event?

The first pilgrims walked the Via Dolorosa to identify themselves with the original moment, not to reduce it to a pious legend; nor even to worship the story of one man and his agony, but to stand witness to the story of each man's agony; the agony that is single, constant, unrelenting, willed—world without end.

> "The ones who are born are to die
> Against thy will art thou formed
> Against thy will art thou born
> Against thy will dost thou live
> Against thy will die."

Jesus surely heard these words from the "Pirke Abot," "The Wisdom of the Fathers."

No one gets anybody's permission to be born. No one asks to live. Who can say he has *more* permission than anybody else?

The following article was written by Newman for Art News *(April 1966). It appeared simultaneously with the first exhibition of The Stations of the Cross.*

THE 14 STATIONS OF THE CROSS, 1958-1966

No one asked me to do these Stations of the Cross. They were not commissioned by any church. They are not in the conventional sense "church" art. But they do concern themselves with the Passion as I feel and understand it; and what is even more significant for me, they can exist without a church.

I began these paintings eight years ago the way I begin all my paintings—by painting. It was while painting them that it came to me (I was on the fourth one) that I had something particular here. It was at that moment that the intensity that I felt the paintings had, made me think of them as the Stations of the Cross.

It is as I work that the work itself begins to have an effect on me. Just as I affect the canvas, so does the canvas affect me.

From the very beginning I felt that I would do a series. However, I had no intention of doing a theme with variations. Nor did I have any desire to develop a technical device over and over. From the very beginning I felt I had an important subject and it was while working that it made itself clear to me that these works involved my understanding of the Passion. Just as the Passion is not a series of anecdotes but embodies a single event, so these fourteen paintings, even though each one is whole and separate in its immediacy, all together form a complete statement of a single subject. That is why I could not do them all at once, automatically, one after another. It took eight years. I used to do my other work and come back to these. When there was a spontaneous, inevitable urge to do them is when I did them.

The cry of *Lema,* for what purpose, this is the Passion and this is what I have tried to evoke in these paintings.

Why fourteen? Why not one painting? The Passion is not a protest but a declaration. I had to explore its emotional complexity. That is, each painting is total and complete by itself yet only the fourteen together make clear the wholeness of the single event.

As for the plastic challenge, could I maintain this cry in all its intensity and in every manner of its starkness? I felt compelled—my answer had to be—to use only raw canvas and to discard all color palettes. These paintings would depend only on the color that I could create myself. There would be no beguiling esthetics to scrutinize. Each painting had to be seen—the visual impact had to be total, immediate—at once.

Raw canvas is not a recent invention. Pollock used it. Miró used it. Manet used it. I found that I needed to use it here not as a color among colors, not as if it were paper against which I would make a graphic image, or as colored cloth—batik—but that I had to make the material itself into true color—as white light—yellow light—black light—that was my "problem."

The white flash is the same raw canvas as the rest of the canvas. The yellow light is the same raw canvas as the other canvases.

And there was, of course, the "problem" of scale. I wished no monuments, no cathedrals. I wanted human scale for the human cry. Human size for the human scale.

Neither did I have a preconceived idea that I would execute and then give a title to. I wanted to hold the emotion, not waste it in picturesque ecstasies. The cry, the unanswerable cry, is world without end. But a painting has to hold it, world without end, in its limits.

© *Art News Magazine,* 1966

NOTES

1. Donald Judd, "Barnett Newman," *Studio International* (London), vol. 179 (February 1970), p. 67.

2. Ben Heller was the first serious collector of Newman's paintings, although the artist had sold pictures previously to Mrs. Burton G. Tremaine (in 1947), to Ruth Stephan, then coeditor of *Tiger's Eye* (in 1949), to Frances Cohen (in 1950) and Tony Smith—the last two both close friends of the Newmans. Heller not only bought paintings, but interested others in Newman's work. It was he who took Arnold Rudlinger of the Basel Kunstmuseum and later Alfred H. Barr, Jr., of The Museum of Modern Art to the artist's studio in 1958; both visits eventually resulted in sales.

3. The exact measurements of the divisions in the two 1958 paintings are 4⅝ inches (left black area), 40¹⁵⁄₁₆ inches (central blank area), ¾ inch (stripe), 14⅜₁₆ inches (right blank area). Both are 60½ inches wide. The first picture is 70⅛ inches high, the second 70³⁄₁₆ inches. I wish to thank Mr. Orrin Riley, conservator at The Solomon R. Guggenheim Museum, New York, for taking these measurements.

4. The general "feel" of the structure of these two works reminds one of the 1945 untitled painting with a tree trunk at the left and a "flower" or "sword" floated in the space to the right. It was Newman's first return to oils of ambitious scale after the long silence of the early and mid-1940s—at least the first one with which he was satisfied. When he broke silence again, after *Outcry,* in 1958, he perhaps consciously, perhaps unconsciously, remembered the liberating vision of thirteen years before.

5. "The Stations of the Cross and the Subjects of the Artist," in exhibition catalogue *The Stations of the Cross: Lema Sabachthani* (New York: The Solomon R. Guggenheim Museum, 1966), p. 11.

6. Barbara Reise, *op. cit.,* p. 58.

7. In 1934–1935, when Barney was courting Annalee, he wrote her love poems, and Newman, champion of avant-garde art and literature, admirer of Joyce and Lorca, phrased them in severely regulated Shakespearean sonnet forms, iambic pentameter, heroic couplets and all.

8. Barnett Newman, "The 14 Stations of the Cross," *Art News* (New York), vol. 65, no. 3 (May 1966), pp. 28, 57.

9. Barnett Newman, *op. cit.,* p. 26.

10. The picture is listed and reproduced as "Resurrection" in the catalogue of Newman's two-man exhibition with Willem de Kooning at the Allan Stone Gallery, New York, October 23–November 17, 1962. In fact, it was not exhibited then, nor was *Uriel,* which was also included in the checklist and reproduced. "Resurrection" was a title Allan Stone liked, and as his catalogue was going to press in a rush, he simply gave it to the picture; for some reason he also retitled *The Third* and called it "Orange Colossus"; he listed *Not There— Here* as "untitled" and he called the vertical, untitled 1946 drawing of a circle, "The Void." These were arbitrary acts by the dealer. However, Newman's own plan for the show also is evident in the catalogue—he planned to exhibit *eighteen* pictures *(Hai).*

11. The Golden Section is a relationship of height to width which can be expressed in the proportion A:B=B:(A+B).

DAVID SMITH:
The Voltri Sculpture

CHECKLIST

1. Voltri I 1962
steel
235.8 × 56.1 × 48.1 cm (92⅞ × 22⅛ × 19 in)
Signed and dated on base: David Smith 5-25-62 VOLTRI I
Hirshhorn Museum and Sculpture Garden, Smithsonian
Institution, Washington

2. Voltri IV 1962
steel
174.0 × 154.0 × 50.0 cm (68½ × 60⅝ × 19¾ in)
Signed and dated on base: David Smith 6/62 VOLTRI IV
Rijksmuseum Kröller-Müller, Otterlo, The Netherlands

3. Voltri VI 1962
steel
261.6 × 261.0 × 64.8 cm (103 × 102¾ × 25½ in)
Signed and dated on one side of horizontal spine: David Smith
1962; on other side: VOLTRI VI
Signed on side with blowtorch: Andiamo a Spoleto Voltri—Sally
Collection, Nelson A. Rockefeller

4. Voltri VII 1962
steel
215.8 × 311.6 × 110.5 cm (85 × 122¾ × 43½ in)
Signed and dated on end of horizontal spine: David Smith 1962;
middle of spine: VOLTRI-VII
National Gallery of Art, Washington, Ailsa Mellon Bruce
Fund, 1977

5. Voltri VIII 1962
steel
201.3 × 103.6 × 81.9 cm (79¼ × 40¾ × 32½ in)
Signed and dated on shoulder: GIUGNO 1962/David Smith VOLTRI
VIII
Collection, Mr. and Mrs. Harold P. Starr, Philadelphia

6. Voltri IX 1962
steel
200.2 × 80.9 × 30.0 cm (78⅞ × 31⅞ × 11⅞ in)
Signed and dated on front base: David Smith 6/62;
side base: VOLTRI IX
Hirshhorn Museum and Sculpture Garden, Smithsonian
Institution, Washington

7. Voltri XII 1962
steel
221.0 × 121.3 × 34.3 cm (87 × 47¾ × 13½ in)
Signed and dated on one end of base: David Smith 6/62;
on other side: VOLTRI XII
Collection, Mr. and Mrs. Gilbert H. Kinney, Washington

8. Voltri XV 1962
steel
228.1 × 196.1 × 57.4 cm (89⅞ × 77¼ × 22⅝ in)
Signed on base: David Smith VOLTRI XV
Hirshhorn Museum and Sculpture Garden, Smithsonian
Institution, Washington

9. Voltri XVII 1962
steel
218.5 × 88.9 × 78.8 cm (86 × 35 × 31 in)
Signed and dated on side: David Smith 6/62 VOLTRI XVII
Collection, Lois and Georges de Ménil, Paris

10. Voltri XIX 1962
steel
139.7 × 114.3 × 127.0 cm (55 × 45 × 50 in)
Signed and dated at top center: David Smith 6-62 VOLTRI XIX
Collection, Mr. and Mrs. Stephen D. Paine, Boston

11. Voltri XVI 1962
steel
111.7 × 101.6 × 96.5 cm (44 × 40 × 38 in)
Signed and dated on top: David Smith 6/62 VOLTRI XVI
Estate of David Smith, Bolton Landing, N.Y.

12. Voltri XVIII 1962
steel
107.7 × 101.6 × 83.2 cm (42⅜ × 40 × 32¾ in)
Signed and dated on one side: David Smith 6/62;
on other side: VOLTRI XVIII
Estate of David Smith, Bolton Landing, N.Y.

13. Voltri XX 1962
steel
197.4 × 69.1 × 23.7 cm (77¾ × 27¼ × 9⅜ in)
Signed and dated on one side of base: David Smith 6-62;
on other side: VOLTRI XX
Collection, Mr. and Mrs. Robert Schwarz, Palm Springs,
Calif.

BIOGRAPHY

Born in 1906 in Decatur, Indiana. Studies at various schools before enrolling as full-time student under John Sloan at the Art Students League between 1927 and 1932. In 1932 sees reproductions of metal sculpture by Picasso and Gonzalez and begins his own welded works. During 1935-1936 travels in Greece, studying ancient and classical art, continuing this interest with study at the British Museum in London. In 1940 moves permanently to Bolton Landing, New York, to a farm purchased in 1929. In 1948, large works of open linear construction are begun. In May 1962 goes to Voltri, Italy, for thirty days to make twenty-six pieces of sculpture subsequently shown in Festival of Two Worlds at Spoleto. In June returns to Bolton Landing and continues Italian series in Voltri-Bolton sculptures, and resumes work on Cubi series. Dies in truck accident in 1965.

DAVID SMITH:
The Voltri Sculpture

E. A. CARMEAN, JR.

"But for me—I never made so much—so good so easy in such condensed time as in my 30 day Italian phase," wrote David Smith about the sculpture he made in Voltri, Italy, in late May and June 1962 for the Spoleto Festival of Two Worlds.[1] The work, the making of it, and its exhibition in the concert amphitheater of Spoleto (figs. 2, 34) have acquired virtually the status of a legend in the history of modern sculpture. "And Vulcan went to Voltri," wrote Giovanni Carandente of Smith.

One spring morning he reached the idle scrapheap, those still skeletons, relics of the flesh of steel, inanimate forms that had, not long before, been living symbols of the latest of the Iron Ages. Glancing around the boneheap, he pondered awhile, and set to work. With his own hands, he improvised a forge and, then, summoned his alter-ego, fire.[2]

Edward Fry, writing in 1969, referred to Smith's Voltri period as "so prolific an outpouring of monumental sculpture . . . without precedent in the history of modern art."[3]

Part of the legend of Voltri, if we can call it that, derives merely from the number of works Smith created: twenty-six sculptures in thirty days. "That was damn near a piece a day," Smith wrote later. "While I work in a concentrated way in [the] USA—I've never done this before."[4] Indeed, the total number of works is staggering, even allowing for the fact that four works—*Voltri XXI* to *XXIV*—are quite small in scale. As Rosalind Krauss has pointed out, less than ten years earlier Smith had referred to making twenty pieces in a year as his record output.[5]

Furthermore, there is the level of quality—and importance—of the Voltri sculpture. The Italian works number among them many of Smith's greatest sculptures, and he was clearly inspired by them in his subsequent art. Leaving Voltri he could not part with the metal—the bits and pieces which had so provoked these works: "I had work in progress and parts started," he wrote upon his return, "so I piled up all the parts—tongs, wrenches, wheels . . . all on the floor in one pile—and said—send them to me in [the] USA—they did and I will finish my Italian period here [1962]."[6] This second series, entitled Voltri-Bolton Landing, consists of twenty-five works which use the Italian parts and was completed in Bolton Landing, New York, between early December 1962 and mid-March 1963.

Another part of the legend derives from the manner in which the Voltri sculptures took command of the Spoleto arena. "Carandente installed it so well that it looked like it belonged," Smith commented.[7] Indeed, the subject of the Voltri sculpture

appears to be involved—in part—both with Smith's level of ambition and with an inspiration drawn from Voltri. But Smith completed the works before the decision was made to use the amphitheater so that the sculpture cannot be seen as intended for its debut setting. Nevertheless, its very appropriateness derives from Smith's larger subject in many of these works, namely the tradition of ancient and classical art. If Smith's inspiration in the Voltri sculptures comes, in part, from his experience in Italy, his level of ambition derives in part from his freedom from financial constraints regarding materials and assistants, which were provided by Italsider. In New York Smith's projects were always limited by financial conditions; he later referred to Voltri as a place where he could realize what he wanted to do.[8]

INVITATION

The Voltri sculptures were made as the result of an invitation to Smith to work, originally, in an Italsider factory near Genoa. Giovanni Carandente originated the idea of Smith's participation in the *Sculpture in the City* exhibition which was part of the larger musical events of the Festival of Two Worlds at Spoleto. Calder, Chadwick, Consagra, Pomodoro, Lipton, Rosati, Chillida, Richier, Moore, Manzu, Franchina, and Marini also participated.[10] Smith was contacted first by Beverly Pepper, then as now living in Italy, and then in New York by the composer Gian Carlo Menotti, who, as further encouragement, offered to dedicate an opera to Smith's daughters Candida and Rebecca. Smith was cabled by Savarese, the director of Italsider, to "realize sculpture for Spoleto exhibition." Smith replied affirmatively with plans to "come May twenty work hard 30 days."[11] Smith's original plan had been to work in stainless steel, but when he arrived in Italy on May 19 he rejected working in the modern Italsider steel factory at Cornegliano. He was then given full use of five abandoned factories at Voltri, nearby, and the rights to use any materials he found there.

Italsider let me roam all the factories—pick out whatever I wanted—let me work without interruption. . . . I was never bothered with officials, questions teas, social affairs or check ups—Somehow word was extended that I had privileges—it was a delight and an honor.[12]

There are still many questions about the exact nature of Smith's expected contribution to the Spoleto exhibition. The other sculptors made only a few works, but Smith made twenty-six because, he explained, "not speaking Italian I had not known I had been asked to make 1-2 pieces. . . ."[13] But as

Figure 2. Installation view of David Smith's Voltri sculpture in the amphitheater at Spoleto, June 1962. [Photo: Ugo Mulas, courtesy of Antonia Mulas, Milan. Reproduced from Carandente, *Voltron* (Philadelphia, 1964)]

Krauss observes, Smith had an interpreter (provided by Italsider), and his friendship with Lynn Chadwick—they "prowled the night life [of] Genoa together"—who knew the nature of the commission, suggests that Smith should have known as well.[14] Furthermore, Smith did complete and send early to Spoleto two works: *Voltri I and II*. These two were joined by *Cubi IX*, which had probably been sent from Bolton Landing as an example of Smith's stainless steel sculpture done in the United States, to be placed in comparison to the expected Italsider pieces in the same material.[15] These three alone met the exhibition requirements.

Sometime after *Voltri I*, Smith planned an enormous railway flatcar piece, and he probably intended to send this to Spoleto. This was to be his major project, a "dream"—to use his word—drawn from his Midwest childhood. "A dream is a dream, never lost," he wrote. "I found an old flat-car [in Voltri], asked for and was given it. Had I used the flat-car for the base and made a sculpture on the top, the dream would have been closer. . . . In a year I could have made a train."[9] Smith had hopped freight trains as a child in Ohio and had worked in locomotive plants during his career. These autobiographical sources were drawn upon in Voltri as ideas for a monumental work; but he could not make the sculpture, as a railway flatcar could not travel to Spoleto, and, if shipped by truck, it would have been too high to clear low tunnels en route. Though Smith then turned to other themes, this dream and the fact that it briefly appeared possible to Smith give evidence of the soaring height of his intentions at Voltri.

As this decision against the flatcar occurred early—before *Voltri VI* was begun—Smith may have decided to shift the ideas for this single project to a series of works, conceived as separate pieces, but interrelated. Or he may simply have been less satisfied with the first two Voltris and, still inspired, continued to produce sculpture. At any rate, six works—five Voltris (*I, II, XIII, XXII,* and *XXIII*) were installed in the city of Spoleto itself, and the remaining large pieces installed in the amphitheater.

CLASSICAL THEMES

The Voltri pieces clearly are embedded within the broader stylistic and thematic scope of Smith's work. They continue themes of Smith's earlier sculpture—unit compositions, figures, and circles—or they realize earlier ideas which had never been made—such as the chariots. They also introduce a new one in his art—the "straight" still life. And Smith would continue these themes after his Italian period, not only in the works made of Italian parts, but in his work in general.

The Voltri works also stand apart from the artist's oeuvre not only because of their Italian materials but also because they have a sense of a classical style. Indeed, it will be proposed here that Smith intentionally made the Voltri works with ancient Sumerian, Greek, Etruscan, and Roman (and Hindu) works in mind, referring to them both in terms of form as well as theme. This linkage bonds the Voltri works together and is the central subject of Smith's Italian sculpture.

Smith himself set his Voltri works apart from his other sculpture and suggested they have their distinction precisely because of the influence of Italy—Voltri—upon them. "I think it was climate—locale," he wrote, "at least it seems to me that my Italian work took on a different feeling than my USA works ever had—yet it was natural and without intention. . . ."[16] But the central question about the Voltris is precisely Smith's intention in them and how they—or at least some of them—relate compositionally and thematically to ancient and classical pre-

Figure 3. David Smith. *Voltri I*, 1962. Steel, 235.8 x 56.1 x 48.1 cm (92⅞ x 22⅛ x 19 in). Hirshhorn Museum and Sculpture Garden, Smithsonian Institution, Washington [photo: Ugo Mulas, courtesy of Antonia Mulas, Milan. Reproduced from Carandente, *Voltron* (Philadelphia, 1964)]. Cat. no. 1

cedents. In this regard, Smith's haunting description of the climate of the Voltri factories more specifically locates the mood of his work within these ideas:

The first Sunday alone in these factories—functional in an era long past, abandoned only a few months—were like Sundays in Brooklyn in 1934 at the Terminal Iron Works, except that here I could use anything I found dragging parts between buildings to find their new identity. . . . The first two Sundays—not even a skeleton crew around—the great quiet of stopped machines—the awe, the pull, exceeded that of visits to museums in Genoa or even the ancient art in other cities.

And,

A factory stripped of its function—leaves on the floor from holes in the roof—quiet except for a bird cheep. . . . I felt the awe and the scared air—like one returning survivor after holocaust, and as I had felt, very young in Decatur, when I went through the window in my first abandoned factory. After the first shock of its immensity and the privilege, I felt at home, and then to work.

And again,

The beauties of the forge shop, parts dropped partly forged, cooled now but stopped in progress—as if the human factor had dissolved and the great dust settled—the found tombs of early twentieth

Figure 4. David Smith. *Cubi IX*, 1961. Stainless steel, 269.9 x 142.3 x 116.9 cm (106¼ x 56 x 46 in). Walker Art Center, Minneapolis, Gift of the T. B. Walker Foundation. Not in exhibition

century, from giants to tweezers headed for the open hearth to feed the world's speediest rolls.

Archaeologists have their iron interests back 5,000 years. In the yard where iron has lain shedding scale and scrap, punchings scraps from shearing, I found parts of my nature not over seventy years old in the first inch, but this flat beside a stream near the sea may, farther down, hold museum iron. I brought back to Bolton handfuls of findings for no greater reason than that they fit with my miscellany and complement the manhole cover from Brooklyn which hangs on my wall. The archaeologists may go as far as L. S. B. Leakey and fill many halls, but my vision is in dreaming the host of events destroyed in their time. It is possible the museums are too small in truth to form historianisms.[17]

VOLTRI I

Smith's arrival at the Voltri factories was less than successful:

Day 1 to be introduced in white collar to my workmen, to whom I couldn't speak—awkward to us both. In equal garb the next day. Request for swept floor not met. I swept floor. Request for moving of heavy objects not moved exact place. I moved to positions. After welding, moving, sweeping, my collar was O.K. We worked together from then on great. An interpreter and unknown work added to the first problems, but for only several days—we understood, and their desire to produce first class and to my need never failed.[18]

Smith completed the first sculpture, *Voltri I* (fig. 3), on May 25, six days after his arrival in Italy. With its vocabulary of repeated shapes and rigid, vertical composition, *Voltri I* stands apart from the other Italian pieces. Smith wrote of it:

This piece probably carried in my consciousness from Bolton since I had been working cube unities since 1955. [and] I had gone to Genoa expecting to make stainless pieces. . . .[19]

Smith "had come with some drawings but abandoned them, seizing opportunity of wholly new world. . . ."[20] But *Voltri I* suggests that these drawings were related to the Cubis Smith had intended to make in Italy. Actually, Smith's great Cubi series had only just been begun when he went to Italy; and of these large, volumetric stainless steel works, only *Cubi III* and *Cubi IX* were completed. Smith would finish the remaining before his death three years later. Smith originally conceived of the Cubis as compositions of "units" and importantly *Voltri I* was also referred to by Smith as "Unit of Six." This relates it directly to earlier pieces from 1956, entitled *Four Units Equal* and *Five Units Equal,* both of which employed boxlike components and which, in turn, served as prototypes for the Cubis.

Although Carandente wrote that *Voltri I* "consists of a number of forms cut with a blowtorch out of steel plate . . . ,"[21] it is clear that the six elements in the sculpture were actually pieces found in the factory. The individual units were a rectangular plate, two projecting arms a quarter way down the side, and two legs, connected to the outer perimeter. The basic unit stands at the bottom, on a round plate, bisected at a right angle by another standing unit. The remaining four units above are turned on their sides, three rotated ninety degrees to the left, one—in the middle of the work—turned ninety degrees to the right. The sense of vertical association in a climbing composition had entered Smith's work in *Cubi III* and was to be repeated in *Cubi I,* which Smith completed after his Italian period; but in *Voltri I* the turning of units, which is more complex, also relate it directly to *Cubi IX* (fig. 4), which was sent to Italy.

The kind of unit composition in *Voltri I* was abandoned by Smith because of the "wholly new world" of forms and ideas he found in Voltri. That world was the environment of the five abandoned factories at Voltri, where Smith was allowed to use in his works any of the machine parts, leftover forgings, rugs, tools, implements, equipment, and machines that were there:

"[I] used every thing that appealed [which had been] left behind in the factories."[22]

Smith also went to Cornegliano (where Chadwick was working) to select steel for his works; "any plate end or found piece I wrote my name on and 'Voltri' was delivered. I . . . had full freedom of the mill and scrap cars."[23] Smith's plate ends were steel outcroppings, which can easily be found in Italy, England, and older factories in Canada.[24] When steel is rolled out to make rectangular plates, it has irregular ends at each width, much like those which result in rolling out pastry dough; these are then cut off in straight lines to make the rectangular plate. The leftover results, steel outcroppings, thus have a straight edge on one side, and a soft, curving profile around the remainder. Probably the first time he had seen them, Smith selected a good many from Cornegliano for use in Voltri:

Voltri II, IV, V, IX, XI, XIV, XV, XVII all have an element in their structure which I'll call a chopped cloud, although in different relationships the visual response varies. When a billet rolls out to a sheet no two ends are the same, as in the edges of clouds. There is great wonder and a beauty of natural growth in these variations. I cut off many ends and flew them many ways. I would like a hundred more. I have never before seen or possessed chopped-iron cloud ends. There are ends on a table. An end on a full cloud. Ends caught on a tower. Ends in a tower. Pennant ends on circles. And ends making a whole. In the mountains, clouds are in my daily unconsciousness, but I've never had one before.[25]

COLLAGE, OBJET-TROUVÉ, AND THEMES

The various found materials of the Voltri sculptures, the parts of machines, scrap steel, or tools, have an initial intrinsic identity, as opposed to metal stock, such as tubes and plates, which are in this sense abstract. Smith had begun the transformation of materials in his work as early as 1933, as part of his interest in the sculpture of Picasso and Gonzalez and its outgrowth from the tradition of the cubist collage. This use of found ingredients is not surprising, for the first *papier collé*, by Braque in 1912, was made following his discovery of a wood-grain wallpaper in a shop window. But *faux-bois* paper and other materials in cubism often retain their referential values, whereas in Smith's art the source materials give up their original identity (or at least generally so) in favor of a new one of figuration or as part of an abstract syntax. Smith's art was also influenced by surrealist works which also used discovered materials. But the surrealist *objet-trouvé-aidé* was often used more for its poetic inspiration in the work than for formal transformation. The surrealist work of Picasso is an exception here, because we do find formal transformation in his *Bull's Head,* 1943 (collection of the estate of the artist, Paris), where a bicycle seat and handlebars form the animal's head, or the *Baboon and Young,* 1951 (The Museum of Modern Art, New York), where toy cars are used to create the ape's cranium. But Picasso's work is marked by both the more traditional or pre-modern appearance of the figures and the ease with which the components may still be identified. Smith's art, to the contrary, is distinguished both by its tendency toward abstraction on the one hand, and its more complete absorption of materials—their loss of recognizable identities—on the other.

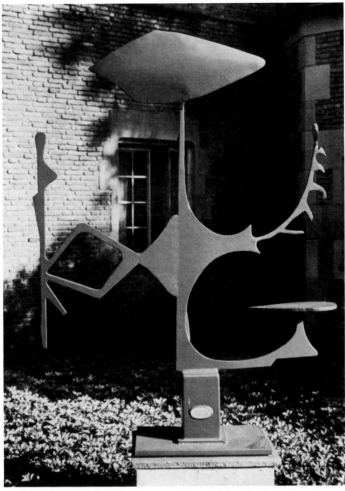

Figure 5. David Smith. *Agricola (Agricola I)*, 1951-1952. Painted steel, 185.5 x 141.0 x 62.3 cm (73 x 55½ x 24½ in). Hirshhorn Museum and Sculpture Garden, Smithsonian Institution, Washington. Not in exhibition

Figure 6. Attributed to Adriaen de Vries. *Mercury*, 1603-1613. Bronze, 177.0 x 48.5 x 94.9 cm (69⅝ x 19 x 37¼ in). National Gallery of Art, Washington, Andrew W. Mellon Collection, 1937. Not in exhibition

Smith's balance between abstraction and metaphorical figuration characterizes much of Smith's mature work. The presence of such a balance is apparent in the Voltri series as well. On one level the Voltris read as internally focused abstract compositions and are fully successful in this comprehension. On another level, while the Voltris are tied to previous thematic, indeed figural concerns of Smith, they narrow them to interpretations more precisely based on ancient and classical sources.

The Voltri sculptures can be divided into four subgroupings: figural works *(Voltri III, V, VIII, IX, XI, XIV, XVII, and XX)*; the chariots *(Voltri VI, VII, and XIII)*; the circle compositions *(Voltri II, X, XII, and XV)*; and the still-lifes *(Voltri XVI, XVIII, and XIX)*. This is the approach taken here in discussing the Italian works, rather than dealing with them in the straight chronological order indicated by their numbering (which may in fact be arbitrary, as Smith's numbering often does not indicate the sequence of expressive ideas but rather marks the successive completion of works). However, a discussion organized around thematic concerns should not be taken as an indication that the Voltri works are any less (nor any more) concerned with formal—or abstract—considerations than Smith's other works.[26]

FIGURATION

Smith's first full series using machine parts was the Agricola works done between 1951 and 1955. Significantly, he records that this series came to mind later when he first discovered the different elements in the Voltri factories: "dragging parts between buildings to find their new identity. I thought of my Agricolas. There was a similarity—but the language was different—and the size bolder."[27]

The Agricola works were made from parts of abandoned farm machinery, as the Latin series title indicates. As Smith described the series,

The Agricola series are like new unities whose parts are related to past tools of agriculture. Forms in function are often not appreciated in their context except for their mechanical performance. With time and the passing of their function and a separation of their past metaphoric changes can take place permitting a new unity, one that is strictly visual.[28]

The Voltris, which were made from abandoned factory machinery elements, or the steel products of those machines, have obvious formal and metaphorical concerns which correspond to those of the earlier series. Moreover, certain of the Agricola

Figure 7. David Smith. *Voltri IX,* 1962. Steel, 200.2 x 80.9 x 30.0 cm (78⅞ x 31⅞ x 11⅞in). Hirshhorn Museum and Sculpture Garden, Smithsonian Institution, Washington. Smith is seen in background of this photograph taken in the Voltri factory. [Photo: Ugo Mulas, courtesy of Antonia Mulas, Milan. Reproduced from Carandente, *Voltron* (Philadelphia, 1964).] Cat. no. 6

Figure 8. Detail from the Ara Pacis Augustae, Rome: processional scene with members of the imperial family, c. 9-14 A.D. [Photo: Anderson, courtesy of Alinari, Florence.] Not in exhibition

works are also figural, and one of them, *Agricola (Agricola I)* (fig. 5), is especially pertinent here. While the exact identity of the farm machinery components is difficult to detect, their transformation into a figure is not: the large head, vertical, central body core, extended arm, and supporting leg are quite immediately legible. What is not so readily apparent is that the figural composition of *Agricola I* is, in fact, a reference to another sculpture, the famous *Mercury* (fig. 6) attributed to Adriaen de Vries at the National Gallery.[29] Smith's work repeats the winged foot (turned to the front), the extended arm, and the cradled caduceus, with its entwined vine; even the lifting rhythm of Mercury's movement is present in Smith's configuration.

The environment produced by the factory materials in Voltri did not suggest simply figures composed of disparate parts. Rather his singling out of the Agricola works, which were a precedent for transforming elements into works which contained, less obviously, references to still other works of art,

suggests that Smith saw in the Voltri materials a similar, more specific thematic undertaking. In the case of the Voltris, they refer to the works of ancient and classical art evoked by the Italian factories.

Voltri IX (fig. 7), although later in the series, joins *Voltri X* in being the only figural works made entirely from the steel outcroppings Smith had selected at Cornegliano. Here there is "an end on a full cloud," the latter made from two outcroppings joined along the straight edge. But the union is not exact. One piece is set slightly back in plane from the other, and raised above so not to rest upon the base but to extend above the top. It is this latter placement which suggests the figuration, the bottom extension indicating a foot for the sculpture, the upper separation implying a neck. This is supported by the half cloud above, which rests as a head upon the lower body.

Smith's piece immediately before this one, *Voltri III* (collection of Giovanni Carandente, Spoleto, Italy), also has figural qualities. Made from a long thin outcropping with a clamp positioned above, the piece suggests a figure in motion. It is likened to a "fleeting nun" by Carandente[30] and "was called the little old lady by one of my workmen," Smith records.[31] The extended curve of the cloud both in *Voltri III* and *IX* does suggest the long fall of cloth associated with the contemporary dress of a nun or an elderly woman. But when combined with the similar quality of the upper cloud of *Voltri IX,* the composite form suggests a long robe covering the figure, with a cowl hood pulled up over the head. While this costume might have been visible to Smith in Italy, the broad and flat surfaces suggest a more specific source for the garments and for the stance: the figures seen in stone reliefs and in vase and wall paintings in Greek and Roman art (fig. 8). Moreover, these classical figures are often seen in procession, and it is this sense of movement and direction—more stately than in *Voltri III*—which characterizes *Voltri IX.*

It is important here to realize that citing classical sources for Smith's work is not an act of projecting an iconography or imagery upon them. As Krauss has observed, Smith had "the sense that his art was parented by the whole of Western culture extending back to Egyptian and Sumerian art,"[32] and his oeuvre is replete with references to other sculpture of other periods, as in *Agricola I.* This is made implicit in certain of his works, which refer to Sumerian seals and inscribed line drawings of Egyptian reliefs, and explicit in others, such as the 1951 *Head* (estate of the artist) which is based directly upon canopic burial jars Smith studied in the early 1940s in the Museum of Fine Arts, Boston.

Smith was well acquainted with classical art, especially Greek, having studied it in Athens when he spent the winter of 1935-1936 in Greece. He had studied classical sculpture at length, even as to coloration:

It is easy to understand the patine on the Greek and Roman statues. The Romans got it all from the Greeks. I've been reading Pliny and Vitruvius and Theophrastus and learning their methods. I intend to take color specimens from the colored statues in the museums for micro slides etc.

The American School starts excavations in a couple of days and it will be interesting to watch the process of uncovering. They are clearing a big slum area of modern houses to get down to the Byzantine level—then thru the Roman level to the Greek. One of the arche's [archeologists] took me through the excavated areas and showed me the maps of the various stratas. . . . The National Museum is near us—and what Jesus good things they have. . . .[33]

This experience had a lasting effect on Smith. Upon his return to New York he adopted the use of ancient Greek letters ΔΣ for his signature, which was used on his sculpture through 1945 and on his drawings to the end of his life. Smith's fifteen Medals for Dishonor, 1939-1940, although based on Sumerian seals Smith had studied at the British Museum in London and on Renaissance plaquettes, nevertheless use Greek letters for the inscription, translated from Smith's own phrases by his friend the painter, John Xceron. Throughout his work other classical—as well as Sumerian and Egyptian—quotations and references can be located. Smith's knowledge of earlier sculpture and his record of seeing it as advisory to his more abstract figuration, when combined with the antique influence of Voltri and his study of classical works at the Genoa museum, make probable the notion that the Voltri sculptures are aligned with classical themes. Even identifying *Voltri IX* with as particular a subject as a cowled woman in a procession is not unlikely. Certainly evidence of classic subjects in other Voltri works would support this argument.

The preceding figural work (in numerical order), *Voltri VIII* (fig. 9), is composed of two elements set at right angles to each other. Smith recorded:

When a sheet runs back and forth under the rolls, before it shoots through quench and to the next rolling reduction, a rarity can happen—it can stub a toe, instead of running, fold up like a great stick of gum. I saw one, sent it to Voltri, watched it in many positions until I found its relationship.[34]

Voltri VIII has figural characteristics—the flat sheet with its long sweeping curve implying the back of the figure and narrowing at the top to suggest the neck, with a rectangular head thrust forward. The curved sheet which crosses at right angles can be read as drapery, as its curves and loops are similar to fabric folds. Even the two rivets at the front suggest breasts beneath the covering fabric. But these observations are general. Associations can be projected onto the figure; for example, Carandente calls it, alternately, "the high priestess," "a baroque angel," and "the steel blue goddess."[35] But no precise, specifically classical, thematic source can here be identified, although the sculpture's sweeping curves recall certain works of the fifth century B.C. (fig. 10). And, the rigidity of the flat plate figure—in contrast to the intricate curves of the frontal sheet—gives it, if nothing else, the hieratic bearing of earlier Greek figures.

THE KORE AND ARCHAIC VOLTRIS

If *Voltri IX* only suggests a classical processional figure, and *Voltri VIII* implies, at most, a correspondence to antiquity, *Voltri XVII* (fig. 11) is far more direct in its references. When viewed from the front the composition of this work consists of two vertically upright supports, bearing between them in the upper half an encasement of horizontal bars, the whole surmounted by a "chopped cloud" fragment. This arrangement makes explicit references to the human figure in legs, trunk, and head. Although the side view differs greatly with softer silhouettes of the steel outcroppings attached perpendicular to the frontal plane, nevertheless they are placed again to correspond to figuration. These curving shapes can also be seen as indicating the figure to be feminine. This would be in keeping with the other Voltri figurations and Smith's own observation that he "never made boy sculptures."[36]

With its union of dominant vertical and horizontal elements there is something architectural—a post and lintel structure—about *Voltri XVII.* Indeed Smith discussed the piece as "[cloud] ends caught on a tower," and Krauss has referred to this piece as "magnificently Doric."[37] Certainly its massive presence, its rigid structure, and its near symmetry, suggest the architectonic rather than the organic. It has a columnlike identity. But further study of its frontal division of legs, torso, and head, when combined with the curves of its side view, suggests

Figure 9. David Smith. *Voltri VIII,* 1962. Steel, 201.3 x 103.6 x 81.9 cm (79¼ x 40¾ x 32½ in). Collection, Mr. and Mrs. Harold P. Starr, Philadelphia. Cat. no. 5

Figure 10. Roman, after Greek work (by Kallimachos?). *Maenad Leaning on her Thyrsos,* 5th century B.C. Marble; height: 143.0 cm (56 5⁄16 in). The Metropolitan Museum of Art, New York, Fletcher Fund, 1935 (35.11.3). Not in exhibition

the sculpture belongs in the figural grouping of other of the Italian works, though this does not deny an architectural sense. After all, Smith's work is replete with figural and landscape images which can be read in multiple ways, as Edward Fry has pointed out.[38] For example, Smith's 1938 *Amusement Park,* though based on a far distant view of Palisades, New Jersey, can also be interpreted as a close-up series of circus artists. The suggested union of column and figure in *Voltri XVII* is, in fact, precedented in one of Smith's major early works, *Reliquary House,* 1945 (collection of David Mirvish, Toronto), where, on the right, a classical column opens at the top—suggesting the bursting open of an acanthus capital—to reveal a tiny female figure based on a classical idiom. Here in *Voltri XVII*

the combination of figure and column is given in one image, rather than depicted as a transformation. And, of course, in Greek art the fusion of imagery between the column and the figure in the Karyatid figure offers a direct source. Unlike the Karyatid, Smith's figure, however much it may suggest architecture, is, nonetheless, a self-contained presence, not a part for a larger ensemble. The boldness of the figure of *Voltri XVII* is startling, but not new.

Smith had used hieratic symmetry and grand presence before in his work, most notably the *Hero* from 1951–1952 (Brooklyn Museum, New York). Here the use of vertical layers in a squared-off torso with head is quite comparable to the later work. But distinctively, *Voltri XVII* offers direct allusion to

Figure 11. David Smith. *Voltri XVII*, 1962. Steel, 218.5 x 88.9 x 78.8 cm (86 x 35 x 31 in). Collection, Lois and Georges de Ménil, Paris [photo: Ugo Mulas, courtesy of Antonia Mulas, Milan. Reproduced from Carandente, *Voltron* (Philadelphia, 1964)]. Not in exhibition

Figure 12. Probably by Antenor. *Kore*, c. 530-525 B.C. Acropolis Museum, Athens [photo: reproduced from Gisela M. A. Richter, *A Handbook of Greek Art* (New York, 1959)]. Not in exhibition

classical sources as well, most particularly the Greek Korai figures (fig. 12), where figuration also has characteristics of hieratic frontality and massive scale but, like *Voltri XVII*, combined with the softer curves associated with femininity. *Voltri XVII*'s use of these stylistic qualities associates it directly with the precedent, and the particularities, of Korai figures. Furthermore, while the horizontal banding in the torso of the work is a form of detailing, in compositional terms, it also can be seen as a more oblique reference to the folds of the chiton worn by the Korai figure; this reference is also suggested in the "clouds" (although the pattern in the Greek works is predominantly vertical and follows the surfaces of the figure). Thus of all of the Voltri sculptures this piece, by means of its massive presence, its feminine figuration, and its detailing, suggests a

definite link with a clear precedent of classical figuration.

In contrast to *Voltri XVII*, the later *Voltri XX* (fig. 13) is distinguished by its thin linear qualities which set it apart from the other Italian pieces as well. Yet its round pelvis, striding legs, projecting arms—or breasts—and rounded head, definitely join *Voltri XX* to the other figural works. The figure of *Voltri XX* is composed entirely of found tools, pliers, clamps, hooks, and the flat disk at the center of the work. Curiously of Smith's figural works made by assembly, *Voltri XX* is one of the few in which the component parts are identifiable—as they were not, for example, in *Agricola I*. It is the sharp and linear character of these parts which Smith promotes in this construction rather than any identification of the elements per se with their original function. His configuration ensures the down-

Figure 13. David Smith. *Voltri XX,* 1962. Steel, 197. 4 x 69.1 x 23.7 cm (77¾ x 27¼ x 9⅜ in). Collection, Mr. and Mrs. Robert Schwarz, Palm Springs, Calif. [photo: Ugo Mulas, courtesy of Antonia Mulas, Milan. Reproduced from Carandente, *Voltron* (Philadelphia, 1964)]. Cat. no. 13

play of the latter tendencies, but it still allows the separateness of the components to register.

Curiously, although it was the last of the major Voltris to be completed, *Voltri XX* relates more directly to Smith's previous work in a figural style. A pertinent example is his *Running Daughter* of 1956-1960 (fig. 14), where Smith joined varying elements together to form the image of a graceful child moving in space. It is significant to note that the seemingly abstract construction of the work not only alludes to a child but that Smith based *Running Daughter* on an external source, a photograph of his daughter running across the lawn at a picnic.[39]

Unfortunately no such precise source for *Voltri XX* can here be cited. But the stylistic traits of the figuration—its attenuated body, its more linear character, and its sharply projected profile—all suggest the archaic style of Greek art, especially as seen in the surviving vase paintings (fig. 15).

VOLTRI CIRCLES

Among the larger sculpture from Voltri are four major works using flat circular rings, *Voltri II, X, XII* (fig. 16), and *XV* (fig. 19). *Voltri XII* and *XV* are closely related in size and in composition, each with its large circle placed atop a thin vertical column, or post, support with smaller, detailing elements attached. Smith's art contains numerous works which use circles; in his Voltri notes he said, "Circles have long been a preoccupation, more primary than squares. Wheels are circles with mobility, from the first wheel of man to wheels on Indian stone temples, to a target on a pyramid I painted in 1934, to all the suns and poetic imagery of movement. . . . "[40] The general idea of a circle lifted as an emblem high in the air had entered Smith's art around 1960 in such works as *Parrot's Circle,* 1958 (Larry Aldrich Museum, Ridgefield, Connecticut), or *Noland's Blues,* 1961 (collection of Mr. and Mrs. Harold P. Starr, Philadelphia). The latter work gives some evidence to the influence on Smith's art made by his close friend Kenneth Noland's target paintings. These compositions might have recalled for Smith "a target on a pyramid I painted in '34. . . ."

Smith's methods of working were varied, and none dominated a particular period of his work. From all evidence we have, certain sculptures were created spontaneously, and the decisions were made directly in the process of constructing the piece. Some works grew out of preliminary studies, but these in turn range from highly finished sketches to simple notations. The ideas for other works actually come from three-dimensional maquettes, such as *Cubi IV* and *V,* which Smith studied first in mock-ups of cardboard boxes.[41] Finally, Smith made still other works on the floor, moving the separate pieces about in a collagelike fashion; and using white chalk, he would also draw in new compositional elements on the floor.

The two related circle Voltris were made in the last fashion, as can be seen from a photograph of them (fig. 17) in an early state. Here, for *Voltri XII,* Smith placed the ring horizontally as the initial layer, subsequently adding other components onto the work—at one side a square plate turned as a diamond and at the bottom a rectangular plate outside the circumference of the circle. Two pieces of steel outcropping have been added, a long piece that forms the stem of the work and a much smaller piece pointing upward at the top. This latter element is used in *Voltri XV* as well, and Smith referred to them as "pennant ends on circles."

This photographic record of *Voltri XII* gives a clear indication of the way in which certain of Smith's sculpture (and particularly the Voltris) were indebted, in their initial states, to the collage technique. We have seen how many of the components of Smith's art—the found objects and abstract plates and pieces—either remain formless or are transformed in the collagelike unions of his eventual construction. As in the making of a *papier collé,* Smith, at this state of *Voltri XII,* treated the elements like thin planar components—pieces of paper—moving and rearranging them on the horizontal plane of the floor until compositional ideas became clearer. But Smith's sculpture is distinct from collage precisely by its three-dimensionality. Unlike the collage where paper is pasted to a continual plane, the pieces in Smith's work are independent because they must always be read as entities in physical space. In this sense, the ring of *Voltri XII* becomes the compositional and focal plane, but one which carries its own sense of form at the same time. Furthermore, unlike the *papier collé,* Smith's constructions introduce layers both in front of and behind this major plane: in *Voltri XV,* for example, the cloud pennants are placed on varying sides, challenging the form's identity as a flat sculpture, although it is still close to being a greatly perforated relief. In *Voltri XII* the accents assume greater spatial presence; Smith turned the chopped-cloud support out at ninety degrees to the right and added two smaller and spatially curved pieces to either side. Other changes from the early stage are also present, the cloud pennant above is reversed so it points downward, and the circular base—drawn in perspective on the floor—has become a rectangular stand.

Because the circular ring and its vertical support play such a dominant role in these two works, both as shapes as well as planes and axes, they have an air of symmetry, which is then challenged by the minor collaged accents. This is especially true for *Voltri XV,* where the vertical element—a flat plane—is oriented to the plane of the ring, and the cloud pennants, which are placed as horizontal elements crossing the perimeter of the circle, weave in and out of this fixed layer.

As with the works we have discussed, comparisons to classical compositions can be made for these two Voltri circles. The raised circle on a vertical support is precedented in Greek mirrors (fig. 18), where a disc surmounts a vertical figure that serves as a handle. Of interest, these works differ from earlier Egyptian examples since they are on a base, as are Smith's circles. Other shared characteristics are also apparent—for example, the subtle asymmetry of the supporting figure or the eccentricity of the structural braces on its shoulders, which suggest the curvilinear elements that flare out below the ring on *Voltri XII.* Indeed, in this piece the chopped cloud, although turned at ninety degrees, still has a figural characteristic which recalls the handles of the mirrors. In contrast to these precedents, however, *Voltri XII* is governed by more sharply asymmetrical detailings. And *Voltri XV,* which is less kinetic, is also less related because of the manner in which the detailing—the use of "collaged" elements—takes place not in the support, but in the upper areas.

But the simplicity of *Voltri XV* with its few applied elements gives rise to another association: that it is a symbolic presentation of the sun. Smith himself makes this association in his Voltri "Report," referring to circles as "all the suns." This reading is supported by the manner in which the "clouds"—to use Smith's term—cross the circle in a horizontal fashion highly suggestive of natural imagery. Furthermore, Smith's art contains numerous references to the moon—*Lunar Arcs on One Leg* of 1959-1960 (estate of the artist), for example, and his 1945 *Reliquary House,* which, while filled with lunar imagery, nevertheless draws some of its iconographic details (eyes and projecting rays especially) from Egyptian art and, in particular, the Tel el Amarna depiction of the sun.[42]

This proposed connection between *Voltri XV* and solar images may seem incidental or strained; however, upon his return from Voltri Smith made stencil drawings which employ circular rings on vertical supports, just as in these two Voltris (fig. 20).[43] But now Smith has added rays projecting outward from the perimeter in a manner even more given to sun imagery. At the risk of even greater speculation, this heraldic device—a sun

Figure 14. David Smith. *Running Daughter,* 1956-1960. Steel, 255.3 x 94.0 x 44.5 cm (100½ x 37 x 17½ in). Collection, Mr. and Mrs. Oscar Kolin, New York [photo: reproduced from *David Smith by David Smith* (New York, 1968)]. Not in exhibition

Figure 15. Workshop of the Edinburgh Painter (Attic). Black-figured Lekythos, c. 500 B.C. Clay; height: 32.1 cm (12⅝ in). Yale University Art Gallery, New Haven, Gift of Rebecca Barlington Stoddard (1913.11). Not in exhibition

Figure 16. David Smith. *Voltri XII,* 1962. Steel, 221.0 x 121.3 x 34.3 cm (87 x 47¾ x 13½ in). Collection, Mr. and Mrs. Gilbert H. Kinney, Washington [photo: Ugo Mulas, courtesy of Antonia Mulas, Milan. Reproduced from Carandente, *Voltron* (Philadelphia, 1964)]. Cat. no. 7

Figure 17. Interior of factory at Voltri showing *Voltri XII* and *XV* in early states on the floor of the shop. [Photo: Ugo Mulas, courtesy of Antonia Mulas, Milan. Reproduced from Carandente, *Voltron* (Philadelphia, 1964)]

image—placed upon a vertical support can be compared with the symbolic standards carried in the processions recorded in Roman art, with which Smith was probably familiar. Even if these correspondences are accidental, it is clear that both circles—and *Voltri XV* especially—are characterized by a more graphic presentation and a more heraldic composition.

The post-Voltri stencils which relate to the two circles raise again the question of the relationship between the Italian works and Smith's Cubi series. Smith had begun making stencil drawings in 1955. Although they are perhaps best termed "paper paintings," these stencils were made by masking out areas of the sheet with blocks and rectangles of paper, Smith then spraying paint onto the remaining surface. In the resultant stencil the "ghosts" of unpainted areas cohere to become studies—or ideas—for vertical compositions. While Smith also

made many tall vertical paintings in this manner, it is the drawings which seem to be directly related to the stainless steel sculpture of the Sentinel and Cubi series. In these works one has the feeling that the density of the resultant sculpture was not only identified with the white unpainted paper areas but that Smith was able to see how it would set against a softer tonality of natural atmosphere, suggested by the surrounding dappled, sprayed surface. That the "ring and cloud" imagery, directly related to the Voltris, should also be painted in this manner—Smith apparently using watermelon rinds and other natural materials as stencils to recreate his "chopped clouds"[44]—again curiously ties the Voltris to the Cubis. It suggests not only parallel compositional concerns but also his interest in learning how (or utilizing) the particular forms developed under Italian light would be seen under different atmospheric conditions. Ultimately the burnished steel of the Cubis reflects the tonalities of the New England landscape, and the flat solid shapes of the Voltris are rooted to the harsh and dry sunlight of Italy.

The circular composition, first fully realized in Voltri by Smith, was continued in three works made in the fall of 1962 at

Figure 18. Greek. Bronze mirror (handle in form of a woman on a recumbent lion), 6th century B.C. Bronze; height: 34.6 cm (13⅝ in). The Metropolitan Museum of Art, New York, Fletcher Fund, 1938 (38.11.3). Not in exhibition

Bolton Landing, *Circle I, II,* and *III* (fig. 21). But in these works, the circle rests directly upon the base and was painted by Smith in softer colors. They were aligned in his fields in Bolton Landing in such a way as to form concentric circles when viewed on end, which further indicates an interest in Kenneth Noland's target paintings.[45] The greater abstraction of the immediately subsequent *Circle I, II,* and *III* further points to the different—and more suggestive—character of the Voltri series.

STILL LIFE

While some Voltri works suggest figuration or heraldic signs, they do so in a metaphorical manner. The implied imagery in them rises out of the more abstract character which dominates, however referential the syntax of the work may be. But three Voltris, *Voltri XVI* (fig. 24), *Voltri XVIII* (fig. 30), and *Voltri XIX* (fig. 22), stand apart from the others for precisely opposite traits: rather than abstract or actual materials (as in *Voltri XX*) composed into abstract constructions which hint, in their un-

ion, at figuration, these works have joined actual materials (springs, tongs, blocks, anvils) to other materials (in two, work benches; the other a cart) in such a way that the still life which is formed fully retains its character as a still life. Although the found properties of these works—and especially *Voltri XVI* and *XIX*—reveal a vocabulary which is traditional, the idea of a still-life sculpture is almost uniquely a part of twentieth-century art.

It is often surprising to realize that there exists no tradition of the still life as theme in sculpture to parallel its counterpart in painting. With the probable exception of only Canova's *Fruit Basket,* c. 1770 (collection Ca' Rezzonico, Venice), the subject in its pure form is unknown until cubism.[46] There are, of course, partial exceptions to this, in the neoclassic tradition of allegorical still lifes which feature musical instruments or palettes and brushes (fig. 23), yet these elements are presented more as symbols of the arts and are enlivened by putti who introduce active life into the compositions.

Several reasons can be advanced for this absence in Western art. The role of the still-life painting was often tied to symbolic presentations, and part of its message—as well as the source of its enlivening appearance—was geared to the color of the objects. Working much to the contrary, the monochromatic tradition of sculpture could not encompass this possibility. Furthermore, the painted still life could—by virtue of illusion—present complicated assemblages of elements, varying from fruit and flowers to dead animals. Sculpture, tied irredeemably to a system of actual spatial construction, in three dimensions, could not contrive to duplicate the energy of composition found in painting. Finally, an aspect of *trompe l'oeil* is probably present here as well. The still life, either painted or sculpted, is *nature morte*—dead life. In a presentation without color and tied to a direct verisimilitude of composition, sculpture would clearly be more static than its visual counterpart—the real still life. Only some feature of technical skill might redeem the work, but it would offer little evidence of artistic presence.

It was then left to cubism to introduce the still life into sculpture, since its fracturing of the surface enlivens the subject externally. This occurred first in the blocklike divisions of surface in Picasso's small wooden *Apple* of 1909 (estate of the artist, Paris) and was quickly followed by Boccioni's *Development of a Bottle in Space,* 1912-1913 (The Lydia and Harry Lewis Winston Collection; Dr. and Mrs. Barnett Malbin, New York), where the spiraling composition of the futurist vocabulary serves further to energize the subject. But these works—joined by Picasso's *Absinthe Glass* pieces of 1914, that introduce color and texture into still-life sculpture—are still of single objects and not the proper still-life assembly. The realization of the latter was again Picasso's, in the original idea for his *Guitar* which included a table and other ancillary items in an ensemble. While Picasso did not execute this project as planned, other constructions do go further toward it, such as the *Glass, Pipe and Playing Card,* 1914 (estate of the artist, Paris), a bas-relief that includes an indication of a back plane wall and the front edge of a tabletop. In 1919-1920(?) Picasso made other still-life works which gather separate objects or present an entire tableau before a window. In Picasso's works,

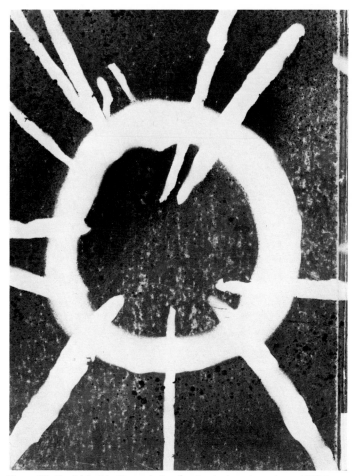

Figure 19. David Smith. *Voltri XV*, 1962. Steel, 228.1 x 196.1 x 57.4 cm (89⅞ x 77¼ x 22⅝ in). Hirshhorn Museum and Sculpture Garden, Smithsonian Institution, Washington. Cat. no. 8

Figure 20. David Smith. Cover design for *Art in America*, winter 1962 issue. [Photo: courtesy of *Art in America*]

however, planes slice through objects thus lessening their volume and depth. Derived from contemporary paintings, such handling of forms allows a pictorial illusionism to enter into the sculpted works, and this is probably why they retain a relieflike character.

As a fully three-dimensional sculpture of a still life we can cite Giacometti's *Table* of 1933 (Musée National d'Art Moderne, Centre Georges Pompidou, Paris). This work clearly contains the spirit of the surrealist *objet-trouvé-aidé*, as William Rubin has observed. The force of its imagery is generated by the poetic joining of a severed left hand, a bottle, an abstract sculpture, and the bust of a woman.[47] Giacometti's tabletop still life is followed by another by David Hare—*Magician's Game*, 1944 (collection of the artist, New York). Smith's *Voltri XVI* and *XIX* differ from these precedents in the distinct manner of his presentation of the elements. Each Voltri "is a workbench recreated in a formal manner as a work of art"[48] but without the formal fracturings of the cubist assembly or the futurist analysis and without the surrealist's poetic gathering of displaced objects. Although Smith introduced the still life into earlier works—his *11 Books, 3 Apples,* 1959 (estate of the artist), for example—these works are clearly indebted to either the cubist collage or to surrealist combina-

tions or distortions. *Voltri XIX* is distinguished precisely by its lack of any formal or thematic alterations; rather the objects—and their workbench support—were simply found at Voltri and left in their original state. Smith brought them together and left them as actual pieces.

The Voltri still lifes are decidedly autobiographical as records of Smith's encounter with the elements of an earlier age of making steel and with the atmosphere in the Voltri factories. He wrote of them:

Speciality tongs were hand-forged at stations. Since this method was abandoned, the work in process was left in varying stages of finish. . . . A thick steel layout table was never white [fig. 25]. I had it painted with lime and water. Ancient in use, practical because it was there, it gave me an order contact which from then on let me work freely without order. . . . From factory to factory I laid out workbenches—I finished two there, left more. . . .[49]

Many of Smith's earlier works have elements of autobiography in them, derived both from the cubist themes of recording daily studio life and the surrealist's more psychological renderings of existence. Smith's *Home of the Welder, Pillar of Sunday* (both, estate of the artist), and *Reliquary House,* all of 1945, have as themes the artist's house, his mother, and his childhood, respectively. The former and the latter clearly draw upon precedents set by Giacometti's work, such as the *Palace*

Figure 21. David Smith. *Circle I, Circle II,* and *Circle III,* 1962. Painted steel. *Circle I:* 200.6 x 273.6 x 43.7 cm (79 x 107¾ x 18 in); *Circle II:* 267.9 x 281.2 x 60.0 cm (105½ x 110¾ x 23⅝ in); *Circle III:* 242.5 x 182.8 x 45.7 cm (95½ x 72 x 18 in). National Gallery of Art, Washington, Ailsa Mellon Bruce Fund, 1977 [photo: Dan Budnik, courtesy of Woodfin Camp & Associates, New York]. Not in exhibition

at 3 A.M. (The Museum of Modern Art, New York). In the 1950s, while Smith's art grew more abstract still, such works as *The Letter* (Munson-William-Proctor Institute, Utica, New York) or *The Bouquet* (private collection, New York) or *Running Daughter* relate to events in his life; later works such as *Hirebecca* and *Hicandida,* using the names of his daughters Rebecca and Candida, indicate his fondness for his children.

In *Voltri XIX* Smith gathers together various tongs and forging tools, which rest upon a table, their handles bent over the edges, the only formal alteration. The only suggested imagery in the work is the juxtaposition of the anvil on the left with the six-pointed burst attached to the back of the bench, suggesting a star or solar symbol, and (although quite speculative) the combination of firing and shaping a sculptor's works. To the right a combination of a circular disk and an *I* beam recalls—indirectly—other elements of other Voltri pieces. Thus with a group of found materials, the artist may have represented the making of art—heating, pounding, etc.—and the results, sculpture. Autobiographical in nature the sculpture also draws a connection between Smith as artist and Smith as workman, a connection he often verbalized in his life. But in the straightness of its telling *Voltri XIX* is curiously removed from the modern tradition of still-life sculpture; it is placed more correctly among the neoclassical, allegorical works which also use artist's materials as attributes of traditions.

Voltri XVI (fig. 24), the other still-life workbench, is far more direct in its composition. Here Smith has joined steel springs and open cubes, placed in an almost casual manner. It is the latter quality which argues against reading *Voltri XVI* in any reference to the works of the Cubi series, which were tightly and complexly organized. The scattering of the block forms, the simple resting of the tongs along the top of one edge

and the direction of the entire piece again place it in a more autobiographic context.

ANVIL

In his notes on Voltri Smith indicates another work in the series which we can properly consider as a still life, *Voltri IV* (fig. 26). The work, with its horizontal plane and cloud ends, is the only one to correspond to Smith's description, "there are ends on a table." *Voltri IV* was finished early in the series, and its combination of irregular found elements with regular material—here the horizontal *I* beam—established ideas and formal touches which were also used in subsequent works. Like the later *Voltri XII* circle, *Voltri IV* was begun on the floor as a collage of separate pieces, including, in this case, the cloud ends and the horizontal beam upon which they rest. The support was not joined to them at this stage. In the final work the horizontal bar is raised up on two clouds—which rest on a rectangular platform and stick out at an angle away from the perpendicular, predicting again the stem and the "tails" in *Voltri XII.* The joining together of clouds along a horizontal axis is repeated in two of the subsequent chariots—*Voltri VI* (fig. 27) and *Voltri XIII* (University of California, Berkeley)—and *Voltri VII* (fig. 30) borrows the general compositional idea of flat elements juxtaposed along an established horizontal plane.

Voltri IV, like the later *Voltri XV* circle, skirts the edge of the pictorial; but by placing the supporting clouds at an angle and by turning the end cloud of the upper form ninety degrees to the others, Smith was able to articulate the composition in greater spatial depth. Nevertheless, a sense of the two-dimensional orchestrates the work, as its parts consistently refer back to the imaginary plane established by the *I* beam.

Although Smith's reference to *Voltri IV* as a "table" does

Figure 22. David Smith. *Voltri XIX*, 1962. Steel, 139.7 x 114.3 x 127.0 cm (55 x 45 x 50 in). Collection, Mr. and Mrs. Stephen D. Paine, Boston [photo: Ugo Mulas, courtesy of Antonia Mulas, Milan. Reproduced from Carandente, *Voltron* (Philadelphia, 1964)]. Cat. no. 10

Figure 23. Jean-Pierre-Antoine Tassaert. *Painting and Sculpture*, 1775-1778. Marble, 98.3 x 87.2 x 63.8 cm (38⅝ x 34¼ x 25⅛ in). National Gallery of Art, Washington, Samuel H. Kress Collection 1952. Not in exhibition

suggest a relationship to the still-life benches, the abstract character of both the elements and the final composition of *Voltri IV* separates it dramatically from the later still lifes. While precedents in Smith's own work—*11 Books, 3 Apples*, for example—would admit an interpretation of the clouds as rounded fruit, both the actual scale of the piece as well as the character of the Voltri series as a whole militates against this interpretation. More in keeping with the broader autobiographical references of the later works and with Smith's experiences in the Voltri factories would be to interpret *Voltri IV* as an anvil, metaphorically stated in the *I* beam, with the product of its work suggested by the cloud shapes resting on it. Mulas' photograph of Smith welding one of the clouds into place on the spine suggests this reading (fig. 1).

CHARIOTS

As we have seen, Smith's dream of making a large sculpture on a railway flatcar was ruled out because of external conditions. This decision was made early, and Smith transferred the idea of a wheeled work to *Voltri VI* (fig. 27) and *VII* (fig. 30). Smith recounts in his Voltri letter: "Since I had to abandon it [the flatcar]—I used wheels in many of the sculptures for mobility and aesthetic reasons."[50] The resulting two works, joined by the later *Voltri XIII* comprise a subset of Voltri wagons which Smith called "chariots." They are perhaps the most remarkable of all of the Italian works.

The use of wheels in sculpture is very rare; the closest prece-

dent to Smith's chariots is Giacometti's *Chariot* of 1950, which sets an attenuated standing female figure on the axis between two antique wheels. While this work might have indirectly influenced Smith, Giacometti's composition is more hieratic, even iconic, and the juxtaposition of differing scales and images clearly continues the surrealist *tableau* tradition. Smith's chariots do curiously relate to the *tableau*, probably drawn from the "table" of *Voltri VI*. But their more abstract images shift the character of the works away from description. Actually wheels had entered Smith's vocabulary as early as 1957 in *Sentinel III* (collection of Mr. and Mrs. Stephen Paine, Boston), and the vertical dominance of this piece is clearly different. Furthermore, unlike the cast and fixed wheels in Giacometti's *Chariot*, those in Smith's works are actual and functional, Smith integrating them into the allover composition of the sculpture. As in his Voltri "Report," he indicated that their use in the chariots was for "the practical fact that my sculpture is getting too big to move without built-in rolling."[51]

The wheels and the spine of the chariots were integral units found in the Voltri factories. Smith reported:

Forgings too big for hand—worked by drop hammers—are transported from ovens to hammer by a tong which is a chariot on two wheels pushed by men. Three remained which I remade for carrying and being a part of in *Voltri VI, Voltri VII, Voltri [XIII]*.[52]

Of the chariots, the first two, *Voltri VI* and *VII*, are the most radical in terms of image. *Voltri VI* is the more dramatic piece,

232

Figure 24. David Smith. *Voltri XVI,* 1962. Steel, 111.7 x 101.6 x 96.5 cm (44 x 40 x 38 in). Estate of David Smith [photo: Robert D. Edwards, courtesy of M. Knoedler & Co., New York]. Cat. no. 9

with its low spine and bold vertical elements above. Smith described it as "a tong with wheels and two end clouds. One cloud rests in the spoon—each cloud end goes up from the tongue unsupported."[53] As with the *I* beam of *Voltri IV,* the spoon thus forms a long horizontal element that here works in opposition to the vertical direction of the two large upper elements.

Voltri VI is quite distinguished from the other works in its scale. Smith used only two cloud elements, but they were of much larger scale and of more character, as large curving "bites" reach into the forms, giving them a dramatic shape unlike the soft rounded profile of the other cloud outcroppings. The artist has intensified the drama in the work by facing the curved edges outward so the "bites" face one another. This tension is increased by the separation of the two sheets, leaving a gap along each chopped line which creates a bold vertical element of negative space. This latter element both reinforces and contests the perpendicular quality of its counterpart, the horizontal spine.

The tension created by the vertical gap with its slightly ragged edges has invited comparison between *Voltri VI* and the vertical stripes which Barnett Newman used in his heroic paintings (see "Barnett Newman: The Stations of the Cross—Lema Sabachthani" in this catalogue).[54] But a more likely comparison for this chariot and other Voltris which use chopped cloud forms on a horizontal plane is to the black ovals and panels of Robert Motherwell's Elegies to the Spanish Republic (see

Figure 25. Smith at workbench in factory at Voltri, Italy, 1962. [Photo: Ugo Mulas, courtesy of Antonia Mulas. Reproduced from Carandente, *Voltron* (Philadelphia, 1964)]

"Robert Motherwell: The Elegies to the Spanish Republic"). Both sets of works not only employ contrasts between rounded shapes and straight edges along a horizontal plane but also are directed to the Mediterranean atmosphere, where the harsh sunlight not only heightens the contrast between light and dark, but casts forms into a vocabulary of silhouettes.[55]

That Smith would look at Motherwell's Elegies as forces he could enroll in sculpture is not surprising. We have seen how Smith used the examples of Noland's target works for his concentric colored circles. Motherwell and Smith were close friends during this period, and Smith had actually encouraged Motherwell to make a sculptured Elegy, which the latter declined because he could "never imagine what an Elegy would look like from the side."[56] Smith himself may have approached this idea, however, in his *Gondola* of 1961 (estate of the artist), which uses a series of overlapping black shapes (and especially a rectangle and a squared-off oval) joined in a lateral arrangement. They form a horizontal pattern which is quite reminiscent of the general composition of Motherwell's works. Furthermore, Smith made the shapes in *Gondola* by painting these black silhouettes onto a white surface and then cutting them

Figure 26. David Smith. *Voltri IV*, 1962. Steel, 174.0 x 154.0 x 50.0 cm (68½ x 60⅝ x 19¾ in). Rijksmuseum Kröller-Müller, Otterlo, The Netherlands. Cat. no. 2

out as one continuous shape.[57] In regard to the relationship of the forms of the later *Voltri VI* to those of the Elegies, it is pertinent to note that *Gondola*'s lateral band of overlapping silhouetted shapes rests upon a horizontal base which in turn is raised above wheels. Of all of Smith's works, it is the only direct precedent for *Voltri VI* and thus a clue to the latter's affinities to the Elegies.

Smith, in discussing his Voltri works emphasized their abstract nature, and especially so for the wheeled pieces: "horse chariots are not in my picture,"[58] he wrote. Yet faced with the forms of the work itself, Smith described them as chariots, and given the pattern of general references to ancient art found throughout the Voltri series, it is important to look at *Voltri VI* with these points in mind.

Carandente noted that Voltri chariots evoke "Etruscan memories. They have the majestic carriage that was a property of classical sculpture."[59] Given his interest in—or more importantly, his knowledge of—ancient art, there is one major work of Etruscan art Smith surely knew—the large ceremonial chariot of the late sixth century B.C., in the collection of the Metropolitan Museum of Art in New York (fig. 28). Its compartment for the rider—formed to curvilinear elements which meet along a vertical joining—might be echoed in Smith's works, just as its spoke wheels and long tongue are recalled in *Voltri VII*. Other possible sources for this work are the hieratic and stylized figural scenes in sixth-century B.C. vase paintings, such as the figures seated in a chariot—or wagon—on the Lekythos by the Amasis Painter, c. 560 B.C. (fig. 29), where the figures facing in opposite directions form an image distantly echoed in the back-to-back chopped clouds in the composition of *Voltri VI*. And there are other ancient and classical repre-

sentations of chariots which might also be mentioned. The important point here is that Smith's works—and in particular *Voltri VI*—call upon the ideas of these earlier works, and even if formed abstractly, they still suggest comparison with these precedents.

But it is also important to note how Smith makes the chariots horseless. In all of the chariots Smith moves the vertical elements to the center of the longitudinal spine, thus balancing the composition and removing exact reference to the chariot idea. While the Etruscan chariot at the Metropolitan—with its compartment placed directly over the wheels—appears incomplete without the horses tied into their places, the Voltri chariots never indicate such an absence.

The final image of *Voltri VI* is that of a whole object, its composition balanced and focused along the dramatic vertical gap between the cloud ends. But, nevertheless, Smith does suggest a potential for movement in the work in the inscription he wrote on the side of the vertical cloud, using a blowtorch: "Andiamo a Spoleto" ("Let's go to Spoleto"). Smith's plate ends, as well as other materials, had been sent to him in Voltri from the steelyards in Cornegliano after he had written his name and "Voltri" on them; "Andiamo A Spoleto" being written out on the work is an indication of the process of completing the creation—a sort of braggadocio: "I'm ready for Spoleto."

PROCESSIONAL

Certainly one of Smith's greatest works is *Voltri VII* (fig. 30), the second chariot piece which was installed as the focal point of the Spoleto arena exhibition. Different from the solid sheets

Figure 27. David Smith. *Voltri VI*, 1962. Steel, 261.6 x 261.0 x 64.8 cm (103 x 102¾ x 25½ in). Collection, Nelson A. Rockefeller [photo: Ugo Mulas, courtesy of Antonia Mulas, Milan. Reproduced from Carandente, *Voltron* (Philadelphia, 1964)]. Cat. no. 3

Figure 28. Etruscan chariot *(Biga)*, c. 550-540 B.C. Wood with bronze sheathing; height: 130.9 cm (51½ in). The Metropolitan Museum of Art, New York, Rogers Fund 1903. Not in exhibition

and smaller wheels and relatively lower compositional levels of *Voltri VI* and *XIII, Voltri VII* is made of thin linear elements placed on a structure with spoked wheels, aligned on an arched axis, with a long extended horizontal spine. "*Voltri VII*," Smith wrote, "is a chariot ram with five bar forgings. They are not personages—they are forgings."[60] Like many of the other elements used at Voltri, these five elements were found by Smith in one of the factories. But their general *S*-shaped form—a vertical greatly pushed away from center line first to one side, then the other, then back again—corresponds to

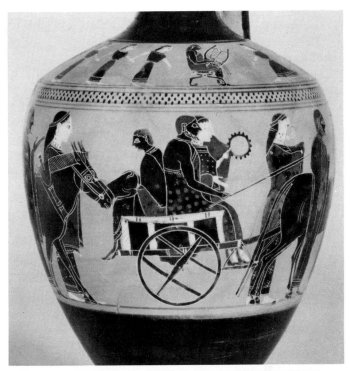

Figure 29. Amasis Painter (Greek). Black-figured Lekythos, c. 560 B.C. Clay; height: 17. 5 cm (6⅞ in). The Metropolitan Museum of Art, New York, Purchase, 1956, Walter C. Baker Gift (56.11.1). Not in exhibition

earlier works Smith made in 1955—each using a single bar—also called the forgings.

Smith made these earlier works based upon a series of ink drawings.

It is a drawing line really. I would never have done that if I hadn't been interested in drawing lines. . . . I don't think I could ever make a sculpture like that without making three hundred or four hundred drawings a year—I think it has to develop that way, if you are interested in making a vertical, simple vertical with the development of a drawing concept.[61]

As Krauss observes, "[The Forgings] are probably the most abbreviated sculpture Smith ever made."[62] And they are probably his most abstract as well. By considering, then, the nature of such precedents for the Voltri forgings, as well as Smith's denial of the Forgings as figuration, and by studying the manner in which they are placed on the chariot's spine—to form an abstract, rhythmic arrangement of A-B-A-B-A—it is correct to read the forgings as sheer design.

Significantly, if we read the bar forgings as abstract patterns—not figuration—we still encounter an association with classical art. The elongated and simplified *S*-shaped forms of the forging, especially when combined in a pattern with a reverse *S*-shape, recalls an almost identical pattern found in the strigilation on the sides of Roman sarcophagi (fig. 31). This Roman *S*-shaped pattern was derived from an instrument used by Greeks and Romans for scraping one's skin at the bath or in the gymnasium. Organized in a horizontal band of facing *S* shapes and reverse *S* shapes, strigilation was employed as decorative fluting in architecture as well as in the side registers of stone coffins. We must presume that Smith knew the use of the form on sarcophagi.[63] Given both the particularity of its

Figure 30. David Smith. *Voltri VII*, 1962. Steel, 215.8 x 311.6 x 110.5 cm (85 x 122¾ x 43½ in). National Gallery of Art, Washington, Ailsa Mellon Bruce Fund, 1977 [photo: Ugo Mulas, courtesy of Antonia Mulas, Milan]. Cat. no. 4, pl. 30

shape and Smith's use of *S* shapes in a similar reversing pattern, this suggests that, at the least, *Voltri VII* makes direct reference to a Roman motif, and at most, the sculpture metaphorically presents an abstracted sarcophagus being born on a cart. This latter reading is supported by the manner in which the elements are placed so as to form—if bracketed in—a long coffinlike rectangle along the horizontal tongue of the sculpture. In this interpretation, *Voltri VII* can then be linked with *Voltri III* and especially *Voltri IX*, in the way its form is associated with procession.

Again Smith's earlier works offer precedents for the *Voltri VII* theme in the *(Canopic) Head* based on the Egyptian burial jars at Boston or the earlier *Reliquary House*. Certain works such as *Sacrifice*, 1952 (estate of the artist), use a horizontal support as an altar, with vertical elements indicating the participants, and in *Table Torso*, 1942 (Rose Art Museum, Brandeis University, Waltham, Massachusetts), Smith identifies directly the imagery of "a body atop a table or platform."[64] Thus the theme of a bier as formed by the horizontal line of the wagon with the vertical elements above referring to a sarcophagus

would not be an isolated subject in Smith's art. The earlier works, however, do not compare to *Voltri VII* in displaying the richness of Smith's inventive powers. While other Voltris combine multiple points of view or dual images, *Voltri VII* indicates a remarkable ability to combine in one work a bold abstract graphic statement with an allusion to a Roman funeral. By stressing only the strigilation pattern on one hand—and leaving the cart in its original state on the other—Smith is able to shift our readings between the two images.

RAILROAD CAR

"Why haven't you made a lot of steel boxes all shapes & piled one upon each other—put together on wheels," Smith wrote above a (related) drawing in a sketchbook from 1959.[65] As Edward Fry was the first to point out, *Voltri XVIII* (fig. 32), the small cart made near the end of the series, relates to this earlier idea.[66] It is composed of anvils and blocks and wrenches set upon a wide platform, which, in turn, rests on four tiny wheels; it thus can be joined to the chariots subset. In the manner in

236

Figure 31. Sarcophagus, Early Christian period. Ospedale di S. Giovanni in Laterano, Rome. [Photo: Anderson, courtesy of Alinari, Florence]

which it combines actual elements without altering them through compositional juxtapositions, this Voltri cart can also be seen as part of the two still lifes, where "tools" are grouped on workbenches. Indeed these three give evidence of a kind of nostalgia, as if S Tith—near the end of this extraordinary month—wanted to record directly, rather than metaphorically, his experiences in the Voltri factories.

But another identity can be proposed for *Voltri XVIII*, one which is still in keeping with Smith's desire to record autobiographical themes; namely that it represents in miniature an image of what Smith's railway flatcar might have been. In discussing his dream Smith's statement reads in full:

A dream is a dream never lost. I've had it inside a 4-8-4 on the top of a Diesel engine, they have been in a size dream. I found an old flat-car, asked for, and was given it. Had I used the flatcar for the base and made a sculpture on the top, the dream would have been closer.

I could have loaded a flatcar with vertical sheets, inclined planes, uprights with holes, horizontals supported—

I could have made a car with the nude bodies of machines, undressed of their details and teeth—

I could have made a flatcar with a hundred anvils of varying sizes and character which I found at forge stations.

I could have made a flatcar with painted skeletal wooden patterns. In a year I could have made a train.[67]

Certainly, the base of the sculpture, a flat, thick platform, and the position and relative scale of the wheels to it correspond to the general configuration of a railway flatcar. Upon the horizontal plane the wrenches and the raised box in the center can be related to the "uprights with holes, horizontals supported," Smith had planned, while "a hundred anvils of varying sizes and characters" can be seen represented in two small examples.

Smith's description of his railroad car dream—and its reflection in *Voltri XVIII*—invites a review of the other Voltri works as well, as certain works can be seen in relationship to the elements Smith would "have loaded" onto the flatcar of this

grand design. *Voltri VIII*, for instance, suggests "vertical sheets," and the Voltri circles can be read as "uprights with holes," with *Voltri IV* as "horizontals supported." This latter work also suggests, as we have seen, the anvil element.

When he had to abandon his dream of a flatcar Smith certainly did not then make its imagined components into the separate Voltri sculpture. Not all of his dream images are included among the Voltri works—no inclined planes, or nude bodies or machines or painted skeletal wooden patterns—and certain Voltri sets are not mentioned by Smith as part of his train—the figures or the workbenches, for example. The Voltri chariots are excluded from mention as components, though, in fact, they can be seen in certain ways as replacements for his larger design.

If there is a relationship to Smith's dream flatcar components in certain Voltri works—not, however, in their individual compositional elements which were drawn from the earlier project—they also relate as an ensemble. Smith wrote of his dream: "The closest to realization came when Mulas chose to put finished work on the flat [car] for his photos."[68] Mulas included Smith with his sculpture in one photograph (see page 14): the expression on his face, the turning up of his head, and his pose display his own awareness of the nearness of realizing his dream, displayed behind him in the Voltri pieces placed across a flatcar, not unlike the arrangement of anvils, blocks, and wrenches in *Voltri XVIII*.

We can find many precursors for Smith's dream, and he may have been aware of some of them. For example, works such as the Greek terra-cotta *Funeral Wagon* of 600 B.C. (fig. 33) with its casket covered with cloth, surrounded by mourning women, all on a flat platform attached to wheels. This work, which Smith could have known in Athens—or from reproductions—offers a clear precedent not only for large compositions on a flatcar but for the figural *Voltri IX* and the funeral wagon of *Voltri VII*.

Another source is one which seems far more speculative,

Figure 32. David Smith. *Voltri XVIII*, 1962. Steel, 107.7 x 101.6 x 83.2 cm (42⅜ x 40 x 32¾ in). Estate of David Smith [photo: Ugo Mulas, courtesy of Antonia Mulas, Milan]. Cat. no. 11

Figure 33. Funeral wagon, c. 600 B.C. Terra-cotta group found at Vari. National Archaeological Museum, Athens [photo: reproduced from Gisela M. A. Richter, *A Handbook of Greek Art* (New York, 1959)]. Not in exhibition

especially as it is removed from the context of classical art. It is mentioned by Smith in his "Report on Voltri" in discussing the circles and the chariots: "Wheels are circles with mobility, from the first wheel of man to wheels on Indian stone temples."[69] Smith was more expansive about this reference in a later discussion of the chariots with Thomas Hess:

Of course I've used wheels a lot. As far as I know, I got the wheel idea from Hindu temples.... They cut them out of stone on the temples to represent the processions where they carry copies of temples down the streets in wagons. Carved stone wheels. It's a fascinating idea.[70]

The work to which Smith refers is the Orissan *Sūrya Deul*—or temple of the sun—at Konārak in the northeast section of Puri (fig. 34). Although conceived as a Hindu temple, this extraordinary work includes large stone-cut wheels along its base walls, thus likening the temple itself to the *Vimāna*, or chariot, of the sun god as it moves through the sky.[71] This reference to the sun god is intriguing, when we recall the possible solar symbol of *Voltri XV*. Clearly, however, the images of the Hindu temple do not correspond in any specific way to what we know of Smith's intentions in his flatcar. Rather it was the image or the idea of the massive *Vimāna* which may have been inspiring to Smith—in its scale and its complexity.

Thus the realization of the dream at full scale was ruled out, and only the small *Voltri XVIII* cart and the Mulas photograph of Smith survive as evidence of its presence: "So many, dreams have been lost to lack of material, workspace, storage, etc., that one more becomes another wish," wrote Smith.

The flatcar I had is now melted in the open hearth and rolled into sheet. The beauty of the ballet of a white-to-red-to-black sheet in a

238

Figure 34. Sun Temple of Kōnarak, Orissa, India (south side), 13th century A.D. [Photo: Eliot Elisofon, *Life Magazine,* copyright © 1949 Time Inc.]

fast-rolling mill at different speeds running back and forth billowing steam with the quenches is a memory for me of automation fed by my flatcar.[72]

Smith's dream was certainly not laid aside, but continued to be his central ambition. Recalling his past, Smith told Hess:

When I was a kid, I had a pretty profound regard for railroads. I used to sit down on the edge of town and watch trains go through. I used to hop trains, ride on the tops of boxcars. We used to play on trains and around factories. I played there just like I played in nature, on hills and creeks. I remember when I first sat in my father's lap and steered a car. In fact, I've always had a high regard for machinery. It's never been an alien element; it's been in my nature. . . .

And don't forget I've worked in locomotive plants. I've sat on those goddamned engines, welding them up, hoping I could someday make sculptures as big. And I will someday. I think.[73]

Hess asked:

There was a certain social setup when you were a kid in Indiana, and you had certain ideas about machinery and materials. And on your farm you've set up those huge "useless" sculptures which, to me, have a certain symbolic effect—like a book in a secret language.

Smith replied:

The secret language, Tom, is very simple: I'm building the biggest, the best goddamned sculptures I can make within my present limits, conceptually and financially. If I could have built sculpture within my conception several years ago, they would have been twenty-five to thirty feet high. . . .[74]

James Rosati has recently recounted comments Smith made shortly before his death about building a flatcar with sculpture on it. Smith called it a "traveling exhibition," suggesting it would go from town to town like a circus.[75] This image of the railroad car and the circus world would again come from Smith's childhood in the Midwest.

Smith transferred his Italian flatcar dream back to a revised Agricola theme in 1964, when he renewed the idea of an enormous sculpture which would be movable, like a train. Motherwell wrote of Smith's plans in February 1965:

Lately he has been buying up ancient tractors with gigantic steel wheels, and even an enormous old road grader. He wants to incorporate them into sculpture, sculpture so tremendous that this industrial machinery will have no larger rôle in the whole sculptures than the clockworks have in a grandfather clock, or the elevator in an elevator shaft.[76]

Smith died in May of that year before this American version of his Voltri flatcar could be begun.

If Smith's dream of a flatcar was abandoned in Italy, the level of inspiration and the recognition of the complexity remained with him throughout the series of individual pieces. That Smith intended them to be kept together as a group—and thus form a series—is clear in his correspondence about them after his return from Italy (now on file in the Archives of American Art). Although they were not formed as a single unit, it can be proposed that the Voltri works as a group represent Smith's closest approach to the enormous scale and complexity of abstract-expressionist painting, which Smith had used for formal ideas in individual Voltri pieces. Abstract-expressionist painting is marked by the manner in which it combines differing stylistic traditions, and Smith's works relate here as well, for the Voltris also draw upon the traditions of ancient Sumeria and Egypt and of Indian art and on cubism and surrealism, where he had more direct roots. Most of all, the central subject of the Voltri works is the merging of Smith's own modern vocabulary and the forms and themes drawn from the classical tradition of Greeks and Romans and other sources in ancient art.

We must be careful not to suggest that Smith based his sculpture on these ancient works but then camouflaged his sources, altering their forms or hiding the imagery. If Smith intended to draw from the antique—as is proposed here—it was in the nature of its providing, on one hand, metaphors for concerns already evident in his works; thus, he chose these subjects for formal and thematic precedents. On the other hand, the antique provided a way to bind his art not only to the modern tradition, but to the entire range of Western and Oriental sculpture. The grandness of this vision—and Smith's approach to his sources—again links Smith's art to that of the abstract-expressionist painters. It is also clear that his vocabulary was so sure that it was able to accommodate these references as metaphors, not as determinants. Given Smith's ambitions, and their realization in the classical works of Voltri, their installation in the Roman amphitheater produced the final unity to the series and the subject. Of Smith's dreams—which were directed to the realizing of a grand subject—Voltri and Spoleto were the closest he actually ever came (fig. 33).

Figure 35. Installation view of David Smith Voltri sculpture in amphitheater at Spoleto, June 1962. [Photo: Ugo Mulas, courtesy of Antonia Mulas, Milan. Reproduced from Carandente, *Voltron* (Philadelphia, 1964)]

NOTES

For their very generous assistance and insight into the Voltri works I would like to thank the estate of David Smith, Garnett McCoy of the Archives of American Art, and Anthony Caro, James Rosati, and Anne Truitt.

1. David Smith, "Letter to David Sylvester," Dec. 11, 1962; quoted in Giovanni Carandente, *Voltron* (Philadelphia: Institute of Contemporary Art, University of Pennsylvania, 1964), 13.

2. Carandente, *Voltron*, 5.

3. Edward F. Fry, *David Smith*, exh. cat. (New York: Solomon R. Guggenheim Museum, 1969): 142.

4. Smith; quoted in Carandente, *Voltron*, 13.

5. Rosalind E. Krauss, *Terminal Iron Works: The Sculpture of David Smith* (Cambridge, Mass.: MIT Press, 1971), 51.

6. Smith; quoted in Carandente, *Voltron*, 13-14.

7. Smith; quoted in Carandente, *Voltron*, 13.

8. Anne Truitt, in conversation with the author, 1978 (on file in the Department of Twentieth-Century Art, National Gallery of Art, Washington). Mrs. Truitt recalls seeing Smith immediately after his return from Italy and noting the extraordinary sense of accomplishment he had of the work, which he related directly to the circumstances in Italy. See also Krauss' discussion, in *Terminal Iron Works*, 51-52.

9. Smith in "Report on Voltri" in *David Smith*, ed. Garnett McCoy (New York: Praeger Publishers, 1973), 161.

10. See Martha Leeb Hadzi, "Sculpture at Spoleto," *Art in America*, 50 (Winter 1962): 116-118.

11. Savarese's cable with Smith's handwritten draft of a reply is illustrated in *David Smith by David Smith*, ed. Cleve Gray (New York: Holt, Rinehart and Winston, 1968), 42.

12. Smith; quoted in Carandente, *Voltron*, 12-13.

13. Smith; quoted in Carandente, *Voltron*, 11.

14. Krauss, *Terminal Iron Works*, 52.

15. Other artists shown at Spoleto did not make pieces in Italy but rather selected from works in their studios, matching them to photographs of prospective sites.

16. Smith; quoted in Carandente, *Voltron*, 14.

17. Smith; quoted in McCoy, *David Smith*, 157 and 159.

18. Smith; quoted in McCoy, *David Smith*, 160.

19. Smith; quoted in McCoy, *David Smith*, 161.

20. Smith; quoted in Carandente, *Voltron*, 11.

21. Carandente, *Voltron*, 5.

22. Smith; quoted in Carandente, *Voltron*, 11.

23. Smith; quoted in McCoy, *David Smith*, 159 and 162.

24. Anthony Caro, in conversation with the author, 1978 (on file in the Department of Twentieth-Century Art, National Gallery of Art, Washington). Caro's Veduggio series of 1972 was made in Italy from similar components.

25. Smith; quoted in McCoy, *David Smith*, 162.

26. Indeed, the Cubis, which are often viewed as Smith's most abstract works and, by some, as the grand point of his career, may have been inspired by—or more precisely, Smith may have seen the possibilities of realizing these works in—the Voltri sculpture. These were, to a degree, an interpretation and a "replacement" for the Cubis Smith had planned to make in Italy. It should be noted in this regard that Smith's idea of making sculpture out of "clouds" did not originate with the Voltris; rather his notation on the first Cubi work—*Cube III* (now entitled *Cubi III*), finished in Nov. 1959, records: "polished—like I feel if I make square *clouds*" [my emphasis]. In this sense, the two series share a major conception of their elements. David Smith on a sketch of the first *Cubi*; quoted in Rosalind Krauss, *The Sculpture of David Smith: A Catalogue Raisonné* (New York: Garland Publishing, Inc., 1977), 116.

27. Smith; quoted in McCoy, *David Smith*, 157.

28. Smith; quoted in Krauss, *The Sculpture of David Smith*, 54-55.

29. The connection between these two works was kindly pointed out to this author by Phyllis Tuchman. As Smith was frequently in Washington during these years—he lectured at American University in 1951, the year *Agricola I* began—it is highly probable he knew the National Gallery's sculpture, exhibited prominently in the central rotunda of the gallery.

30. Carandente, *Voltron*, 10.

31. Smith; quoted in McCoy, *David Smith*, 162.

32. Krauss, *The Sculpture of David Smith*, 51.

33. Smith, letter to Lucille and Edgar Levy, from Athens, c. Jan. 1936; in McCoy, *David Smith*, 190. Thus the problems of colored or painted sculpture, which Smith interestingly revives in *Circle I, II,* and *III* after Voltri, dates from this early study of Greek art.

34. Smith; quoted in McCoy, *David Smith*, 162.

35. Carandente, *Voltron*, 10.

36. Smith; quoted in Gray, *David Smith by David Smith*, 87.

37. Krauss, *Terminal Iron Works*, 152.

38. Fry, *David Smith*, 31.

39. Illustrated in Gray, *David Smith by David Smith*, 94.

40. Smith; quoted in McCoy, *David Smith*, 162.

41. Illustrated in *The Terminal Iron Works: Photographs of David Smith*, exh. cat. (New York: American Federation of Arts, 1974), n.p.

42. See Krauss, *The Sculpture of David Smith*, 35.

43. Illustrated on the front and back covers of *Art in America*, 50 (Winter 1962), for Hilton Kramer, "David Smith: Stencils for Sculpture,"32-43.

44. Kramer, "David Smith," 41-42.

45. Noland has confirmed Smith's interest in the targets and in color combinations during the fall of 1962. The subtle color of Smith's circles and the way the paint is applied to allow some of the white primer coat to show through suggests another connection with the stain-painted surfaces of Noland's targets. *Circle II* and *III*, with their composition of the circular form and straight bars, recall the composition of Noland's target paintings, whereas the union of the circle and arc of *Circle I* does not. Here the forms are related more to the enclosed ovals of Jules Olitski's works from 1962. These Olitskis were shown at Bennington College in the fall of 1962, and Noland recalls going with Smith to see the exhibition and Smith's interest in Olitski's work. Noland, in conversation with the author, Sept. 1975 and May 1976 (on file in the Department of Twentieth-Century Art, National Gallery of Art, Washington).

46. C. Douglas Lewis, Jr., curator of sculpture at the National Gallery of Art, kindly pointed out the Canova exception.

47. William Rubin, *Anthony Caro* (New York: Museum of Modern Art, 1975), 141.

48. Rubin, *Anthony Caro*, 140.

49. Smith; quoted in McCoy, *David Smith*, 158-159.

50. Smith; quoted in Carandente, *Voltron*, 12.

51. Smith; quoted in McCoy, *David Smith*, 162.

52. Smith; quoted in McCoy, *David Smith*, 162.

53. Smith; quoted in McCoy, *David Smith*, 162.

54. Miranda McClintic suggested this relationship in conversation with the author, Sept. 1977 (on file in the Department of Twentieth-Century Art, National Gallery of Art, Washington).

55. Anthony Caro commented on this effect of the light in Voltri, in conversation with the author, Feb. 1978 (on file in the Department of Twentieth-Century Art, National Gallery of Art, Washington).

56. Robert Motherwell in conversation with the author, Apr. 1976 (on file in the Department of Twentieth-Century Art, National Gallery of Art, Washington).

57. A photograph of Smith making *Gondola* is illustrated in Krauss, *Terminal Iron Works*, fig. 3A. *Gondola* also turns an open rectangle at ninety degrees to the black shapes, suggesting a "notation" for pictorial space.

58. Smith; quoted in McCoy, *David Smith*, 162.

59. Carandente, *Voltron*, 7.

60. Smith; quoted in McCoy, *David Smith*, 162.

61. David Smith, in "Some Late Words from David Smith," ed. Gene Baro, *Art International*, 9 (Oct. 1965): 50.

62. Krauss, *The Sculpture of David Smith*, 66.

63. Robert Motherwell and Helen Frankenthaler had a Roman sarcophagus—but with a different pattern—in their garden in New York, outside the room where Smith often stayed when he was in the city.

64. Krauss, *The Sculpture of David Smith*, 26-27.

65. David Smith, in his sketchbook of 1959, illustrated in Krauss, *The Sculpture of David Smith*, fig. 838 (from Smith Archive IV 247).

66. Fry, *David Smith*, 31.

67. Smith; quoted in McCoy, *David Smith*, 161.

68. Smith; quoted in McCoy, *David Smith*, 161.

69. Smith; quoted in McCoy, *David Smith*, 162.

70. Smith, in an interview with Thomas Hess, in McCoy, *David Smith*, 185.

71. See Benjamin Rowland's discussion in *The Art and Architecture of India* (Baltimore: Penguin Books, 1953), 171.

72. Smith; quoted in McCoy, *David Smith*, 161.

73. Smith; quoted in McCoy, *David Smith*, 176.

74. Smith; quoted in McCoy, *David Smith*, 179.

75. In conversation with the author, Mar. 1978 (on file in the Department of Twentieth-Century Art, National Gallery of Art, Washington).

76. Robert Motherwell, "A Major American Sculptor: David Smith," *Vogue*, Feb. 1, 1965, 140.

MARK ROTHKO:

The Brown and Gray Paintings

Figure 1. Mark Rothko in his studio, April 1964. [Photo: Alexander Liberman]

CHECKLIST

1. Brown and Gray   1969
   acrylic on paper
   122.5 × 182.9 cm (48¼ × 72 in)
   Anonymous loan

2. Brown and Gray   1969
   acrylic on paper
   122.4 × 182.9 cm (48³⁄₁₆ × 72 in)
   Private collection

3. Brown and Gray   1969
   acrylic on paper
   123.1 × 182.9 cm (48⁷⁄₁₆ × 72 in)
   Estate of Mark Rothko, New York

4. Brown and Gray   1969
   acrylic on paper
   122.9 × 173.0 cm (48⅜ × 68⅛ in)
   Anonymous loan

5. Brown and Gray   1969
   acrylic on paper
   122.5 × 182.3 cm (48¼ × 71¾ in)
   Estate of Mark Rothko, New York

6. Brown and Gray   1969
   acrylic on paper
   122.9 × 173.7 cm (48⅜ × 68⅜ in)
   Anonymous loan

7. Brown and Gray   1969
   acrylic on paper
   120.8 × 152.9 cm (47⁹⁄₁₆ × 60³⁄₁₆ in)
   Private collection

8. Brown and Gray   1969
   acrylic on paper
   122.9 × 172.8 cm (48⅜ × 68 in)
   Private collection

BIOGRAPHY

Mark Rothko (Marcus Rothkowitz). Born in Dvinsk, Russia in 1903. Settles with family in Portland, Oregon, 1913. Studies at Yale University, 1921-1923, and in 1925 under Max Weber at Art Students League. In 1935, is cofounder of The Ten. Has one-man exhibition at Art of This Century Gallery in 1945, and is a founding member of the Subjects of the Artist School in 1948. In 1958-1959 paints murals for Seagram Building, New York. Has retrospective at the Museum of Modern Art in 1961, and does murals for Holyoke Center, Harvard University, 1961-1962. In 1965-1967 paints murals for chapel of Institute of Religion and Human Development, Houston, Texas. In 1969, makes gift to Tate Gallery, London, of eight of Seagram murals (making a total of nine, including one given the year before). In 1969, paints Brown and Gray series, in acrylic on paper, of which there are approximately thirteen. Commits suicide in New York City in 1970.

MARK ROTHKO:
The Brown and Gray Paintings

ELIZA E. RATHBONE

INTRODUCTION

Mark Rothko's status among the foremost artists of this century is assured. That he was also deeply wedded to the shared aspiration of the abstract expressionists to convey meaning in his work is perhaps not so firmly established. Yet, as a founding member of the school on Eighth Street in New York, given the name *The Subjects of the Artist*, his inclusion in this exhibition was a natural one. Rothko is further distinguished as one of the first of the abstract expressionists to make a public statement on the importance of subject matter in his work. In the oft-quoted letter to Edward Alden Jewell of the *New York Times* in 1943, he and Adolph Gottlieb (with the help of Barnett Newman) pronounced as one of their artistic principles, "We assert that the subject is crucial. . . ."

In an exhibition intended to explore each artist's pursuit of his subject in the light of a particular series of works, Rothko presents a special case. Like Clyfford Still, Barnett Newman, or Adolph Gottlieb, all of Rothko's work deals with one central theme.[1] A particular subject, however, does not stand apart as in the case of Motherwell's Elegies or Gorky's The Plow and the Song. Moreover, by 1948, the year of the founding of the school, Rothko gave up completely the titling of his works, the clearest means of designating a theme. From then on he identified his paintings by number or color.

Any exploration of what Rothko intended to express in his work leads us quickly to realize that not only the breadth but also the very nature of his subject would make any verbal titling inadequate and restricting. Yet series or groups of works do exist in Rothko's oeuvre and provide a key to the understanding of his work. From his first series of paintings for the Seagram Building in New York to the paintings for the Rothko Chapel in Houston, Rothko executed such groups of works for a particular place. While Clyfford Still has had his work installed at the San Francisco Museum of Modern Art and in the Albright-Knox Gallery in Buffalo, in galleries exclusively devoted to his work, Rothko is the only abstract expressionist to be commissioned exclusively to execute an entire group of works for a predetermined public space. Such commissions provided the fulfillment of his artistic ideal. They played an important formative role in his artistic evolution and realization of his subject.

The Brown and Gray paintings of 1969 have never been exhibited before. And, indeed, they would take one with more than a passing acquaintance with Rothko's work by surprise. In an oeuvre of such consistency, the Brown and Gray paint-

ings, done the year before he died, are a testimony to the resource of ideas and feelings that continued, until the end of his life, to stimulate new departures. In a show which presents, in the case of every other artist included, series of works of major importance, Rothko should ideally be represented by the Houston chapel or the Seagram paintings. Yet we hope that this bringing together of eight of the approximately thirteen Brown and Gray paintings will not only present a hitherto unknown aspect of the artist's late work but also, by showing them as a group, present them as Rothko himself might have wished. This essay, in addressing the whole question of Rothko's subject matter, does not concern itself solely with the Brown and Gray works. Rather it examines the way in which particular groups of works had been a fulfillment of his vision and in what respect such commissioned works prior to the Brown and Gray paintings were steps in the development that led to those paintings in the exhibition.

Rothko's expression of his subject emerged through a continuous dialogue between the artist and his work. In aspiring to express in his painting an equivalent to music and poetry, his themes, as he himself stated, were vast themes of human emotion—tragedy and ecstasy. Such themes, broadly applied and interpreted through the ages, are also given a breadth of expression by Rothko. They were themes charted in the past but previously uncharted in abstract painting.

One of the outstanding characteristics of Mark Rothko's art is its continuity. His preoccupation—even obsession—with one image, and the consequent subtleties of its growth and transformation attest to the depth of its source and the eloquence and refinement of its manifestation. Among his last works, the Brown and Gray paintings shed light on the past evolution of his art and its meaning, as well as inaugurating a new direction that led to the so-called "Black" paintings of 1970 (fig. 2). Rothko committed suicide on February 25 of that year. Although the last painting in progress in his studio when he died was red,[2] the Black paintings, for their marked differences from his preceding works, are often considered his final statement.

The Black paintings consist of an upper register of black and a lower register that ranges from golden ochre to shades of gray and blue. Likewise, in the Brown and Gray paintings, a greater range of treatment occurs in the gray portion below (fig. 3). The gray was probably mixed with a flesh tone that Rothko often used in these last years. They are nevertheless spare and somber works in contrast to the luminous hues ranging from

Figure 2. Mark Rothko. *Black on Gray*, 1970. Oil on canvas, 175 x 233.5 cm (69 x 92 in). Estate of Mark Rothko. Not in exhibition

yellows to reds, greens to blues, of the works for which he is best known and which comprise the large part of his oeuvre. For all their consistency with his earlier work, the Brown and Gray paintings exhibit what are, in the context of such continuity, notable differences in size, technique, and composition.

Rothko painted three other distinctly definable series prior to the Brown and Gray paintings. In every case he had a project already in mind. The twelve predominantly maroon and black paintings, for the Seagram Building in New York, were executed in 1958-1959; a smaller and more diversely colored group of five paintings were made in 1961-1962 for a room in the new Holyoke Center of Harvard University; and finally the four-teen deep crimson, plum, and black wall-size paintings for the chapel of the Institute of Religion and Human Development in Houston, Texas, were begun in 1965 and finished, except for minor touches, the following year. While he had no such ap-pointed destination for the Brown and Gray paintings, he deliberately created another series. As in the case of the other grouped works, he reduced his palette to just a few colors. Gathered together, they have a like capacity to create an envi-ronment dominated by one mood.

It was soon after he completed the murals for the chapel in Houston that Rothko suffered a heart attack.[3] He spent the summer of 1968 in Provincetown, on Cape Cod. In his debili-tated state, he could work on a scale no larger than forty inches high.[4] This resulted in many small works on paper, a dramatic shift from the scale of the Houston chapel murals, all of which were about twice his height or more (fig. 4). Soon, however, he saw in these small works the potential for larger paintings and, on his return to his 69th Street studio in New York, went on to execute the somewhat larger (most of them approximately six feet high) Brown and Gray paintings. Despite their larger scale, he continued to use paper and acrylic as his medium.

The most noticeable new direction Rothko took in these works is their division into two fields and their clean peripheral demarcation by a white border. Rothko made the border, averaging a width of one-half to three-quarters of an inch, by

Figure 3. Mark Rothko. *Brown and Gray*, 1969. Acrylic on paper, 120.8 x 152.9 cm (47⁹⁄₁₆ x 60³⁄₁₆ in). Private collection. Cat. no. 7, pl. 28

taping the sheet along each edge before beginning the painting. Removing the masking tape left a clean edge and the untouched white of the paper. Rothko had used masking tape to establish the edges of the forms in some of the paintings for the chapel. Here, however, the border itself was an innovation which he retained in some subsequent larger oils. The more important departure in these works was that of extending both fields to this border, eliminating the one unifying painted ground in which forms are suspended, characteristic of earlier work. In some cases, Rothko perfected this margin, to make it precise. The margin left bare, hence identified with the paper itself, declares these works as objects—flat painted surfaces.[5]

In Rothko's earlier work, two basic compositions recur. In some works a large shape occupies the center with a much smaller shape above and below. Others consist of three or four shapes (fig. 5). In the latter case, the largest or the most intense rectangle of color is usually in the upper portion of the paint-ing. This adds pictorial presence at the top of the composition and arrests the illusion of ascension in forms already floating. This capping of the weightless signals the pictorial dialectic that permeates every aspect of Rothko's conception. Thus he opposes any landscape reading of the painting—earth below, vaporous sky above. The strong presence of the uppermost form prevents the intensity of the whole from diffusing. That quality of containment provides the tension that holds the spectator spellbound.

In the Brown and Gray paintings, and in the Black paintings that follow, Rothko employed similar means. The darker portion is consistently on top. The straight, broad strokes, visibly vertical and horizontal, give the upper register in brown a more fixed quality than the more irregular brushwork—sometimes in sweeping curves—of the gray area below. The top weighs down and serves to contain, as if to suppress, the more turbulent passages in gray. While the upper margin is more consistently clean, Rothko allowed the gray in some cases to spill over into the white border (fig. 6). Yet, despite any general similarity of means, these paintings differ dramatically from Rothko's previous work. One is not immediately aware of, but senses, the layers of paint in Rothko's mature oils, but in the Brown and Gray paintings the artist used broad strokes of water-thinned acrylic that occasionally allow the paper itself to show through. Obscure spatial depths are thus suggested in the Rembrandtesque penumbra of the upper portion. The subtle admixture of pink endows the gray portion with equal warmth.

Surely Rothko's early works in watercolor laid the foundation for his mature work in oil where the paint, thinned with turpentine, created a like luminosity. His return to working on paper in a water-based medium reminds one of the extraordinary continuity of technique, and indeed intention, that threads through Rothko's entire oeuvre. Rothko kept a few of these early watercolors in the studio.[6] The underwater realm of the early works—a world of growth and formation, which is in keeping with the medium—is evoked again in the lower portion of the Brown and Gray paintings. Rothko's apparent return to that earlier surrealist-derived analogy with the subconscious is embodied in this mature and more direct manifestation of his own state of mind. Since the series of small works preceding the Brown and Gray paintings was painted in Provincetown, by the sea, it could in part account for their similar suggestion of a watery domain. Indeed, these paintings are more suggestive of landscape than any of Rothko's work since his early watercolors, more aptly described as "submarine-scapes." Like many of the early watercolors, however, they are vertical paintings. And while their verticality, coupled with the absence of any descriptive forms, does not deny an association with landscape, it works against it. Early works, *Baptismal Scene* of 1945 (fig. 7), for example, allow the biomorphic forms to evoke growth and change. In the lower register of the Brown and Gray paintings, Rothko again explores a fluidity of handling. A sense of change, lack of resolution, sets these works apart from both the mature works in oil that precede them and from the more iconic works that follow with his resumed use of oil.

Although the Brown and Gray paintings grew out of Rothko's previous work, they provide a more intimate and personal glimpse of the burgeoning of a new idea. They are consummate in Rothko's mastery of his vision and his medium. Nevertheless, in relation to the grand achievement of the chapel, they present the artist on a human scale once more—not the titanic visionary, the artist of an iconic absolute. In the Brown and Gray paintings, the forms of his preceding works in oil have been dissolved into a more overt expression of the unrest they always contained. Rothko was very depressed and introspec-

Figure 4. Mark Rothko with Houston chapel paintings, May 1967. [Photo: Alexander Liberman]

tive these last two years of his life, and this state of mind is revealed in the brooding quality of these works.

The Brown and Gray, and the Black, paintings are by no means the only works of his final years, nor do they represent a denial of the theme of his earlier work. Every reduction Rothko made, starting with the elimination of the figure (which he regretted), was to the same end; he found it to be the only route to the breadth and depth of his subject.[7] Indeed, he never deviated from the statement he made with Gottlieb in 1943:

It is a widely accepted notion among painters that it does not matter what one paints as long as it is well painted. This is the essence of academicism. There is no such thing as good painting about nothing. We assert that the subject matter is crucial and only that subject matter is valid which is tragic and timeless.[8]

In stating that there is no such thing as good painting about nothing, the artists might as well have added, but there *is* such a thing as good painting about *something*.[9] It is obvious that their pursuit of meaningful subject also involved the evolution of a pictorial language that, in effect, constituted a rebirth of modern painting. And it is just as essential to recognize that without subject matter (different for each of the artists involved), the new language would not have been born. Rothko was adamant about the content of his work. Although widely considered one of America's finest colorists, he was disturbed by his constant reception as a colorist above all. In 1958, Dore Ashton wrote in reference to Rothko's first works in the dark manner,

I suspect that in part, Rothko struck out with exasperation at the general misinterpretation of his earlier work—especially the effusive yellow, orange and pinks of three years back. He seems to be saying in these new foreboding works that he was never painting luxe, calme and volupte if we had only known it![10]

Rothko's increasingly somber palette of the sixties reflects not a subjugation but an intensification of certain aspects of the spirit that had guided him throughout his oeuvre. The nature of his subject, which he himself stated in general terms to be tragedy and ecstasy, and the evolution of this one central theme is the subject of this essay. It is essential to the understanding of the Brown and Gray paintings.

Figure 5. Mark Rothko. *Four Darks in Red*, 1958. Oil on canvas, 259.1 x 294.7 cm (102 x 116 in). Whitney Museum of American Art, New York, Gift of the Friends of the Whitney Museum of American Art, Mr. and Mrs. Eugene M. Schwartz, Mrs. Samuel A. Seaver, Charles Simon (and purchase) [photo: Geoffrey Clements]. Not in exhibition

Perhaps more than that of any other abstract expressionist, Rothko's work bears an aspect of self-portraiture. The constancy of the image encourages this observation. For one so sensitive to the understanding, the communication, of his work to others, how devastating must have been the telling remark of Maurice Sievan, who, at Rothko's prompting, told the artist what he thought of his late work. Only a week before Rothko died, Sievan on a visit to the artist in his studio "told him that they didn't look like Rothkos."[11] Yet Rothko's sense of his life's involvement in these works we might learn from his own words. On the occasion of the 1961 exhibition at the Museum of Modern Art, he had been asked by a reporter how long it had taken him to paint one of the most recent large works. Although Rothko could, and sometimes did, finish a painting in a morning,[12] he replied, "I am 57 years old and it took me all that time to paint this picture."[13]

Thus it was a long period of development that led to Rothko's last statements of profound personal belief. A concern with ultimate philosophical questions was already the stimulus behind his work of the forties. The abstract expressionists all, in one way or another, abandoned the figure as they realized that the myths of the past and the past modes of expressing them could no longer provide the vehicle for the content they sought.

WORKS FOR AN ENVIRONMENT

Rothko's entire mature oeuvre can be, and has been, considered a consistent statement of one theme. Yet certain groups of works form discrete series, and significantly the first of these, the paintings he executed for the Seagram Building in New York, marks the turn toward the darker palette that charac-

Figure 6. Mark Rothko. *Brown and Gray*, 1969. Acrylic on paper, 122.4 x 182.9 cm (48 3/16 x 72 in). Private collection. Cat. no. 2, pl. 23

terized much of his work of the sixties and dominated the paintings of his last two years. The three series of works that he did in the course of the last twelve years of his life seem to have propelled him toward an intensification of an obsessive vision.

None of the other abstract expressionists, except perhaps Clyfford Still, was so sensitive about the conditions under which his work was seen as Rothko was. Still and Rothko were reluctant to let their work travel to Europe where they would be unable to oversee their installation. Rothko disliked being in group shows. Doing such a commissioned group of works not only allowed him a decisive hand in their installation but also that exclusive dominion, over the space and spectator, he desired.

Rothko was not alone in his awareness of the dialogue between artist and public necessary to the life of his work. It was an attitude shared by the other artists of the New York School. It was not only intrinsic to the nature of the work itself but was also provoked by the artistic climate of the formative years of the movement.

Robert Goldwater wrote of the artists of the New York School that

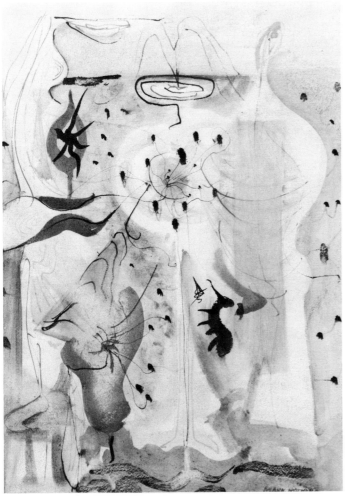

Figure 7. Mark Rothko. *Baptismal Scene*, 1945. Watercolor on paper, 50.5 x 35.6 cm (19⅞ x 14 in). Whitney Museum of American Art, New York [photo: Geoffrey Clements]. Not in exhibition

during the decade 1945-55, and especially during its first five years, [they were] a small and embattled minority, misunderstood and unappreciated. . . .

The result of all this was that they adopted an attitude at once uncompromising and possessive. . . . They seemed to view them [their creations] as extensions of themselves, whose understanding was given to few. The appreciation of others somehow compromised the work's existence, as if, after the manner of primitive belief, something of its vigor was drawn into the eye of the observer; popularity was suspect, and success (not yet achieved) a major crime. (How different the atmosphere today!) Since the artist identified with his work, intentions and result were fused, and he who questioned the work, in however humble a fashion, was taken to be doubting the man.[14]

It was Rothko who expressed this belief during those formative years in words more applicable to his own work than to that of any of the other artists of the group—words that express his particular sensitivity in this regard:

A picture lives by companionship, expanding and quickening in the eyes of the sensitive observer. It dies by the same token. It is, therefore, a risky business to send it out into the world. How often it must be permanently impaired by the eyes of the vulgar and the cruelty of the impotent who would extend their affliction universally.[15]

This sensitivity continued throughout his life, years after the

success and acclaim of the movement as a whole as well as of his work in particular. The year Rothko died, Max Kozloff wrote: "He refused to show any of the work he had done since his 1961 retrospective at the Museum of Modern Art, for fear it would be hostilely received. No one could persuade him otherwise, though many tried."[16]

Although there had always been long periods when Rothko refused to exhibit his work, when he accepted the invitation for the one-man show at the Museum of Modern Art in 1961, he selected the paintings himself and insisted on overseeing their installation. Particularly important was the lighting that he requested be dimmer than customary. He didn't want his paintings seen by the hard overbright lighting customary in museums, that would inevitably have a flattering effect. It was his way of drawing attention away from the means and of heightening instead the effect. Rothko even tried to control the conditions of shows at commercial galleries. Philip Guston's account of Rothko's efforts in this regard at the Sidney Janis Gallery is revealing.

Philip Guston remembers the time when he and Rothko went to see the installation of one of Rothko's shows at Janis. They strolled into the gallery and Mark, without a word, switched off half the lights. When Janis emerged from his office, the three of them chatted a bit and, in a pause in the conversation, Janis slid off and turned all the lights back on. Rothko didn't say anything. They finished their visit; Janis went back to work, Guston and Rothko waited for the elevator, and just before they entered it, Rothko turned half the lights back off again.

"I'm positive," Guston says, "that Mark sneaked up there every day and turned the lights down—without ever complaining or explaining."[17]

As a man, Rothko showed the same reserve as his works. He was as disinclined to protest overtly such treatment of his work as he was stubborn to assert his own intention. He saw no point in discussing what to him was self-evident. He had little tolerance for those who were blind to it, but he believed equally in the importance of an understanding that might come independent of any explanation on his part. He once said to Elaine de Kooning with regard to his work, "Silence is so accurate."[18]

Rothko's concern about letting his work out into the world does not reflect an insecurity about their worth but rather the very opposite; more than anything he wanted them to be seen and understood as he saw them. But, as in magic or religion, he saw the world as consisting of true believers and those who professed belief. He would encourage younger artists and could be generous in praise of the work of his contemporaries, but he had no patience with anyone whom he felt was not true to himself.

Often it was for its exquisite color sensibility that Rothko's work was admired. It disturbed him that his reception in the public eye was that of an abstract painter whose primary concern was relations of color and form. In an interview with Seldon Rodman, he made clear his frustration in this regard:

"You're an abstractionist to me," [Rodman] said. "You're a master of color harmonies and relationships on a monumental scale. Do you deny that?"

"I do. I'm not interested in relationships of color or form or anything else."

Figure 8. Mark Rothko. *Triptych,*
1962: center panel. Oil on canvas,
267.0 x 457.2 cm (105⅛ x 180 in).
The President and Fellows of Harvard
College, Cambridge, Mass. Not in
exhibition

"Then what is it you're expressing?"

"I'm interested only in expressing basic human emotions—tragedy,
ecstasy, doom, and so on—and the fact that lots of people break down
and cry when confronted with my pictures shows that I *communicate*
these basic human emotions. I communicate them more directly than
your friend Ben Shahn, who is essentially a journalist with, sometimes,
moderately interesting overtones. The people who weep before my
pictures are having the same religious experience I had when I painted
them, and if you, as you say, are moved only by their color relationships, then you miss the point." [19]

The one-man show at the Museum of Modern Art (1961)
pointed up the fact that the gathering together of many
Rothkos that do not form a series can belie their shared intention and accentuate, rather, the range and beauty of Rothko's
color. The formal differences from canvas to canvas, particularly with regard to color, could too easily overcome the need
for each painting to be encountered as a presence in itself.
Robert Goldwater, whom Rothko felt was especially sensitive
to his work,[20] noted this in his review of the exhibition, and
observed: "the most successful arrangement is the small
chapel-like room in which have been hung three of the mural
series of 1958-59. Partaking of the same somber mood, they
reinforce each other, as they were designed to do." [21]

Even before the exhibition (or installation of any of Rothko's commissioned series), however, Lawrence Alloway had
written in 1959 that Rothko "prefers his pictures to be hung in
groups, not spaced out in conventional good hanging; their
united effect stresses their environmental function." [22]

At this time Duncan and Marjorie Phillips, who already had
bought one Rothko (from Sidney Janis, in 1957), after visiting
the artist in his studio, soon purchased another. They gave him
a one-man exhibition in 1960, and began to plan the room at
the Phillips Collection containing nothing but four Rothkos—one on each wall—as it exists today. All four works of the
fifties, they are close in size to one another though they vary in
combinations of hue. Rothko visited the Phillips Collection in
Washington more than once and was delighted with the room.
The paintings were not, however, specially executed for the
space as in the case of other grouped works.[23] In the case of the
Tate paintings, the Harvard murals, and the chapel in Houston, the artist studied the space at length, specified not only the
lighting (it was in an argument over lighting that the design of
the chapel passed from the hands of Philip Johnson into those
of the Houston architects Howard Barnstone and Eugene Au-
bry) but also the color of the walls and floor. In every case,
however, such specifications were made to minimize every
intruding aspect of the existing environment.

When Rothko decided that the paintings he did for the
Seagram Building did not suit the designated space of the Four
Seasons Restaurant, he paid off the commission and kept the
paintings. Soon after, however, in 1961, he accepted Harvard's
invitation to do murals for the Holyoke Center designed by
Jose Luis Sert.[24] The paintings were exhibited at the Guggenheim in April 1963, before they were installed in Cambridge.
"Rothko comments that he has been preoccupied for a number
of years with the idea of translating his 'pictorial concepts into
murals which would serve as an image for a public space.' "[25]
Consisting of a large painting, flanked by two medium-sized
ones (which Rothko referred to as a triptych), and two independent paintings on the opposite wall, each of which displays
two or three vertical rectangles (figs. 8, 9), they relate in composition to the Seagram paintings and adumbrate, in the triptych formation, the three "triptychs" in the chapel in Houston.

While Rothko continued through the sixties to execute
paintings using the format of his work of the previous
decade—a format in which two or three or four areas of color

250

Figure 9. Mark Rothko. *Triptych,* 1962: left panel. Oil on canvas, 266.4 x 297.2 cm (104⅞ x 117 in). The President and Fellows of Harvard College, Cambridge, Mass. Not in exhibition

Figure 10. Mark Rothko in East Hampton, 1964. The painting to the left is probably *Brown on Red,* 1960. [Photo: Hans Namuth]

are suspended in an essentially uniform field—his works that exist in series reflect an intensification of certain concerns that such projects encouraged him to explore. The power of Rothko's work to create a pervasive mood has been called a theatrical experience, unfolding in time. An isolated series promised to fulfill the conditions for such a sustained experience. Rothko himself would sit before his work at the end of a day as the light in his studio dwindled, lost in contemplation (fig. 10).[26] The opportunity to create such an environment provoked a certain reduction of means in a given painting, and, at the same time, broadened the scope of his intent. From the beginning, Rothko's style evolved out of a continual process of reduction. His work in series opened a new chapter in this evolution—to explore further questions of scale, of flatness versus depth, of the relationship of one painting to another. In these environmental series both the formal and the spiritual concerns that absorbed the artist became a necessary part of the development that led to the late Brown and Gray paintings.

FROM THE SEAGRAM PAINTINGS TO THE ROTHKO CHAPEL

Rothko's first commission, the Seagram murals, provoked a number of significant changes in his work. While the intense reds of the Seagram works, ranging from orange to maroon, together with black, is adumbrated in a number of paintings of 1957, in the entire series he narrowed his palette to shades of two basic colors, red and black. In tandem with Rothko's restricted palette emerged subtle compositional variations.

In one of the Seagram paintings, *Two Openings in Black over Wine* (fig. 11), Rothko gave the entire canvas a wine ground. Black plays a structural role in the composition unprecedented in Rothko's work. Because the color of the forms that

it frames is the same as that of the ground, they do not appear suspended in one field. Rather they suggest openings through the black.

Rothko's work had always dealt with ambiguity, both inviting the spectator in and shutting him out. His forms both advance and recede, not alternately—like an optical illusion that one can perceive at will first one way, then the other—but simultaneously. Nor can it be compared to the kind of surface ambiguity that occurs in de Kooning's black and white paintings of 1948 and all of Kline's black and white work. Rothko had never denied the spectrum of color in his earlier work for black and white in the manner of Pollock, Motherwell, de Kooning, or Kline. This contrast points up the essence of Rothko's particular dialectic, and the distinct direction to which the use of "monochrome" would lead in his work. In the black and white paintings of Kline and de Kooning the duality lies in the dialogue between figure and ground. The white is not a ground for a black form but cuts into the black, asserting the picture plane in a play between the two in a shallow, cubist-derived space.

The impact of cubism plays no such significant role in the development of Rothko's work. The artists whose work shares closest formal affinity with his (Avery, Matisse, Bonnard) either never worked in a cubist idiom, or, in the case of Matisse, only for a short period and in a manner that was not fundamental to his style. Rothko's dialectic lies, rather, between the painting as object—as a flat surface into which paint has been stained—and as an illusion, in the spatial recession effected by the actual handling of paint in thin atmospheric layers. The frontality of the forms reinforces the former, while their indeterminate edges creates the residual optical sensation of expansion beyond its defined (or concrete) boundaries.

In *Two Openings in Black over Wine,* the two rectangular forms are vertical and thus create a particularly direct rapport with the spectator, further enabling the forms to be experienced as openings. This concentration of Rothko's dialectic (flat surface and illusion of depth) provoked an equally more intense response from the viewer. Peter Selz wrote in 1961:

The open rectangles suggest the rims of flame in containing fires, or

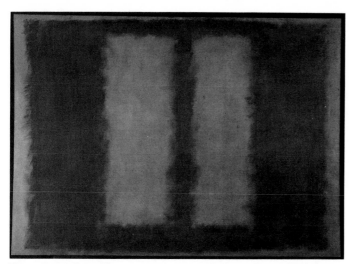

Figure 11. Mark Rothko. *Two Openings in Black over Wine* (sketch for *Mural No. 6*), 1958. Oil on canvas, 267.0 x 365.8 cm (105 x 144 in). The Tate Gallery, London. Not in exhibition

the entrances to tombs, like the doors to the dwellings of the dead in Egyptian pyramids, behind which the sculptors kept the kings "alive" for eternity in the *ka*. But unlike the doors of the dead, which were meant to shut out the living from the place of absolute might, even of patrician death, these paintings—open sarcophagi—moodily dare, and thus invite the spectator to enter their orifices.[27]

The unique effect on the spectator of Rothko's composition and handling has continually provoked special comment. Rothko's paintings, like a kind of intangible apparition, tend to locate the viewer at a particular point. Brian O'Doherty noted the manner in which the works exert this ineffable control: "Before a Pollock, people wander to and fro. Before a Rothko each finds a spot appropriate to his own size and tends to stay there, or leave and return. It is uncanny to watch this. The picture eventually locates the spectator at a particular distance."[28]

It is not only the lack of surface incident in a Rothko that provokes this singular reaction. In such a Newman as *Vir Heroicus Sublimus*, clear of the intricasies of a Pollock that engage the eye, the vertical elements mark a progression the length of the canvas. There is no implied center as in a Rothko. William Seitz described this rapport in his dissertation of 1955 in such a manner as to almost predict the extension of this unique relation of the work to its audience in the culminating statement of the chapel in Houston.

There is almost no reason for a close-up study of the spare surface of a late Rothko [that is, of the mid-fifties], nor does the painter want his audience at a great distance. These canvases should be seen at a relatively close range, or in a room that (judged by the popular idea of the placing of large compositions) is "too small," and in which the painting might occupy an entire wall. The spectator is not lured into the picture space—he is in fact excluded; yet he must remain close enough so that the surface of the canvas constitutes his entire visual environment. Rothko values the quality of "immanence": of a spirit which is indwelling, unified and complete. The edges of the canvas are the borders of a finite but expanding environment whose limits lie on the periphery of perception. If one moved back far, the picture would become (what it must not be) a unit of another, larger, configuration. Pinned down laterally by the similarity of right and left, moreover,

what can one do but stand half-way between, at the center?[29]

In his late commissioned works, Rothko went beyond what seemed a self-evident and intrinsic aspect of his style—that of each painting's demand for a single one-to-one encounter—to do exactly that: make it additionally "a unit of another, larger, configuration," but, significantly, without losing the individual presence of each canvas.

The Seagram paintings were originally intended to be installed high on the wall above the heads of the diners. Eight of the twelve that Rothko had in his studio when Tate director Sir Norman Reid visited him in 1969 were chosen with much deliberation and were later installed in accordance with Rothko's plans at eye level in a room of the Tate Gallery in London. The paintings originally comprised three groups. Such groupings inaugurated a whole new set of concerns that preoccupied Rothko regarding the interrelationship of one painting to another. At the Tate two horizontal paintings, each six feet high and fifteen feet long, and each comprising one rectangular opening, were installed one above the other. As a pair, they establish a correspondence with the one large horizontal painting in which two vertical openings occur (*Two Openings in Black over Wine*). Although he never saw his paintings hanging in the Tate nor in the chapel in Houston, in both cases Rothko gave utmost consideration to the dimensions of the space for his work. For the Harvard and the chapel murals, he requested that the ceiling be low, the paintings be without frames and mounted on thin stretchers—all to the end that they are identified as much as possible with the walls. While such close identification of the paintings with the wall might have detracted from the ambiguity of each painting as both self-contained object and the illusion of expansion beyond such boundaries, Rothko did not allow the total environment to sap any of the dialectic inherent in his art. For the chapel in Houston, the artist arrived at a brilliant solution to this problem. The nearly monochrome paintings dominate the space—both define it architecturally and create a unifying mood. At the same time, the indefinite space of the paintings dissolves the architectural boundaries of the room. As Rothko said to Dore Ashton, with regard to the chapel, what he wanted to do was to "paint both the finite and the infinite."[30]

Three "triptychs," four single monochrome panels, and a panel between the two entrance doors, comprise the fourteen paintings of the chapel (figs. 12, 13). The artist combined crimson, black, raw umber, even small amounts of blue, to produce closely related tones ranging from deep maroon to a "purplish lighter maroon." "Half of the paintings have a black field. These fields were outlined by Rothko in charcoal directly on the painting. . . . Rothko could work a whole month experimenting on half an inch." Dominique de Ménil has described the stages of transformation of these black fields: "At first, the field occupied only the central part—an opening into a wall into the night. Step by step, the field was enlarged, leaving only a narrow margin of color. The night had invaded the wall."[31]

In the relationship of one painting to another, he carried the schema of the two preceding projects a step further. With the reduction of his palette to even closer hues, further denying the internal dialogue of color form to field, the relations of scale

Figure 12. Rothko Chapel, Houston, dedicated February 27, 1971. [Photo: courtesy of Rothko Chapel, Houston]

Figure 13. Rothko Chapel, Houston. [Photo: courtesy of Rothko Chapel, Houston]

took on added importance. The center panel of two of the triptychs is raised, and Rothko reduced by two and a half inches the two paintings to either side of the apse, in order to establish the relationship he wanted (fig. 14). In an even more subtle modification, he added one-half inch to a ten-foot canvas, "and decided it made a substantial difference."[32] It was through such imperceptible refinements (and by dint of their imperceptibility) that Rothko managed to maintain the individual presence of each painting and its relation to the others in orchestrating the whole ensemble. Whereas Barnett Newman's Stations of the Cross were conceived and executed to be interpreted sequentially, Rothko's chapel paintings are both hierarchical in themselves (built up as they are in gradual layers) *and* as a group. It is as if the assembled whole were an extension or fulfillment of the part. Thus the interrelation of forms within one painting evolved to include larger relationships of canvas to canvas that reach a culmination in the Rothko Chapel in Houston.

It is Rothko's immediately preceding experience in such subtle modifications of proportion that continue to evolve in the variations of the Brown and Gray paintings, in which scale and proportion took on increased importance. With every reduction of palette and composition, the possibilities became infinite. Unlike the other series, however, the Brown and Gray paintings were not destined for a particular environment. For this reason they appear, gathered together, more along the lines of variations on a theme. It is as though Rothko took pleasure in the freedom from the restrictions of the chapel project and enjoyed pursuing the new directions it suggested in terms of scale and proportion.

The special nature of large-scale painting introduced by the abstract expressionists is virtually impossible to account for in terms of any visual sources. While the WPA murals provided a direct antecedent in size, and Picasso's *Guernica* had a large impact when first shown in this country in 1939 at the Valentine Gallery,[33] the abstract expressionists introduced an entirely new attitude toward internal scale. Size became endemic to their artistic goals. Rothko and Gottlieb had stated in 1943

their concern with the "large shape,"[34] but Jackson Pollock is generally credited for being the first to make a wall-size painting entitled *Mural* that same year for Peggy Guggenheim, with regard to which he stated in 1947:

I intend to paint large movable pictures which will function between the easel and mural. I have set a precedent in this genre in a large painting for Miss Peggy Guggenheim. . . .

I believe the easel picture to be a dying form, and the tendency of modern feeling is towards the wall picture or mural. I believe the time is not yet ripe for a *full* transition from easel to mural. The pictures I contemplate painting would constitute a half-way state and an attempt to point the direction of the future, without arriving there completely.[35]

As this shared attitude began to jell as an essential ingredient of their art, it became increasingly aligned with the idea of public art. Each artist's personal quest to express a universal (the antithesis of the regionalism of American art of the thirties)—a universal that had its closest precedent in the artistic and philosophical goals of Mondrian—quite quickly led to, and naturally incorporated, religious projects. The idea of executing works for a religious environment appealed to many of these artists. In 1951, for a new synagogue of the B'nai Israel Congregation in Millburn, New Jersey, Robert Motherwell executed a mural, Adolph Gottlieb an altar curtain, and Herbert Ferber a sculpture. The outstanding model for such a project at the time, however, was entirely done by one artist.

Figure 14. Rothko Chapel, Houston. [Photo: courtesy of Rothko Chapel, Houston]

Matisse had just finished the Chapel of the Rosary at Vence, which was consecrated on June 25, 1951. Jackson Pollock had evidenced particular interest in the Matisse chapel and at one point made plans to do a chapel himself.[36] Newman toyed with the idea of designing a synagogue for many years before Richard Meier asked him to participate in an exhibition, *Recent American Synagogue Architecture,* for which, with the sculptor Robert Murray, he made a model.[37] Rothko was the only one of the abstract expressionists whose work was permanently installed in such a religious context to the exclusion of any other artist's participation. Such a project seems, moreover, more of a fulfillment of Rothko's ideals and more especially suited to his work than to that of any of the others.

Having recently returned from seeing the Matisse Chapel of the Rosary at Vence, John and Dominique de Ménil, on visiting Rothko's studio in 1964, immediately grasped the suitability of Rothko's work for a chapel. The paintings they saw in his studio at the time were those he had done for the Seagram Building. By the end of 1964, Rothko had rented a studio, on East 69th Street, large enough for him to construct inside a full-scale model of a section of the chapel to be built in Houston (fig. 15). By June 1966, the paintings were largely completed (fig. 16). Rothko made a trip to Europe and, on his return, added some finishing touches, with particular attention to the subtleties of the interrelationship of the paintings, one to another.[38]

This was his third trip to Europe, preceded by a trip to England, France, and Italy in 1950 and a return to all three countries in 1959, in addition to Holland and Belgium.[39]

The monuments that are recorded as having impressed Rothko most during his travels were, significantly, examples of religious architecture in which the paintings or mosaics are intimately related to the architectural space. Rothko is said to have been especially moved by the frescoes of Fra Angelico at San Marco in Florence.[40] It seems that these frescoes may well have been in the back of his mind when he was working on the Seagram murals. In most of these frescoes, large flat areas of color fill the background space to the edges. Their tonalities, richly suggestive of mood, are very close to those of the Seagram paintings, and they must have struck Rothko as kindred means to a kindred end. In a large crucifixion fresco by Fra Angelico, the three crucified are situated against a maroon sky that fills the upper register. In three other frescoes of the crucifixion—an isolated Christ on the cross with saints below—the sky is black.[41] Fra Angelico tended to simplify shapes and to compose in a shallow space parallel to the picture plane and, in the case of the San Marco frescoes, to divide the space into two registers almost devoid of indication of land and sky in an image that thereby becomes more iconic and absolute. Rothko's explanation to Harvard president Nathan Pusey of the paintings for Harvard University, which follow the Seagram murals, reveals his intent not to illustrate such subjects but rather to evoke a similarly intense experience. "Rothko explained that the dark mood of the monumental triptych was meant to convey Christ's suffering on Good Friday; and the brighter hues of the last mural, Easter and the Resurrection."[42]

Rothko also harbored special love for the Byzantine church at Torcello. It was apparently his memory of this small island of the Veneto and presumably the central plan of Santa Fosca nearby the church that made Philip Johnson's octagonal plan for the chapel appeal to him. The mosaics of the church depict the Madonna and Child in dark blue, isolated on a gold ground, in the apse, and the Last Judgment on the west entrance wall.[43] Rothko also alluded to the impact that Michelangelo's design for the hallway and stairs of the Laurentian Library in Florence had had on him: "He [Michelangelo] achieved just the kind of feeling I'm after—he makes the viewers feel that they are trapped in a room where all the doors and windows are bricked up so that all they can do is butt their heads forever against the wall."[44]

Despite the atmospheric "depth" of Rothko's paintings, in surrounding the viewer the chapel paintings appear irresolute, unrelieved in the unity and frontality of the image. Rothko's intention in hanging his paintings close together in a small room became more pronounced in the planned environment of the chapel, where the claustrophobic atmosphere creates an intensification of the "immanence" to which Seitz refers (not unlike Michelangelo's hallway). That Rothko felt a special rapport with examples of Byzantine and Renaissance art in Italy is not surprising. The iconic command of the austere frontal images of Byzantine art, and the humanism—the view of man as the measure—central to the culture of the Renais-

Figure 15. Mark Rothko in his studio on East 69th Street, New York, in 1964. [Photo: Hans Namuth]

sance—are mysteriously fused as both fundamental elements of Rothko's vision.

In Rothko's attempt to penetrate to the core the viability of myth in our time and the faith required for myth to live, his own approach to his art became an expression of faith. The consistency of its inward growth and distillation reflects the dedication that has no closer parallel than that of a kind of religious devotion.

The Rothko Chapel points up how exceptionally Rothko's paintings depend on the surrounding conditions of space and light. The more subtly adjusted and attuned to their environment (of his New York studio) they became, the greater their estrangement when moved.[45] The late series of paintings (the Seagram-Tate murals, the Harvard murals, and the chapel) depend, more than any earlier work, on each other and on their environment for their effect. Thus it is because all his previous work seemed to be directed toward the goal of creating an environment with his paintings that his eventual engagement in several projects became central to his stylistic development, and to the fulfillment of his ideal.

DUALITY AND THE ROLE OF THE SPECTATOR

The role of the spectator vis-à-vis Rothko's work is an essential dimension that one must appreciate in order to understand the implications of the duality in the work itself. Perhaps more than any other abstract expressionist, Rothko created works that seem to require the presence of the spectator to come into their own. As in theater the life of a work depends on how it engages and affects the spectator. Rothko elevated this dimension to a level of particular importance. He liked to live with his paintings and felt exceptionally possessive toward them. His paintings have a private, personal quality that Motherwell, for example, would reserve for his collages. It was not only, however, Rothko's sensitivity to his work's fate outside his studio, in the world, that made him consider the spectator such a crucial dimension. His awareness of this dimension is implicit

Figure 16. Mark Rothko in his studio on East 69th Street, New York, in October 1964(?). [Photo: Hans Namuth]

in the works themselves. While all abstract-expressionist painting asserts the unequivocal two-dimensionality of the surface, Rothko carried this attitude to the furthest extent. His paintings are single frontal images. There is virtually no dialogue within the work itself—of figure versus ground, of contrasts of forms or color. All such internal play of pictorial opposites or dichotomies has been subsumed into one unified presence. It is by virtue of this aspect of a single presence that a dialogue is created beyond the confines of the painting, between it and the spectator.

Herein lies the personal quality of Rothko's work. His work is not descriptive or symbolic nor, by any previous definition, metaphorical. His content is at once more vague or open to interpretation and more plainly succinct. He invites us to experience his experience.

As a young man Rothko had been involved in the theater. He loved to act and, for a while, painted scenery as well.[46] He was most likely familiar with the theories of the Russian producer Meyerhold, whose approach to theater finds a parallel in the pictorial ideas soon to emerge among the abstract expressionists.[47] Meyerhold, in the first quarter of this century, created a theater revolutionary in its time. He conceived of a stark stage (no curtain, minimal props), the focus on the actor, who was restricted by no conventional boundaries or sequence of space or time, and the audience as a fourth dimension. All these factors are paralleled in Rothko's work.

Rothko indeed made frequent reference, in his writings, to drama. In one of his early pieces of writing, published in *Possibilities* (1947/48) and entitled "The Romantics Were Prompted," he wrote of his paintings as "dramas"; "the shapes in the pictures are the performers."[48] In the same essay, he stated, "For me the great achievements of the centuries in which the artist accepted the probable and familiar as his subjects were the pictures of the single human figure—alone in a moment of utter immobility."

From the beginning Rothko had conceived of his paintings as dramas, but as his pictorial style evolved it grew to identify more and more with the single human figure. The drama became an internal one—self-contained. Rothko wanted to express the human drama as had those giants he most highly esteemed, Aeschylus and, later, Shakespeare—a drama that transcends time and place. As his vision became increasingly distilled, each canvas became a "performer," as it were, a single portrait of a temperament or mood. One experiences their command as one does that of a portrait, whose gaze arrests, calling for a dialogue. Years after the small irregular shapes in his paintings of 1947-1948 had expanded to fill the field, in a lecture at Pratt Institute in 1958 Rothko expressed his interest in the role of the human figure as the agent of a larger, timeless ideal:

There is, however, a profound reason for the persistence of the word "portrait" because the real essence of the great portraiture of all time is the artist's eternal interest in the human figure, character, and emotions—in short in the human drama. That Rembrandt expressed it by posing a sitter is irrelevant. We do not know the sitter but we are intensely aware of the drama. The Archaic Greeks, on the other hand used as their models the inner visions which they had of their gods. And in our day, our visions are the fulfillment of our own needs.

It must be noted that the great painters of the figure had this in common. Their portraits resemble each other far more than they recall the peculiarities of a particular model. In a sense they have painted one character in all their work. What is indicated here is that the artist's real model is an ideal which embraces all of human drama rather than the appearance of a particular individual.[49]

Rothko was a humanist. His respect for past masters was engendered by his own ideal—to realize his vision in terms of universal truths of human experience. In as much as he was inspired by Matisse and Avery, his response to the work of Rembrandt and Soutine, from whom he derived little in formal terms, reveals his sensitivity to artists for whom psychology and feeling was a fundamental source of their inspiration.[50] As objects and and as façades Rothko's paintings reflect an aura of solitude and silence and, at the same time, in their engagement of the viewer, an attempt to overcome that state. Rothko's "theater" thus deals with an inner drama that is least apparent in conventional terms of dramatic gesture and yet is of greatest consequence.

In his review of the 1961 exhibition, Robert Goldwater drew attention to the duality of presence and absence that lies at the heart of Rothko's work. In describing the room that contained a selection of the Seagram murals, he wrote, "It is significant that at the entrance to this room one pauses, hesitating to enter. Its space seems both occupied and empty."[51]

Each painting appears both as filled with a living presence and as an empty space. While they engage the spectator on both levels, the paintings also assert themselves unequivocally as objects, precisely by virtue of the formal means by which this dichotomy is achieved. Thus the dual content of these works is both intrinsic to the works themselves and also finds its necessary fulfillment in the relationship between the spectator and the painting.

Those who have written about Rothko's work have often turned to literature, largely philosophy, by way of explaining them. The experience of Rothko's paintings as objects (as well as images) is fundamental to our experience of them as icons of a kind and, hence, is an equally fundamental and important ingredient of their content. Yet if one considers the polarities of subjective and objective in a larger context as the way in which we experience all of life, one could perhaps find no better, or more poetic, explication of the duality in Rothko's work than in the *I-Thou* philosophy of the modern theologian Martin Buber. Buber essentially divided experience into two relations: *I-Thou* as that of "natural combination"; *I-It* as that of "natural separation." The *I-Thou* is man's primary experience—the child's experience. Buber wrote:

But whenever the sentence "I see the tree" is so uttered that it no longer tells of a relation between the man—*I*—and the tree—*Thou*—, but establishes the perception of the tree as object by the human consciousness, the barrier between subject and object has been set up. The primary word *I-It*, the word of separation, has been spoken.

And conversely, he explains that the *Thou* "appears . . . simultaneously as acting and as being acted upon—not, however, linked to a chain of causes, but, in its relation of mutual action with the *I*, as the beginning and the end of the event."

The world which appears to you in this way is unreliable, for it takes on a continually new appearance; you cannot hold it to its word. It has no density, for everything in it penetrates everything else; no duration, for it comes even when it is not summoned, and vanishes even when it is tightly held. It cannot be surveyed, and if you wish to make it capable of survey you lose it. It comes, and comes to bring *you* out; if it does not reach you, then it vanishes; but it comes back in another form. It is not outside you, it stirs in the depth of you.[52]

Buber's analysis of two sides of experience is reflected in the two basic premises on which Rothko's work is based: the painting to be encountered as a presence in an *I-Thou* relation and as an object, or what Buber describes as the *I-It* relation. As soon as thought and an intent to analyze these works breaks in upon one's intuitive response, they vanish as experiences. The understanding of his work that Rothko so deeply desired requires the *I-Thou* relation, without which the painting's meaning is lost. Yet their content eludes definition, forcing one to confront them as enigmatic concrete objects. While one may analyze these works formally, Rothko's paintings stubbornly refuse dissection. They force one to encounter them as a whole.

Rothko's work acquired this aspect of individual presences through his process of integrating all the parts into one. In his early work, the field, sometimes clearly demarcated into registers, sometimes transforming imperceptibly from top to bottom, embraced a diversity of biomorphic forms. His mature style did not spring full blown into his work. Rothko's early

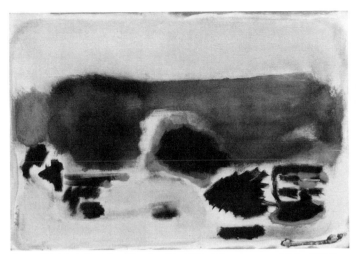

Figure 17. Mark Rothko. *Number 24*, 1948. Oil on canvas, 86.4 x 127.6 cm (34 x 50¼ in). The Museum of Modern Art, New York, Gift of the Artist [photo: Geoffrey Clements]. Not in exhibition

paintings never employed symbols or images as concrete as those of Pollock or Gottlieb for example. In 1947-1948, the forms became irregular patches of color—a somewhat tentative probing of relationships. In those transitional years, he seemed to move intuitively further from the specific than even his vague biomorphic allusions and was already more involved in exploring the power of suggestion, as opposed to symbolic statement. The wonder of this transformation lies in the declarative strength that did nevertheless emerge in his mature work. In 1949, the patches of color seemed to grow and expand (almost of their own volition) blocking out the underlying forms, although lighter hues were applied on top to allow the underlying forms to hint at their presence (fig. 14). Gradually Rothko aligned the contours of the forms more and more with the rectilinearity of the canvas. As both factors—the size and the contour of the shapes—increasingly identified with the field of canvas, the diversity dissolved into a new unity.[53] A new dialectic replaced that of the whole versus its parts in the dual identity of the painting as both object and image. It is on the basis of this dialectic that Rothko was able to orchestrate the complex interrelation of one work to another in the Houston chapel.

Rothko's paintings thus acquired their aspect of individual living presences in tandem with the artist's concerns for pictorial unity. Henri Focillon's *Life of Forms in Art*, published in English in 1948 by George Wittenborn Inc., as one of the Documents of Modern Art (director: Robert Motherwell), was one of a number of selected publications that New York artists read and discussed among themselves. It is highly likely that Focillon's book provided encouragement to the evolution of Rothko's "living" forms. In "The Romantics Were Prompted," Rothko echoes passages from Focillon—passages eloquently illustrated by his paintings of the years to follow. Rothko's description of shapes in this essay as "organisms with volition and a passion for self-assertion," bears comparison with Focillon's thesis:[54]

We must never think of forms, in their different states, as simply suspended in some remote, abstract zone, above the earth and above

man. They mingle with life; whence they come; they translate into space certain movements of the mind. But a definite style is not merely a state in the life of forms, nor is it that life itself: it is a homogeneous, coherent, formal environment, in the midst of which man acts and breathes.[55]

Rothko's further description of shapes is not only supported by Focillon's, but Focillon continues with words that evoke to an extraordinary degree Rothko's own interpretation and use of forms.

Rothko ("On Shapes"):

They move with internal freedom, and without need to conform with or to violate what is probable in the familiar world.

They have no direct association with any particular visible experience, but in them one recognizes the principle and passion of organisms.[56]

Focillon:

We are always tempted to read into form a meaning other than its own, to confuse the notion of form with that of image and sign. But whereas an image implies the representation of an object, and a sign signifies an object, form signifies only itself. . . . For form is surrounded by a certain aura: although it is our most strict definition of space, it also suggests to us the existence of other forms. It prolongs and diffuses itself throughout our dreams and fancies: we regard it, as it were, as a kind of fissure through which crowds of images aspiring to birth may be introduced into some indefinite realm—a realm which is neither that of physical extent nor that of pure thought.[57]

Focillon's interpretation of the self-defined and self-motivated form as alive (born of and giving birth to other forms) as opposed to an image or sign, which, by implied contrast, is fixed or dead, states in terms of form the magic of Rothko's pictorial language. Thus Rothko's forms both stand for nothing but themselves and exist as presences that "expand and quicken." Rothko's abandoning of the figure, and every subsequent reduction, constituted a simplification toward not a narrower but a broader statement. In its succinct embodying of an essential philosophical position, his work can embrace a wealth of response.

The abstract expressionists inherited from the surrealists the theory and technique of automatism and used it in a manner parallel to the romantic ideals of the early nineteenth century—of Géricault and Delacroix. The elevation of the sketch to a level of unprecedented importance—the desire to express the artist's creative passion and individuality, by the directly expressive and immediate handling of the paint—finds a descendant in the paintings of Robert Motherwell or Franz Kline, both of whom realized powerful images by blowing up a drawing to a heroic scale. (Motherwell's Elegies were born in such a way;[58] Kline blew up sketches with a Bell opticon.) As an abstract expressionist, Rothko is uniquely absent, as it were, in this regard. In most of his work, his active presence is scarcely evident in the brushstrokes themselves, but that, paradoxically, does not diminish the individual resonance of the work. The layers of paint endow each painting with a pulsating quality. Thus the element of time, which so often in abstract-expressionist works pits the time*ful* element of facture against the timelessness of the image, has been contracted into not a present moment but a continual presence. In the openness of their

Figure 18. Mark Rothko. *Brown and Gray,* 1969. Acrylic on paper, 122.5 x 182.9 cm (48¼ x 72 in). Anonymous loan. Cat. no. 1, pl. 22

Figure 19. Mark Rothko. *Brown and Gray,* 1969. Acrylic on paper, 122.9 x 173.0 cm (48⅜ x 68⅛ in). Anonymous loan. Cat. no. 4, pl. 25

handling, the Brown and Gray paintings are exceptional in their immediacy and accessibility (figs. 18, 19).

More than even Clyfford Still or Barnett Newman, Rothko eliminated line and gesture—stated or implied. While his surface handling appears to lie somewhere between that of the two artists (the irregular, sometimes thick, impasto of Still and the clean surface of Newman), Rothko's forms elude that quality of rhetorical statement of either Still or Newman. Rothko often used rags to apply oil that results in a mat surface with little incident that can be perceived except at close range. He later used sponges and wide brushes to apply acrylic.[59] Automatic gesture and line, which were central to the emergence of abstract expressionism, dropped out of Rothko's vocabulary in the late forties. After allowing the initial influence of Miró in his biomorphic forms suspended in the watercolors of the mid-forties (1945 especially)—which proved his skill as a draftsman—Rothko grew stylistically closer to Matisse and Bonnard. The drama of the artist's gesture itself and the immediacy implicit in the technique of automatism was only initially a route he chose to unlock his inner motivation. It was in terms of Focillon's interpretation of forms in art as a natural emanation that must be intuitively understood that Rothko found an equivalent for automatism to release the subconscious image. Yet, paradoxically, drama—drama in the sense of theater—is perhaps closer to the heart of Rothko's vision than to that of any of the others.

Rothko's method evolved naturally out of his early use of watercolor. When he used oil he thinned it with turpentine. His method of staining it into the cotton duck resulted in the furthest remove from the *matière,* or impasto, the physical presence of pigment that resulted in the viewer's awareness of the action involved in its application—essential to the work of Pollock or de Kooning. The paint in most mature Rothkos seems not to lie on the surface but rather to be wed to it. Rothko's handling, coupled with the resulting luminosity, deliberately opposes the tactile. For all the marriage of paint and canvas, Rothko's paintings are the abstract-expressionist works that most deny their own material presence. For that reason his work perhaps embodies the greatest contradiction or dichotomy in abstract-expressionist painting. The works both confront the viewer, yet dematerialize, and they seem, at the same time, to transcend their physicality.

While all Rothko's work may be perceived in terms of façades (and have often been referred to as such—and by Rothko himself),[60] they might also be considered a baring of his soul, to which the constancy of the image and of its gradual and organically consistent transformations testify. All the ingredients were there from the start. His late work is adumbrated in embryonic stages in his earliest work. The capacity for growth and change in an idiom of such restrictions is due to the depth of its source. It is, moreover, precisely that quality of contained expression that maintains the tension and hence the life of the work. In some respects the manner in which the paintings function as façades is not dissimilar from other abstract-expressionist works in which a highly individual sensibility (in some cases released through automatic gesture) is translated into a statement of larger implications (witness Motherwell). By virtue of its remove, or transcendence of the individual impulse, the meaning of the work is broadened, and, at the same time, it becomes a more powerful carrier of the individual feeling than any automatic record of it could be (witness Masson). Rothko does not present a dramatic moment nor a heroic statement of a theme. Ecstacy in his work depends on the remarkable quality of sustained tension, in the works themselves and in the viewer's experience. Intimacy, combined with indefinite suspension, raises to the level of drama the fusion (both intrinsic and extrinsic) that is at the heart of Rothko's theme of ecstasy.

Rothko's formal dialectic and his content must be recognized as one. Each painting embodies a duality that, by analogy, lies at the heart of the human condition—man's deepest yearning to transcend the physical. They appear to invoke the human spirit which, despite its subjection to physical boundaries, is also free of them. The tension in the works results from that conflict—formally expressed, to be humanly experienced.

Rothko's response to Shakespeare's use of irony became a facet of this duality. In the Pratt Lecture of 1958, and again in an interview with Peter Selz in 1960, he made special mention of irony in relation to his own work:

As I have grown older, Shakespeare has come closer to me than Aeschylus, who meant so much to me in my youth. Shakespeare's tragic concept embodies for me the full range of life from which the artist draws all his tragic materials, including irony; irony becomes a weapon against fate.[61]

The essence of irony lies in a dichotomy, in the opposition of literal or accepted truth, to a deeper, sensed truth. For his seemingly vague, atmospheric handling of paint and the feeling it evokes, Rothko's work has been considered the expression of a romantic individual. For his formal innovations and his achievements as a colorist, however, his work has brought praise that overlooks its content.[62] Rothko's formal conception evolved hand-in-hand with the desire to express, and evoke, a felt response.

The closer Rothko came to a personally meaningful statement, the more past modes of expression—be it of myth or other—dropped away like crutches, to offer a new point of departure—a new interpretation of an age-old "given" subject. The abstract expressionists as a group traded in all such "given subjects" for themselves as points of departure. As throughout

the history of Western art, myths of classical antiquity were reinvested with meaning in accordance with their relevance to the time; Freud, Jung, and modern existential philosophers had proven that the truth of these myths was to be found in every individual. And the implication in terms of Jung's collective unconscious was that a profoundly individual expression could also be of universal meaning. Thus Aeschylus and Shakespeare indicated to Rothko fundamental concepts which he looked to find within his own personal relation to his art.

Rothko was aware of the particular nature of the gap his work would seek to close—one of the first being the assumed notion of the incompatibility of the large and the intimate. At a symposium on how to combine architecture, painting, and sculpture, at the Museum of Modern Art in 1951, he made a statement in which he reverses the conventional perception to propose the immediacy of the large painting and, by implication, the distance maintained by the scale of the small. Most importantly, he stresses that the immediacy of response called for by the large painting is also the artist's own experience in the process of making it.

I paint very large pictures. I realize that historically the function of painting large pictures is painting something very grandiose and pompous. The reason I paint them, however—I think it applies to other painters I know—is precisely because I want to be very intimate and human. To paint a small picture is to place yourself outside your experience, to look upon an experience as a stereopticon view or with a reducing glass. However you paint the larger picture, you are in it. It isn't something you command.[63]

Rothko believed that any depiction that stimulates historical, descriptive, or literal associations in the viewer only distract from the essential content. Yet, paradoxically, this purification of means is not intended to deny participation on the part of the viewer. By distilling the content, its impact is enforced. Although Rothko found any form of naming or categorizing a misrepresentation and would have considered the term *mystical*, when applied to his art, as tainted with associations he didn't like, his intention could hardly be considered other than that of a mystical experience. Equally he wrote of "sensuality, the basis for being concrete about the world" as one of his "ingredients" for painting.[64]

While the variety of feeling in Rothko's work is directly produced by his choice of color, its effect is released through the particular decisions of technique and composition from work to work. Indeed it is not only on the basis of color that Rothko's work has been compared to that of two great colorists, Matisse and Bonnard. Rothko believed that one of the greatest revolutions in the treatment of pictorial space was instigated by Henri Matisse (and he paid tribute to the French master in a painting of 1954, *Homage to Matisse*). Matisse's *Red Studio* (acquired by the Museum of Modern Art in 1948) presented an alternative to the shallow faceted space proposed by cubism. On a uniform ground of red, a linear skeleton defines the space—a virtual ghost of a space, as if suspended like a curtain, in which, to its contradiction, real objects (Matisse's own paintings and studio paraphernalia) exist. Yet the spatial duality shared by Matisse and Rothko is achieved through different means and to different ends. Matisse's play between a surface, asserted by a uniform field or linear arabesque (more pronounced in other works), and depth, suggested representationally through perspective diagonals or openings (a door or, more often, a window), is tranformed into a different dialectic by Rothko. Matisse's duality between real and unreal, tangible and intangible, between space and no space, lies within the painting itself. Rothko created a like duality, but extended it beyond the boundaries of the painting itself, in a play between the immeasurable image and the measurable or concrete object.

Rothko's touch has been compared to Bonnard's,[65] but again it is perhaps more significantly Bonnard's treatment of space and his use of color in handling his subject, intimate in nature, that create the intimacy of feeling for which, with Vuillard, he was called an *intimist,* and to which Rothko also aspired. The space in a Bonnard has none of the structural clarity of Matisse. Bonnard avoided such spatial definition, and often employed a wide-angle treatment of his field, making the viewer aware of peripheral vision and, in such a way, inviting him to enter the space.[66] Rothko's avoidance of spatial definition, combined with scale and an absence of vanishing point or focus, creates a similar breadth of visual field. It is the quality of felt or sensed, as opposed to defined, space that Rothko shares with Bonnard.

Yet it is undeniable that Rothko also understood color as the principal means of evoking sensation in both these artists' work. It was Bonnard, however, who juxtaposed close tonalities of reds, pinks, oranges and, in other cases, blues and greens, that together produce the sensual luminosity similarly achieved by Rothko. It was at about the time of Bonnard's retrospective in honor of his eightieth birthday, at the Museum of Modern Art in 1948, that Rothko discarded the subdued palette of his surrealistic, biomorphic paintings for the patches of color that would grow into the large forms of his mature work.

Robert Motherwell has described the variety of mood in Rothko's work as akin to Renaissance humors.[67] The four humors were characterized in ancient physiology by four fluids: blood, phlegm, choler (yellow bile), and melancholy (black bile). Despite his consistency of subject, Rothko's moods, or humors, span such a range. As Rothko himself said, "I exclude no emotion from being actual and therefore pertinent," and "I take the liberty to play on any string of my existence. I might as an artist, be lyrical, grim, maudlin, humorous, tragic. I allow myself all possible latitude. Everything is grist for the mill."[68]

Much has been said about the quality of light in Rothko's work. He did not achieve this effect of light by any traditional means. Neither does he employ effects of contrast (light and shadow), nor does he use impressionist means of juxtaposing hues to be mixed optically. Even Delaunay's way of creating pictorial light in such abstractions as his *Disc* of 1912 (collection of Mr. and Mrs. Burton Tremaine, Meriden, Connecticut), relies upon brilliant contrasts that are closer to impressionist means than to Rothko's. Rothko's paintings emanate a quality of light that depends not on luminosity alone (Barnett Newman's paintings are as luminous as Rothko's) but rather on

their quality of atmosphere. Although it has been compared to the atmospheric light of Whistler and of Turner, this light arises only in association with the unprecedented formal means Rothko employs to create a consistent and permeating defiance of any measurable substance—a weightless expansion, immeasurable in depth. It is this particular role of light in Rothko's works that suggests their relation to transcendence in the traditional religious sense.

Both Rothko and Gottlieb began in the forties to make frequent visits to the studio of Milton Avery. The poetry of Avery's work, its restraint in handling that allows color and form to exist as primary agents of his lyrical vision, evoked a kindred response in Rothko. These visits to Avery's studio may well have inspired Rothko to use rags, as Avery did, in applying paint, to achieve a similar absence of *matière*.[69] The sense of a continuous but fluid environment, in which biomorphic forms are suspended, in Rothko's earlier work, is retained in his use of a continuous ground that covers the entire canvas in his mature oils.[70] In accommodating the forms in subtle modifications from top to bottom, this underlying coat grants each one a life of its own. Once this approach is perceived, the gap between Rothko and Albers, for example, becomes obvious and instructive. Albers' relations of color and form appear as absolutes and result in rational and geometric relations of pure optical harmony. Rothko's absolute arose from his concern with content. His clarity lies not in the realm of formal precision; rather the clarity Rothko sought was clarity of idea. At the Artists Session, in 1951, Ad Reinhardt, in addressing the issue of "romantic" and "classic," stated, "Let's straighten out our terminology if we can. Vagueness is a 'romantic' value, and clarity and 'Geometricity' are 'classic' values." Barnett Newman's rejoinder, that speaks also for Rothko, was: "The question of clarity is one of intention."[71]

One might suspect, nevertheless, that Rothko's use of black owes something to the black paintings of Ad Reinhardt. Reinhardt had turned to black years before Rothko, in the mid-fifties. Yet their differing approaches to dark monochromatic painting brings into focus fundamental differences in intention.[72] While Rothko's use of black entered his work gradually, Ad Reinhardt began painting entirely black paintings in the 1950s and executed only black paintings during the last decade of his life. Rothko's black paintings, in the Houston chapel as well as in the last series of 1970, despite every reduction and restriction, every development toward a more absolute statement, continue to concern themselves with a humanly felt experience. Even in those cases where Rothko seems closest to denying color, the most austere works are rich in felt permutations that one does not have to see—by examining pentimenti at close hand—to feel. Reinhardt's choice of black was the ultimate step in an avoidance of any use of color—contaminated, as it were, by associations, or enlivened by vibrations of hue. His paintings deal in pure value relations in an unequivocal format. Reinhardt believed "black is interesting not as a color but as a non-color and as the absence of color" (1967).[73] Nothing could be farther from Rothko's use of black; instead it forms a continuity of intention with his earlier more colorful work. While Reinhardt's black paintings usually employ one other hue to create pure tonal relations, Rothko's black is really an admixture, including plum, maroon, or other hues. Rothko's single idea is an experience that may expand in the response of the viewer, whereas Reinhardt's refutes any such exchange or interpretative possibilities. In dealing with the physical and its transcendence, Rothko maintains an essentially Western philosophical position (embodied for example in Christian theology). In Reinhardt's paintings, on the other hand, all tension is resolved, eliminated. They transcend any such dialectic and, in doing so, express an Eastern, rather than Western, ideal. The polarity of intention between the two artists is clearly implied by Nicolas Calas' perception of Reinhardt's work: "Reinhardt's last paintings have become icons for agnostics who prefer veils covering the obvious to signs indicating the presence of an enigma."[74]

Yet neither Rothko nor Reinhardt used black by itself as a pure hue. Rothko's use of black accentuates the way in which his use of color differs from that of Matisse. Indeed Motherwell's use of color is closer to Matisse's in this regard—in his use of fully saturated hues, each, by virtue of its relation to the next, allowed its individual resonance. In the work of both Motherwell and Matisse a formal clarity of statement is achieved by allowing each hue all its pictorial strength. Both artists used black as a color that acquires its intensity by way of contrast. Not only Rothko's method, that of laying on pigment in thin layers, but also his choice of colors work together to the same end: that of deflecting the experience of his work as pure relations of color and form. He continually modified his hues to the end that they became relegated to a role of lesser individual importance than the felt experience of the whole. Thus, his use of black, arrived at through a gradual development of increasingly closer relations of hue and tonality, constitutes a distinctly opposing approach to that of the other abstract expressionists. Rothko's means of reducing his pictorial composition in the late 1940s reveal the way in which his eventual use of black would differ from that of the other abstract expressionists. They, for the most part, introduced black in conjunction with white, either for its contrasted intensity or as a means to open new avenues in their formal development. Barnett Newman stated in 1958, with regard to the first of the Stations of the Cross:

Black is what an artist uses . . . when he is trying to break into something new, when he is clearing the decks for experiment, when he wants to find a new way to his image and a way out of the restrictions his old paintings have imposed.[75]

It was only after the completion of the chapel that Rothko found new potential inherent in the restrictions of his palette—to be explored not specifically as a means of creating a unified environment but as an end of and by itself, as we find in the Brown and Gray paintings.

Rothko employed such reductions to unique purpose. His concern for the feeling that black, as a color, can convey is only perhaps shared to some extent by Motherwell. For de Kooning and Kline, for example, black may be used virtually like a color, but not intentionally for its mood. While Motherwell discovered, in the process of making the first Elegy, the resonance of black as a light-absorbant and, indirectly, a symbol of death,

Rothko's gradual move toward it reveals his own distinct means and intention. Rothko's black is never as inky as Motherwell's; the accrued effect of his thin layers of pigment is that of an actual experience of darkness that asks to be probed, though what lies in or behind it will never reveal itself.

A MYTH FOR OUR TIME

While the pictorial duality that has given rise to opposing comments and responses to Rothko's work is also the very essence of its content, in a larger context this duality can be seen as a resolution of two foregoing traditions—a resolution that was central to the emergence of abstract expressionism. Despite their own initial disputes over how they, a group of artists of tremendous stylistic diversity, might be labeled as a movement, the two stylistic strains that contributed to its formation might indeed be loosely termed *abstraction* and *expressionism*. The revolution they brought about revolved upon a subjective and inherently romantic motivation, to be manifested through an entirely new (and ideally objective and universal) formal language. Formal solutions arose as an inextricable part of the content their work was intended to embody.

Robert Motherwell, in an issue of *Tiger's Eye* (1948), which included contributions from several artists and writers on "What Is Sublime in Art?", expressed what was a shared ideal of transcending the violence or personal anguish of expressionism:

Perhaps—I say perhaps because I do not know how to reflect, except by opening my mind like a glass-bottomed boat so that I can watch what is swimming below—painting becomes Sublime when the artist transcends his personal anguish, when he projects in the midst of a shrieking world an expression of living and its end that is silent and ordered. That is opposed to expressionism. So is the beauty and perfection of the school of Paris. Like the latter, all of us must reject the Sublime in the social sense, in its association with institutional authority, regardless of one's relation to beauty as an ideal. In the metaphysical sense, it cannot be a question of intent, one experiences the Sublime or not, according to one's fate and character.[76]

Rothko began his painting career in an expressionist idiom. His earliest studies (in 1925) were with Max Weber, who had studied with Matisse in Paris but who also worked in cubist and expressionist styles. In 1935, Rothko was a cofounder of The Ten (which included also Gottlieb), which Jacob Kainen described at the time as "the best organized group of young Expressionists functioning in New York."[77]

While Rothko's paintings of the period, of which his subway station scenes are the best known, foreshadow his later work formally in the architectonic handling of frontal planes of color, they also do so in their quality of silence, the containment and isolation of each of the figures; a kind of subdued angst creates the mood of these works. William Rubin opened his obituary article in the *New York Times* with "Mark Rothko sometimes spoke of himself as a violent artist. . . ."[78] And Dore Ashton reported in 1957, "Rothko claims that his is the most violent painting in America today."[79] Such a claim could only baffle that body of critics who see Rothko's work purely in formal terms. It is only in the content Rothko intended to convey that this attitude may be comprehended. Rothko channeled this intensity of feeling into an increasingly direct statement. With every apparent reduction of means, he did not empty his work of its content. He distilled it.

The abstract expressionists seconded the surrealists in their own revolt against existing pictorial convention. Their desire to elevate their art to the level of a sublime statement necessitated a transcendence of the anecdotal or material. While the works of the surrealists, however, often attacked openly society's conventions, both of perception and belief, the abstract expressionists removed themselves from such pointed comment or provocation to concerns at once loftier and more fundamental.

The artistic climate of the late thirties and early forties was characterized not only by the influx of European artists to New York and a keen desire among these New York artists to elevate their art to an equal level of international artistic consequence, but also by an interest in primitive art which was recognized as an important source of European modernism. Primitive art had provided the surrealists with one stimulus to the shucking off of artistic convention and affectation. Miró wrote, "Art has been in decadence since the caveman." The abstract expressionists, however, sought to go to the heart of the intrinsic and societal import of those primitive works and to infuse their own art, born of a panoply of recent traditions, with a like quality—something of the hypnotic and direct appeal to the "gut" response of the viewer. Their shared expressionist outlook led them to both reinterpret the possibilities of automatism on the one hand and, on the other, to make their references to primitive art, unlike the surrealists, generalized ones. The earliest indication of the abstract expressionists' search for a language of equivalent impact was in the fetishistic images, pictographs, and biomorphic forms of the forties. These, however, were still burdened with references to cultures not his own that only served to impede the direct expression of the artist's feelings as well as inhibit (or burden) the immediate response of the viewer. As their individual styles developed, they abandoned even general references to symbols and totems to allow the work in its entirety to become totemic.

Throughout the 1930s and 1940s the Museum of Modern Art organized several exhibitions of primitive art and thus presented to American artists the opportunity to draw upon the example of primitive art as their immediate predecessors in Paris had done.[80] James Johnson Sweeney, in the catalogue for the exhibition *African Negro Art* (1935), pointed out that not only ideas but also emotions could be married to, and conveyed by, abstract means in African sculpture by an emphasis on the essential and a truth to material.[81] It was Barnett Newman, however, who played the most important role in clarifying what relevance ancient and primitive art might have to him and his fellow artists. He wrote the forewords to exhibition catalogues of primitive art at Betty Parsons' Gallery: in 1944, *Pre-Columbian Stone Sculpture*, and in 1946, *Northwest Coast Indian Painting*. In making a case for the relevance of primitive art to contemporary artists, Newman seemed to pick up where John Graham left off. The Russian expatriate theorist and artist, who came to New York from Paris in the late 1920s (and revisited Paris frequently), contributed significantly to the awareness of primitive art among New York artists. In an article of 1937, "Primitive Art and Picasso," he outlined two distinct traditions. The first of these traditions he called the Greco-African, that is "geometric . . . synthetic . . . evocative . . . spontaneous"; the second was the Persian-Indian-Chinese, that is "analytic . . . decorative . . . literary . . . [with a] deliberate machine-like technique."[82] The former he allied with Picasso, Ingres, and Mondrian; the latter with, among others, Soutine and Kandinsky. He then extols the primitive artist for his "readier access" to his unconscious, which is the "creative factor and the source and the storehouse of power and of all knowledge, past and future." Graham thus introduced the possibility of analyzing recent artistic manifestation in an historical perspective reaching back to the roots of art, in a diversity of primitive or ancient cultures. Barnett Newman's studies of primitive art and its recent influence, however, led him to suggest that "we are living in a time without legend or mythos that can be called sublime."[83]

In an essay inspired by the exhibition *Arts of the South Seas* at the Museum of Modern Art (1946), Newman, as had Graham, traced the influence of two opposing traditions on the art of the immediate past. He opened by stating that "primitive art has become for artists the romantic dream of our time" from the impressionists to Matisse, Picasso, Mondrian, and the surrealists. He stated that the distinguishing feature of African art is that "it is an art of terror, terror before nature . . . ," and "the distinguishing character of Oceanic art . . . is its sense of magic." Moreover, "unlike the African terror before nature this is terror before nature's meaning, the terror involved in a search for answers to nature's mysterious forces." He then hails in the work of his contemporaries evidence of an intent to create a language that might provoke the same magic response on the part of the spectator. Indeed, these artists not only tapped the subconscious in their methods but also created an art that transported the irrational (central to the surrealist approach) to a realm of far greater inexplicables, or what Newman would term the "sublime." Newman then declared in reference to the exhibition:

It was almost as if the object lesson of this important exhibition was to demonstrate the failure of the Surrealists correctly to interpret the meaning of magic—that they comprehended only its superficial aspects. By insisting on a materialistic presentation of it rather than a plastic one, by attempting to present a transcendental world in terms of realism, in terms of Renaissance plasticity and Renaissance space, by so to speak, mixing the prevailing dream of the modern artist with the outworn dream of academic Europe, they hoped to make *acceptable* (the Surrealists prefer the term Sur-real) what they consciously knew was unreal.[84]

Having defined the problem of the surrealists as being one of representation and, moreover, representation in an out-worn academic style, he stated that "they practised illusion because they did not themselves feel the magic." Whereas, of course, modern man has no mythology, "the primitive artist attempted no deception. He believed his magic." Thus the problem that confronted these artists, and which seemed, from Newman's argument, ripe for resolution, was to create an art that could have through its formal qualities (qualities that these artists had necessarily inherited from their recent past) the same impact—be the bearer of magic through some expression of the human condition of modern man—that is, to find and create a myth for our time. If certain principles of abstract form could carry such meaning before, to a broad span of primitive cultures, could they not again? In 1943, Rothko and Gottlieb had stated that the nature of their subject matter made them feel a "spiritual kinship with primitives and archaic art."[85]

Gottlieb described the search for mythological subject matter that he and Rothko embarked upon in the early forties.

In 1941 (it) started with some conversations that I had with Rothko in which I said . . . that one of the ways to solve this problem . . . is to find some sort of subject matter other than that which is around us. Because everyone was painting the American scene—Mark was painting people in subway stations . . . I said, well, why not try to find a good subject matter like mythological themes? And, well, we agreed to do that, and Mark chose to do some themes from the plays of Aeschylus and I . . . played around with the Oedipus myth which was both a classical theme and a Freudian theme. (As a result) we very quickly discovered that by a shift in subject matter we were getting into formal problems that we hadn't anticipated. Because obviously we weren't going to try to illustrate these themes in some sort of a Renaissance style. We were exploring. So we suddenly found that there were formal problems that confronted us for which there was no precedent. We were in unknown territory.[86]

Indeed it is at this point that Rothko's style comes closest to Gottlieb's. While Rothko derived his early oil of 1942, *The Omen of the Eagle,* from Aeschylus, he characteristically stated, "The picture deals not with the particular anecdote, but rather with the Spirit of Myth, which is generic to all myths at all times."[87]

By the mid-forties, Rothko's dependence on any outside source had become vague and obscure—his style markedly unaggressive in a consistent expression of a private and lyrical vision. And in 1948, he reiterated Newman's standpoint that "not everything strange or unfamiliar is transcendental."[88] Much of Rothko's and Gottlieb's work of the forties exhibits underwater qualities. Significantly, *Tiger's Eye* featured quite a number of poems and essays about nature, many to do with the sea and its inhabitants. Paul Valéry's "Man and the Shell" describes the emanation of a shell from a mollusk that suggests a parallel to man's creative processes. This underwater quality had an inherited significance from the surrealists: that of a kind of dream world, a metaphor for subconscious recesses, where feelings and ideas are born and take shape. Nevertheless, while Orozco also painted a scene of the subway (1928), and Gottlieb painted such marine scenes as *Sea Chest,* Rothko's interpretations of both subjects evoked a silent, remote, and unfathomable world. In his mature work, he no longer describes such a world. He confronts us with it.[89]

Rothko's few statements about his work (including inherent contradictions) are as consistent as the works themselves. In a lecture at Pratt Institute (1958) he listed among the "ingredients" of his paintings: "A clear preoccupation with death. All art deals with intimations of mortality."[90]

Ten years earlier, when his mature style was just emerging, he had stated: "But the solitary figure could not raise its limbs in a single gesture that might indicate its concern with the fact of mortality and an insatiable appetite for ubiquitous experience in face of this fact."[91]

The artist Bud Hopkins related a story told to him regarding an image that had haunted Rothko that seems to reflect a preoccupation with the ultimate solitariness of man in the face of existence.

In the 50's a friend of mine told me something that Rothko once described to him. It was a childhood memory of his family and relatives talking about a Czarist pogrom. The Cossacks took the Jews from the village to the woods and made them dig a large grave. Rothko said he pictured that square grave in the woods so vividly that he wasn't sure that the massacre hadn't happened in his lifetime. He said he'd always been haunted by the image of that grave, and that in some profound way it was locked into his painting. Though I knew Rothko for years, I felt that this was too personal a subject to ever broach to him myself. The point is that our response to his painting, on some subliminal level, involves our sensing his feeling about that rectangle. It's one demonstration of the greatness of his work and the power of its obsessive imagery.[92]

Robert Motherwell relates that Rothko thought of his paintings as individual voices in an opera.[93] Indeed, to consider his paintings in terms of music helps to clarify the manner in which meaning may and may not be found in his work. Music surrounds one, evokes a direct response. Its mood depends on resonance, tonal relations; it has no tangible substance. What closer parallel to the means Rothko chose to create mood and move the spectator directly! Rothko adored Mozart and felt that many fail to recognize and experience the intensity of emotion—indeed tragedy—Mozart expressed in his music. Thus the duality of material and immaterial in his painting is not a metaphor or symbol of the gulf between life and death or being and nonbeing. Rather his desire was to invest his art with the impact and mystery of such a confrontation. In his late work he seems to confront himself with the impenetrability of the mystery.

Because of the subdued palette of the Brown and Gray paintings (figs. 20, 21), the flatness so strongly asserted by their composition, and because of their scale, they do not expand and envelop the viewer as his previous work had done. While a certain intimacy results from their openness of handling, at the same time they recede—they appear withdrawn. Yet the tension that is maintained in these works and the warmth they nevertheless exude recall the extraordinary fusion of the gentle and intimate yet powerful and remote—polarities of all Rothko's mature work. The one constant throughout Rothko's work, throughout its many moods, does indeed appear to reflect a philosophical dialectic: being and nonbeing, the physical standing for the metaphysical. Every assertion of the painting as object led simultaneously to its denial as such. In materializing the idea, he dematerialized the object. Rather than endowing the concrete, the representational, or the known with otherworldly characteristics, he made the unknown concrete.

With the Seagram murals of 1958, Rothko's work shows the first signs of becoming increasingly objectlike. As we have seen, his works for an environment encouraged this direction. The

Figure 20. Mark Rothko. *Brown and Gray*, 1969. Acrylic on paper, 122.9 x 172.8 cm (48⅜ x 68 in). Private collection. Cat. no. 8, pl. 29

Figure 21. Mark Rothko. *Brown and Gray*, 1969. Acrylic on paper, 122.9 x 173.7 cm (48⅜ x 68⅜ in). Anonymous loan. Cat. no. 6, pl. 27

apparent irony is that as the sensuality of his colors diminished, the more concrete—material—the works became. Thus his earlier work comprises a greater polarity—of the finite and the sensual vs. the infinite and the spiritual. With his later work (in good part as a result of the considerations that his commissioned environments brought to bear) the two poles are brought closer together: the paintings become both more finite and more insistently impenetrable and mysterious. As Robert Goldwater observed, "All at once [with his heart attack] he had been moved close, physically, to the edge above the abyss where emotionally he had lived for so long."[94]

Thus the Brown and Gray paintings are like meditations on mortality. By contrast, they show how much color, as well as composition, made his earlier work come forward and expand. The edges of forms in Rothko's work had become increasingly absolute, evolving from the blurred edges in the Seagram murals to the sharper definition of forms in those of the chapel. Their lack of this degree of atmospheric expansion makes them more objectlike. Nevertheless, despite the flattening effect of the white border of the Brown and Gray paintings, Rothko's varied use of the acrylic introduces subtle spatial dimensions. A

soft light appears to emanate from these works. Within the limitations of his palette (of only two colors), one is struck by the range of effect that results from subtle differences of proportion and handling (figs. 22, 23). The relation of brown to gray quickens where they meet. In thus heightening the importance of a modicum of pictorial relations, the essence of Rothko's spirit comes through. Color variations are no longer salient. As a group, in their shared absence of a wide range of hue, they reveal Rothko's mastery in conveying an extraordinary range of feeling. Thus the Brown and Gray paintings provide a poignant and revealing reflection on the meaning of Rothko's earlier work. In motivation (and so in content) we can see Rothko's works as violent or expressionist to the end. However controlled, however much they appear as façades, Rothko's works bear direct witness to his own state of being—not just his state of mind, his philosophical outlook, nor just his emotional state, but that point where the two meet.

There is something particularly moving about the decision of an artist of such a consistent oeuvre to turn his hand to something new after coming perilously close to death—as though, given a reprieve, he realized there were many things he had

Figure 22. Mark Rothko. *Brown and Gray*, 1969. Acrylic on paper, 122.5 x 182.3 cm (48¼ x 71¾ in). Estate of Mark Rothko. Cat. no. 5, pl. 26

Figure 23. Mark Rothko. *Brown and Gray*, 1969. Acrylic on paper, 123.1 x 182.9 cm (48⁷⁄₁₆ x 72 in). Estate of Mark Rothko. Cat. no. 3, pl. 24

neglected to try. Nevertheless, the Brown and Gray paintings, for all their differences, not only stem from his previous development but also continue to be a direct expression of his state of mind.

Why are all Rothko's series dark paintings? That they were all executed in the latter half of his mature career, when he had already turned to a more and more frequent use of a somber palette, is the first and most obvious explanation. Certainly Robert Goldwater's special acclaim of the Seagram paintings in the 1961 MOMA show must also have been an important factor to his continuing in that vein. Almost for the first time he was receiving the kind of critical understanding of his work that he desired—a recognition of its utter seriousness. It was the Seagram paintings that first produced this response and later that persuaded the de Ménils to ask Rothko to do the Houston chapel.

The content of Rothko's work is inevitably, as Brian O'Doherty has proposed, each individual's experience. Dore Ashton has stated that Rothko's subject is "the expression of the condition of being moved."[95] With regard to the chapel, she has been more specific: "No one could have summarized birth,

dissolution and death so well. It was his theme from the beginning."[96] Rothko's Brown and Gray paintings are an intimate, personal expression that attests both to the continual growth and renewal of his artistic expression and to its emanation from his deepest conviction. Barnett Newman once spoke, in words evocative of Rothko's Brown and Gray paintings and the Black paintings that follow, of "the idea-complex that makes contact with mystery—of life, of men, of nature, of the hard, black chaos that is death, or the grayer softer chaos that is tragedy."[97] Thus Rothko's commissioned series of works are of utmost importance in understanding the content of his work and the evolution of its expression.

The Black paintings that follow the paper works are more monumental, more austere, flatter, more iconic than any before, and more than ever before, they shut out the viewer and recede into themselves as Rothko himself did these last two years of his life.[98] They are like an ultimate confrontation and recall the words of one of Rothko's first stated ambitions: "the impact of the unequivocal."

Mrs. William Scharf tells a haunting and poignant story, revealing of Rothko's state of mind the last two years of his life.

By way of introduction, she relates that they were good friends, that should she encounter Rothko on the street in New York, she wouldn't hesitate to hail him. On one occasion, however, some months before he died, she saw him by chance at the carousel in Central Park, alone. He seemed utterly self-absorbed, remote, his introspection so intense that this time she didn't approach him or even let him know she was there and had seen him.[99] Rothko's art had always focused on the single individual's experience. The richness of his formal development arose from his own perpetual self-questioning, to which the intensity of his late work attests. De Kooning once remarked to Rothko that of all the abstract expressionists, he was the most modern of them all. Rothko replied: "What do you mean? I'm straight out of Rembrandt."[100]

NOTES

1. Barnett Newman stated as early as 1950 his belief in such a consistency of theme: "I think the idea of a 'finished' picture is a fiction. I think a man spends his whole lifetime painting one picture or working on one piece of sculpture." From "Artists' Sessions at Studio 35 (1950)" in *Modern Artists in America*, 1st ser. (New York: Wittenborn Schulz, 1951); quoted in Maurice Tuchman, ed., *New York School: The First Generation: Paintings of the 1940s and 1950s* (Los Angeles: Los Angeles County Museum of Art, 1965), 33.

2. William Scharf, conversation with the author, Jan. 31, 1978 (on file in the Department of Twentieth-Century Art, National Gallery of Art, Washington).

3. Jacob Kainen, *Potomac*, Apr. 11, 1971, 28: "Self-destruction, the final, tragic act of a principled man driven into a corner."

4. See Robert Goldwater, "Rothko's Black Paintings," *Art in America*, 59 (Mar.-Apr. 1971): 58-63.

5. William Scharf recalls once referring to Rothko's paintings as "slab-like," and that Rothko seemed to like that (fellow artist Scharf assisted Rothko with the chapel paintings). Conversation with the author, Jan. 31, 1978.

6. Thomas B. Hess, "Rothko: A Venetian Souvenir," *Art News*, 69 (Nov. 1970).

7. Rothko: "It was with the utmost reluctance that I found the figure could not serve my purposes. . . . But a time came when none of us could use the figure without mutilating it." Quoted by Dore Ashton, "Art: Lecture by Rothko," *The New York Times*, Oct. 31, 1958, 26.

8. See Dore Ashton, *The New York School* (New York: Viking Press, 1973), 128.

9. See Robert Goldwater, "Reflections on the New York School," *Quadrum*, 8 (1960).

10. Dore Ashton, "Recent Show at the Sidney Janis," *Arts and Architecture*, 75 (Apr. 1958): 8.

11. Maurice Sievan, painter (b. Russia, Ukraine); quoted in Jacob Kainen, "Self-destruction," 28.

12. Hess, "Venetian Souvenir," 72.

13. Georgine Oeri, "Marc Rothko," *Quadrum*, 10 (1961): 67.

14. Goldwater, "Reflections," 29.

15. Rothko quoted in "The Ides of Art: 6 Opinions on What Is Sublime in Art," *Tigers Eye*, 1, no. 2 (Dec. 1947): 44.

16. Max Kozloff, "Mark Rothko (1903-1970)," *Artforum*, 8 (Apr. 1970): 88.

17. Thomas B. Hess, "Mark Rothko, 1903-1970" [editorial], *Art News*, 69 (Apr. 1970): 29.

18. Rothko; quoted in Elaine de Kooning's "Two Americans in Action: Kline and Rothko," *Art News Annual*, 27 (1958): 174. Rothko: "Forgive me if I continue with my misgivings, but I feel that it is important to state them. There is the danger that in the course of this correspondence an instrument will be created which will tell the public how the pictures should be looked at and what to look for. While on the surface this may seem an obliging and helpful thing to do, the real result is paralysis of the mind and imagination (and for the artist a premature entombment). Hence my abhorrence of forewards and explanatory data" (quoted by Katherine Kuh, "Mark Rothko," *Art Institute of Chicago Quarterly*, 48 [Nov. 15, 1954]: 68).

19. Rothko and Seldon Rodman; quoted in Seldon Rodman, *Conversations with Artists* (New York: Devin-Adair Co., 1957), 93-94.

20. William Scharf, in conversation with the author, Jan. 31, 1978. Scharf also said that Rothko hoped that Goldwater would write a book on his work.

21. Robert Goldwater, "Reflections," 45.

22. Lawrence Alloway, "The New American Painting," *Art International*, 3, nos. 3-4 (1959): 23.

23. John Gernand, registrar at the Phillips Collection, Washington; in conversation with the author, Mar. 1978 (on file in the Department of Twentieth-Century Art, National Gallery of Art, Washington).

24. It was through his friendship with Wassily Leontif, who became head of Harvard's Society of Fellows (1960-1961), that Rothko came to do the paintings for Holyoke Center. Rothko would not accept a commission anonymously. In every case a personal interest and understanding was essential to him.

25. "Rothko Murals for Harvard," *Art Journal*, 22 (Summer 1963): 254.

26. Robert Motherwell said that Rothko usually painted in the morning and that he used bright lights. The nuances of tone that he had to *see* to paint he wanted to be *sensed*, more than *perceived*, by the spectator (conversation between E. A. Carmean, Jr., and Robert Motherwell, Aug. 1977, on file in Department of Twentieth-Century Art, National Gallery of Art, Washington). Mrs. Barnett Newman said that Rothko would call Newman at 11:00-12:00 in the morning, having already worked several hours (in conversation with E. A. Carmean, Jr., Nov. 1977, on file in Department of Twentieth-Century Art).

27. Peter Selz, *Mark Rothko* (New York: Museum of Modern Art, 1961), 12-14.

28. Brian O'Doherty, "Rothko," *Art International*, 14 (Oct. 1970): 37.

29. William Seitz, "Abstract Expressionist Painting in America" (Ph.D. diss., Princeton University, 1955), 230-231.

30. Dore Ashton, "The Rothko Chapel in Houston," *Studio International*, 181 (June 1971): 274.

31. Dominique de Ménil, "The Rothko Chapel," *Art Journal*, 30 (Spring 1971): 250.

32. Brian O'Doherty, "The Rothko Chapel," *Art in America*, 61 (Jan. 1973): 16.

33. See Dore Ashton, *New York School*, 102.

34. Ashton, *New York School*, 128.

35. Francis V. O'Connor, *Jackson Pollock* (New York: Museum of Modern Art, 1967), 39-40.

36. See E. A. Carmean, Jr.'s essay on Pollock in this catalogue: "Jackson Pollock: Classic Paintings of 1950."

37. Thomas B. Hess, *Barnett Newman* (New York: Museum of Modern Art, 1971), 109-114.

38. De Ménil, "Rothko Chapel," 250.

39. Selz, *Mark Rothko*, 8.

40. Selz, *Mark Rothko*, 9.

41. It is quite conceivable that the terra verde of Italian Renaissance painting, which becomes increasingly visible with time, had some influence on Rothko's thin application of a base coat.

42. Lee Seldes, *Legacy of Mark Rothko* (New York: Holt, Rinehart and Winston, 1978), 51.

43. De Ménil, "Rothko's Chapel," 250.

44. Seldes, *Legacy of Mark Rothko*, 44.

45. See Ashton, "Rothko Chapel," and O'Doherty, "Rothko Chapel."

46. Hess, "Mark Rothko," 29.

47. Vsevolod Emilievich Meyerhold (1874-1942), Russian producer, was head of the Communist theater in the USSR, and, during the Russian Revolution, he was in charge of Bolshevik (propaganda) theater. On Meyerhold, see Marjorie L. Hoover, *Meyerhold, The Art of Conscious Theatre* (Amherst: University of Massachusetts, 1974); and James M. Symons, *Meyerhold's Theatre of the Grotesque* (Miami: University of Miami, 1971). Dore Ashton introduces this connection in *New York School*, 36.

48. Rothko, "The Romantics Were Prompted," *Possibilities*, 1 (Winter 1947/48):84.

49. Rothko; excerpts from Pratt Lecture quoted in Tuchman, *New York School*, 30.

50. William Rubin, "Rothko 1903-70," *New York Times*, Mar. 8, 1970, 22.

51. Goldwater, "Reflections," 45. Brian O'Doherty refers to Rothko's paintings as both actors and stages (see "Rothko Chapel," 15).

52. This is not to suggest that Rothko read, or even knew of, Buber. Buber here quoted from: Martin Buber, *I and Thou*, 2nd ed., trans. Ronald Gregor Smith (New York: Charles Scribner's Sons, 1958), 23, 30, 32-33.

53. For a brief discussion of the transition that occurred in Rothko's work from 1947 to 1948, see Lawrence Alloway, "Notes on Rothko," *Art International*, 4 (Summer 1962), 90-94.

54. Rothko, "The Romantics," 84.

55. Henri Focillon, *The Life of Forms in Art* (1942; 2nd ed. rev., New York: George Wittenborn, Inc., 1958), 14.

56. Rothko, "The Romantics."

57. Focillon, *Forms in Art*, 3. E. C. Goosen makes brief reference to the connection between Rothko's pictorial language and the principles expounded by Focillon (Goosen, "Rothko: The Omnibus Image," *Art News*, 59 [Jan. 1961]).

58. See also Lawrence Alloway, "Signs and Surface: Notes on Black and White Painting in New York," *Quadrum*, 9 (1960).

59. Hess, "Venetian Souvenir," 73.

60. Rothko (quoted in Tuchman, *New York School*, 30): "There are some artists who want to tell all, but I feel it is more shrewd to tell little. My paintings are sometimes described as facades, and indeed, they are facades."

61. Rothko; quoted in Selz, *Mark Rothko*, 12.

62. Brian O'Doherty, whose writing on Rothko has been an important source for the direction I have taken in exploring the stylistic evolution in Rothko's late work, has pointed out two discernibly distinct responses to Rothko's art. The dichotomy may be reduced essentially to that of form versus content and, by association, to the paradox of the depth and variety of personal responses to what appear to be succinct and direct statements.

The most cursory glance at the Rothko literature reveals two responses. Most of the writers see the work through the literature of their own feelings. Mystical and dramatic images occur frequently. They have projected an extravisual universe and are in the interesting state of being exalted and blind. I think this response bears witness to the persuasiveness of Rothko's muted rhetoric, that voice confined to a single word, mood, color. These writers are perhaps Rothko's proper audience, for they have forgotten art.

For this they are despised by the second group, which takes the clear view that Rothko was an artist and that what he did is obviously art. They explicate his formal emancipations, his debts to others and to history. They are not blind, but rather deaf to the voice in the work.

O'Doherty quotes Erich Heller on Casper David Friedrich and the beginnings of romanticism, and what Hegel called "absolute art." He mentions

the paradoxes which Romanticism, in its beginnings, experienced with clarity. Rothko's two audiences embody these paradoxes. One, which has forgotten itself, writes obscure poetry. The other, which remembers itself, writes lucid prose. These audiences represent the breakdown of what Rothko put together: the poetic and the analytic, the imaginative and the rational, the transcendent and the historical, alternatives of which early Romanticism was very conscious.

O'Doherty, *American Masters, The Voice and the Myth* (New York: Random House, 1973), 153-154.

63. Rothko; quoted in "A Symposium on how to combine architecture, painting and sculpture," *Interiors, 110* (May 1951):104.

64. Rothko; quoted in Tuchman, *New York School*, 30.

65. Lawrence Alloway, "Notes on Rothko," 93. Alloway agrees with Rubin, "in relation to Rothko's characteristic handling: his touch is unexpectedly abrupt, the majority of his works reveal a harder and sharper surface than I expected. Pentimenti abound.... Thus the patchy and staccato aspect of Bonnard's touch seems nearer to Rothko than one had at first supposed."

66. See James Elliott, "Bonnard and his Environment," in *Bonnard and his Environment* (New York: Museum of Modern Art, 1964), 28.

67. Robert Motherwell, in conversation with E. A. Carmean Jr., Aug. 1977.

68. Rothko; quoted by Elaine de Kooning, "Two Americans," 177.

69. See Rothko's memorial address, reprinted as the "Commemorative Essay" in *Milton Avery, Prints and Drawings, 1930-1964* (New York: Brooklyn Museum, 1966), 15. It's possible that the influence between Avery and Rothko worked both ways. In the later fifties, Avery did an increasing number of very spare landscapes, including *Tangerine Moon and Wine Dark Sea* (1959), in which his palette closely approximates that of Rothko's Seagram murals.

70. Exceptions to this general procedure do exist. In the case of *Red, Black, White on Yellow*, 1955 (collection, Paul Mellon), three shapes—red, black, and white—are painted on unprimed beige canvas.

71. Tuchman, *New York School*, 32-33.

72. The different orientations of these two artists, Rothko and Reinhardt, dates back to the 1930s when Reinhardt was a member of the American Abstract Artists, whereas Rothko was a member of an expressionist group, The Ten.

73. Ad Reinhardt, "Black as Symbol and Concept," in Barbara Rose, *Art-as-Art, The Selected Writings of Ad Reinhardt* (New York: Viking Press, 1975), 86.

74. Nicolas Calas and Elena Calas, *Icons and Images of the Sixties* (New York: E. P. Dutton and Co., Inc., 1971), 214.

75. Hess, *Barnett Newman*, 94.

76. Motherwell, in "The Ides of Art," 48; his description of the sublime echoes the passage from Nietzsche's *The Birth of Tragedy* that Peter Selz has quoted with regard to Rothko: "There is need for a whole world of torment in order for the individual to produce the redemptive vision and to sit quietly in rocking row-boat in mid-sea, absorbed in contemplation"; Selz, *Mark Rothko*, 14.

77. Jacob Kainen, "Our Expressionists," *Art Front, 1-3* (Nov. 1934-Dec. 1937): 14-15. Kainen describes the characteristics of the "Expressionist outlook" as:

1. The attempt to reduce the interpretation of nature or life in general to the rawest emotional elements.

2. A complete and utter dependence on pigment as an expressive agency rather than an imitative or descriptive one.

3. An intensity of vision which tries to catch the throb of life, necessarily doing violence to external facts to lay bare internal facts.

He went on to state:

Now, after six shattering years of economic crisis which have destroyed the myth of American immunity to the general decay of bourgeois society, the stage is set for Expressionism, the direction par excellence for social disillusion and individual nihilism. Expressionism is also the vehicle for a socially revolutionary consciousness.

The Ten included Yankel Kufeld, Louis Schanker, Joseph Solman, Adolph Gottlieb, Marcus Rothkowitz (Mark Rothko), David Burliuk. Kainen includes as painters of expressionist persuasion: Milton Avery, Karl Knaths.

78. Rubin, "Rothko," 21, 22.

79. Dore Ashton, *Arts and Architecture*, 74 (Aug. 1957):8.

80. Museum of Modern Art exhibitions: *African Negro Art* (1935), *Prehistoric Rock Pictures in Europe and Africa* (1937), and *Arts of the South Seas* (1946).

81. James Johnson Sweeney, *African Negro Art* (New York: Museum of Modern Art, 1935), 21.

82. John Graham, "Primitive Art and Picasso," *Magazine of Art*, Apr. 1937, 236-237.

83. Barnett Newman; quoted in "The Ides of Art," 53.

84. Barnett Newman, "Las Formas artisticas del Pacifico," *Ambos Mundos, 1* (June 1946):51-55; reprinted in English in "Art of the South Seas," *Studio International, 179* (Feb. 1970):70-71 (see Hess, *Barnett Newman*, in "Bibliography," p. 151).

85. Letter to *New York Times* editor Jewell, in Ashton, *New York School*, 128. In a radio broadcast, on Oct. 13, 1943, Rothko and Gottlieb further described this "kinship": "If our titles recall the known myths of antiquity, we have used them again because they are eternal symbols. . . . They are the symbols of man's primitive fears and motivations, no matter in which land, at what time, changing only in detail but never in substance." And: "Those who think that the world of today is more gentle and graceful than the primeval and predatory passions from which these myths spring, are either not aware of reality or do not wish to see it in art" (quoted in Ashton, *New York School*, 129).

86. Adolph Gottlieb; quoted from an interview with Andrew Hudson, 1968, in Karen Wilkin, "Adolph Gottlieb: The Pictographs," *Art International, 21* (Dec. 1977):28.

87. Mark Rothko; quoted in Sidney Janis, *Abstract and Surrealist Art in America* (New York: Reynal and Hitchcock, 1944), 118.

88. Rothko, "The Romantics."

89. Artist Stephen Pace remembers that when he once asked Rothko if the landscape of Oregon where he spent his childhood had not somehow influenced his work, Rothko's re-

tort was, "Absolutely not; there is no landscape in my work." Paraphrased by Pace, in conversation with the author, Apr. 7, 1978 (on file in the Department of Twentieth-Century Art, National Gallery of Art, Washington).

90. Rothko; quoted in Tuchman, *New York School.*

91. Rothko, "The Romantics."

92. "Bud Hopkins on Bud Hopkins," *Art in America*, 61 (Summer 1973):92-93.

93. Robert Motherwell; in conversation with E. A. Carmean, Jr., Apr. 1978 (on file in the Department of Twentieth-Century Art, National Gallery of Art, Washington).

94. Robert Goldwater, "Rothko's Black Paintings," 58.

95. Dore Ashton, "Beyond the Arabesque," in *A Reading of Modern Art*, rev. ed. (New York: Harper and Row, 1971), 21.

96. Dore Ashton, "Rothko Chapel," 275.

97. Barnett Newman; quoted by Ashton, *New York School,* 133.

98. See Goldwater, "Rothko's Black Paintings."

99. Conversation with the author, Jan. 31, 1978 (on file in the Department of Twentieth-Century Art, National Gallery of Art, Washington).

100. Paraphrased by Lee Eastman, in conversation with the author, Apr. 10 (?), 1978 (on file in the Department of Twentieth-Century Art, National Gallery of Art, Washington).